John Calvin's Commentary on the Letter to the Hebrews

Translated by
John Owen
Vicar of Thrussington, Leicestershire

GLH Publishing
Louisville, KY

Originally published as *Commentaries on the Epistle of Paul the Apostle to the Hebrews*.
Edited and Translated by John Owen, Edinburgh, 1853.

Republished by GLH Publishing, 2020.

ISBN:
 Paperback 978-1-64863-008-8
 Epub 978-1-64863-009-5

CONTENTS

Translator's Preface 1
To the Right Honourable Robert Earle of Salisbury, Vicount 10
To The Reader 13
Epistle Dedicatory 14
The Argument on the Epistle to the Hebrews 21
Chapter 1 26
Chapter 2 47
Chapter 3 72
Chapter 4 88
Chapter 5 108
Chapter 6 126
Chapter 7 150
Chapter 8 173
Chapter 9 189
Chapter 10 216
Chapter 11 255
Chapter 12 306
Chapter 13 335
Appendix of Additional Annotations 355
A Translation of Calvin's Version of The Epistle to the Hebrews 408

TRANSLATOR'S PREFACE

No doubt the Epistle next in importance to that to the Romans is this to the Hebrews. The truths explained in it might, indeed, have been deduced from other portions of Scripture; but it is a vast advantage and a great satisfaction to find them expressly set forth, and distinctly stated by an inspired Apostle.

In condescension to our ignorance, it has pleased God, not only to give us what might have been deemed sufficient for our information, but also to add "line upon line," so that there might be every help given to those who have a desire to know the truth, and every reasonable accuse taken away from such as resolve to oppose it, and to follow the guidance of self-will, and the delusions of their own proud minds and depraved hearts. It might then, seem strange to us that defect, insufficiency, and obscurity have been ascribed to the Scriptures, did we not know that these have been made by such as wish Revelation to be otherwise than it is; they having imbibed errors and adopted superstitions to which it yields no countenance, but which it condemns in terms so plain, that they must be represented as defective or obscure in order to be evaded.

There are especially two parties who find this Epistle in no way favorable to them — the Papists and the Socinians. The Sole Priesthood of Christ, and his Sole Sufficient Sacrifice, are here so distinctly stated, that the former cannot resist the evidence except by the subtle arts of the most consummate sophistry; and the latter find it a very difficult task to neutralize the strong and clear testimony here given as to the Divinity of our Savior and his Atonement. Though these parties are wholly opposed to one another, yet, like Herod and Pilate, they unite in degrading the Savior — the one indirectly, by substituting others in his place; and the other in open manner, by denying his dignity and the character and efficacy of his death. But by both the Savior is equally dishonored.

There have been more disputes about this Epistle than any other portion of Scripture; but many of the questions which have been raised have been of a very trifling character, as though learned men were idle and had nothing else to do; and this has been the case, especially with the divines of the German school, not only with regard to this Epistle, but with respect to many other subjects.

Disquisitions called learned, have been written as to the character of this Epistle, whether it be properly an Epistle, or something that ought to be called by some other name![1] Then it has been a subject learnedly discussed, to whom in particular the Epistle was sent, whether to the dispersed Jews, or to those in Palestine — whether to a particular Congregation, or to the Hebrews in general?[2] Such questions are comparatively of very little importance; and to spend time and talent in discussing them, is a work frivolous and useless; and not only so, but also mischievous, calculated to serve the purposes of Popery and Infidelity; for to render thus apparently important what is not so, and on which no degree of certainty can be obtained, is to involve men in a mist which may lead them astray.

Another subject has been much discussed, which is of no great consequence, as the inspiration of the Epistle is not thereby endangered, and that is the language in which the Epistle

---

1   To say that it has not the unusual introductory form of an Epistle, is no valid objection; for we find the case to be the same with regard to the First Epistle of John. It begins in a way very similar to this, while in the two following the usual mode is adopted.

2   The following account seems sufficiently satisfactory on this point: — "Clement of Alexandria, Jerome, Euthalius [Epiphanius?], Chrysostom, Theodoret, Theophylact and others, were of opinion that the Epistle to the Hebrews was sent to the Jews living in Judea, who in the Apostle's time were called *Hebrews* to distinguish them from the Jews in the Gentile countries, who were called *Hellenists* or Grecians, Acts vi. 1; ix. 29; xi. 20. In that opinion these ancient authors were well founded, because as Lardner observes, this letter appears to have been written to persons dwelling in one place, Hebrews xiii. 19, 23, 24, namely, to the inhabitants of Judea, and to those of them especially who lived in Jerusalem." — *Macknight*

was originally written. An opinion prevailed among some of the Early Fathers that it was written in Hebrew, or rather in Syro-Chaldee language, and that it was translated into Greek by Luke, Clement, or Barnabas. It was stated as an *opinion*, confirmed by no authority, and founded mainly on two circumstances — that it was written to Hebrews, and that its style is different from that of Paul in his other Epistles. Almost all modern divines regard this opinion as not well founded. The Greek language was in Paul's time well known throughout Palestine; the "General Epistles," intended for the Jews as well as the Gentiles, were written in Greek; and *there is no record of any copy of this Epistle in Hebrew*. As to the style, it differs not more from that of the other Epistles than what may be observed in writers in all ages, or what might be expected in Paul when advanced in years, compared with what he wrote in his younger days. It may be further added, that the Epistle itself contains things which seem to show that it was written in Greek: Hebrew words are interpreted, Hebrews vii. 2; the passages quoted are mostly from the *Septuagint*, and not from the Hebrew; and there is the use of a word, rendered "Testament," in Hebrews ix. 17, in the sense of a Will, which the Hebrew word never means.

There are only two questions of real importance — the canonicity of the Epistle, and its Author.

As to the first, it has never been doubted except by some of the strange heretics in the first ages. There is quite as much external testimony in its favor as most portions of the New Testament. It was from the first received by the Churches, Eastern and Western, as a portion of the Inspired Volume. It is found in the very first versions of the New Testament, the *Syriac* and the *Italic*. These versions were made as early as the end of the second century, about 140 years after the date of this Epistle.[3] The testimony of the Fathers from the earliest time is uniformly the same in this respect. The Epistle is acknowledged by them all as a portion of Holy Writ.

But with regard to the Author there has been a diversity of opinion, though, when all things are duly weighed, without reason. From the *earliest times*, the Eastern Church acknowledge

---

3   It is indeed thought, as stated by *Horne* in his Introduction, that the *Syriac* version was made at the end of the *first*, or at the beginning of the *second* century. In that case, it was made less than 40 years after the Epistle was written.

Paul as the Author. Some in the Western Church, in the third and the fourth century, did not regard Paul as the Author, but Luke, or Clement, or Barnabas. Jerome and Augustine in the fifth century, a more enlightened age than the two preceding centuries, ascribed to Paul the authorship; and since their time the same opinion has prevailed in the Western, as it did from the beginning in the Eastern Church. How to account for a different opinion in the Western Church during the third and the fourth century, is difficult. Some think it was owing to the Novalien Heresy, which some parts of this Epistle were supposed to favor, though without any good reason.

As far then as the testimony of history goes, almost the whole weight of evidence is in favor of Paul being the Author.

With regard to modern times, the prevailing opinion has been that it is the Epistle of Paul. Luther, indeed, ascribed it to Apollos — a mere conjecture. Calvin, as we find, supposed that either Luke or Clement was the author; for which there are no satisfactory reasons. Beza differed from his illustrious predecessor, and regarded Paul as the writer; and such has been the opinion entertained by most of the successors of the Reformers, both in this country and on the Continent, as proved by their confessions of Faith.

About the middle of the seventeenth century there seems to have been a revival of the controversy; for in the year 1658 the younger Spanheim wrote an elaborate treatise on the subject, in which he canvasses the whole evidence, both historical and internal, and affords the strongest ground for the conclusion that Paul was the writer of this Epistle. Since that time, till late years, his arguments were regarded by most as conclusive. But some of the German divines, who seem to have a taste for exploded opinions, have again revived the question, produced afresh the old arguments, and added some new ones to them. But a second Spanheim has appeared in the person of Professor Stuart, of America, who has published a learned Commentary on this Epistle, and prefixed to it a long Introduction, in which he has fully entered into the subject, and more fully than his predecessor. The labor and toil which this Introduction must have cost its author, were no doubt very great; for every argument, however frivolous, (and some of the arguments are *very* frivolous indeed,) is noticed, and everything plausible is most clearly exposed.

The evidence both external and internal is so satisfactory, that an impression is left on the mind, that Paul was the author of this Epistle, nearly equal to what his very name prefixed to it would have produced. Indeed the writer can truly say, that he now entertains no more doubt on the subject than if it had the Apostle's own superscription.[4]

As to the date of this Epistle, it is commonly supposed to have been written late in 62 or early in 63, about the time that Paul was released from his first imprisonment at Rome.

There seem to be especially two reasons why Paul did not commence this Epistle in his usual manner: first, because he was not specifically an Apostle to the Jews, but to the Gentiles; and secondly, because the contents of the Epistle are such that it was not necessary for him to assume his Apostolic character; for the arguments are founded on testimonies found in the Old Testament, and not on his authority as a commissioned Apostle. His main object appears to have been to show and prove that the Gospel is but a fulfillment of the ancient Scriptures, which the Jews themselves received as divine. His arguments and his examples are throughout borrowed from the Old Testament. This is a fact that is too often overlooked, to which Macknight, in an especial manner, very justly refers.

The Epistle begins by indicating a connection between the Old and the New Testament: both are revelations from the same God; He who spoke by the Prophets in the Old, speaks by His Son in the New. Then the obvious and inevitable conclusion is, that the New is but the Old completed. It is on this ground that the whole argument of the Epistle proceeds.

Having thus clearly intimated the connection between the two Testaments, the Apostle immediately enters on his great subject — the superiority of Him who introduced the perfected dispensation over all connected with the previous incomplete, elementary, and, in a great measure, symbolical dispensation, even over angels and Moses and the Levitical high-priest. And

---

[4] The arguments in favor of Paul being the author of this Epistle are briefly found in Horne's Introduction to the Critical Study of the Scriptures; but those who wish to see the subject fully handled, and that with great discrimination and judgment, must read Stuart's Introduction to his Commentary on this epistle. Dr. Bloomfield uses no exaggerated language when he says, that is "very elaborate and invaluable."

this subject occupies the largest portion of the Epistle, extending from the *first* chapter to the 19th verse of the *tenth* chapter. From that verse to the end of the Epistle, we have exhortations, warnings, examples of faith and patience, admonitions, directions, and salutations.

Then the Epistle divides itself into two main parts: —

1. The didactic, including the *ten* first chapters, with the exception of the latter part of the tenth.

2. The parainetic or hortative, from the 19th verse of the tenth chapter to the end of the Epistle.

The first part may be thus divided, —

1. Christ's superiority over angels — warnings — objections answered, ch. i. and ii.

2. Christ's superiority over Moses — warnings as to faith and the promised rest, ch. iii. and iv. 13.

3. Christ's superiority over the Levitical high-priest, as to his appointment, the perpetuity of his office, his covenant, and the efficacy of his atonement, ch. iv. 14, to x. 19.

The second part admits of these divisions, —

1. Exhortation to *persevere*, derived from the free access in a new way to God; from the awful fate of apostates; and from their own past example, ch. x. 19-37.

2. Exhortation to *faith* and *patience*, derived from the example of the ancient saints, ch. x. 38, to the end of ch. xi.

3. Exhortation to encounter *trials* and *afflictions*, derived from the example of Christ; and from the love of God, as manifested by afflictions, ch. xii. 1-13.

4. Exhortation to *peace* and *holiness*, derived from our superior privileges, and the aggravated guilt of no electing Him who speaks to us from heaven, ch. xii. 14-29.

5. Various directions and cautions, requests and salutations, ch. xiii.

The former part, the didactic, has many digressions, and hence the difficulty sometimes of tracing the course of the Apostle's reasoning. But it was his practice as appears from his other epistles, to apply, as it were, the subject, as he proceeds. Having in the *first* chapter proved the superiority of Christ over angels, he points out at the beginning of the *second* the great danger of disregarding his doctrine, and of neglecting his salvation, an inference drawn from what had been previously proved. He then proceeds with the same subject, Christ's superiority over angels, answers an objection derived from his human nature, and shows the necessity there was that he should become man; as he could not otherwise have sympathized with lost creatures, nor have atoned for their Sins. Here he first refers to him in express terms as a priest.

Then in ch. iii. he proceeds to show Christ's superiority over Moses; and having done so, he goes on in verse 7 to warn the Hebrews against following the example of their forefathers, who, through unbelief, lost the land of promise; and he pursues this subject to the end of the 13th verse of ch. iv.

The last section of the didactic part commences at ch. iv. and extends to verse 19 of the tenth chapter; it occupies nearly *six* chapters, and contains several episodes, so that it is sometimes no easy matter to trace the connection.

He begins this portion by calling attention to Christ as a high-priest, whom he had before represented as such at the end of ch. ii.; where he mentions *two* things respecting him — that he became man, in order that he might atone for sin, and in order that he might be capable of sympathizing with his people. But here he refers mainly to the *last*, to his sufferings; and in order to anticipate an objection from the fact that he was a suffering Savior, he mentions his appointment, which, according to the testimony of David in the Book of Psalms, was to be according to the order of Melchisedec. Without going on with this subject, he makes a digression, and evidently for the purpose of making them more attentive to the explanation he was going to give of Melchisedec as a type of Christ in his priesthood.

This digression contains several particulars. To arouse their attention and stimulate them, he blames them for their ignorance, mentions the danger of continuing satisfied with the knowledge of first principles, and the impossibility of restoration in case of apostasy; he gives an illustration of this from unproductive land after culture and rain; reminds them of their past commendable conduct, and encourages them to activity and zeal by an assurance respecting the certainty of Gods promises, ch. v. 12, to the end of ch. vi.

In chap. vii. he proceeds with Melchisedec as the type of Christ in his priestly office. Christ is a priest according to his order, not according to that of Aaron; then Aaron *must* have been superseded. According to the testimony of David, Christ's priesthood excelled that of Aaron in two things — it was established by an *oath*, and it was to he perpetuated "forever," ch. vii. to the end of the 25th verse.

He now goes on to the other part of this subject, to speak of Christ as making an atonement for sin, ch. vii. 26, having before spoken of him as a sympathizing priest from the circumstance of having been a sufferer. While speaking of his expiation, he refers to the covenant of which he was the Mediator, for expiations depended on the covenant. Respecting the new covenant, he quotes the express words of Jeremiah; and it included the remission of sins, and remission of sins necessarily implies an expiation. Then in the *ninth* chapter he refers to the old covenant, the tabernacle, and its services, and proves the insufficiency of these services, they being only typical of what was to come. From the *tenth* chapter to the 19th verse he pursues the same subject, and shows that the sacrifices under the Law were insufficient for the remission of sins, and that this could only be obtained through the Mediator of the new covenant promised by God through his prophet Jeremiah, chapter. vii. 26, to chapter.10:19.[5]

Here the Apostle completes the *first* part, having stated at large in the last portion of it the claims of Christ as a high-priest, and these claims are fully confirmed by the testimonies of the ancient Scriptures. His arguments are such that it is impossible really to understand and believe the Old Testament and to deny the New; the latter being most evidently the fulfillment of the former. The Old Testament distinctly speaks of another priesthood different from that of Aaron, and of another covenant different from that made with the children of Israel, and of one which would confer the remission of sins, which the other could not do. Now these are the testimonies not of the New but of the Old Testament; and the New exhibits a priest and a cov-

---

5   There is an elaborate analysis of the subject from chapter iv. 14, to chapter x. 19, by Stuart at the commencement of his notes on Chapter v.; but it is not satisfactory. He seems to have overlooked that there are two sections to this part, the one referring mainly to the appointment of Christ as a priest, which stands connected with this sufferings, and His capability of sympathy, chapter iv. 14 to vii. 25; and the other referring to the expiation he made as Mediator of the new covenant, chapter vii. 26 to chapter x. 9. The text which is the ground of the first section is Psalm cx. 4; the passage on which the second section is built is Jeremiah xxxi. 31-34, in connection with Psalm xl. 6.

enant exactly answerable to the priest and the covenant which the Old Testament refers to and describes. Nothing can be more plain and more conclusive than the Apostle's arguments on this subject.

The parainetic or hortative portion of the Epistle, extending from chap. x. 19 to the end, requires no further explanation.

We especially learn from this Epistle that the distinctive character of the old dispensation was symbolical, and of the new spiritual. The old abounded in forms, rituals, and ceremonies; the new exhibits what these things signified and typified. To have recourse again to symbols and rituals, is to prefer darkness to light, to reverse the order of things, and to disregard a favor which kings and prophets in ancient times desired to enjoy. This is not only an evidence of fatuity, but it is also ingratitude and sin, and it ought never to be deemed as innocent or harmless. Having the glorious light of the Gospel, let us walk in the light, and never regard "beggarly elements" as things to be perpetuated and admired.

This Commentary was translated into English by Clement Cotton, from the French Version, and was published in 1605 under the following title: — "A Commentarie on the whole Epistle to the Hebrews. By Iohn Calvin. Translated ovt of French. *The Lawe was given by Moses, but grace and truth came by Iesus Christ* John i. 17. Imprinted at London by Felix Kingston, for *Arthur Iohnson*, and are to be sold at his shop neere the great North doors of Pauls, at the signs of the white Horse. 1605." Like his translation of Isaiah, that of the Commentary on the Hebrews, "though not altogether suitable to modern taste, is faithful, vigorous, idiomatic, and not inelegant."

The "Epistle Dedicatorie" to Cotton's patron, Robert Cecil, Earl of Salisbury, and his Address "to the Reader," have been reprinted as a specimen of the style of such performances at that period.

J. O.
Thrussington, August 1853

TO THE RIGHT HONOURABLE ROBERT EARLE OF SALISBURY, VICOUNT

CRANBOURNE, BARON OF ESSENDON, PRINCIPAL SECRETARY TO THE KINGS MOST EXCELLENT MAJESTY, MASTER OF THE COURT OF WARDS AND LIVERIES, AND ONE OF HIS HIGHNESS MOST HONOURABLE PRIVY COUNSEL.

Grace and peace be multiplied

Right Honorable, such has been the singular care and fatherly providence of God over his church in these last times: that according to his own most gracious promise (through the means of preaching and writing) knowledge has overflowed in all places, as the waters that cover the sea. Hence it is come to pass, that even this nation also, albeit utterly unworthy to receive so much as the least sprinklings of this knowledge, has not withstanding been replenished and filled therewith, almost from corner to corner. Many chosen and worthy instruments has the Lord raised up here and there for this purpose. But amongst the rest, none for whom there is greater cause of thankfulness, than for that rare and excellent light of this age, *Mr. Calvin*: whether in respect of the large and many volumes, which with unwearable pains he has written, or the exceeding fruits which the Churches have thereby gained. So that all of sound judgment will acknowledge, that God had poured out upon him a principal portion and measure of his spirit to profit with all, 1 Corinthians xii. 7. Whereof, as his whole works give sufficient proofs, so his Commentaries especially. For besides his sincerity and faithfulness in delivering the true and natural sense of the holy Scriptures; he has this as peculiar to himself, that with his faithfulness and sincerity he always matches an exceeding plainness and gravity: whereby his Reader may obtain that he seeks, both with great ease, and with very little loss of time.

Divers of these his Commentaries, Right Honorable, have been already translated to the great benefit of this nation: others yet remain untranslated, which doubtless would be no less beneficial. The which, as I have earnestly desired; so, had gifts and means been in any measure answerable, it had been performed ere this. For the present, I have been bold to give your Honor a small taste thereof in these my poor first fruits: wherein although my pains are no way sufficient to commend the same unto your Honor, yet I doubt not but the matter itself will be found worthy of your H. patronage. For where are the natures and offices of Christ so largely described; the doctrine of the free remission of sins in Christ's blood better established, or faith with her effects more highly commended, than in this Epistle to the Hebrews?

Now as touching the reasons, Right Honorable, that have moved me hereunto, they are briefly these; First, I was not ignorant what singular love and affection your Honor bare to the author of this Commentary for his work's sake, whereof many also are witnesses. Unto which, if your Honor should be pleased to add a second favor in Patronizing these his labors, I thought it would be a special means to revive his memory again, now almost decayed amongst us.

Secondly, I was persuaded that if your Lordship, whom it has pleased the Almighty so highly to advance, being also a favorer and defender of the truth, and of all good causes; would permit this works to pass under your Honors protection: that it would be both better esteemed, and the more acceptably received of all.

Lastly, my good Lord. As I cannot conceal that deep and inward affection of love and duties which I owe unto your Honor, in regard of the near employments which sometimes a dear friend of mine had about your Lordship in your young years: so by this dedication it was my desire to testify part of a thankful mind, in respect that you have not suffered neither length of time, nor your H. weighty affairs in matters of state, to wear the same out of your Honorable remembrance: as by the great favors your H. has lately showed in that behalf, does plainly appear.

Thus in most humble manner craving pardon for my great boldness, I humbly end; beseeching the most high God, possessor of heaven and earth, to pour out the abundance of all blessings both upon you and yours in this life, and to crown your H. and them with immortal blessedness in his kingdom of glory, through Christ.

Your Honours in all humble and dutifull affection ever to be commanded,
      Clement Cotton

TO THE READER

Dear Christian Reader, among the many helps wherewith God has furnished thee for the furtherance of thy godly Meditations and spiritual growth in Christ, I pray thee accept of this amongst the rest; of which (if I may so speak) thou has been too long unfurnished. Diverse good and godly men have labored, some by their own writings, and some again by translating the works of others, to store thee with Sermons and Expositions in English, upon all the books of the New Testament, this Epistle to the Hebrews lonely excepted: which lack, rather than it should be unsupplied, has caused me (the unfittest I confess at many thousands) to undertake the translation of the Commentary ensuing: which being finished, I have been bold (for thy benefit Christian Reader) now to publish. Hoping therefore of thy friendly allowance and acceptance of these my poor endeavors: I beseech thee, if thou reap that benefit thereby, which I heartily with thou may, to give God the praise, and to help me with thy prayers. Thus commending thee and thy studies to the grace of God, I bid thee farewell.

Thine ever in Christ,
C.C.

EPISTLE DEDICATORY

JOHN CALVIN

TO THE MOST MIGHTY AND MOST SERENE PRINCE, SIGISMUND AUGUSTUS, BY THE GRACE OF GOD, THE KING OF POLAND, GREAT DUKE OF LITHUANIA, RUSSIA, PRUSSIA, AND LORD AND HEIR OF MUSCOVY, ETC.

There are at this day many foolish men, who everywhere, through a vain desire for writing, engage the minds of ignorant and thoughtless readers with their trifles. And to this evil, most illustrious King, is added another indignity — that while they inscribe to kings and princes their silly things, to disguise, or at least to cover them by borrowed splendor, they not only profane sacred names, but also impart to them some measure of their own disgrace. Since the unreasonable temerity of such men makes it necessary for serious and sober writers to frame an excuse, when they publicly dedicate their labors to great men, while yet there is nothing in them but what corresponds with the greatness of those to whom they are offered, it was necessary to make this remark, lest I should seem to be of the number of those who allow themselves, through the example of others, to render public anything they please, however foolish it may be. But it has not escaped me how much it has the appearance of foolish confidence, that I, (not to speak of other things,) who am an unknown and obscure man, should not hesitate to address your royal Majesty. Let my reasons be heard, and if you, O King, approve of what I do, what others may judge will cause me no great anxiety.

First, then, though I am not forgetful of mine insignificance, nor ignorant of the reverence due to your Majesty, yet the fame of your piety, which has extended almost to all who are zealous for the sincere doctrine of Christ, is alone sufficient to remorse any fear; for I bring with me a present which that piety will not allow you to reject. Since the Epistle inscribed to the Hebrews contains a full discussion respecting the eternal divinity of Christ, his government, and only priesthood, (which are the main points of celestial wisdom,) and as these things are so explained in it, that the whole power and work of Christ are set forth in the most graphic manner, it deservedly ought to obtain in the Church the place and the honor of an invaluable treasure. By you also, who desire that the Son of God should reign alone and be glorified, I doubt not but that it will be valued.

In the interpretation which I have undertaken, I say not that I have succeeded; but I feel confident that when you have read it you will approve at least of my fidelity and diligence. And as I claim not the praise of great knowledge or of erudition, so what has been given me by the Lord for the purpose of understanding the Scripture, (since this is to glory in him,) I am not ashamed to profess; and if in this respect I have any capacity to assist the Church of God, I have endeavored to give an evident proof of it in these my labors. I therefore hope that the present (as I have said) which I offer will not only avail, O King, as an excuse to your Majesty, but also procure for me no small favor.

This may possibly be also a new encouragement to your Majesty, who is already engaged in the work of restoring the kingdom of Christ, and to many who live under your government to further the same work. Your kingdom is extensive and renowned, and abounds in many excellences; but its happiness will then only be solid, when it adopts Christ as its chief ruler and governor, so that it may be defended by his safeguard and protection; for to submit your scepter to him, is not inconsistent with that elevation in which you are placed; but it would be far more glorious than all the triumphs of the world. For since among men gratitude is deemed the proper virtue of a great and exalted mind, what in kings can be more unbecoming than to be ungrateful to the Son, by whom they have been raised to the highest degree of honor? It is, therefore, not only an honorable, but more than a royal service, which raises us to the rank of angels, when the throne of Christ is erected among us, so that his celestial voice becomes the only rule for living and dying both to the highest and to the lowest. For though at this day to obey the authority of Christ is the common profession, made almost by all, yet there are very few who render this obedience of which they boast.

Now this obedience cannot be rendered, except the whole of religion be formed according to the infallible rule of his holy truth. But on this point strange conflicts arise, while men, not only inflated with pride, but also bewitched by monstrous madness, pay less regard to the unchangeable oracles of our heavenly Master than to their own vain fictions; for whatever pretenses they may set up, who oppose us and strive to assist the Roman Antichrist, the very fountain of all the contentions, by which the Church for these thirty years has been so sorely disturbed, will be found to be, that they who seek to be deemed first among Christ's disciples, cannot bear to submit to his truth. Ambition as well as audacity has so far prevailed, that the truth of God lies buried under innumerable lies, that all his institutions are polluted by the basest corruptions; his worship is in every part vitiated, the doctrine of faith is wholly subverted, the sacraments are adulterated, the government of the Church is turned into barbarous tyranny, the abominable sale of sacred things has been set up, the power of Christ has been abused for the purpose of sustaining the tyranny of the ungodly, and in the place of Christianity is substituted a dreadful profanation, full of the grossest mummeries of every kind. When for these so many and so atrocious evils we bring this one remedy — to hear the Son of God speaking from heaven, we are instantly opposed by these Atlases, not those who support the Church on their shoulders, but who elevate on high by vain boastings of empty titles an idol devised and formed by themselves. They also adduce this as a pretext for their fierce recriminations, that we by our appeals disturb the peace of the Church. When we come to know things aright, we see that these subtle artifices devise for themselves a Church wholly different from that of Christ! And what else is this but a wicked and sacrilegious attempt to separate the body from its head? It hence appears how frivolous is the boasting of many as to Christianity; for the greatest part suffer themselves to be governed by nothing less than by the pure teaching of the Gospel.

But what you acknowledge, O King, that in order that Christ may take an entire possession of his own kingdom, it is necessary to clear away all superstitions, is a proof of singular wisdom; and to undertake and attempt what you judge to be thus necessary, is an evidence of rare virtue. That you are indeed like another Hezekiah or Josiah, destined by God to restore shortly to the kingdom of Poland a purer teaching of that gospel, which has been throughout the world vitiated by the craft of Satan and perfidy of men, there are many things which give almost a certain hope to all good men. For, to omit other superior qualities, which even foreigners proclaim and men of your own kingdom observe with great advantage, there has ever appeared in you a wonderful concern for religion, and religion itself appears eminent in you in the present day. But the chief thing is, that Christ, the Sun of Righteousness, has so irradiated your mind with the light of his Gospel, that you understand that the true way of governing the Church is no other than what is to be derived from him, and that you at the same time know the difference between that genuine form of religion which he has instituted, and that fictions and degenerate form which was afterwards introduced; for you wholly understand that God's worship has been corrupted and deformed, as innumerable superstitions have crept in, that the grace of Christ has been unworthily involved in great darkness, that the virtue of his death has been annihilated, that he himself has been almost lacerated and torn in pieces, that assurance of salvation has been plucked up by the roots, that consciences have been miserably and even horribly vexed and tormented, that wretched men have been led away from the sincere and right worship of God into various and perplexed labyrinths, that the Church has been cruelly and tyrannically oppressed; and, in short, that no real Christianity has been left.

It is not to be believed, O most noble King, that you have been in vain endowed by God with this knowledge; doubtless he has chosen you as his minister for some great purposes. And it has hitherto happened through God's wonderful Providence that no innocent blood has been shed in the renowned kingdom of Poland — no, not a drop, which by calling for vengeance might retard so great a benefit. It was through the clemency and gentleness of King Sigismund, of happy memory, the father of your Majesty, that this did not take place; for, while the contagion of cruelty was spreading through the whole of the Christian world, he kept his hands pure. But now your Majesty and some of the most eminent of your princes not only receive Christ willingly when offered to them, but anxiously desire him. I also see John a Lasco, born of a noble family, carrying the torch to other nations.

The presumption of Eckius is by no means to be endured, who dedicated to King Sigismund, the father of your Majesty, his book on The Sacrifice of the Mass; for he thus, as far as he could, affixed a base blot to your illustrious kingdom! At the same time, it was nothing strange in that *Silenus*, who, being the prince of drunkards, was wont to vomit at the altar as well as at the dunghill. Now, by dedicating this my labor to your Majesty, I shall at least effect this, that I shall wash away from the name of Poland the base filth of *Eckius*, so that it may not stick where it has been so unworthily fixed. And by doing so I shall not, as it seems to me, attain a small object; and no book of Scripture could hardly be chosen so suitable for such a purpose. For here our Apostle shows in an especial manner, that the sacrifice which *Eckius* advocates is manifestly inconsistent with the priesthood of Christ. There is here, indeed, no mention of the mass, which Satan had not then vomited out of hell. But by bidding the Church to be satisfied with the one only true sacrifice which Christ offered on the cross, that all rites of sacrificing might cease forever, he doubtless closes the door against all their new glosses. The Apostle cries aloud that Christ was sacrificed on the cross once for all, while *Eckius* feigns that this sacrifice is daily renewed! The Apostle declares that the only Son of God was the fit priest to offer himself to the Father, and hence he was constituted by an oath; but *Eckius* denies that he alone is the priest, and transfers that function to hired sacrificers! At the same time, I am not ignorant of the evasions by which they elude these and similar arguments; but there is no fear that he will deceive any but those who are blind or who shun the light. He was at the same time so inebriated with Thrasonic haughtiness that he labored more in insolent boasting than in subtle demonstration. That I may not, however, seem to triumph over a dead dog, I will add nothing more at present than that my Commentary may serve to wipe off the filthy stain which that unprincipled and Scottish man attempted to fix on the name of Poland; and there is no fear that they who will read will be taken by his baits.

Moreover, as I wish not in offering this my labor to your Majesty, only to show privately a regard for you, O King, but especially to make it known to the whole world, it remains now for me humbly to implore your Majesty not to repudiate what I do. If indeed a stimulus be thereby given to encourage your pious endeavors, I shall think it an ample remuneration. Undertake, then, I pray, O magnanimous King, under the auspicious banner of Christ, a work so worthy of your royal elevation, as well as of your heroic virtue, so that the eternal truth of God, by which his own glory and the salvation of men are promoted, may, wherever thy kingdom spreads, recover its own authority, which has been taken away by the fraudulent dealings of Antichrist. It is truly an arduous work, and of such magnitude as is sufficient to fill even the wisest with solicitude and fear.

But first, there is no danger which we ought not cheerfully to undergo, no difficulty which we ought not resolutely to undertake, no conflicts in which we ought not boldly to engage, in a cause so necessary. Secondly, as it is the peculiar work of God, we ought not in this case to regard so much the extent of human powers as the glory due to his power; so that, relying on that not only to help us, but also to guide us, we may venture on things far beyond our own strength; for the work of restoring and establishing the church is not without reason everywhere assigned in Scripture to God. Besides, the work itself is altogether divine; and as soon as any beginning is made, whatever arts of injury Satan possesses, he employs them all either to stop or to delay a further progress. And we know that the prince of this world has innumerable agents who are ever ready to oppose the kingdom of Christ. Some are instigated by ambition, others by gain. These contests try us in some degree in our humble condition; but your majesty will have, no doubt, to experience far greater difficulties. Therefore, all those who undertake to promote the doctrine of salvation and the well-being of the Church must be armed with invincible firmness. But as this business is above our strength, aid from heaven will be granted to us.

It is in the meantime our duty to have all these promises which everywhere occur in Scripture inscribed on our hearts.

The Lord who has himself as it were by his own hand laid the foundations of the Church, will not suffer it to remain in a decayed state, for he is represented as solicitous to restore it and to repair its ruins; for, by speaking thus, he in effect promises that he will never fail us when engaged in this work. As he would not have us to sit down as idle spectators of his power, so the presence of his aid in sustaining the hands which labor, clearly proves that he himself is the chief architect. What, therefore, he so often repeats and inculcates, and not without reason, is, that we are not to grow weary, however often we may have to contend with enemies, who continually break forth into hostility; for they are, as we have said, almost infinite in number, and in kinds various. But this one thing is abundantly sufficient, that we have such an invincible Leader, that the more he is assailed the greater will be the victories and triumphs gained by his power.

Farewell, invincible King. May the Lord Jesus rule you by the spirit of wisdom, sustain you by the spirit of valor, bestow on you all kinds of blessings, long preserve your Majesty in health and prosperity, and protect your kingdom. Amen.

GENEVA, May 23, 1549

THE ARGUMENT ON THE EPISTLE TO THE HEBREWS

Not only various opinions were formerly entertained as to the author of this Epistle, but it was only at a late period that it was received by the Latin Churches. They suspected that it favored Novatus in denying pardon to the fallen;[6] but that this was a groundless opinion will be shown by various passages. I, indeed, without hesitation, class it among apostolical writings; nor do I doubt but that it has been through the craft of Satan that any have been led to dispute its authority. There is, indeed, no book in the Holy Scriptures which speaks so clearly of the priesthood of Christ, so highly exalts the virtue and dignity of that only true sacrifice which he offered by his death, so abundantly treats of the use of ceremonies as well as of their abrogation, and, in a word, so fully explains that Christ is the end of the Law. Let us not therefore suffer the Church of God nor

---

6   *Novatus* was a priest in Carthage about the middle of the third century, and came to Rome as an advocate on *Novation*, who was the leader in this opinion. What gave the first occasion to this sentiment was the case of some who fell away from the faith during the Decian persecution. *Novatian* resisted their restoration, and afterwards extended the same denied repentance to all such, and regarded them as forever unfit to be received into the Church. He opposed the election of *Cornelius* to the see of Rome, who differed from his jurisdiction, and formed a sect of his own. He was consequently excommunicated, together with his party, (of which Novatus seems to have been one,) by a council assembled by Cornelius in the year 251. He was then made a bishop by his own party, and was followed by many; and his sect continued to flourish till the fifth century. But Novation, a Roman priest, rather than Novatus, a priest from Carthage, was its founder. — See Mosheim's Eccl. Hist., volume. 1 page 249. — *Ed.*

ourselves to be deprived of so great a benefit, but firmly defend the possession of it.

Moreover, as to its author, we need not be very solicitous. Some think the author to have been Paul, others Luke, others Barnabas, and others Clement, as Jerome relates; yet Eusebius, in his sixth book of his Church History, mentions only Luke and Clement. I well know that in the time of Chrysostom it was everywhere classed by the Greeks among the Pauline Epistles; but the Latins thought otherwise, even those who were nearest to the times of the Apostles.

I indeed, can adduce no reason to show that Paul was its author; for they who say that he designedly suppressed his name because it was hateful to the Jews, bring nothing to the purpose; for why, then, did he mention the name of Timothy as by this he betrayed himself. But the manner it of teaching, and the style, sufficiently show that Paul was not the author; and the writer himself confesses in the second chapter that he was one of the disciples of the Apostles, which is wholly different from the way in which Paul spoke of himself. Besides, what is said of the practice of catechizing in the sixth chapter, does not well suit the time or age of Paul. There are other things which we shall notice in their proper places.

What excuse is usually made as to the style I well know that is, that no opinion can be hence formed, because the Greek is a translation made from the Hebrew by Luke or someone else. But this conjecture can be easily refuted: to pass by other places quoted from Scripture, on the supposition that the Epistle was written in Hebrew, there would have been no allusion to the word Testament, on which the writer so much dwells; what he says of a Testament, in the ninth chapter, could not have been drawn from any other fountain than from the Greek word; for διαθήκη has two meanings in Greek, while ברית in Hebrew means only a covenant. This reason alone is enough to convince men of sound judgment that the epistle was written in the Greek languages. Now, what is objected on the other hand, that it is more probable that the Apostle wrote to the Jews in their own language, has no weight in it; for how few then understood their ancient language? Each had learned the language of the country where he dwelt. Besides, the Greek was then more widely known than all other languages. We shall proceed now to the Argument.

The object at the beginning is not to show to the Jews that Jesus, the son of Mary, was the Christ, the Redeemer promised to them, for he wrote to those who had already made a profession of Christ; that point, then, is taken as granted. But the design of the writer was to prove what the office of Christ is. And it hence appears evident, that by his coming an end was put to ceremonies. It is necessary to draw this distinction; for as it would have been a superfluous labor for the Apostle to prove to those who were already convinced that he was the Christ who had appeared, so it was necessary for him to show what he was, for they did not as yet clearly understand the end, the effect, and the advantages of his coming; but being taken up with a false view of the Law, they laid hold on the shadow instead of the substance. Our business with the Papists is similar in the present day; for they confess with us that Christ is the Son of God, the redeemer who had been promised to the world: but when we come to the reality, we find that they rob him of more than one-half of his power.

Now, the beginning is respecting the dignity of Christ; for it seemed strange to the Jews that the Gospel should be preferred to the Law. And first indeed he settles that point which was in dispute, that the doctrine brought by Christ had the preeminence, for it was the fulfillment of all the prophecies. But as the reverence in which they held Moses might have been a hindrance to them, he shows that Christ was far superior to all others. And after having briefly referred to those things in which he excelled others, he mentions by name the angels, that with them he might reduce all to their proper rank. Thus he advanced prudently in his course; for if he had begun with Moses, his comparison would have been more disliked. But when it appears from Scripture that celestial powers are subordinated to Christ, there is no reason why Moses or any mortal being should refuse to be classed with them, so that the Son of God may appear eminent above angels as well as men.

After having thus brought the angels under the power and dominion of Christ, the Apostle having, as it were, gained confidence, declares that Moses was so much inferior to him as a servant is to his master.

By thus setting Christ in the *three first chapters* in a supreme state of power, he intimates, that when he speaks all ought to be silent, and that nothing should prevent us from seriously attending to his doctrine. At the same time he sets him forth in the second chapter as our brother in our flesh; and thus he allures us to devote ourselves more willingly to him; and he also blends exhortations and threatening in order to lead those to obedience who are tardy or perversely resist; and he continues in this strain nearly to the end of the fourth chapter.

At the end of the *fourth chapter* he begins to explain the priesthood of Christ, which abolishes all the ceremonies of the Law. But after having briefly showed how welcome that priesthood ought to be to us, and how gladly we ought to acquiesce in it, he shortly turns aside to reprove the Jews, because they stopped at the first elements of religion like children; and he also terrifies them with a grievous and severe denunciation, that there was danger lest they, if slothful to make progress, should at length be rejected by the Lord. But he presently softens this asperity by saying, that he hoped better things of them, in order that he might encourage them, whom he had depressed, to make progress.

Then [in the *seventh* chapter] he returns to the priesthood; and first shows that it differed from the ancient priesthood under the Law; secondly, that it was more excellent, because it succeeded it, and was sanctioned by an oath, — because it is eternal, and remains for ever efficacious, — because he who performs its duties is superior in honor and dignity to Aaron and all the rest of the Levitical tribe; and he shows that the type which shadowed forth all things was found in the person of Melchisedec.

And in order to prove more fully that the ceremonies of the Law were abrogated he mentions that the ceremonies were appointed, and also the tabernacle, for a particular end, even that they might get forth the heavenly prototype. Hence it follows, that they were not to be rested in unless we wish to stop in the middle of our course, having no regard to the goal. On this subject he quotes a passage from Jeremiah, in which a new covenant is promised, which was nothing else than an improvement on the old. It hence follows, that the old was weak and fading.

Having spoken of the likeness and similitude between the shadows and the reality exhibited in Christ, he then concludes that all the rituals appointed by Moses have been abrogated by the one only true sacrifice of Christ, because the efficacy of this sacrifice is perpetual, and that not only the sanction of the New

Testament is made by it complete, but that it is also a true and a spiritual accomplishment of that external priesthood which was in force under the Law.

To this doctrine he again connects exhortation like a goad, that putting aside all impediments they might receive Christ with due reverence.

As to the many examples he mentions in the *eleventh* chapter concerning the fathers, they seem to me to have been brought forward for this purpose, — that the Jews might understand, that if they were led from Moses to Christ, they would be so far from departing from the fathers, that they would thus be especially connected with them. For if the chief thing in them was faith, and the root of all other virtues, it follows that this is especially that by which they should be counted the children of Abraham and the Prophets; and that on the other hand all are bastards who follow not the faith of the fathers. And this is no small commendation of the Gospel, that by it we have union and fellowship with the universal Church, which has been from the beginning of the world.

The *two last* chapters contain various precepts as to the way in which we ought to live: they speak of hope, of bearing the cross, of perseverance, of gratitude towards God, of obedience, of mercy, of the duties of love, of chastity, and of such like things. And lastly, he concludes with prayer, and at the same time gives them a hope of his coming to see them.

CHAPTER 1

HEBREWS I. 1-2

1. God, who at sundry times and in divers manners spake in time past unto the fathers by the prophets,
2. Hath in these last days spoken unto us by *his* Son, whom he hath appointed heir of all things, by whom also he made the worlds;

God formerly, etc. This beginning is for the purpose of commending the doctrine taught by Christ; for it shows that we ought not only reverently to receive it, but also to be satisfied with it alone. That we may understand this more clearly, we must observe the contrast between each of the clauses. First, the Son of God is set in opposition to the prophets; then we to the fathers; and, thirdly, the various and manifold modes of speaking which God had adopted as to the fathers, to the last revelation brought to us by Christ. But in this diversity he still sets before us but one God, that no one might think that the Law militates against the Gospel, or that the author of one is not the author of the other. That you may, therefore, understand the full import of this passage, the following arrangement shall be given, —

GOD SPAKE
FORMERLY BY THE PROPHETS. . . NOW BY THE SON;
THEN TO THE FATHERS. . . BUT NOW TO US;
THEN AT VARIOUS TIMES. . . NOW AS AT THE END OF THE TIMES.

This foundation being laid, the agreement between the Law and the Gospel is established; for God, who is ever like himself, and whose word is the same, and whose truth is unchangeable, has spoken as to both in common.

But we must notice the difference between us and the fathers; for God formerly addressed them in a way different from that which he adopts towards us now. And first indeed as to them he employed the prophets, but he has appointed his Son to be an ambassador to us.[7] Our condition, then, in this respect, is superior to that of the fathers. Even Moses is to be also classed among the prophets, as he is one of the number of those who are inferior to the Son. In the manner also in which revelation was made, we have an advantage over them. For the diversity as to visions and other means adopted under the Old Testament, was an indication that it was not yet a fixed state of things, as when matters are put completely in order. Hence he says, *multifariously and in many ways*". God would have indeed followed the same mode perpetually to the end, had the mode been perfect and complete. It hence follows, that this variety was an evidence of imperfection.

The two words I thus understand: I refer *multifariously* to a diversity as to times; for the Greek word πολυμερῶς which we may render, "in many parts," as the case usually is, when we intend to speak more fully hereafter; but πολυτροπῶς points out a diversity, as I think, in the very manner itself.[8] And when

---

[7] The absence of the definite article before υἱῷ is not unusual in the New Testament, it being often omitted before all sorts of nouns. In many instances it is Hebrewism, and so here; for Chrysostom in his comment supplies it, and mentions that ἐν here is διὰ, which is another Hebrewism. — *Ed.*

[8] Some of the fathers, such as Chrysostom, regarded the two words as meaning the same thing; but there is no reason for this. On the contrary, each word has a distinct meaning; one expresses a variety as to parts or portions, and the other variety as to the mode or manner. The "parts" clearly refer to the different portions of revelation communicated to "holy men" in different ages of the world. Hence the meaning, though not the literal rendering, is given in our version, "at sundry time;" or "often", as by Stuart; or "at many times", as by Doddridge. A more literal version is given by Macknight, "in sundry parts".

Most agree as to the second word, that it designates the various modes of communication, — by visions, dreams, interposition of angels, and speaking face to face, as the case was with

he speaks of *the last times*, he intimates that there is no longer any reason to expect any new revelation; for it was not a word in part that Christ brought, but the final conclusion. It is in this sense that the Apostles take *the last times* and *the last days*. And Paul means the same when he says, "Upon whom the ends of the world are come." (1 Corinthians x. 11.) If God then has spoken now for the last time, it is right to advance thus far; so also when you come to Christ, you ought not to go farther: and these two things it is very needful for us to know. For it was a great hindrance to the Jews that they did not consider that God had deferred a fuller revelation to another time; hence, being satisfied with their own Law, they did not hasten forward to the goal. But since Christ has appeared, an opposite evil began to prevail in the world; for men wished to advance beyond Christ. What else indeed is the whole system of Popery but the overleaping of the boundary which the Apostle has fixed? As, then, the Spirit of God in this passage invites all to come as far as Christ, so he forbids them to go beyond the last time which he mentions. In short, the limit of our wisdom is made here to be the Gospel.[9]

2. *Whom he has appointed, heir, etc.* He honors Christ with high commendations, in order to lead us to show him reverence; for since the Father has subjected all things to him, we are all under his authority. He also intimates that no good can be found apart from him, as he is the heir of all things. It hence follows that we must be very miserable and destitute of all good things except he supplies us with his treasures. He further adds that this honor of possessing all things belongs by right to the Son, because

---

Moses; see Numbers xii. 6-8. And there was another variety in the manner, sometimes in plain language, and at another time in similitudes and parables. — *Ed.*

[9] It is said that the MSS, are in favor of ἐσχάτου "in the last of these days." Were it not for "these", this might be allowed, as the literal rendering of these Hebrew words often used, באחרית הימים, "at the extremity of the days", (see Isaiah ii. 2; Hosea iii. 5, etc.) but the sentence, as changed by Griesbach and others, makes no sense, and is inconsistent with the words as elsewhere used by Paul; see 2 Timothy iii. 1. A mere majority of MSS, is no sufficient authority for a reading. — *Ed.*

by him have all things been created. At the same time, these two things[10] are ascribed to Christ for different reasons.

The world was created by him, as he is the eternal wisdom of God, which is said to have been the director of all his works from the beginning; and hence is proved the eternity of Christ, for he must have existed before the world was created by him. If, then, the duration of his time be inquired of, it will be found that it has no beginning. Nor is it any derogation to his power that he is said to have created the world, as though he did not by himself create it. According to the most usual mode of speaking in Scripture, the Father is called the Creator; and it is added in some places that the world was created by wisdom, by the word, by the Son, as though wisdom itself had been the creator, [or the word, or the Son.] But still we must observe that there is a difference of persons between the Father and the Son, not only with regard to men, but with regard to God himself. But the unity of essence requires that whatever is peculiar to Deity should belong to the Son as well as to the Father, and also that whatever is applied to God only should belong to both; and yet there is nothing in this to prevent each from his own peculiar properties.

But the word *heir* is ascribed to Christ as manifested in the flesh; for being made man, he put on our nature, and as such received this heirship, and that for this purpose, that he might restore to us what we had lost in Adam. For God had at the beginning constituted man, as his Son, the heir of all good things; but through sin the first man became alienated from God, and deprived himself and his posterity of all good things, as well as of the favor of God. We hence only then begin to enjoy by right the good things of God, when Christ, the universal heir, admits to a union with himself; for he is an heir that he may endow us with his riches. But the Apostle now adorns him with this title, that we may know that without him we are destitute of all good things.

If you take *all* in the masculine gender, the meaning is, that we ought all to be subject to Christ, because we have been given to him by the Father. But I prefer reading it in the neuter gender; then it means that we are driven from the legitimate possession of all things, both in heaven and on earth, except we be united to Christ.

---

10 That is, heirship and creation.

HEBREWS I. 3

3. Who being the brightness of *his* glory, and the express image of his person, and upholding all things by the word of his power, when he had by himself purged our sins, sat down on the right hand of the Majesty on high.

3. *Who being the brightness of his glory, etc.* These things are said of Christ partly as to his divine essence, and partly as a partaker of our flesh. When he is called *the brightness of his glory and the impress of his substance,* his divinity is referred to; the other things appertain in a measure to his human nature. The whole, however, is stated in order to set forth the dignity of Christ.

But it is for the same reason that the Son is said to be "the brightness of his glory", and "the impress of his substance:" they are words borrowed from nature. For nothing can be said of things so great and so profound, but by similitudes taken from created things. There is therefore no need refinedly to discuss the question how the Son, who has the same essence with the Father, is a brightness emanating from his light. We must allow that there is a degree of impropriety in the language when what is borrowed from created things is transferred to the hidden majesty of God. But still the things which are indent to our senses are fitly applied to God, and for this end, that we may know what is to be found in Christ, and what benefits he brings to us.

It ought also to be observed that frivolous speculations are not here taught, but an important doctrine of faith. We ought therefore to apply these high titles given to Christ for our own benefit, for they bear a relation to us. When, therefore, thou hear that the Son is the brightness of the Father's glory, think thus with thyself, that the glory of the Father is invisible until it shines forth in Christ, and that he is called the impress of his substance, because the majesty of the Father is hidden until it shows itself impressed as it were on his image. They who overlook this connection and carry their philosophy higher, weary themselves to no purpose, for they do not understand the design of the Apostle; for it was not his object to show what likeness the Father bears to the Son; but, as I have said, his purpose was really to build up our faith, so that we may learn that God is made known to us in no other way than in Christ:[11] for as to the essence of God, so immense is the brightness that it dazzles our eyes, except it shines on us in Christ. It hence follows, that we are blind as to the light of God, until in Christ it beams on us. It is indeed a profitable philosophy to learn Christ by the real understanding of faith and experience. The same view, as I have said is to be taken of "the impress;" for as God is in himself to us incomprehensible, his form appears to us only in his Son.[12]

The word ἀπαύγασμα means here nothing else but visible light or refulgence, such as our eyes can bear; and χαρακτὴρ is the vivid form of a hidden substance. By the first word we are reminded that without Christ there is no light, but only darkness; for as God is the only true light by which it behoves us all to be illuminated, this light sheds itself upon us, so to speak, only by irradiation. By the second word we are reminded that God is truly and really known in Christ; for he is not his obscure or shadowy image, but his impress which resembles him, as money the impress of the die with which it is stamped. But

---

11 The fathers and some modern divines have held that these words express the eternal relation between the Father and the Son. But Calvin, with others, such as Beza, Dr. Owen, Scott and Stuart, have regarded the words as referring to Christ as the Messiah, as the Son of God in human nature, or as Mediator, consistently with such passages as these, — "He that hath seen me hath seen the Father." John xiv. 9; "He that hath seen me hath seen him that sent me." (John xii. 45). By this view we avoid altogether the difficulty that arises from the expressions, "the impress of his substance," or essence, he being so, not as to his eternal divinity, but as a Mediator. — Ed.

12 The remarkable wisdom of the preceding remarks must be approved by every enlightened Christian. There is an "Excursus" in Professor Stuart's Commentary on this Epistle, on the same subject, which is very valuable, distinguished for caution, acuteness, and sound judgment. Well would it be were all divines to show the same humility on a subject so remote from human comprehension. The bold and unhallowed speculations of some of the fathers, and of the schoolmen, and divines after them, have produced infinite mischief, having occasioned hindrances to the reception of the truth respecting our Savior's divinity, which would have otherwise never existed. — Ed.

the Apostle indeed says what is more than this, even that the substance of the Father is in a manner engraven on the Son.[13]

The word ὑπόστασις which, by following others, I have rendered substance, denotes not, as I think, the being or essence of the Father, but his person; for it would be strange to say that the essence of God is impressed on Christ, as the essence of both is simply the same. But it may truly and fitly be said that whatever peculiarly belongs to the Father is exhibited in Christ, so that he who knows him knows what is in the Father. And in this sense do the orthodox fathers take this term, *hypostasis*, considering it to be threefold in God, while the essence (οὐσία) is simply one. *Hilary* everywhere takes the Latin word substance for person. But though it be not the Apostle's object in this place to speak of what Christ is in himself, but of what he is really to us, yet he sufficiently confutes the Asians and Sabellians; for he claims for Christ what belongs to God alone, and also refers to two distinct persons, as to the Father and the Son. For we hence learn that the Son is one God with the Father, and that he is yet in a sense distinct from him, so that a subsistence or person belongs to both.

And upholding (or bearing) all things, etc. To uphold or to bear here means to preserve or to continue all that is created in its own state; for he intimates that all things would instantly come to nothing, were they not sustained by his power. Though the pronoun *his* may be referred to the Father as well as to the Son, as it may be rendered "his own," yet as the other exposition is more commonly received, and well suits the context, I am disposed to embrace it. Literally it is, "by the word of his power;" but the genitive, after the Hebrew manner, is used instead of an adjective; for the perverted explanation of some, that Christ sustains all things by the word of the Father, that is, by himself who is the word, has nothing in its favor: besides, there is no need of such forced explanation; for Christ is not wont to be called ῥῆμα, saying, but λόγος, word.[14] Hence the "word" here

---

13 See Appendix A.

14 Stuart following Chrysostom, renders the words φέραν, "controlling" or governing, and so does Schleusner; but the sense of "upholding" or sustaining, or supporting, is more suitable to the words which follow — "by the word of his power," or by his powerful word. Had it been "by the word of his wisdom," then

means simply a nod; and the sense is, that Christ who preserves the whole world by a nod only, did not yet refuse the office of effecting our purgation.

Now this is the second part of the doctrine handled in this Epistle; for a statement of the whole question is to be found in these two chapters, and that is, that Christ, endued with supreme authority, ought to be head above all others, and that as he has reconciled us to his Father by his own death, he has put an end to the ancient sacrifices. And so the first point, though a general proposition, is yet a twofold clause.

When he further says, *by himself,* there is to be understood here a contrast, that he had not been aided in this by the shadows of the Mosaic Law. He shows besides a difference between him and the Levitical priests; for they also were said to expiate sins, but they derived this power from another. In short, he intended to exclude all other means or helps by stating that the price and the power of purgation were found only in Christ.[15]

---

controlling or governing would be compatible; but as it is "power", doubtless sustension or preservation is the most congruous idea. Besides, this is the most obvious and common meaning of the word, and so rendered by most expositors; among others by Beza, Doddridge, Macknight and Bloomfield.

Doddridge gives this paraphrase, — "Upholding the universe which he hath made by the efficacious word of his Father's power, which is ever resident in him as his own, by virtue of that intimate but incomparable union which renders them one." This view is consistent with the whole passage: "his substance" and "his power" corresponds; and it is said, "by whom he made the world," so it is suitable to say that he sustains the world by the Father's power. — *Ed*

15 The word here used means properly "purification," but is used for expiation by the Sept.; see Exodus xxx. 10. The same truth is meant as when in chapter x. 12, that Christ, "after he had offered on sacrifice for sins, for ever sat down on the right hand of God." The reference here cannot be to the actual purification of his people; for what was done by Christ when he died is what is spoken of, even when he "put away sin" as it is said in chapter ix. 26, "by the sacrifice for himself." The word then, may be forgiveness proceeds from the atonement: see 1 John i. 9.

Dr. Owen gives three reasons for considering the word in the sense of expiation or atonement, — It is so rendered in some instances by the Septuagint; the act spoken is past, while cleansing

Sat down on the right hand, etc.; as though he had said, that having in the world procured salvation for men, he was received into celestial glory, in order that he might govern all things. And he added this in order to show that it was not a temporary salvation he has obtained for us; for we should otherwise be too apt to measure his power by what now appears to us. He then reminds us that Christ is not to be less esteemed because he is not seen by our eyes; but, on the contrary, that this was the height of his glory, that he has been taken and conveyed to the highest seat of his empire. *The right hand* is by a similitude applied to God, though he is not confined to any place, and has not a right side nor left. The session then of Christ means nothing else but the kingdom given to him by the Father, and that authority which Paul mentions, when he says that in his name every knee should bow. (Philippians ii. 10) Hence to sit at the right hand of the Father is no other thing than to govern in the place of the Father, as deputies of princes are wont to do to whom a full power over all things is granted. And the word *majesty* is added, and also *on high,* and for this purpose, to intimate that Christ is seated on the supreme throne whence the majesty of God shines forth. As, then, he ought to be loved on account of his redemption, so he ought to be adored on account of his royal magnificence.[16]

HEBREWS I. 4-6

4. Being made so much better than the angels, as he hath by inheritance obtained a more excellent name than they.

---

or purification is what is effected now; and "himself" shows that it is not properly sanctification as that is effected by means of the word, (Ephesians v. 26,) and by the regenerating Spirit. (Titus iii. 5)

The version of Stuart is, "made expiation for our sins," which is no doubt the meaning. — *Ed.*

16 It has been observed by some that in these verses the three offices of Christ are to be found: the Father spoke by him as a prophet; he made expiation for our sins as a priest; and he sits at God's right hand as a king. — *Ed.*

5. For unto which of the angels said he at any time, Thou art my Son, this day have I begotten thee? And again, I will be to him a Father, and he shall be to me a Son?

6. And again, when he bringeth in the first begotten into the world, he saith, And let all the angels of God worship him.

4. *Being made so much better, etc.* After having raised Christ above Moses and all others, he now amplifies His glory by a comparison with angels. It was a common notion among the Jews, that the Law was given by angels; they attentively considered the honorable things spoken of them everywhere in Scripture; and as the world is strangely inclined to superstition, they obscured the glory of God by extolling angels too much. It was therefore necessary to reduce them to their own rank, that they might not overshadow the brightness of Christ. And first he proves from his name, that Christ far excelled them, for he is called the Son of God;[17] and that he was distinguished by this title he shows by two testimonies from Scripture, both of which must be examined by us; and then we shall sum up their full import.

5. *Thou art my Son,* etc. It cannot be denied but that this was spoken of David, that is, as he sustained the person of Christ. Then the things found in this Psalm must have been shadowed forth in David, but were fully accomplished in Christ. For that he by subduing many enemies around him, enlarged the borders of his kingdom, it was some foreshadowing of the promise, "I will give thee the heathen for thine inheritance." But how little was this in comparison with the amplitude of Christ's kingdom, which extends from the east to the west? For the same reason David was called the son of God, having been especially chosen to perform great things; but his glory was hardly a spark, even the smallest, to that glory which shone forth in Christ, on whom the Father has imprinted his own image. So the name of Son belongs by a peculiar privilege to Christ alone, and cannot in this

---

17 Some by "name" understand dignity, but not correctly, as it appears from what follows; for the name, by which he is proved here to be superior to angels, was that of a Son, as Calvin here states. — *Ed.*

sense be applied to any other without profanation, for him and no other has the Father sealed.

But still the argument of the Apostle seems not to be well-grounded; for how does he maintain that Christ is superior to angels except on this ground, that he has the name of a Son? As though indeed he had not this in common with princes and those high in power, of whom it is written, "Ye are gods and the sons of the most", (Psalm l. 6;) and as though Jeremiah had not spoken as honorably of all Israel, when he called them the firstborn of God. (Jeremiah xxxi. 9.) They are indeed everywhere called children or sons. Besides, David calls angels the sons of God;

> "Who," he says, "is like to Jehovah among the sons of God?" (Psalm lxxxix. 6.)

The answer to all this is in no way difficult. Princes are called by this name on account of a particular circumstance; as to Israel, the common grace of election is thus denoted; angels are called the sons of God as having a certain resemblance to him, because they are celestial spirits and possess some portion of divinity in their blessed immortality. But when David without any addition calls himself as the type of Christ the Son of God, he denotes something peculiar and more excellent than the honor given to angels or to princes, or even to all Israel. Otherwise it would have been an improper and absurd expression, if he was by way of excellence called the son of God, and yet had nothing more than others; for he is thus separated from all other beings. When it is said so exclusively of Christ, "Thou art my Son," it follows that this honor does not belong to any of the angels.[18]

If any one again objects and says, that David was thus raised above the angels; to this I answer, that it is nothing strange for him to be elevated above angels while bearing the image of

---

18 "If it be objected," says Stuart, "that angels are also called sons, and men too, the answered is easy: No one individual, except Jesus, is ever called by way of eminence, the Son of God, i.e., the Messiah or the King of Israel," John i. 49. By "The Son of God" is to be understood here His kingly office: He was a Son as one endowed with superior power and authority; and angels are not sons in this respect. — *Ed.*

Christ; for in like manner there was no wrong done to angels when the high-priest, who made an atonement for sins, was called a mediator. They did not indeed obtain that title as by right their own; but as they represented the kingdom of Christ, they derived also the name from him. Moreover, the sacraments, though in themselves lifeless, are yet honored with titles which angels cannot claim without being guilty of sacrilege. It is hence evident that the argument derived from the term Son, is well grounded.[19]

As to his being *begotten*, we must briefly observe, that it is to be understood relatively here: for the subtle reasoning of Augustine is frivolous, when he imagines that *today* means perpetuity or eternity. Christ doubtless is the eternal Son of God, for he is wisdom, born before time; but this has no connection with this passage, in which respect is had to men, by whom Christ was acknowledged to be the Son of God after the Father had manifested him. Hence that declaration or manifestation which Paul mentions in Romans i. 4, was, so to speak, a sort of an external begetting; for the hidden and internal which had preceded, was unknown to men; nor could there have been any account taken of it, had not the Father given proof of it by a visible manifestation.[20]

---

19 The foregoing is a sufficient answer to Doddridge, Stuart, and others, who hold that the texts quoted must refer exclusively to Christ, else the argument of the Apostle would be inconclusive. David is no doubt called a son in the 2nd Psalm, but as a king, and in that capacity as a type of Christ; and what is said of him as a king, and what is promised to him, partly refers to himself and to his successors, and partly to Christ whom he represented. How to distinguish these things is now easy, as the character of Christ is fully developed in the New Testament. We now see the reason why David was called a son, and why Solomon, as in the next quotation, was called a son; they as kings of Israel, that is, of God's people, were representatives of him who is alone really or in a peculiar sense the Son of God, the true king of Israel, an honor never allotted to angels. (See Appendix B) — *Ed*.

20 Many have interpreted to-day as meaning eternity; but there is nothing to countenance such a view. As to the type, David, his "to-day" was his exaltation to the throne; the "to-day" of Christ, the antitype, is something of a corresponding character; it was his resurrection and exaltation to God's right hand, where he sits, as

I will be to him a Father, etc. As to this second testimony the former observation holds good. Solomon is here referred to, and though he was inferior to the angels, yet when God promised to be his Father, he was separated from the common rank of all others; for he was not to be to him a Father as to one of the princes, but as to one who was more eminent than all the rest. By the same privilege he was made a *Son;* all others were excluded from the like honor. But that this was not said of Solomon otherwise than as a type of Christ, is evident from the context; for the empire of the whole world is destined for the Son mentioned there, and perpetuity is also ascribed to his empire: on the other hand, it appears that the kingdom of Solomon has confined within narrow bounds, and was so far from being perpetual, that immediately after his death it was divided, and some time afterwards it fell altogether. Again, in that Psalm the sun and moon are summoned as witnesses, and the Lord swears that as long as they shall shine in the heavens, that kingdom shall remain safe: and on the other hand, the kingdom of David in a short time fell into decay, and at length utterly perished. And further, we may easily gather from many passages in the Prophets, that that promise was never understood otherwise than of Christ; so that no one can evade by saying that this is a new comment; for hence also has commonly prevailed among the Jews the practice of calling Christ the Son of David.

6. *And again, when he bringeth or introduceth*[21] , *etc.* He now proves by another argument that Christ is above the angels, and that is because the angels are bidden to worship him. (Psalm xcvii. 7.) It hence follows that he is their head and Prince. But it may seem unreasonable to apply that to Christ which is spoken of God only. Were we to answer that Christ is the eternal God, and therefore what belongs to God may justly be applied to him, it would not perhaps be satisfactory to all; for it would avail but little in proving a doubtful point, to argue in this case from the common attributes of God.

The subject is Christ manifested in the flesh, and the Apostle expressly says, that the Spirit thus spoke when Christ was introduced into the world; but this would not have been said

---

it were, on the throne of David. See Acts ii. 30; v. 30, 31; xiii. 33. — *Ed.*

21 See Appendix C.

consistently with truth except the manifestation of Christ be really spoken of in the Psalm. And so the case indeed is; for the Psalm commences with an exhortation to rejoice; nor did David address the Jews, but the whole earth, including the islands, that is, countries beyond the sea. The reason for this joy is given, because the Lord would *reign*. Further, if you read the whole Psalm, you will find nothing else but the kingdom of Christ, which began when the Gospel was published; nor is the whole Psalm anything else but a solemn decree, as it were, by which Christ was sent to take possession of His kingdom. Besides, what joy could arise from His kingdom, except it brought salvation to the whole world, to the Gentiles as well as to the Jews? Aptly then does the Apostle say here, that he was introduced into the world, because in that Psalm what is described is his coming to men.

The Hebrew word, rendered angels, is Elohim — gods; but there is no doubt but that the Prophet speaks of angels; for the meaning is, that there is no power so high but must be in subjection to the authority of this king, whose advent was to cause joy to the whole world.

HEBREWS I. 7-9

7. And of the angels he saith, Who maketh his angels spirits, and his ministers a flame of fire.
8. But unto the Son *he saith*, Thy throne, O God, *is* for ever and ever: a scepter of righteousness *is* the scepter of thy kingdom.
9. Thou hast loved righteousness, and hated iniquity; therefore God, *even* thy God, hath anointed thee with the oil of gladness above thy fellows.

7. *And to the angels, etc.* To the angels means *of* the angels. But the passage quoted seems to have been turned to another meaning from what it appears to have; for as David is there describing the manner in which we see the world to be governed, nothing is more certain than the winds are mentioned, which he says are made messengers by the Lord, for he employs them as his runners; so also, when he purifies the air by lightnings, he shows what quick and swift ministers he has to obey his orders. But

this has nothing to do with angels. Some have had recourse to an allegory, as though the Apostle explained the plain, and as they say, the literal sense allegorically of angels. But it seems preferable to me to consider this testimony is brought forward for this purpose, that it might by a similitude be applied to angels, and in this way David compares winds to angels, because they perform offices in this world similar to what the angels do in heaven; for the winds are, as it were, visible spirits. And, doubtless, as Moses, describing the creation of the world, mentioned only those things which are subject to our senses, and yet intended that higher things should be understood; so David in describing the world and nature, represented to us on a tablet what ought to be understood respecting the celestial orders. Hence I think that the argument is one of likeness or similarity, when the Apostle transfers to angels what properly applies to the winds.[22]

8. *But to the Son, etc.* It must indeed be allowed, that this Psalm was composed as a marriage song for Solomon; for here is celebrated his marriage with the daughter of the king of Egypt;[23] but it cannot yet be denied but that what is here related, is much too high to be applied to Solomon. The Jews, that they may not be forced to own Christ to be called God, make an evasion by saying, it at the throne of God is spoken of, or that the verb "established" is to be understood. So that, according to the first exposition, the word Elohim, God, is to be in construction with throne, "the throne of God;" and that according to the second, it is supposed to be a defective sentence. But these

---

22 Many have been the explanations of this sentence; but this is the most suitable to the passage as it occurs in Psalm civ. 4, and to the design of the Apostle; it is the one adopted by Doddridge, Stuart, and Bloomfield.

The meaning would be thus more apparent, — "Who maketh like his angels the winds, and like his ministers the flaming fire," that is, the winds are subject to him as the angels are, and also the flaming fire as his ministers or attendants. The particle ב is sometimes omitted in Hebrew. — *Ed.*

23 It is generally admitted to be a kind of epithalamium, but not on the occasion here specified, as there was nothing in that marriage that in any degree correspond with the contents of the Psalm. Such was the opinion of Beza, Dr. Owen, Scott, and Horsley. — *Ed.*

are mere evasions. Whosoever will read the verse, who is of a sound mind and free from the spirit of contention, cannot doubt but that the Messiah is called God. Nor is there any reason to object, that the word Elohim is sometimes given to angels and to judges; for it is never found to be given simply to one person, except to God alone.[24]

Farther, that I may not contend about a word, whose throne can be said to be established *forever*, except that of God only? Hence the perpetuity of his kingdom is an evidence of his divinity.

The *scepter* of Christ's kingdom is afterwards called the scepter of righteousness; of this there were some, though obscure, lineaments in Solomon; he exhibited them as far as he acted as a just king and zealous for what was right. But righteousness in the kingdom of Christ has a wider meaning; for he by his gospel, which is his spiritual scepter, renews us after the righteousness of God. The same thing must be also understood of his *love* of righteousness; for he causes it to reign in his own people, because he loves it.

9. *Wherefore God has appointed him, etc.* This was indeed truly said of Solomon, who was made a king, because God had preferred him to his brethren, who were otherwise his equals, being the sons of the king. But this applies more suitably to Christ, who has adopted us as his joint heirs, though not so in our own right. But he was anointed above us all, as it was beyond measure, while we, each of us, according to a limited portion, as he has divided to each of us. Besides, he was anointed for our sake, in order that we may all draw out of his fatness. Hence he is the Christ, we are Christians proceeding from him, as rivulet from a fountain. But as Christ received this unction when in the flesh, he is said to have been anointed by his God; for it would

---

24 The Hebrew will admit of no other construction than that given in our version and by Calvin. The Greek version, the Sept., which the Apostle adopts, seems at first view to be different, as "God" is in the nominative case, ὁ Θεὸς; but the Sept. used in commonly instead of the vocative case. We meet with two instances in the seventh Psalm, verses 1 and 3, and in connection with "Lord," κύριε in the vocative case. See also Psalm x. 12; xli. 1, etc.

The Vulgate, following literally the Sept., without regarding the preceding peculiarity, has rendered "God" in the nominative, "*Deus*," and not "*O Deus.*" — *Ed.*

be inconsistent to suppose him inferior to God, except in his human nature.[25]

HEBREWS I. 10-14

10. And, Thou, Lord, in the beginning hast laid the foundation of the earth; and the heavens are the works of thine hands:
11. They shall perish; but thou remainest; and they all shall wax old as doth a garment;
12. And as a vesture shalt thou fold them up, and they shall be changed: but thou art the same, and thy years shall not fail.
13. But to which of the angels said he at any time, Sit on my right hand, until I make thine enemies thy footstool?
14. Are they not all ministering spirits, sent forth to minister for them who shall be heirs of salvation?

10. *And, Thou, Lord, in the beginning, etc.* This testimony at first sight may seem to be unfitly applied to Christ, especially in a doubtful matter, such as is here handled; for the subject in dispute is not concerning the glory of God, but what may be fitly applied to Christ. Now, there is not in this passage any mention

---

25 He is evidently throughout spoken of in his mediatorial character. To keep this in view will enable us more fully to understand the chapter. It is more agreeable to this passage, to regard "the anointing," not that of consecration, but that of refreshment to guests according to a prevailing custom, see Luke vii. 46. The word "gladness" favors this, and also the previous words of the passage; Christ is addressed as already on his throne, and his administration is referred to; and it is on account of his just administration, that he is said to have been anointed with the perfuming oil of gladness, see Acts x. 38.

The words, "above thy fellows," are rendered by Calvin, "above thy partners," and by Doddridge and Macknight, "above thine associates." Christ is spoken of as king, and his associates are those in the same office; but he is so much above them that he is the "king of kings;" and yet his superior excellencies are here represented as entitling him to higher honors. — *Ed.*

made of Christ, but the majesty of God alone is set forth. I indeed allow that Christ is not named in any part of the Psalm; but it is yet plain that he is so pointed out, that no one can doubt but that his kingdom is there avowedly recommended to us. Hence all the things which are found there, are to be applied to his person; for in none have they been fulfilled but in Christ, such as the following, — "Thou shalt arise and have mercy on Sion, that the heathens may fear the name, and all the kings of the earth thy glory." Again, — "When the nations shall be gathered together, and the kingdoms, to serve the Lord." Doubtless, in vain shall we seek to find this God through whom the whole world have united in one faith and worship of God, except in Christ.

All the other parts of the Psalm exactly suit the person of Christ, such as the following, that he is the eternal God, the creator of heaven and earth, that perpetuity belongs to him without any change, by which his majesty is raised to the highest elevation, and he himself is removed from the rank of all created beings.

What David says about the heavens perishing, some explain by adding, "Were such a thing to happen," as though nothing was affirmed. But what need is there of such a strained explanation, since we know that all creatures are subjected to vanity? For to what purpose is that renovation promised, which even the heavens wait for with the strong desire as of those in travail, except that they are now verging towards destruction?

But the perpetuity of Christ which is here mentioned, brings no common comfort to the godly; as the Psalm at last teaches us, they shall be partakers of it, inasmuch as Christ communicates himself and what he possesses to his own body.[26]

13. *But to whom of the angels, etc.* He again by another testimony extols the excellency of Christ, that it might hence be evident how much he is above the angels. The passage is taken from Psalms cx. 1, and it cannot be explained of any but of Christ. For as it was not lawful for kings to touch the priesthood, as is testified by the leprosy of Uzziah; and as it appears that neither David, nor any other of his successors in the kingdom, was ordained a priest, it follows, that a new kingdom as well as a new priesthood is here introduced, since the same person is

---

26 See Appendix D.

made a king and a priest. Besides, the eternity of the priesthood is suitable to Christ alone.

Now, in the beginning of the Psalm he is set at God's right hand. This form of expression, as I have already said, means the same, as though it was said, that the second place was given him by the Father; for it is a metaphor which signifies that he is the Father's vicegerent and his chief minister in exercising authority, so that the Father rules through him. No one of the angels bears so honorable an office; hence Christ far excels all.

Until I make, etc. As there are never wanting enemies to oppose Christ's kingdom, it seems not to be beyond the reach of danger, especially as they who attempt to overthrow it possess great power, have recourse to various artifices, and also make all their attacks with furious violence. Doubtless, were we to regard things as they appear, the kingdom of Christ would seem often to be on the verge of ruin. But the promise, that Christ shall never be thrust from his seat, takes away from us every fear; for he will lay prostrate all his enemies. These two things, then, ought to be borne in mind, — that the kingdom of Christ shall never in this world be at rest, but that there will be many enemies by whom it will be disturbed; and secondly, that whatever its enemies may do, they shall never prevail, for the session of Christ at God's right hand will not be for a time, but to the end of the world, and that on this account all who will not submit to his authority shall be laid prostrate and trodden under his feet.

If any one asks, whether Christ's kingdom shall come to an end, when all his enemies shall be subdued; I give this answer, — that his kingdom shall be perpetual, and yet in such a way as Paul intimates in 1 Corinthians xv. 25; for we are to take this view, — that God who is not known to us in Christ, will then appear to us as he is in himself. And yet Christ will never cease to be the head of men and of angels; nor will there be any diminution of his honor. But the solution of this question must be sought from that passage.

14. *Are they not all, etc.* That the comparison might appear more clearly, he now mentions what the condition of angels is. For calling them *spirits*, he denotes their eminence; for in this respect they are superior to corporal creatures. But the office (λειτουργία) which he immediately mentions reduces them to their own rank, as it is that which is the reverse of dominion;

and this he still more distinctly states, when he says, that they are sent to *minister*. The first word means the same, as though he had said, that they were officials; but to *minister* imports what is more humble and abject.[27] The service which God allots to angels is indeed honorable; but the very fact that they serve, shows that they are far inferior to Christ, who is the Lord of all.

If any one objects and says, that Christ is also called in many places both a servant and a minister, not only to God, but also to men, the reply may be readily given; his being a servant was not owing to his nature, but to a voluntary humility, as Paul testifies, (Philippians ii. 7;) and at the same time his sovereignty remained to his nature; but angels, on the other hand, were created for this end, — that they might serve, and to minister is what belongs to their condition. The difference then is great; for what is natural to them is, as it were, adventitious or accidental to Christ, because he took our flesh; and what necessarily belongs to them, he of his own accord undertook. Besides, Christ is a minister in such a way, that though he is in our flesh nothing is diminished from the majesty of his dominion.[28]

From this passage the faithful receive no small consolation; for they hear that celestial hosts are assigned to them as ministers, in order to secure their salvation. It is indeed no common pledge of God's love towards us, that they are continually engaged in our behalf. Hence also proceeds a singular confirmation to our faith, that our salvation being defended by such guardians, is beyond the reach of danger. Well then has God provided for our infirmities by giving us such assistants to op-

---

27 There is no doubt a distinction between the two words here used, but not exactly that which is intimated; the first, λειτουργικὰ refers to an official appointment; and the other, διακονίαν, to the work which was to be done. Angels are said to be officially appointed, and they are thus appointed for the purpose of doing service to the heirs of salvation; "Are they not all ministrant (or ministerial) spirits, sent forth for service, on account διὰ of those who are to inherit salvation?" Then they are spirits, having a special office allotted them, being sent forth to do service in behalf of those who are heirs of salvation. It hence appears that they have a special appointment for this purpose See Acts v. 19, and xii. 7. — *Ed.*

28 See Appendix E.

pose Satan, and to put forth their power in every way to defend us!

But this benefit he grants especially to his chosen people; hence that angels may minister to us, we must be the members of Christ. Yet some testimonies of Scripture may on the other hand be adduced, to show that angels are sometimes sent forth for the sake of the reprobate; for mention is made by Daniel of the angels of the Persians and the Greeks. (Daniel x. 20.) But to this I answer, that they were in such a way assisted by angels, that the Lord might thus promote the salvation of his own people; for their success and their victories had always a reference to the benefit of the Church. This is certain, that as we have been banished by sin from God's kingdom, we can have no communion with angels except through the reconciliation made by Christ; and this we may see by the ladder shown in a vision to the patriarch Jacob.

CHAPTER 2

HEBREWS II. 1-4

1. Therefore we ought to give the more earnest heed to the things which we have heard, lest at any time we should let *them* slip.
2. For if the word spoken by angels was steadfast, and every transgression and disobedience received a just recompense of reward;
3. How shall we escape, if we neglect so great salvation; which at the first began to be spoken by the Lord, and was confirmed unto us by them that heard *him*;
4. God also bearing *them* witness, both with signs and wonders, and with divers miracles, and gifts of the Holy Ghost, according to his own will?

1. *Therefore we ought, etc.* He now declares what he had before in view, by comparing Christ with angels, even to secure the highest authority to his doctrine. For if the Law given through angels could not have been received with contempt, and if its transgression was visited with severe punishment, what is to happen, he asks, to the despisers of that gospel, which has the Son of God as its author, and was confirmed by so many miracles? The import of the whole is this, that the higher the dignity of Christ is than that of angels, the more reverence is due to the Gospel than to the Law. Thus he commends the doctrine by mentioning its author.

But should it seem strange to any one, that as the doctrine both of the Law and of the Gospel is from God, one should be preferred to the other; inasmuch as by having the Law lowered the majesty of God would be degraded; the evident answer would be this, — that he ought indeed always to be heard with equal attention whenever he may speak, and yet that the fuller he reveals himself to us, it is but right that our reverence and attention to obedience should increase in proportion to the extent of his revelations; not that God is in himself less at one time than at another; but his greatness is not at all times equally made known to us.

Here also another question arises. Was not the Law also given by Christ? If so, the argument of the Apostle seems not to be well grounded. To this I reply, that in this comparison regard is had to a veiled revelation on one side, and to that which is manifest on the other. Now, as Christ in bringing the Law showed himself but obscurely or darkly, and as it were under coverings, it is nothing strange that the Law should be said to have been brought by angels without any mention being made of his name; for in that transaction he never appeared openly; but in the promulgation of the Gospel his glory was so conspicuous, that he may justly be deemed its author.

Lest at any time we should let them slip, or, "lest we should at any time flow abroad," or, if you prefer, "let dip," though in reality there is not much difference. The true sense is to be gathered from the contrast; for to give heed, or to attend and to let slip, are opposites; the first means to hold a thing, and the other to let off like a sieve, or a perforated vessel, whatever may be poured into it. I do not indeed approve of the opinion of those who take it in the sense of dying, according to what we find in 2 Samuel xv. 14, "We all die and slide away like water." On the contrary, we ought, as I have said, to regard the contrast between attention and flowing out; an attentive mind is like a vessel capable of holding water; but that which is roving and indolent is like a vessel with holes.[29]

2. *Steadfast,* or "firm," or *sure, etc.;* that is, it was the word of authority, for God required it to be believed; and that it was authoritative, was made more evident by its sanctions; for no one despised the law with impunity. Then firmness means authority; and what is added respecting punishment ought to be understood as explanatory; for it is evident the doctrine of which God shows himself to be the avenger, is by no means unprofitable or unimportant.

---

29 See Appendix F.

3. *If we neglect so great a salvation, etc.* Not only the rejection of the Gospel, but also its neglect, deserves the heaviest punishment, and that on account of the greatness of the grace which it offers; hence he says, *so great a salvation.* God would indeed leave his gifts valued by us according to their worth. Then the more precious they are, the baser is our ingratitude when we do not value them. In a word, in proportion to the greatness of Christ will be the severity of God's vengeance on all the despisers of his Gospel.[30]

And observe that the word salvation is transferred here metonymically to the doctrine of salvation; for as the Lord would not have men otherwise saved than by the Gospel, so when that is neglected the whole salvation of God is rejected; for it is God's power unto salvation to those who believe. (Romans i. 16.) Hence he who seeks salvation in any other way, seeks to attain it by another power than that of God; which is an evidence of extreme madness. But this encomium is not only a commendation of the Gospel, but is also a wonderful support to our faith; for it is a testimony that the word is by no means unprofitable, but that a sure salvation is conveyed by it.[31]

Which at first began, etc. Here he sets the Son of God, the first herald of the Gospel, in opposition to angels, and also anticipates what was necessary to remove a doubt which might have crept into the minds of many; for they had not been taught by the mouth of Christ himself, whom the greatest part had never seen. If then they regarded only the man by whose ministry they had been led to the faith, they might have made less of what they had learnt from him; hence the Apostle reminded them, that the doctrine which had been delivered them by others, yet proceeded from Christ; for he says that those who had faithfully declared what had been committed to them by Christ, had been his disciples. He therefore uses the word, *was confirmed,*

---

30 To "neglect," is literally, not to care for; not to care for our salvation is to neglect it. It is rendered, to "make light of," in Matthew xxii. 5; and "not to regard," in chapter viii. 9. — *Ed.*

31 So great, observes Dr. Owen is this salvation, that is a deliverance from Satan, from sin, and from eternal sin, and from eternal death. The means also by which it has been procured, and is now effected, and its endless results, prove in a wonderful manner its greatness. — *Ed.*

as though he had said, that it was not a random report, without any author, or from witnesses of doubtful credit, but a report which was confirmed by men of weight and authority.

Moreover, this passage indicates that this epistle was not written by Paul; for he did not usually speak so humbly of himself, as to confess that he was one of the Apostles' disciples, nor did he thus speak from ambition, but because wicked men under a pretense of this kind attempted to detract from the authority of his doctrine. It then appears evident that it was not Paul who wrote that he had the Gospel by hearing and not by revelation.[32]

4. *God also bearing them witness, etc.* In addition to the fact, that the Apostles had what they preached from the Son of God, the Lord also proved his approbation of their preaching by miracles, as by a solemn subscription. Then they who do not reverently receive the Gospel recommended by such testimonies, disregard not only the word of God, but also his works.

He designates miracles, for the sake of amplifying their importance, by three names. They are called *signs* because they rouse men's minds, that they may think of something higher that what appears; and *wonders*, because they present what is rare and unusual; and *miracles*, because the Lord shows in them a singular and an extraordinary evidence of his power.[33]

---

32 The same objection has been advanced by Grotius and others, but it has no weight in it; for the Apostle here distinctly refers to the facts in connection with the twelve Apostles, as this alone was necessary for his purpose here; and the same reason for concealing his name accounts for no reference being made here to his own ministry. And "we" and "us" as employed by the Apostle, often refer to things which belong to all in common as Christians. See chapter iv. 1, 11; xi. 40, etc. And he uses them sometimes when he himself personally is not included. See 1 Corinthians xv. 51. — *Ed.*

33 These three words occur twice together in other places, Acts ii. 22, and 2 Thessalonians ii. 9; only they are found in Acts in a different order — miracles wonders and signs. Signs and wonders are often found together both in the Old Testament, and in this order except in three places, Acts ii. 19, 43; and vii. 36. The same things, as Calvin says, are no doubt meant by three words under different views. They are called "signs" or as tokens as evidence of a divine interposition; "wonders" or prodigies, as being not

As to the word, *bearing witness*, or attesting, it points out the right use of miracles, even that they serve to establish the Gospel. For almost all the miracles done in all ages were performed as we find for this end, that they might be the seals of Gods word. The more strange then is the superstition of the Papists, who employ their own fictitious miracles for the purpose of overthrowing the truth of God.

The conjunction συν, *together with*, has this meaning, that we are confirmed in the faith of the Gospel by the joint testimony of God and men; for God's miracles were testimonies concurring with the voice of men.

He adds, *by the gifts* or distributions *of the Holy Spirit*, by which also the doctrine of the Gospel was adorned, of which they were the appendages.[34] For why did God distribute the gifts of his Spirit, except in part that they might be helps in promulgating it, and in part that their might move through admiration the minds of men to obey it? Hence Paul says, that tongues were a sign to unbelievers. The words, *according to his will*, remind us, that the miracles mentioned could not be ascribed to any except to God alone, and that they were not wrought undesignedly, but, for the distinct purpose of sealing the truth of the Gospel.

---

natural, but supernatural, and as having the effect of filling men with terror, Acts ii. 43; and "miracles" or powers, as being the effects of a divine power. So that "signs" betoken their intention; "wonders" their characters; and "miracles" their origin, or the power which produces them. — *Ed.*

34 By referring to 1 Corinthians xii. 4-11, we shall be able to see the meaning of "distributions of the Spirit," which seems to have been different from signs and wonders, for in that passage there are several gifts mentioned distinct from signs and wonders, such as the word of wisdom, the word of knowledge, the gift of prophecy, and the discerning of spirits. These were the distributions, or the portions, which the Spirit divined to every one "according to his will;" for the "will" here, as in 1 Corinthians xii. 11, is the will of the Spirit. The most suitable rendering of the last clause would be "and by the gifts of the Holy Spirit distributed according to his will." There is an evident metonymy in the word "distributions;" it is used abstractly for things distributed or divided. — *Ed.*

HEBREWS II. 5-9

5. For unto the angels hath he not put in subjection the world to come, whereof we speak.
6. But one in a certain place testified, saying, What is man, that thou art mindful of him? or the son of man, that thou visitest him?
7. Thou madest him a little lower than the angels; thou crownedst him with glory and honor, and didst set him over the works of thy hands:
8. Thou hast put all things in subjection under his feet. For in that he put all in subjection under him, he left nothing *that is* not put under him. But now we see not yet all things put under him.
9. But we see Jesus, who was made a little lower than the angels for the suffering of death, crowned with glory and honor; that he by the grace of God should taste death for every man.

5. *For unto the angels, etc.* He again proves by another argument that Christ ought to be obeyed; for the Father has conferred on him the sovereignty of the whole world, while the angels are wholly destitute of such an honor. It hence follows that none of the angels should stand in the way of his preeminence who alone possesses supremacy.

But first, the Psalm which he quotes must be examined, for it seems to be unfitly applied to Christ. David there mentions the benefits which God bestows on mankind; for after having contemplated God's power as manifested in heaven and the stars, he comes to man, among whom the wonderful goodness of God appears in a peculiar manner. He does not, then, speak of any particular person, but of all mankind. To this I answer, that all this affords no reason why the words should not be applied to the person of Christ. I indeed allow that man was at first put in possession of the world, that he might rule over all the works of God; but by his own defection he deserved the loss of his dominion, for it was a just punishment for ingratitude as to one thus favored, that the Lord, whom he refused to acknowledge and faithfully to worship, should have deprived him of a right previously granted to him. As soon, then, as Adam alienated himself from God through sin, he was justly deprived of the good things which he had received; not that he was denied the use of them, but that he would have had no right to them after he had forsaken God. And in the very use of them God intended that there should be some tokens of this loss of right, such as these, — the wild beasts ferociously attack us, those who ought to be awed by our presence are dreaded by us, some never obey us, others can hardly be trained to submit, and they do us harm in various ways; the earth answers not our expectations in cultivating it; the sky, the air, the sea, and other things are often adverse to us. But were all creatures to continue in subjection, yet whatever the sons of Adam possessed would be deemed a robbery; for what can they call their own when they themselves are not God's?

This foundation being laid, it is evident that God's bounty belongs not to us until the right lost in Adam be restored by Christ. For this reason Paul teaches us that food is sanctified to us by faith, (1 Timothy iv. 5;) and in another place he declares that to the unbelieving nothing is clean, for they have a polluted conscience. (Titus i. 16.)

We found at the beginning of this epistle that Christ has been appointed by the Father the heir of all things. Doubtless, as he ascribes the whole inheritance to one, he excludes all others as aliens, and justly too, for we are all become exiles from God's kingdom. What food, then, God has destined for his own family, we leave no right to take. But Christ, by whom we are admitted into this family, at the same time admits us into a participation of this right, so that we may enjoy the whole world, together with the favor of God. Hence Paul teaches us that Abraham was by faith made an heir of the world, that is, because he was united to the body of Christ. (Romans iv. 13) If men, then, are precluded from all God's bounty until they receive a right to it through Christ, it follows that the dominion mentioned in the Psalm was lost to us in Adam, and that on this account it must again be restored as a donation. Now, the restoration begins with Christ as the head. There is, then, no doubt but that we are to look to him whenever the dominion of man over all creatures is spoken of.

To this the reference is made when the Apostle mentions *the world to come,* or the future world, for he understands by it the renovated world. To make the thing clearer, let us suppose two worlds, — the first the old, corrupted by Adam's sin; the other, later in time, as renewed by Christ. The state of the first creation has become wholly decayed, and with man has fallen as far as man himself is concerned. Until, then, a new restitution be made by Christ, this Psalm will not be fulfilled. It hence now appears that here the world to come is not that which we hope for after the resurrection, but that which began at the beginning of Christ's kingdom; but it will no doubt have its full accomplishment in our final redemption.

But why he suppressed the name of David does not appear to me. Doubtless he says *one*, or some one, not in contempt, but for honor's sake, designating him as one of the prophets or a renowned writer.

7. *Thou madest him, etc.* A new difficulty now arises as to the explanation of the words. I have already shown that the passage is fitly applicable to the Son of God; but the Apostle seems now to turn the words from that meaning in which David understood them; for *a little*, βραχύ τι seems to refer to time, as it means a little while, and designates the abasement of Christ's humiliation; and he confines the glory to the day of resurrection, while David extends it generally to the whole life of man.

To this I answer, that it was not the Apostle's design to give an exact explanation of the words. For there is nothing improperly done, when verbal allusions are made to embellish a subject in hand, as Paul does in quoting a passage in Romans x. 6, from Moses, "Who shall ascend into heaven," *etc.*, he does not join the words "heaven and hell" for the purpose of explanation, but as ornaments. The meaning of David is this, — "O Lord, thou hast raised man to such a dignity, that it differs but little from divine or angelic honor; for he is set a ruler over the whole world." This meaning the Apostle did not intend to overthrow, nor to turn to something else; but he only bids us to consider the abasement of Christ, which appeared for a short time, and then the glory with which he is perpetually crowned; and this he does more by alluding to expressions than by explaining what David understood.[35]

To be *mindful* and to *visit* mean the same thing, except that the second is somewhat fuller, for it sets forth the presence of God by the effect.

---

35 See Appendix G.

8. *For in that he put all in subjection under him;* or, doubtless in subjecting all things to him, *etc.* One might think the argument to be this, — "To the man whom David speaks all things are subjected, but to mankind all things are not made subject; then he does not speak of any individual man." But this reasoning cannot stand, for the minor proposition is true also of Christ; for all things are not as yet made subject to him, as Paul shows in 1 Corinthians xv. 28. There is therefore another sentence; for after having laid down this truth, that Christ has universal dominion over all creatures, he adds, as an objection, "But all things do not as yet obey the authority of Christ." To meet this objection he teaches us that yet now is seen completed in Christ what he immediately adds respecting *glory* and *honor,* as if he had said, "Though universal subjection does not as yet appear to us, let us be satisfied that he has passed through death, and has been exalted to the highest state of honor; for that which is as yet wanting, will in its time be completed."

But first, this offends some, that the Apostle concludes with too much refinement, that there is nothing not made subject to Christ, as David includes all things generally; for the various kinds of things which he enumerates afterwards prove no such thing, such as beasts of the field, fishes of the sea, and birds of the air. To this I reply, that a general declaration ought not to be confined to these species, for David meant no other thing than to give some instances of his power over things the most conspicuous, or indeed to extend it to things even the lowest, that we may know that nothing is ours except through the bounty of God and our union with Christ. We may, therefore, explain the passage thus, — "Thou hast made subject to him all things, not only things needful for eternal blessedness, but also such inferior things as serve to supply the wants of the body." However this may be, the inferior dominion over animals depends on the higher.

It is again asked, "Why does he say that we see not all things made subject to Christ?" The solution of this question you will find in that passage already quoted from Paul; and in the first chapter of this Epistle we said a few things on the subject. As Christ carries on war continually with various enemies, it is doubtless evident that he has no quiet possession of his kingdom. He is not, however, under the necessity of waging war; but it happens through his will that his enemies are not to be subdued till the last day, in order that we may be tried and proved by fresh exercises.

9. *But we see Jesus, etc.* As the meaning of the words, βραχύ τι "a little" is ambiguous,[36] he looks to the thing itself, as exhibited in the person of Christ, rather then to the exact meaning of the words, as I have already said; and he presents to our meditation the glory after the resurrection, which David extends to all the gifts by which man is adorned by God's bounty; but in this embellishment, which leaves the literal sense entire, there is nothing unsuitable or improper.

For the suffering of death, etc. It is the same as though it was said that Christ, having passed through death, was exalted into the glory which he has obtained, according to what Paul teaches us in Philippians ii. 8-10; not that Christ obtained anything for himself individually, as sophists say, who have devised the notion that he first earned eternal life for himself and then for us; for the way or means, so to speak, of obtaining glory, is only indicated here. Besides, Christ is crowned with glory for this end, that every knee should bow to him. (Philippians ii. 10.) We may therefore reason from the final cause that all things are delivered into his hand.

That he by the grace of God, [37] *etc.* He refers to the cause and the fruit of Christ's death, lest he should be thought to detract anything from his dignity. For when we hear that so much good has been obtained for us, there is no place left for contempt, for admiration of the divine goodness fills the whole mind. By saying *for every man*, he means not only that he might be ample to others, as Chrysostom says, who brings the example of a phy-

---

36 There is no doubt but that the expression is capable of being understood as "little" in degree, or as "little" in time; but in the Psalm the former is evidently the meaning, and there is no reason for a different meaning here: Christ, in becoming man, assumed a nature inferior to that of angels. Many of the fathers, indeed, and some moderns, have thought that time is what is intended "for a little while;" but this is not true, for Christ continues in the nature which has assumed, though it be now refined and perfected. The inferiority of nature is admitted, but that inferiority is as it were compensated by a superiority of honor and glory. Our version is the Vulgate, which Doddridge has also adopted, and also Stuart and Bloomfield. — *Ed.*

37 See Appendix H.

sician tasting first a bitter draught, that the patient might not refuse to drink it; but he means that Christ died for us, and that by taking upon him what was due to us, he redeemed us from the curse of death. And it is added, that this was done through the *grace of God,* for the cause of redemption was the infinite love of God towards us, through which it was that he spared not even his own Son. What Chrysostom says of *tasting of death,* as though he touched it with his lips, because Christ emerged from death a conqueror, I will not refute nor condemn, though I know not whether the Apostle meant to speak in a manner so refined.[38]

HEBREWS II. 10-13

10. For it became him, for whom *are* all things, and by whom *are* all things, in bringing many sons unto glory, to make the captain of their salvation perfect through sufferings.
11. For both he that sanctifieth and they who are sanctified *are* all of one: for which cause he is not ashamed to call them brethren,
12. Saying, I will declare thy name unto my brethren, in the midst of the church will I sing praise unto thee.
13. And again, I will put my trust in him. And again, Behold I and the children which God hath given me.

10. *For it became him, etc.* His object is, to make Christ's humiliation to appear glorious to the godly; for when he is said to have been clothed with our flesh, he seems to be classed with the common order of men; and the cross brought him lower than

---

38 There is no doubt but that is a fanciful refinement. To taste food, according to the language of Scripture, is to eat it. See Acts x. 11; xx. 11; xxiii. 14. To taste death is to die, to undergo death, and nothing else. See Matthew xvi. 28; Luke ix. 27. Stuart observes that the word for taste in Hebrew is taken in the same sense, and also in classic Greek authors. "For every man," ὑπὲρ πάντος, that is "man," mentioned in verse 6; and the "man" there means all the faithful, to whom God in Noah restored the dominion lost in Adam; but this dominion was not renewed to man as a fallen being, but as made righteous by faith. — *Ed.*

all men. We must therefore take heed, lest Christ should be less esteemed, because he willingly humbled himself for us; and this is what is here spoken of. For the Apostle shows that this very thing ought to be deemed honorable to the Son of God, that he was by these means consecrated the Captain of our salvation.

He first assumes it as granted, that we ought to be satisfied with God's decree; for as all things are sustained by his power, so all things ought to serve to his glory. No betters cause, then, can be found out than the good pleasure of God. Such is the purport of the circumlocution which he employs, *for whom, and by whom, are all things.* He might by one word have named God; but his purpose was to remind us, that what is to be deemed best is that which he appoints, whose will and glory is the right end of all things.[39]

It does not, however, appear as yet what he intends by saying, that it became Christ to be thus consecrated. But this depends on the ordinary way which God adopts in dealing with his own people; for his will is to exercise them with various trials, so that they may spend their whole life under the cross. It was hence necessary that Christ, as the first-begotten, should by the cross be inaugurated into his supremacy, since that is the common lot and condition of all. This is the conforming of the head with the members, of which Paul speaks in Romans viii. 29.

It is indeed a singular consolation, calculated to mitigate the bitterness of the cross, when the faithful hear, that by sorrows and tribulations they are sanctified for glory as Christ himself was; and hence they see a sufficient reason why they should lovingly kiss the cross rather than dread it. And when this is the case, then doubtless the reproach of the cross of Christ immediately disappears, and its glory shines forth; for who can despise what is sacred, nay, what God sanctifies? Who can deem that

---

39 Having vindicated Christ's superiority over angels, he being "crowned with glory and honor," notwithstanding his assumption of human nature, and for his sufferings, the Apostle now, as it were, goes back, and proves the necessity of what has been done; showing how needful it was for him to become man, and to suffer as he did; and we find he states two especial reasons — that he might reconcile us to God and be able to sympathize with his people. — *Ed.*

ignominious, by which we are prepared for glory? And yet both these things are said here of the death of Christ.

By whom are all things, etc. When creation is spoken of, it is ascribed to the Son as his own world, for by him were all things created; but here the Apostle means no other thing than that all creatures continue or are preserved by the power of God. What we have rendered *consecrated,* others have rendered *made perfect.* But as the word, τελειῶσαι which he uses, is of a doubtful meaning, I think it clear that the word I leave adopted is more suitable to the context.[40] For what is meant is the settled and regular way or method by which the sons of God are initiated, so that they may obtain their own honor, and be thus separated from the rest of the world; and then immediately sanctification is mentioned.

11. *For both he that sanctifieth, etc.* He proves that it was necessary that what he had said should be fulfilled in the person of Christ on account of his connection with his members; and he also teaches that it was a remarkable evidence of the divine goodness that he put on our flesh. hence he says, that they are *all of one,* that is, that the author of holiness and we are made partakers of it, are all of one nature, as I understated the expres-

---

40 Our version seems more intelligible — "to make perfect." As it appears afterwards his perfection consisted in his having made an atonement for sin, and in being capable of sympathy with his people. God made him perfectly qualified to be the Captain or leader in our salvation, that is, in the work of saving us, even through sufferings, as thereby he procured our salvation and became experimentally acquainted with the temptations and trials of humanity.

The sense given by Stuart and some others, borrowed from the use of the word in the classics, which is that of crowning or rewarding the victor at the games is not suitable here; for what follows clearly shows that its meaning is what has been stated.

Both Scott and Stuart connect "the bringing many sons unto glory" with "the captain of their salvation." One thing is indeed thus gained, the cases seem to suit better; but then the sense is violated. When the sentence is thus rendered, there is no antecedent to "their" connected with "salvation;" and the faithful are not called the "sons" of Christ, but his brethren. As to the case of the participle for "bringing," an accusative for a dative, it is an anomaly, says Bloomfield, that sometimes occurs in Paul's writings and also in the classics. — *Ed.*

sion. It is commonly understood of one Adam; and some refer it to God, and not without reasons; but I rather think that one nature is meant, and *one* I consider to be in the neuter gender, as though he had said, that they are made out of the same mass.[41]

It avails not, indeed, a little to increase our confidence, that we are united to the Son of God by a bond so close, that we can find in our nature that holiness of which we are in want; for he not only as God sanctifies us, but there is also the power of sanctifying in his human nature, not that it has it from itself, but that God had poured upon it a perfect fullness of holiness, so that from it we may all draw. And to this point this sentence refers, "For their sakes I sanctify myself." (John xvii. 19.) If, then we are sinful and unclean, we have not to go far to seek a remedy; for it is offered to us in our own flesh. If any one prefers to regard as intended here that spiritual unity which the godly have with the Son of God, and which differs much from that which men commonly have among themselves, I offer no objection, though I am disposed to follow what is more commonly received, as it is not inconsistent with reason.

He is not ashamed to call them brethren. This passage is taken from Psalm xxii. 22. That Christ is the speaker there, or David in his name, the evangelists do especially testify, for they quote from it many verses, such as the following, — "They parted my garments," — "They gave gall for my meat," — "My God, my

---

41 Though many, ancient and modern, such as Chrysostom, Beza, Grotius and Bloomfield, regard "God" as meant here by "one", yet the context is in favor of the view taken by Calvin, which is also adopted by Dr. Owen and Stuart. The 14th verse seems to decide the question.

The word to sanctify ἁγιάζω, means — 1. To consecrate, to set apart to a holy use or to an office, Matthew xxiii. 19; John xvii. 19; — 2. To purify from pollution, either ceremonially, Hebrew ix. 13, or morally and spiritually, 1 Thessalonians v. 23; — 3. To purify from the guilt of sin by a free remission, Hebrews x. 10, compared with verses 14 and 18. Now, which of these meanings are we to take here? Calvin takes the second, that is to purify from pollution, or to make spiritually holy; others, such as Stuart and Bloomfield, take the last meaning, and the latter gives the rendering, "the expiator and the expiated," This is more consistent with the general tenor of the passage. The subject is not sanctification properly so called, but expiation or atonement. See verses 9 and 17. — *Ed.*

God, why hast thou forsaken me?" And further, the other parts of the chapter prove the same; for we may see in the history of the passion a delineation of what is there related. The end of the Psalm, which speaks of the calling of the Gentiles, can be applied to none but to Christ alone, "Turn to the Lord shall all the ends of the world; adore before him shall all the families of the nations," — "The Lord's is the kingdom, and he will reign over the nations." These things are found accomplished only in Christ, who enlarged the kingdom of God not over a small space, as David did, but extended it over the whole world; it was before confined as it were within narrow limits. There is, then, no doubt but that his voice is what is referred to in this passage; and appropriately and suitably does he say that he is *not ashamed;* for how great is the distance between us and him? Much, then, does he let down himself, when he dignifies us with the name of brethren; for we are unworthy that he should deem us his servants. And this so great an honor conferred on us is amplified by this circumstance — Christ does not speak here as a mortal man while in the form of a servant, but when elevated after the resurrection into immortal glory. Hence this title is the same, as though he had raised us into heaven with himself. And let us remember, whenever we hear that we are called brethren by Christ, that he has clothed us, so to speak, with this honor, that together with this fraternal name we may lay hold on eternal life and every celestial blessing.[42]

We must further notice the office which Christ assumes, which is that of *proclaiming the name of God;* and this began to be done when the gospel was first promulgated and is now done daily by the ministry of pastors. We hence learn, that the gospel has been presented to us for this end, that we may be brought to the knowledge of God, in order that his goodness may be celebrated by us, and that Christ is the author of the gospel in whatever manner it may be offered to us. And this is what Paul

---

42 "If Christ was merely a man and nothing more, where (we may ask with Abresch) would be either the great condescension, or particular kindness manifested in calling men his brethren? If however, he possessed a higher nature, if ἑαυτὸν ἐκένωσεν μορφὴν δούλου λαβών, Philippians ii. 7, if ἐκένωσε ἑαυτὸν μορφὴν δούλου λαβών, Philippians ii. 8; then was it an act of particular kindness and condescension in him to call men his brethren?" — *Stuart*

says, for he declares that he and others were ambassadors for Christ; and he exhorted men as it were in the name of Christ. (2 Corinthians v. 20.) And this ought to add no small reverence to the gospel, since we ought not so much to consider men as speaking to us, as Christ by his own mouth; for at the time when he promised to publish God's name to men, he had ceased to be in the world; it was not however to no purpose that he claimed this office as his own; for he really performs it by his disciples.

12. *In the midst of the Church.*[43] It hence appears plainly, that the proclamation of God's praises is always promoted by the teaching of the gospel; for as soon as God becomes known to us, his boundless praises sound in our hearts and in our ears; and at the same time Christ encourages us by his own example publicly to celebrate them, so that they may be heard by as many as possible. For it would not be sufficient for each one of us to thank God himself for benefits received, except we testify openly our gratitude, and thus mutually stimulate one another. And it is a truth, which may serve as a most powerful stimulant, and may lead us most fervently to praise God, when we hear that Christ leads our songs, and is the chief composer of our hymns.

13. *I will put my trust in him*, or, I will confide in him. As this sentence is found in Psalm xviii. 2, it was probably taken from that place;[44] and Paul, in Romans xv. 9, applies another verse to Christ respecting the calling of the Gentiles. In addition to this, it may be said that the general contents of that Psalm show

---

43 This quotation is made from Psalm xxii. 22, and from the Sept., except that the Apostle changes διηγήσομαι into ἀπαγγελῶ. The words are often used synonymously, only the latter includes the idea of a message, as it literally means to declare something from another. — *Ed.*

44 The words are found literally, according to the Sept., in 2 Samuel xxii. 3; which chapter is materially the same with Psalm 18, and also in Isaiah viii. 17. The words are somewhat different in Psalm xviii. 2, though the Hebrew is the same as in 2 Samuel xxii. 3, אחסה בו, "I will trust in him." The words in Hebrew are wholly different in Isaiah viii. 17, rendered literally, from Isaiah, because they see nothing in the 18th Psalm respecting the Messiah; but the whole Psalm is respecting him who was eminently a type of the Messiah; and in that sense no doubt the Messiah is found there. As God was to David his trust in all trials, so he was to the Son of David. See chapter v. 7. — *Ed.*

clearly that David spoke in the person of another. There indeed appeared in David but a faint shadow of the greatness which is there set forth in terms so magnificent. He boasts that he was made the head of the heathens, and that even aliens and people unknown willingly surrendered themselves to him at the report of his name. David subdued a few neighboring and well-known nations by the force of arms, and made them tributaries. But what was this to the extensive dominions of many other kings? And further, where was voluntary submission? Where were the people that were so remote that he knew them not? In short, where was the solemn proclamation of God's glory among the nations mentioned at the end of the Psalm? Christ then is he who is made head over many nations, to whom strangers from the utmost borders of the earth submit, and roused by hearing of him only; for they are not forced by arms to undertake his yoke, but being subdued by his doctrine, they spontaneously obey him.

There is also seen in the Church that feigned and false profession of religion, which is there referred to; for many daily profess the name of Christ, but not from the heart.

There is then no doubt but that the Psalm is rightly applied to Christ. But what has this to do with the present subject? For it seems not to follow that we and Christ are of one, in order that he might especially put his trust in God. To this I answer, that the argument is valid, because he would have no need of such trust, had he not been a man exposed to human necessities and wants. As then he depended on God's aid, his lot is the same with ours. It is surely not in vain or for nothing that we trust in God; for were we destitute of his grace, we should be miserable and lost. The trust then which we put in God, is an evidence of our helplessness. At the same time we differ from Christ in this — the weakness which necessarily and naturally belongs to us he willingly undertook. But it ought not a little to encourage us to trust in God, that we have Christ as our leader and instructor; for who would fear to go astray while following in his steps? Nay, there is no danger that our trust should be useless when we have it in common with Christ; who, we know, cannot be mistaken.

Behold, I and the children, etc. It is indeed certain that Isaiah was speaking of himself; for when he gave hope of deliverance to the people, and the promise met with no credit, lest being broken down by the perverse unbelief of the people he should despond, the Lord bade him to seal the doctrine he had announced among a few of the faithful; as though he had said, that though it was rejected by the multitude, there would yet be a few who would receive it. Relying on this answer, Isaiah took courage, and declared that he and the disciples given to him would be ever ready to follow God. (Isaiah viii. 18.)

Let us now see why the Apostle applied this sentence to Christ. First, what is found in the same place, that the Lord would become a rock of stumbling and a stone of offense to the kingdom of Israel and of Judas, will not be denied by any one of a sound mind, to have been fulfilled in Christ. And doubtless as the restoration from the Babylonian exile was a sort of prelude to the great redemption obtained by Christ for us and the fathers; so also the fact that so few among the Jews availed themselves of that kindness of God, that a small remnant only were saved, was a presage of their future blindness, through which it happened that they rejected Christ, and that they in turn were rejected by God, and perished. For we must observe that the promises extant in the Prophets respecting the restoration of the Church from the time the Jews returned from exile, extend to the kingdom of Christ, as the Lord had this end in view in restoring the people, that his Church might continue to the coming of his Son, by whom it was at length to be really established.

Since it was so, God not only addressed Isaiah, when he bade him to seal the law and the testimony, but also in his person all his ministers, who would have to contend with the unbelief of the people, and hence Christ above all, whom the Jews resisted with greater contumacy than all the former Prophets. And we see now that they who have been substituted for Israel, not only repudiate his Gospel, but also furiously assail him. But how much soever the doctrine of the Gospel may be a stone of stumbling to the household of the Church, it is not yet God's will that it should wholly fail; on the contrary, he bids it to be sealed among his disciples: and Christ, in the name of all his teachers as the head of them, yea, as the only true Teacher, who rules us by their ministry, declares that amidst this deplorable ingratitude of the world, there shall still be some always who shall be obedient to God.[45]

See then how this passage may be fitly applied to Christ: the Apostle concludes, that we are one with him, because he unites us to himself, when he presents himself and us together to God the Father: for they form but one body who obey God under the same rule of faith. What could have been said more suitably to commend faith, than that we are by it the companions of the Son of God, who by his example encourages us and shows us the way? If then we follow the Word of God, we know of a certainty that we have Christ as our leader; but they belong not at all to Christ, who turn aside from his word. What, I pray, can be more desired than to agree with the Son of God? But this agreement or consent is in faith. Then by unbelief we disagree with him, than which nothing is a greater evil. The word "children", which in many places is taken for servants, means here disciples.

Which God hath given me. Here is pointed out the primary cause of obedience, even that God has adopted us. Christ brings none to the Father, but those given him by the Father; and this donation, we know, depends on eternal election; for those whom the Father has destined to life, he delivers to the keeping of his Son, that he may defend them. This is what he says by John, "All that the Father has given me, will come to me." (John vi. 37.) That we then submit to God by the obedience of faith, let us learn to ascribe this altogether to his mercy; for otherwise we shall never be led to him by the hand of Christ. Besides, this doctrine supplies us with strong ground of confidence; for

---

45 Stuart suggests that these texts are applicable to Christ as the antitype of those to whom they most immediately refer. "As the type," he says, "put his confidence in God, so did the antitype: as the type had children who were pledges for the deliverance of Judah, so has the antitype 'many sons and daughters,' the pledges of his powerful grace, and sureties that his promises in regard to future blessings will be accomplished."

Christ was promised as the Son of David in his office as king: he was therefore to be like David: and the trials and support of David as a king were typical of his trials and support. Hence the Apostle applies to him the language of David. Christ was also promised as a Prophet; and is applied to the antitype. This must have been admitted as a valid reasoning by the Jews who regarded the Messiah both as king and as a prophet. — *Ed.*

who can tremble under the guidance and protection of Christ? Who, while relying on such a keeper and guardian, would not boldly disregard all dangers? And doubtless, while Christ says, "Behold, I and the children," he really fulfills what he elsewhere promises, that he will not suffer any of those to perish whom he has received from the Father. (John x. 28.)[46]

We must observe lastly, that though the world with mad stubbornness reject the Gospel, yet the sheep ever recognize the voice of their shepherd. Let not therefore the impiety of almost all ranks, ages, and nations, disturb us, provided Christ gathers together his own, who have been committed to his protection. If the reprobate rush headlong to death by their impiety, in this way the plants which God has not planted are rooted up. (Matthew xv. 13.) Let us at the same time know that his own are known to him, and that the salvation of them all is sealed by him, so that not one of them shall be lost. (2 Timothy ii. 19.) Let us be satisfied with this seal.

HEBREWS II. 14-15

14. Forasmuch then as the children are partakers of flesh and blood, he also himself likewise took part of the same; that through death he might destroy him that had the power of death, that is, the devil;

---

46 Be it observed that throughout the whole of this passage, from 5 to 14 inclusive, the representation is, that God had a people prior to the coming of Christ, first called "man," afterwards "sons" and "children," and Christ's "brethren," — that those were promised "dominion," glory and honor," — and that the Son of God assumed their nature became lower than the angels, in order to obtain for them this dominion, glory and honor.

This statement bears a similarity to what the Apostle says in the 4th chapter of the Epistle to the Romans, and in the 3rd and 4th to the Galatians: only he seems to go back here to Noah, to whom was restored the dominion and the glory lost in Adam, while in the chapters referred to, he begins with Abraham: and there seems to have been a reason for this; for the posterity of Noah soon departed from the faith; and Abraham became alone the father of the faithful, and through faith "the heir of the world," and had the land of Canaan as a special pledge of a "better country." And the Apostle here also comes to Abraham, verse 16. — Ed.

15. And deliver them who through fear of death were all their lifetime subject to bondage.

14. *Forasmuch then as the children, etc.,* or, *since then the children, etc.* This is an inference from the foregoing; and at the same time a fuller reason is given than what has been hitherto stated, why it behooved the Son of God to put on our flesh, even that he might partake of the same nature with us, and that by undergoing death he might redeem us from it.

The passage deserves especial notice, for it not only confirms the reality of the human nature of Christ, but also shows the benefit which thence flows to us. "The Son of God," he says, "became man, that he might partake of the same condition and nature with us." What could be said more fitted to confirm our faith? Here his infinite love towards us appears; but its overflowing appears in this — that he put on our nature that he might thus make himself capable of dying, for as God he could not undergo death. And though he refers but briefly to the benefits of his death, yet there is in this brevity of words a singularly striking and powerful representation, and that is, that he has so delivered us from the tyranny of the devil, that we are rendered safe, and that he has so redeemed us from death, that it is no longer to be dreaded.

But as all the words are important, they must be examined a little more carefully. First, the destruction of the devil, of which he speaks, imports this — that he cannot prevail against us. For though the devil still lives, and constantly attempts our ruin, yet all his power to hurt us is destroyed or restrained. It is a great consolation to know that we have to do with an enemy who cannot prevail against us. That what is here said has been said with regard to us, we may gather from the next clause, *that he might destroy him that had the power of death;* for the apostle intimates that the devil was so far destroyed as he has power to reign to our ruin; for "the power of death" is ascribed to him from the effect, because it is destructive and brings death. He then teaches us not only that the tyranny of Satan was abolished by Christ's death, but also that he himself was so laid prostrate, that no more account is to be made of him than as though he were not. He speaks of the *devil* according to the usual practice of Scripture, in the singular number, not because there is but one, but because they all form one community which cannot be supposed to be without a head.[47]

15. *And deliver them who*, etc. This passage expresses in a striking manner how miserable is the life of those who fear death, as they must feel it to be dreadful, because they look on it apart from Christ; for then nothing but a curse appears in it: for whence is death but from God's wrath against sin? Hence is that bondage throughout life, even perpetual anxiety, by which unhappy souls are tormented; for through a consciousness of sin the judgment of God is ever presented to the view. From this fear Christ has delivered us, who by undergoing our curse has taken away what is dreadful in death. For though we are not now freed from death, yet in life and in death we have peace and safety, when we have Christ going before us.[48]

But it any one cannot pacify his mind by disregarding death, let him know that he has made as yet but very little proficiency in the faith of Christ; for as extreme fear is owing to ignorance as to the grace of Christ, so it is a certain evidence of unbelief.

Death here does not only mean the separation of the soul from the body, but also the punishment which is inflicted on us by an angry God, so that it includes eternal ruin; for where there is guilt before God, there immediately hell shows itself.

HEBREWS II. 16-18

16. For verily he took not on *him the nature of* angels; but he took on *him* the seed of Abraham.

17. Wherefore in all things it behooved him to be made like unto *his* brethren, that he might be a merciful and faithful high priest in things *pertaining* to God, to make reconciliation for the sins of the people.

18. For in that he himself hath suffered being tempted, he is able to succor them that are tempted.

---

47 See Appendix I

48 The same seem to be meant here as before, — "the sons, the children." Before Christ came, though heirs, yet they were in a state of bondage; so the Apostle represents them in Galatians iv. 1-3. See Romans viii. 15. — *Ed.*

16. *For verily,* or, *For nowhere, etc.* By this comparison he enhances the benefit and the honor with which Christ has favored us, by putting on our flesh; for he never did so much for angels. As then it was necessary that there should be a remarkable remedy for man's dreadful ruin, it was the design of the Son of God that there should be some incomparable pledge of his love towards us which angels had not in common with us. That he preferred us to angels was not owing to our excellency, but to our misery. There is therefore no reason for us to glory as though we were superior to angels, except that our heavenly Father has manifested toward us that ampler mercy which we needed, so that the angels themselves might from on high behold so great a bounty poured on the earth. The present tense of the verb is to be understood with reference to the testimonies of Scripture, as though he set before us what had been before testified by the Prophets.

But this one passage is abundantly sufficient to lay prostrate such men as Marcion and Manicheus, and fanatical men of similar character, who denied Christ to have been a real man, begotten of human seed. For if he bore only the appearance of man, as he had before appeared in the form of an angel, there could have been no difference; but as it could not have been said that Christ became really an angel, clothed with angelic nature, it is hence said that he took upon him man's nature and not that of angels.

And the Apostle speaks of nature, and intimates that Christ, clothed with flesh, was real man, so that there was unity of person in two natures. For this passage does not favor Nestorius, who imagined a twofold Christ, as though the Son of God was not a real man but only dwelt in man's flesh. But we see that the Apostle's meaning was very different, for his object was to teach us that we find in the Son of God a brother, being a partaker of our common nature. Being not therefore satisfied with calling him man, he says that he was begotten of human seed; and he names expressly the *seed of Abraham,* in order that what he said might have more credit, as being taken from Scripture.[49]

17. *Wherefore in all things it behooved him to be made like unto his brethren,* or, *to be like his brethren, etc.* In Christ's human nature there are two things to be considered, the real flesh and the affections or feelings. The Apostle then teaches us, that he had

---

49 See Appendix K

not only put on the real flesh of man, but also all those feelings which belong to man, and he also shows the benefit that hence proceeds; and it is the true teaching of faith when we in our case find the reason why the Son of God undertook our infirmities; for all knowledge without feeling the need of this benefit is cold and lifeless. But he teaches us that Christ was made subject to human affections, *that he might be a merciful and faithful high priest;* which words I thus explain, "that he might be a merciful, and therefore a faithful high priest."[50]

For in a priest, whose office it is to appease God's wrath, to help the miserable, to raise up the fallen, to relieve the oppressed, mercy is especially required, and it is what experience produces in us; for it is a rare thing, for those who are always happy to sympathize with the sorrows of others. The following saying of Virgil was no doubt derived from daily examples found among men:

"Not ignorant of evil, I learn to aid the miserable."[51]

The Son of God had no need of experience that he might know the emotions of mercy; but we could not be persuaded that he is merciful and ready to help us, had he not become acquainted by experience with our miseries; but this, as other things, has been as a favor given to us. Therefore whenever any evils pass over us, let it ever occur to us, that nothing happens

---

50 Here is, as I conceive, an instance of an arrangement similar to what is often found in the prophets, and to what occurs in verse 9; this would be seen were a part of this verse and the following verse put in lines, —

That compassionate he might be
And a faithful high priest in the things of God
To make an atonement for the sins of the people;
For as he suffered, being himself tempted, he can help the tempted.

The first and last line correspond, and the second and the third. He is compassionate, because he can sympathize with the tempted, having been himself tempted; and he is a true and faithful high priest, because he really expiated the sins of the people: and that he might be all this, he became like his brethren that is, by taking their nature. — *Ed.*

51 *Non ignara mali, miseris succurrere disco.*

to us but what the Son of God has himself experienced in order that he might sympathize with us; nor let us doubt but that he is at present with us as though he suffered with us.[52]

Faithful means one true and upright, for it is one opposite to a dissembler; and to him who fulfils not his engagements. An acquaintance with our sorrows and miseries so inclines Christ to compassion, that he is constant in imploring God's aid for us. What besides? Having purposed to make atonement for sins, he put on our nature that we might have in our own flesh the price of our redemption; in a word, that by the right of a common nature he might introduce us, together with himself, into the sanctuary of God. By the words, *in things pertaining to God*, he means such things as are necessary to reconcile men to God; and as the first access to God is by faith, there is need of a Mediator to remove all doubting.

18. *For in that he himself has suffered, etc.* Having been tried by our evils, he is ready, he says, to bring us help. The word *temptation* here means no other thing than experience or probation; and to be *able,* is to be fit, or inclined, or suitable.

---

52 This paragraph, which begins at verse 5, commences with what belongs to the kingly office — dominion, and what accompanies it, glory and honor; but it ends with the priestly office; and it is shown that it was necessary for the Savior to be a priest in order that he might be a king, and might make his people kings as well as priests to God. The dominion and glory promised to the faithful from the beginning intimated even in the first promise made to fallen man, and more fully developed afterwards, was what they had no power to attain of themselves: Hence it became necessary for the Son of God to become the son of man, that he might obtain for his people the dominion and glory. This seems to be the view presented to us in this passage. The children of God, before Christ came into the world, were like heirs under age, though lords of all. He came, took their flesh and effected whatever was necessary to put them in full possession of the privileges promised them. See Galatians iv. 1-6. — *Ed.*

CHAPTER 3

HEBREWS III. 1-6

1. Wherefore, holy brethren, partakers of the heavenly calling, consider the Apostle and High Priest of our profession, Christ Jesus;
2. Who was faithful to him that appointed him, as also Moses *was faithful* in all his house.
3. For this *man* was counted worthy of more glory than Moses, inasmuch as he who hath builded the house hath more honor than the house.
4. For every house is builded by some *man*; but he that built all things *is* God.
5. And Moses verily *was* faithful in all his house, as a servant, for a testimony of those things which were to be spoken after;
6. But Christ as a son over his own house; whose house are we, if we hold fast the confidence and the rejoicing of the hope firm unto the end.

1. *Wherefore, holy brethren, etc.* He concludes the preceding doctrine with a necessary exhortation, that the Jews should attentively consider what sort of being and how great Christ is. As he had before, by naming him a teacher and a priest, briefly compared him with Moses and Aaron, so he now includes both clauses; for he adorns him with two titles, as he sustains a twofold character in the Church of God. Moses was a prophet and a teacher, and Aaron was a priest; but the two offices belong to Christ. If then we seek rightly to know him, we must inquire what sort of being he is; yea, he must be clothed with his own power, lest we lay hold on an empty shadow and not on him.[53]

First, the word *consider*, is important, for it intimates that singular attention is required, as he cannot be disregarded with impunity, and that at the same time the true knowledge of Christ is sufficient to dissipate the darkness of all errors. And to encourage them the more to pursue this study, he reminds them of their *calling*; as though he had said, "God favored you with no common grace when He called you into his kingdom;[54] it now remains that you have your eyes fixed on Christ as your leader in the way."[55] For the calling of the godly cannot be otherwise confirmed than by a thorough surrender of themselves to Christ. We ought not therefore to regard this as said only to the Jews, but that it is a general truth addressed to all who desire to come into the kingdom of God; they ought sedulously to attend to Christ, for he is the sole instructor of our faith, and has confirmed it by the sacrifice of himself; for *confession*, or profession, is to be taken here for faith, as thought he had said, that

---

[53] He calls them "holy brethren." Stuart takes holy as meaning "consecrated, devoted, i.e. to Christ, set apart as Christians." The people of Israel were called holy in the same sense, not because they were spiritually holy, but because they were set apart and adopted as God's people. The word saints, at the commencement of Paul's Epistles, means the same thing. — Ed.

[54] The word heavenly, may also mean a call from heaven. See chapter xii. 25. It is no doubt both, it is a call to the enjoyment of heavenly things, as well as a call that comes from heaven. — Ed.

[55] This is the only place in which Christ is called an Apostle, the design no doubt was to institute a comparison between him and Moses, who is often said to have been sent by God, as Christ is said to have been sent by the Father: they might both therefore be rightly called Apostles, i.e., messengers sent by God. And then he adds, high priest, that he might afterwards make a comparison between him and Aaron.

He had before exalted Christ as a teacher above all the prophets, including no doubt Moses among the rest; but here refers to Moses as the leader of the people, as one sent especially by God to conduct them from Egypt through the wilderness to the land of Canaan. But as our call is from heaven and to heaven, Christ is sent as a messenger to lead us to the heavenly country. We hence see that in this connection the "heavenly calling" is to be taken most suitably as a call to heaven. — Ed.

the faith we profess is vain and of no avail, unless Christ be its object.[56]

2. *Who was,* or *is faithful, etc.* This is a commendation of the apostleship of Christ, in order that the faithful may securely acquiesce in him; and he commends it on two grounds, because the Father has set him to be over us as our teacher, and because Christ himself has faithfully performed the office committed to him. These two things are always necessary to secure authority to a doctrine; for God alone ought to be attended to, as the whole Scripture testifies; hence Christ declares, that the doctrine which he delivered was not his own, but the Father's, (John vii. 16;) and in another place he says, "He who received me, receiveth him who has sent me." (Luke ix. 48.) For we say of Christ, that as he is clothed with our flesh, he is the Father's minister to execute his commands. To the calling of God is added the faithful and upright performance of duty on the part of Christ; and this is required in true ministers, in order that they may obtain credence in the Church. Since these two things are found in Christ, doubtless he cannot be disregarded without despising God in him.

As also Moses, etc. Omitting for a while the priesthood, he speaks here of his apostleship. For as there are two parts in God's covenant, the promulgation of the truth, and so to speak, its real confirmation, the full perfection of the covenant would not appear in Christ, were not both parts found in him. Hence the writer of the epistle, after having mentioned both, roused attention by a brief exhortation. But he now enters on a longer discussion, and begins with the office of a teacher: he therefore now compares Christ only with Moses. The words, *in all his house,* may be applied to Moses; but I prefer to apply them to Christ, as he may be said to be faithful to his Father in ruling his whole house. It hence follows, that none belong to the Church of God except those who acknowledge Christ.[57]

---

56 The simpler meaning of this phrase is to view it as sort of Hebraism, when a noun is put for an adjective or a participle; and it is so rendered by Schleusner and Stuart, "professed by us," or, "whom we profess." See similar instances in chapter x. 23, and in 2 Corinthians ix. 13. — *Ed.*

57 This testimony as to Moses is found in Numbers xii. 7. God says there "in all mine house;" we ought therefore to consider "his" here as referring to God or to Christ, and not to Moses.

3. *For this man* (or, *he*) *was counted worthy, etc.* Lest he might appear to make Moses equal to Christ, he reminds us of his superior excellency; and this he proves by two arguments, -Moses so ruled the Church, that he was still a part and member of it; but Christ being the builder, is superior to the whole building, — Moses while ruling others, was ruled also himself, as he was a servant; but Christ being a Son possesses supreme power.

It is a frequent and well-known metaphor used in Scripture to call the Church the house of God. (1 Timothy iii. 15.) And as it is composed of the faithful, each of them is called a living stone. (1 Peter ii. 5.) They are also sometimes called the vessels with which the house is furnished. (2 Timothy ii. 20.) There is then no one so eminent that he is not a member, and included in the universal body. God being the builder, alone is to be set above his own work; but God dwells in Christ, so that whatever is said of God is applicable to him.

If any one objects and says that Christ is also a part of the building because he is the foundation, because he is our brother, because he has a union with us and then that he is not the master-builder because he himself was formed by God: in reply to these things we say that our faith is so founded on him that he still rules over us that he is in such a way our brother that he is yet our Lord, that he was so formed by God as man that he nevertheless by his Spirit revives and restores all things as the eternal God. The Scripture employs us various metaphors to set forth Christ s grace towards us; but there is no one which derogates from his honor mentioned here by the Apostle; for what is stated here is that all ought to be brought down to their own state because they ought to be in subjection to the head and that Christ alone is exempt from this submission, because he is the head.

If it be again objected and said that Moses was no less a master-builder than Paul who gloried in this title: to this I reply that this name is applied to prophets and teachers but not with strict correctness; for they are only the instruments and indeed dead instruments, except the Lord from heaven gives efficacy

---

"For this man," οὗτος; it is better to render it here he, as it is sometimes rendered, and is so rendered in this place by Doddridge, Macknight and Stuart. The connection is with "consider," in the first verse; "for," a reason is given for the exhortation; "for he," i.e., the apostle and high priest before mentioned, etc. — *Ed.*

to what they do; and then they so labor in building the Church, that they themselves form a part of the structure; but the case is wholly different as to Christ, for he ever builds up the Church by the power of his own Spirit. Besides, he stands far above the rest, for he is in such a way the true temple of God, that he is at the same time the God who inhabits it.

4. *He that built, etc.* Though these words may be extended to the creation of the whole world, yet I confine them to the present subject. We are then to understand that nothing is done in the Church which ought not to he ascribed to Gods power; for he alone has founded it by his own hand, (Psalm lxxxvii. 5;) and Paul says of Christ that he is the head, from whom the whole body, joined together and connected by every subservient juncture, makes an increase according to what is done proportionally by every member. (Ephesians iv. 16.) Hence he often declares that the success of his ministry was God's work. In a word, if we take a right view of things, it will appear that how much soever God may use the labors of men in building his Church, yet he himself performs everything — the instrument derogates nothing from the workman.[58]

5. *And Moses verily was faithful in all his house, as a servant, etc.* The second difference is, that to Moses was committed a doctrine to which he, in common with others, was to submit; but Christ, though he put on the form of a servant, is yet Master and Lord, to whom all ought to be subject; for, as we found in chap. i. 2, he is constituted heir of all things.

For a testimony of those things which were to be spoken after, or *which were afterwards to be said* or *declared.* I explain this simply in this way, — that Moses, while a herald of that doctrine which was to be published for a time to the ancient people, did at the same time render a testimony to the Gospel, the publication of which was not as yet to be made; for it is doubtless evident, that the end and completion of the Law is that perfection of wisdom contained in the Gospel. This exposition seems to comport with the future tense of the participle. The meaning indeed is, that Moses faithfully delivered to the people what the Lord had committed to him, but that limits were prescribed to him which it was not lawful for him to pass. God formerly spoke at different times and in various ways by the prophets, but he deferred to the fullness of time the complete revelation of the Gospel.

---

58 See Appendix L

6. *Whose house are we, etc.* As Paul in his Epistle to the Romans, after having prefaced that he was appointed to be the Apostle of the Gentiles, adds, for the sake of gaining credit among them, that they were of that number; so now the author of this epistle exhorts the Jews who had already made a profession of Christ to persevere in the faith, that they might be deemed as being in Gods household. He had said before that God's house was subject to the authority of Christ. Suitably to this declaration is added the admonition that they would then have a place in God's family when they obeyed Christ. But as they had already embraced the gospel, he mentions their condition if they persevered in the faith. For the word *hope* I take for faith; and indeed hope is nothing else but the constancy of faith. He mentions *confidence* and *rejoicing,* or glorying, in order to express more fully the power of faith.[59] And we hence conclude that those who assent to the Gospel doubtfully and like those who vacillate, do not truly and really believe; for faith cannot be without a settled peace of mind, from which proceeds the bold confidence of rejoicing. And so these two things, confidence and rejoicing, are ever the effects of faith, as we stated in explaining Romans the 5th chapter, and Ephesians the 3rd chapter.

But to these things the whole teaching of the Papists is opposed; and this very fact, were there nothing else, sufficiently

---

59 It is better for "hope" here to be retained in its proper meaning; for in verse 12 the defect of it is traced to unbelief. Were the words "confidence" and "rejoicing" rendered adjectivally, the meaning would be more evident, — "If we hold firm our confident and joyful hope to the end." So we may render a similar form of expression in verse 13, "through deceitful sin," as "newness of life" in Romans vi. 4, means "new life." The most common practice is to render the genitive in such instances as an adjective, but this is not always the case.

Hope is "confident" or assured, while it rests on the word of God, and is "joyful" while it anticipates the glory and happiness of the heavenly kingdom.

But Beza and Doddridge take words apart, "freedom of profession and boasting of hope," or according to Beza, "the hope of which we boast." Macknight renders them "the boldness and the glorifying of the hope." The secondary meaning of the word παρρησία is confidence, and of καύχημα, joy or rejoicing, and the most suitable here, as it comports better with holding fast, or firm. — *Ed.*

proves that they pull down the Church of God rather than build it. For the certainty by which alone we are made, as the Apostle teaches us, holy temples to God, they not only darken by their glosses, but also condemn as presumption. Besides, what firmness of confidence can there be when men know not what they ought to believe? And yet that monstrous thing, implicit faith, which they have invented, is nothing else than a license to entertain errors. This passage reminds us that we are always to make progress even unto death; for our whole life is as it were a race.

HEBREWS III. 7-13

7. Wherefore (as the Holy Ghost saith, To day if ye will hear his voice,
8. Harden not your hearts, as in the provocation, in the day of temptation in the wilderness:
9. When your fathers tempted me, proved me, and saw my works forty years.
10. Wherefore I was grieved with that generation, and said, They do always err in *their* heart; and they have not known my ways.
11. So I sware in my wrath, They shall not enter into my rest.)
12. Take heed, brethren, lest there be in any of you an evil heart of unbelief, in departing from the living God.
13. But exhort one another daily, while it is called To day; lest any of you be hardened through the deceitfulness of sin.

He proceeds in his exhortation, that they were to obey Christ speaking to them; and that he might add more weight to it, he confirms it by the testimony of David; for since they were to be sharply goaded, it was better, for the sake of avoiding offense, to bring forward another person. Had he simply reproached them for the unbelief of the fathers, they would have less favorably attended to him; but when he brought forward David, it was less offensive. Now, the import of the whole is, — As God from the beginning would his voice obeyed, and could not endure perverseness without punishing it severely, so at this day he will not lightly punish our stubbornness, unless we become teachable. But the discourse is suspended until we come to the words, "Take heed, brethren, lest there be at any time in any of you," etc. That the passage, then, may flow better, it would be proper to include the rest in a parenthesis.[60] Let us now consider the words in order.

7. *As the Holy Ghost saith,* etc. This availed much more to touch their hearts than if he had quoted David by name. And it is useful for us to familiarize ourselves with such expressions, so that we may remember that the words adduced from the books of the prophets are those of God and not of men.

But as this sentence, *Today, if ye will hear his voice,* is a part of a former verse, some have not unsuitably rendered it thus, "Would to God you would this day hear his voice." It is indeed certain that when David called the Jews God's people, he immediately drew this conclusion, that the voice of God ought to have been heard by them; for as to those whom he there invited to sing praises to God and to celebrate his goodness, he reminded them at the same time that obedience was the chief worship which he required, and that it was better than all sacrifices. The chief thing, then, was to obey the word of God.

8. Then follows, *Harden not your hearts.* By which words is intimated that our rebellion against God flows from no other fountain than willful wickedness, by which we obstruct the entrance of his grace. We have indeed by nature a heart of stone, and there is in all an innate hardness from the womb, which God alone can mollify and amend. That we, however, reject the voice of God, it happens through a spontaneous obstinacy, not through an external impulse, a fact of which every one is a witness to himself. Rightly, then, does the Spirit accuse all the unbelieving that they resist God, and that they are the teachers and authors of their own perverseness, so that they can throw the blame on none else. It is hence, however, absurdly concluded that we have, on the other hand, a free power to form the heart for God's service; nay rather, it must ever be the case with men, that they harden their heart until another be given them from heaven; for as we are bent towards wickedness, we shall

---

60 There is the same parenthesis in our version; but Beza, Doddridge, Macknight, and Stuart, do not use it, but connect "therefore" or wherefore with "harden not," which seems more suitable. — *Ed.*

never cease to resist God until we shall be tamed and subdued by his hand.

As in the provocation, etc. It was for two reasons necessary for them to be reminded of the disobedience of their fathers; for as they were foolishly inflated on account of the glory of their race, they often imitated the vices of their fathers as though they were virtues, and defended themselves by their examples; and further, when they heard that their fathers were so disobedient to God, they were thus more fully taught that this admonition was not superfluous. As both these reasons existed even in the Apostle's time, he readily accommodated to his own purpose what had been formerly said by David, in order that those whom he addressed might not imitate their fathers too much.

And hence may be learnt a general truth, that we are not to defer too much to the authority of the fathers lest it should draw us away from God; for if any fathers have ever been worthy of honor, no doubt the Jews possessed that preeminence; and yet David distinctly commanded their children to beware of being like them.

And I have no doubt but that he referred to the history recorded in Exodus 17: for David uses here the two names which Moses relates were given to a certain place, מרבה Meribah, which means strife or provocation, and מסה Massah, which means temptation. They tempted God by denying that he was in the midst of them, because they were distressed for want of water; and they also provoked him by contending with Moses. Though indeed they gave many examples of unbelief, yet David selected this in an especial manner, because it was more memorable then any other, and also, because in order of time it followed for the most part the rest, as it evidently appears from the fourth book of Moses, where from chap. x. to xx. a series of many temptations is described; but this narrative is given in the twentieth chapter. This circumstance increased not a little the atrocity of their wickedness; for they had often experienced the power of God, and yet they perversely contended with him, and renounced all confidence in him: how great was their ingratitude! He then mentioned one particular instance instead of many.

9. *Tempted,* etc. This word is to be taken in a bad sense; it means to provoke in a proud and insulting manner, which we express in French by saying, *defier comme en depitant* For though

God had often brought them help, yet they forgot all, and scornfully asked, where was his power. *Proved, etc.* This clause is to be thus explained, "When yet they had proved me and seen my works". For it enhanced the guilt of their impiety, that having been taught by so many evidences of divine power, they had made so bad a progress. For it was a marvelous supineness and stupidity to esteem God's power as nothing, which had been so fully proved.[61]

Forty years. These are connected by David with what follows. But we know that the Apostles in quoting passages attend more to the general meaning than to the words. And no doubt God complained that the people had been vexatious to him for forty years, because so many benefits had availed nothing for the purpose of teaching them; for though God did good continually to them who were wholly unworthy, they yet never ceased to rise up against him. Hence arose his continual indignation, as though he had said "Not once or for a short time have they provoked me, but by their incessant wickedness for forty years." *Generation* means race, or men of one age.

10. *And I said, etc.* This was God's sentence, by which he declared that they were destitute of a sound mind, and he adds the reason, *For they have not known my ways.* In short, he regarded them as past hope, for they were without sense and reason. And here he assumed the character of man, who at length after long trials declares that he has discovered obstinate madness, for he says that they always went astray, and no hope of repentance appeared.

11. *So I sware, etc.* It was the punishment of their madness, that they were deprived of the rest promised them. Moreover, the Lord calls the land, where they might have had their dwelling, *his rest.* For they had been sojourners in Egypt and wanderers in the wilderness; but the land of Canaan was to be, according to the promise, their perpetual inheritance; and it was in reference to this promise that God called it *his* rest: for nowhere can we have a settled dwelling, except where we are fixed by his hand. But their right to a sure possession was founded on what God said to Abraham,

"To thy seed will I give this land." (Genesis xii. 7.)

---

61   See Appendix M.

By God swearing, *If they shall enter, etc.,* the atrocity of their evil conduct is made more evident and is more forcibly set forth, for it is an evidence of wrath greatly inflamed. "If they shall enter," is in the form of an oath, in which something is to be understood, as an imprecation, or some such thing, when men speak; but when God speaks, it is the same as though he said, "Let me not be deemed true,", or, "Let me not be hereafter believed, if such a thing shall not be so." However, this defective mode of speaking recommends fear and reverence to us, so that we may not rashly swear, as many do, who are often in the habit of pouring forth dreadful curses.

But as to the present passage, we ought not to think that they were then for the first time denied entrance into the land by God's oath, when they tempted him in Rephidim; for they had long before been excluded, even from the time they had refused to march forward at the report of the spies. God then does not here ascribe their expulsion from the land to this instance of tempting him as to the first cause; but he intimates that by no chastisement could they have been restored to a sound mind, but that they continually added new offenses: and thus he shows that they fully deserved to be thus severely punished, for they never ceased to increase more and more his wrath by various sins, as though he had said, "This is the generation to which I denied the possession of the promised land, for during whole forty years afterwards it betrayed its obstinate madness by innumerable sins."

12. *Take heed,* (or *See,*) *brethren, lest there be at any time in any of you a wicked heart of unbelief, etc.* I have preferred to retain literally what the Apostle states, rather than to give a paraphrase as to the wicked or depraved *heart of unbelief,* by which he intimates that unbelief would be connected with depravity or wickedness, if after having received the knowledge of Christ they departed from his faith. For he addressed them who had been imbued with the elements of Christianity; hence he immediately added, *By departing;* for the sin of defection is accompanied with perfidy.[62]

---

62   The word connected with "heart" is ἐν τῷ, which properly means diseased and hence corrupted, depraved, wicked. Depraved or wicked would perhaps be the best rendering of it here. "Unbelief" is a genitive used for an adjective or a participle, — "a wicked unbelieving heart." It is unbelieving owing to its wickedness

13. He also pointed out the remedy, so that they might not fall into this wickedness, and that was, to *exhort one another*. For as by nature we are inclined to evil, we have need of various helps to retain us in the fear of God. Unless our faith be now and then raised up, it will lie prostrate; unless it be warmed, it will be frozen; unless it be roused, it will grow torpid. He would have us then to stimulate one another by mutual exhortations, so that Satan may not creep into our hearts, and by his fallacies draw us away from God. And this is a way of speaking that ought to be especially observed; for we fall not immediately by the first assault into this madness of striving against God; but Satan by degrees accosts us artfully by indirect means, until he holds us ensnared in his delusions. Then indeed being blinded, we break forth into open rebellion.[63]

We must then meet this danger in due time, and it is one that is nigh us all, for nothing is more possible than to be deceived; and from this deception comes at length hardness of heart. We hence see how necessary it is for us to be roused by the incessant goads of exhortations. Nor does the Apostle give only a general precept, that all should take heed to themselves, but he should have them also to be solicitous for the salvation of every member, so that they should not suffer any of those who had been once called to perish through their neglect, and he who feels it his duty so to watch over the salvation of the whole flock as to neglect no one sheep, performs in this case the office of a good shepherd.

---

or depravity. Grotius says, that there are two kinds of unbelief, — The first the rejection of the truth when first offered, — and the second the renouncing of it after having once professed it. The latter is the more heinous sin.

"The departing," etc.; ἐν τῷ is rendered "by" by Macknight: it is considered by Grotius to be for εἰς τὸ, which word makes the meaning more evident, "so as to depart," etc. — *Ed.*

[63] "Deceitfulness of sin" is rendered by Stuart "sinful delusion." It ought rather to be "deceitful (or seductive) sin" as "deceitfulness of riches" in Matthew xiii. 22, means "deceitful riches." The "sin" was evidently that of apostasy: and it was deceitful, because there was a present prospect of relief from troubles and persecutions. The power of any sin to deceive and seduce, consists in some present gratification or interest. See note on verse 6. — *Ed.*

While it is called today. He now applies what David said more particularly to his own subjects; for he reminds us that the word *today*, mentioned in the Psalm, ought not to be confined to the age of David, but that it comprehends every time in which God may address us. As often, then, and as long as he opened his sacred mouth to teach us, let this sentence come to our minds, "Today, if ye will hear his voice". In the same way Paul teaches us that when the Gospel is preached to us, it is the accepted time in which God hears us, and the Day of salvation in which he helps us. (2 Corinthians vi. 2.)

Now, of this opportunity we ought to avail ourselves; for if through our sloth we suffer it to pass by, we shall hereafter in vain deplore its loss. So Christ says,

"Walk while ye have the light; come shortly shall the night." (John xii. 35.)

The particle *while*, then, or as long as, intimates that, The seasonable time will not continue always, if we be too slothful to follow when the Lord calls us. God knocks at our door; unless we open to him he will no doubt in his turn close against us the gate of his kingdom. In a word, too late will be their groans who despise the grace offered to them today. As, then, we know not whether God will extend his calling to tomorrow, let us not delay. Today he calls us; let us immediately respond to him, for there is no faith except where there is such a readiness to obey.

HEBREWS III. 14-19

14. For we are made partakers of Christ, if we hold the beginning of our confidence steadfast unto the end;
15. While it is said, To day if ye will hear his voice, harden not your hearts, as in the provocation.
16. For some, when they had heard, did provoke: howbeit not all that came out of Egypt by Moses.
17. But with whom was he grieved forty years? *was it* not with them that had sinned, whose carcases fell in the wilderness?
18. And to whom sware he that they should not enter into his rest, but to them that believed not?

19. So we see that they could not enter in because of unbelief.

14. *For we are made partakers, etc.* He commends them for having begun well; but lest, under the pretext of the grace which they had obtained, they should indulge themselves in carnal security, he says that there was need of perseverance; for many having only tasted the Gospel, do not think of any progress as though they had reached the summit. Thus it is that they not only stop in the middle of their race, yea, nigh the starting-posts, but turn another way. Plausible indeed is this objection, "What can we wish more after having found Christ?" But if he is possessed by faith, we must persevere in it, so that he may be our perpetual possession. Christ then has given himself to be enjoyed by us on this condition, that by the same faith by which we have been admitted into a participation of him, we are to preserve so great a blessing even to death.[64]

Hence he says *beginning,* intimating that their faith was only begun. As *hypostasis* sometimes means *confidence,* it may be so taken here; yet the term *substance,* as some have rendered it, I do not dislike, though I explain it in a way somewhat different. They think that faith is thus called, because the whole of what man may have without it is nothing but vanity; but I so regard it, because we recumb on it alone, as there is no other support on which we can rely. And suitable to this view is the word *steadfast* or firm; for we shall be firmly fixed and beyond the danger of vacillating, provided faith be our foundation. The sum of the whole then is, that faith whose beginnings only appear in us, is to make constant and steady progress to the end.[65]

15. *While it is said, etc.* He intimates that the reason for making progress never ceases as long as we live, because God calls us daily. For since faith responds to the preaching of the Gospel, as preaching continues through the whole course of our life, so

---

64 What is implied here is that we may professedly be partakers of Christ: that is of his blessings as a Savior, and yet be not really so: the proof of the reality is perseverance. — *Ed.*

65 Here is another instance of the genitive being the main subject, "the beginning of our confidence," i.e., our first confidence, which the Apostle calls "first faith" in 1 Timothy v. 12. Macknight renders it "the begun confidence." — *Ed.*

we ought to continue growing in faith. The phrase, then, *while it is said*, is the same as though he had said, "Since God never makes an end of speaking, it is not enough for us readily to receive his doctrine, except we exhibit the same teachableness and obedience tomorrow and every following day."[66]

16 *For some, when they had heard, etc.* David spoke of the fathers as though that whole generation were unbelieving; but it appears that some who truly feared God mingled with the wicked. The apostle mentions this to modify what had been more severely said by David, in order that we may know that the word is preached to all for this end, that all may obey it with one consent, and that the whole people were justly condemned for unbelief, when the body was torn and mutilated by the defection of the greatest part.

But by saying that some *provoked*, while yet they were by far the greatest part, this object was not only to avoid giving offense, but also to encourage the Jews to imitate those who believed; as though he had said, "As God forbids you to follow the unbelief of the fathers, so he sets before you other fathers whose faith is to be your example". Thus is mitigated what otherwise might have appeared too hard; that is, had they been commanded wholly to dissent from their fathers. *To come out by Moses*, means by the hand of Moses, for he was the minister of their deliverance. But there is an implied comparison between the benefit which God had bestowed on them by Moses, and the participation of Christ previously mentioned.

---

66 Most connect this verse with the preceding, as in our version, and as Doddridge thus "forasmuch as it is said;" and Macknight thus "as ye may know by the saying." So does Beza; and Calvin seems to do the same; but some connect it with the 13th and others with the 14th verse. Modern authors, such as Stuart and Blooomfield, regard it as the commencement of a paragraph, and connect it with what follows. Stuart's version is —

15. With regard to the saying, "today while ye hear his voice, harden

16. Not your hearts as in the provocation;" who now were they that when they heard did provoke? Nay, did not all who came out of Egypt under Moses? Etc.

Bloomfield approves of this version, only he considers the quotation is confined to the words, "Today, while ye hear his voice," and regards what follows, "harden not," etc., as said by the writer: See Appendix N. — *Ed.*

17. *But with whom was he grieved,* or *angry, etc.* He means that God had never been angry with his people except for just causes, as Paul also reminds us in 1 Corinthians x. 5, 6. Therefore as many chastisements of God as we read were inflicted on the ancient people, so many grievous sins shall we find which provoked God's vengeance. At the same time we must come to this conclusion, that unbelief was the chief of all their evils; for though he mentions this the last, he yet means that it was the primary cause of their curse; and no doubt from the time they once became unbelievers, they never ceased to add one sin to another, and thus they brought on themselves new scourges continually. Hence those very persons who through unbelief rejected the possession of the land offered to them, pursued their own obstinacy, now lusting, then murmuring, now committing adultery, then polluting themselves with heathen superstitions, so that their depravity became more fully manifested.

The unbelief, then, which they showed from the beginning, prevented them from enjoying the kindness of God; for the contempt of his word ever led them to sin. And as at first they deserved through their unbelief that God should deprive them of the promised rest, so whatever sin they committed afterwards flowed from the same fountain.

It may be further asked, whether Moses, and Aaron, and those like them, were included in this number? To this I answer, that the Apostle speaks of the whole community rather than of individuals. It is certain that there were many godly men who were either not entangled in the general impiety or soon repented. Moses' faith was once shaken and only once, and that for a moment. The Apostle's words, therefore, contain a statement of the whole instead of a part, a mode of speaking frequently employed when a multitude or body of people are spoken of.

CHAPTER 4

HEBREWS IV. 1-2

1. Let us therefore fear, lest, a promise being left *us* of entering into his rest, any of you should seem to come short of it.
2. For unto us was the gospel preached, as well as unto them: but the word preached did not profit them, not being mixed with faith in them that heard *it*

1. *Let us therefore fear, etc.* He concludes that there was reason to fear lest the Jews to whom he was writing should be deprived of the blessing offered to them; and then he says, *lest anyone,* intimating that it was his anxious desire to lead them, one and all, to God; for it is the duty of a good shepherd, in watching over the whole flock so to care for every sheep that no one may be lost; nay, we ought also so to feel for one another that every one should fear for his neighbors as well as for himself

But the fear which is here recommended is not that which shakes the confidence of faith but such as fills us with such concern that we grow not torpid with indifference. Let us then fear, not that we ought to tremble or to entertain distrust as though uncertain as to the issue, but lest we be unfaithful to God's grace.

By saying *Lest we be disappointed of the promise left us,* he intimates that no one comes short of it except he who by rejecting grace has first renounced the promise; for God is so far from repenting to do us good that he ceases not to bestow his gifts except when we despise his calling. The illative *therefore,* or *then* means that by the fall of others we are taught humility and watchfulness according to what Paul also says,

"These through unbelief have fallen; be not thou then high-minded, but fear."[67] (Romans xi. 20.)

2. *For to us, etc.* He reminds us that the doctrine by which God invites us to himself at this day is the same with that which he formerly delivered to the fathers; and why did he say this? That we may know that the calling of God will in no degree be more profitable to us than it was to them, except we make it sure by faith. This, then, he concedes, that the Gospel is indeed preached to us;[68] but lest we should vainly glory, he immediately adds that the unbelieving whom God had formerly favored with the participation of so great blessings, yet received from them no fruit, and that therefore we also shall be destitute of his blessing unless we receive it by faith. He repeats the word *hear* for this end, that we may know that hearing is useless except the word addressed to us be by faith received.

But we must here observe the connection between the word and faith. It is such that faith is not to be separated from the word, and that the word separated from faith can confer no good; not indeed that the efficacy or power of the word depends on us; for were the whole world false, he who cannot lie would still never cease to be true, but the word never puts forth its power in us except when faith gives it an entrance. It is indeed the power of God unto salvation, but only to those who believe. (Romans i. 16.) There is in it revealed the righteousness of God, but it is from faith to faith. Thus it is that the word of God is always efficacious and saving to men, when viewed in itself or

---

67 Calvin renders the last verb "be disappointed," (*frustratus,*) though the verb means properly to be behind in time, to be too late; yet it is commonly used in the sense of falling short of a thing, of being destitute; of being without. See Romans iii. 23; 1 Corinthians i. 7; chapter xii. 15. To "come short" of our version fitly expresses its meaning here, as adopted by Doddridge and Stuart; or "to fall short," as rendered by Macknight.

"Seem" is considered by some to be pleonastic. The verb δοκέω is so no doubt sometimes, but not always; but here appears to have a special meaning, as the Apostle would have no one to present even the appearance of neglecting to secure the rest promised. — *Ed.*

68 See Appendix O

in its own nature; but no fruit will be found except by those who believe.

As to a former statement, when I said that there is no faith where the word is wanting, and that those who make such a divorce wholly extinguish faith and reduce it to nothing, the subject is worthy of special notice. For it hence appears evident that faith cannot exist in any but in the children of God, to whom alone the promise of adoption is offered. For what sort of faith have devils, to whom no salvation is promised? And what sort of faith have all the ungodly who are ignorant of the word? The hearing must ever precede faith, and that indeed that we may know that God speaks and not men.

HEBREWS IV. 3-10

3. For we which have believed do enter into rest, as he said, As I have sworn in my wrath, if they shall enter into my rest: although the works were finished from the foundation of the world.
4. For he spake in a certain place of the seventh *day* on this wise, And God did rest the seventh day from all his works.
5. And in this *place* again, If they shall enter into my rest.
6. Seeing therefore it remaineth that some must enter therein, and they to whom it was first preached entered not in because of unbelief:
7. Again, he limiteth a certain day, saying in David, To day, after so long a time; as it is said, To day if ye will hear his voice, harden not your hearts.
8. For if Jesus had given them rest, then would he not afterward have spoken of another day.
9. There remaineth therefore a rest to the people of God.
10. For he that is entered into his rest, he also hath ceased from his own works, as God *did* from his.

He now begins to embellish the passage which he had quoted from David. He has hitherto taken it, as they say, according to the letter, that is, in its literal sense; but he now amplifies and decorates it; and thus he rather alludes to than explains the words of David. This sort of decoration Paul employed in

Romans x. 6, in referring to these words of Moses, "Say not, who shall ascend into heaven!" *etc.* Nor is it indeed anything unsuitable, in accommodating Scripture to a subject in hand, to illustrate by figurative terms what is more simply delivered. However, the sum of the whole is this, that what God threatens in the Psalm as to the loss of his rest, applies also to us, inasmuch as he invites us also at this day to a rest.

The chief difficulty of this passage arises from this, that it is perverted by many. The Apostle had no other thing in view by declaring that there is a rest for us, than to rouse us to desire it, and also to make us to fear, lest we should be shut out of it through unbelief He however teaches us at the same time, that the rest into which an entrance is now open to us, is far more valuable than that in the land of Canaan. But let us now come to particulars.

3. *For we which have believed do enter into rest,* or, *for we enter into the rest after we have believed, etc.* It is an argument from what is contrary. Unbelief alone shuts us out; then faith alone opens an entrance. We must indeed bear in mind what he has already stated, that God being angry with the unbelieving, had sworn that they should not partake of that blessing. Then they enter in where unbelief does not hinder, provided only that God invites them. But by speaking in the first person he allures them with greater sweetness, separating them from aliens.

Although the works, etc. To define what our rest is, he reminds us of what Moses relates, that God having finished the creation of the world, immediately rested from his works and he finally concludes, that the true rest of the faithful, which is to continue forever, will be when they shall rest as God did.[69] And

---

69 The general drift of the passage is evident, yet the construction has been found difficult. Without repeating the various solutions which have been offered, I shall give what appears to me the easiest construction, —

3. We indeed are entering into the rest who believe: as he hath said, "So that I sware in my wrath, They shall by no means enter into my rest," when yet the works were finished since the foundation of

4. the world; (for he hath said thus in a certain place of the seventh day, "And God rested on the seventh day from all his works,"

5. and again in this place, "They shall by no means enter into my

doubtless as the highest happiness of man is to be united to his God, so ought to be his ultimate end to which he ought to refer all his thoughts and actions. This he proves, because God who is said to have rested, declared a long time after that he would not give his rest to the unbelieving; he would have so declared to no purpose, had he not intended that the faithful should rest after his own example. Hence he says, *It remaineth that some must enter in:* for if not to enter in is the punishment of unbelief, then an entrance, as it has been said, is open to believers.

7. But there is some more difficulty in what he immediately subjoins, that there is another today appointed for us in the Psalm, because the former people had been excluded; but the words of David (as it may be said) seem to express no such thing, and mean only this, that God punished the unbelief of the people by refusing to them the possession of the land. To this I answer, that the inference is correct, that to us is offered what was denied to them; for the Holy Spirit reminds and warns us, that we may not do the same thing so as to incur the same punishment. For how does the matter stand? Were nothing at this day promised, how could this warning be suitable, "Take heed lest the same thing happen to you as to the fathers." Rightly then does the Apostle say, that as the fathers' unbelief deprived them of the promised possession, the promise is renewed to their children, so that they may possess what had been neglected by their fathers.

8. *For if Jesus had given them rest,* or, *had obtained rest for them, etc.* He meant not to deny but that David understood by rest the land of Canaan, into which Joshua conducted the people; but he

---

6. rest;") it then remains therefore that some do enter in because of unbelief.

The particle ἐπεί has created the difficulty, which I render in the sense of ἔπειτα, then consequently the argument is simply this: Inasmuch as God had sworn that the unbelieving should not enter into his rest long after the rest of the sabbath was appointed; it follows as a necessary consequence that some do enter into it, though the unbelieving did not enter. The argument turns on the word "rest;" It was to show that it was not the rest of the Sabbath. The argument in the next verses turns on the word "today," in order to show that it was not the rest of Canaan.

The fourth and fifth verses are only explanatory of the concluding sentence of the preceding, and therefore ought to be regarded as parenthetic. — *Ed.*

denies this to be the final rest to which the faithful aspire, and which we have also in common with the faithful of that age; for it is certain that they looked higher than to that land; nay, the land of Canaan was not otherwise so much valued except for this reason, because it was an image and a symbol of the spiritual inheritance. When, therefore, they obtained possession of it, they ought not to have rested as though they had attained to the summit of their wishes, but on the contrary to meditate on what was spiritual as by it suggested. They to whom David addressed the Psalm were in possession of that land, but they were reminded of the duty of seeking a better rest.

We then see how the land of Canaan was a rest; it was indeed but evanescent, beyond which it was the duty of the faithful to advance. In this sense the Apostle denies that that rest was given by Joshua; for the people under his guidance entered the promised land for this end, that they might with greater alacrity advance forward towards heaven.

And we may hence easily learn the difference between us and them; for though the same end is designed for both, yet they had, as added to them, external types to guide them; not so have we, nor have we indeed any need of them, for the naked truth itself is set before our eyes. Though our salvation is as yet in hope, yet as to the truth, it leads directly to heaven; nor does Christ extend his hand to us, that he may conduct us by the circuitous course of types and figures, but that he may withdraw us from the world and raise us up to heaven. Now that the Apostle separates the shadow from the substance, he did so for this reason, — because he had to do with the Jews, who were too much attached to external things.

He draws the conclusion, that there is a sabbathizing reserved for Gods people, that is, a spiritual rest; to which God daily invites us.

10. *For he that is entered into his rest,* or, *For he who has rested, etc.* This is a definition of that perpetual Sabbath in which there is the highest felicity, when there will be a likeness between men and God, to whom they will be united. For whatever the philosophers may have ever said of the chief good, it was nothing but cold and vain, for they confined man to himself, while it is necessary for us to go out of ourselves to find happiness. The chief good of man is nothing else but union with God; this is attained when we are formed according to him as our exemplar.

Now this conformation the Apostle teaches us takes place when we rest from our works. It hence at length follows, that man becomes happy by self-denial. For what else is to cease from our works, but to mortify our flesh, when a man renounces himself that he may live to God? For here we must always begin, when we speak of a godly and holy life, that man being in a manner dead to himself, should allow God to live in him, that he should abstain from his own works, so as to give place to God to work. We must indeed confess, that then only is our life rightly formed when it becomes subject to God. But through inbred corruption this is never the case, until we rest from our own works; nay, such is the opposition between God's government and our corrupt affections, that he cannot work in us until we rest. But though the completion of this rest cannot be attained in this life, yet we ought ever to strive for it.[70] Thus believers enter it but on this condition, — that by running they may continually go forward.

But I doubt not but that the Apostle designedly alluded to the Sabbath in order to reclaim the Jews from its external observances; for in no other way could its abrogation be understood, except by the knowledge of its spiritual design. He then treats of two things together; for by extolling the excellency of grace, he stimulates us to receive it by faith, and in the meantime he shows us in passing what is the true design of the Sabbath, lest the Jews should be foolishly attached to the outward rite. Of its abrogation indeed he does expressly speak, for this is not his subject, but by teaching them that the rite had a reference to something else, he gradually withdraws them from their superstitious notions. For he who understands that the main object of the precept was not external rest or earthly worship, immediately perceives, by looking on Christ, that the external rite was abolished by his coming; for when the body appears, the shadows immediately vanish away. Then our first business always is, to teach that Christ is the end of the Law.

---

70 Many, like Calvin, have made remarks of this kind, but they are out of place here; for the rest here mentioned is clearly the rest in heaven. — *Ed.*

HEBREWS IV. 11-13

11. Let us labor therefore to enter into that rest, lest any man fall after the same example of unbelief.
12. For the word of God *is* quick, and powerful, and sharper than any two-edged sword, piercing even to the dividing asunder of soul and spirit, and of the joints and marrow, and *is* a discerner of the thoughts and intents of the heart.
13. Neither is there any creature that is not manifest in his sight: but all things *are* naked and opened unto the eyes of him with whom we have to do.

Having pointed out the goal to which we are to advance, he exhorts us to pursue our course, which we do, when we habituate ourselves to self-denial. And as he compares entering into rest to a straight course, he sets falling in opposition to it, and thus he continues the metaphor in both clauses, at the same time he alludes to the history given by Moses of those who fell in the wilderness, because they were rebellious against God. (Numbers xxvi. 65.) Hence he says, *after the same example,* signifying as though the punishment for unbelief and obstinacy is there set before us as in a picture; nor is there indeed a doubt but that a similar end awaits us, if there be found in us the same unbelief.

Then, "to fall" means to perish; or to speak more plainly, it is to fall, not as to sin, but as a punishment for it. But the figure corresponds as well with the word to "enter", as with the sad overthrow of the fathers, by whose example he intended to terrify the Jews.

12. *For the word of God is quick,* or *living, etc.* What he says here of the efficacy or power of the word, he says it, that they might know, that it could not be despised with impunity, as though he had said, "Whenever the Lord addresses us by his word, he deals seriously with us, in order that he may touch all our inmost thoughts and feelings; and so there is no part of our soul which ought not to be roused."[71]

---

71 It has been a matter of dispute whether the "word" here is Christ, or the Scripture. The fathers as well as later divines are divided. The former is the opinion of Augustin, Ambrose, and also of Dr. Owen and Doddridge: and the latter is held by Chrysostom, The-

But before we proceed further, we must inquire whether the Apostle speaks of the effect of the word generally, or refers only to the faithful.

It indeed appears evident, that the word of God is not equally efficacious in all. For in the elect it exerts its own power, when humbled by a true knowledge of themselves, they flee to the grace of Christ; and this is never the case, except when it penetrates into the innermost heart. For hypocrisy must be sifted, which has marvelous and extremely winding recesses in the hearts of men; and then we must not be slightly pricked or torn, but be thoroughly wounded, that being prostrate under a sense of eternal death, we may be taught to die to ourselves. In short, we shall never be renewed in the whole mind, which Paul requires, (Ephesians iv. 23,) until our old man be slain by the edge of the spiritual sword. Hence Paul says in another place, (Philippians ii. 17,) that the faithful are offered as a sacrifice to God by the Gospel; for they cannot otherwise be brought to obey God than by having, as it were, their own will slain; nor can they otherwise receive the light of God's wisdom, than by having the wisdom of the flesh destroyed. Nothing of this kind is found in the reprobate; for they either carelessly disregard God speaking to them, and thus mock him, or clamour against his truth, and obstinately resist it. In short, as the word of God is a hammer, so they have a heart like the anvil, so that its hardness repels its strokes, however powerful they may be. The word of God, then, is far from being so efficacious towards them as to penetrate into them to *the dividing of the soul and the spirit*. Hence it appears, that this its character is to be confined to the faithful only, as they alone are thus searched to the quick.

The context, however, shows that there is here a general truth, and which extends also to the reprobate themselves; for though they are not softened, but set up a brazen and an iron heart against God's word, yet they must necessarily be restrained by their own guilt. They indeed laugh, but it is a sardonic laugh; for they inwardly feel that they are, as it were, slain; they make evasions in various ways, so as not to come be-

---

ophylact, and also by Calvin, Beza, Macknight, Scott, Stuart and Bloomfield. The latter is clearly the most suitable to the words of the passage. The only difficulty is in verse 13; but there a transition is evidently made from the word of God to God himself; and thus both are in remarkable manner connected together. — *Ed.*

fore God's tribunal; but though unwilling, they are yet dragged there by this very word which they arrogantly deride; so that they may be fitly compared to furious dogs, which bite and claw the chain by which they are bound, and yet can do nothing, as they still remain fast bound.

And further, though this effect of the word may not appear immediately as it were on the first day, yet it will be found at length by the event, that it has not been preached to any one in vain. General no doubt is what Christ declares, when he says, When the Spirit shall come, he will convince the world, (John xvi. 8 9.) for the Spirit exercises this office by the preaching, of the Gospel. And lastly, though the word of God does not always exert its power on man, yet it has it in a manner included in itself. And the Apostle speaks here of its character and proper office for this end only, — that we may know that our consciences are summoned as guilty before God's tribunal as soon as it sounds in our ears, as though he had said, "If any one thinks that the air is beaten by an empty sound when the word of God is preached, he is greatly mistaken; for it is a living thing and full of hidden power, which leaves nothing in man untouched." The sum of the whole then is this, — that as soon as God opens his sacred mouth, all our faculties ought to be open to receive his word; for he would not have his word scattered in vain, so as to disappear or to fall neglected on the ground, but he would have it effectually to constrain the consciences of men, so as to bring them under his authority; and that he has put power in his word for this purpose, that it may scrutinize all the parts of the soul, search the thoughts, discern the affections, and in a word show itself to be the judge.

But here a new question arises, "Is this word to be understood of the Law or of the Gospel?" Those who think that the Apostle speaks of the Law bring these testimonies of Paul, — that it is the ministration of death, (2 Corinthians iii. 6, 7,) that it is the letter which killeth, that it worketh nothing but wrath, (Romans iv. 15,) and similar passages. But here the Apostle points out also its different effects; for, as we have said, there is a certain vivifying killing of the soul, which is effected by the Gospel. Let us then know that the Apostle speaks generally of the truth of God, when he says, that it is living and efficacious. So Paul testifies, when he declares, that by his preaching there went forth an odor of death unto death to the unbelieving, but of life unto life to believers, (2 Corinthians ii. 16,) so that God never speaks in vain; he draws some to salvation, others he drives into ruin. This is the power of binding and loosing which the Lord conferred on his Apostles. (Matthew xviii. 18.) And, indeed, he never promises to us salvation in Christ, without denouncing, on the other hand, vengeance on unbelievers; who by rejecting Christ bring death on themselves.[72]

It must be further noticed, that the Apostle speaks of God's word, which is brought to us by the ministry of men. For delirious and even dangerous are those notions, that though the internal word is efficacious, yet that which proceeds from the mouth of man is lifeless and destitute of all power. I indeed admit that the power does not proceed from the tongue of man, nor exists in mere sound, but that the whole power is to be ascribed altogether to the Holy Spirit; there is, however, nothing in this to hinder the Spirit from putting forth his power in the word preached. For God, as he speaks not by himself, but by men, dwells carefully on this point, so that his truth may not be objected to in contempt, because men are its ministers. So Paul, by saying, that the Gospel is the power of God, (Romans i. 16.) designedly adorned with this distinction his own preaching, though he saw that it was slandered by some and despised by others. And when in another place, (Romans x. 8,) he teaches us that salvation is conferred by the doctrine of faith, he expressly says that it was the doctrine which was preached. We indeed find that God ever commends the truth administered to us by men, in order to induce us to receive it with reverence.

Now, by calling the word *quick* or living he must be understood as referring to men; which appears still clearer by the second word, *powerful*, for he shows what sort of life it possesses, when he expressly says that it is efficacious; for the Apostle's object was to teach us what the word is to us.[73] The *sword* is a metaphorical word often used in Scripture; but the Apostle not content with a simple comparison, says, that God's word is *sharper than any sword*, even than a sword that cuts on both sides, or *two-edged*; for at that time swords were in common use, which were blunt on one side, and sharp on the other. *Piercing even to the dividing asunder of the soul and spirit*, or to the dividing

---

72 See Appendix P.

73 See Appendix Q.

of the soul and spirit, etc. The word *soul* means often the same with *spirit;* but when they occur together, the first includes all the affections, and the second means what they call the intellectual faculty. So Paul, writing to the Thessalonians, uses the words, when he prays God to keep their spirit, and soul, and body blameless until the coming of Christ, (1 Thessalonians v. 23,) he meant no other thing, but that they might continue pure and chaste in mind, and will, and outward actions. Also Isaiah means the same when he says,

> "My soul desired thee in the night; I sought thee with my spirit." (Isaiah xxvi. 9.)

What he doubtless intends to show is, that he was so intent on seeking God, that he applied his whole mind and his whole heart. I know that some give a different explanation; but all the sound-minded, as I expect, will assent to this view.

Now, to come to the passage before us, it is said that God's word *pierces,* or reaches to the dividing of soul and spirit, that is, it examines the whole soul of man; for it searches his thoughts and scrutinizes his will with all its desires. And then he adds *the joints and marrow,* intimating that there is nothing so hard or strong in man, nothing so hidden, that the powerful word cannot pervade it.[74] Paul declares the same when he says, that prophecy avails to reprove and to judge men, so that the secrets of the heart may come, to light. (1 Corinthians xiv. 24.) And as it is Christ's office to uncover and bring to light the thoughts from the recesses of the heart, this he does for the most part by the Gospel.

Hence God's word is a *discerner,* (κριτικὸς, one that has power to discern,) for it brings the light of knowledge to the mind of man as it were from a labyrinth, where it was held before entangled. There is indeed no thicker darkness than that of unbelief, and hypocrisy is a horrible blindness; but God's word scatters this darkness and chases away this hypocrisy. Hence the separating or discerning which the Apostle mentions; for

---

74 The metaphor of a sword is evidently carried on; the word is like the sword which "penetrates so as to separate the soul (the animal life) and the spirit, (the immortal part,) the joints also and the marrows, being even a strict judge of the thoughts and purposes of the heart." — *Ed.*

the vices, hid under the false appearance of virtues, begin then to be known, the varnish being wiped away. And if the reprobate remain for a time in their hidden recesses, yet they find at length that God's word has penetrated there also, so that they cannot escape God's judgment. Hence their clamour and also their fury, for were they not smitten by the word, they would not thus betray their madness, but they would seek to elude the word, or by evasion to escape from its power, or to pass it by unnoticed; but these things God does not allow them to do. Whenever then they slander God's word, or become enraged against it, they show that they feel within its power, however unwillingly and reluctantly.[75]

13. *Neither is there any creature, etc.* The conjunction here, as I think, is causal, and may be rendered *for;* for in order to confirm this truth, that whatever is hid in man is discerned and judged by God's word, he draws an argument from the nature of God himself. There is no creature, he says, which is hid from the eyes of God; there is, therefore, nothing so deep in man's soul, which cannot be drawn forth into light by that word that resembles its own author, for as it is God's office to search the heart, so he performs this examination by his word.

Interpreters, without considering that God's word is like a long staff by which he examines and searches what lies deep in our hearts, have strangely perverted this passage; and yet they have not relieved themselves. But all difficulty disappears when we take this view, — that we ought to obey God's word in sincerity and with cordial affection, because God, who knows our hearts, has assigned to his word the office of penetrating even into our inmost thoughts. The ambiguous meaning of the last words has also led interpreters astray, which they have rendered, "Of whom we speak;" but they ought, on the contrary, to be rendered, *With whom we have to do.* The meaning is, that it is God who deals with us, or with whom we have a concern; and that, therefore, we ought not to trifle with him as with a mortal man, but that whenever his word is set before us, we ought to tremble, for nothing is hid from him.

---

75 See Appendix R.

HEBREWS IV. 14-16

14. Seeing then that we have a great high priest, that is passed into the heavens, Jesus the Son of God, let us hold fast *our* profession.
15. For we have not an high priest which cannot be touched with the feeling of our infirmities; but was in all points tempted like as *we are, yet* without sin.
16. Let us therefore come boldly unto the throne of grace, that we may obtain mercy, and find grace to help in time of need.

14. *Seeing then that we have,* or, *Having then, etc.* He has been hitherto speaking of Christ's apostleship, But he who passes on to his second office. For we have said that the Son of God sustained a twofold character when he was sent to us, even that of a teacher and of a priest. The Apostle, therefore, after having exhorted the Jews obediently to embrace the doctrine of Christ, now shows what benefit his priesthood has brought to us; and this is the second of the two points which he handles. And fitly does he connect the priesthood with the apostleship, since he reminds us that the design of both is to enable us to come to God. He employs an inference, *then;* for he had before referred to this great truth, that Christ is our high priest;[76] but as the character of the priesthood cannot be known except through teaching, it was necessary to prepare the way, so as to render men willing to hear Christ. It now remains, that they who acknowledge Christ as their teacher, should become teachable disciples, and also learn from his mouth, and in his school, what is the benefit of his priesthood, and what is its use and end.

---

76 That is, in the latter part of chapter ii. In the beginning of chapter iii. he exhorted us to "consider" the apostle and high priest of our profession, and then proceeded to speak of him as an apostle. He now returns to the high priesthood, and says that as we have a great high priest, we ought to hold fast our profession. Such, according to Calvin, is the connection, and is adopted by Stuart and Bloomfield. — *Ed.*

In the first place he says, *Having a great high priest,* [77] *Jesus Christ, let us hold fast our profession,* or confession. Confession is here, as before, to be taken as a metonymy for faith; and as the priesthood serves to confirm the doctrine, the Apostle hence concludes that there is no reason to doubt or to waver respecting the faith of the Gospel, because the Son of God has approved and sanctioned it; for whosoever regards the doctrine as not confirmed, dishonors the Son of God, and deprives him of his honor as a priest; nay, such and so great a pledge ought to render us confident, so as to rely unhesitantly on the Gospel.

15. *For we have not, etc.* There is in the name which he mentions, *the Son of God,* such majesty as ought to constrain us to fear and obey him. But were we to contemplate nothing but this in Christ, our consciences would not be pacified; for who of us does not dread the sight of the Son of God, especially when we consider what our condition is, and when our sins come to mind? The Jews might have had also another hindrance, for they had been accustomed to the Levitical priesthood; they saw in that one mortal man, chosen from the rest, who entered into the sanctuary, that by his prayer he might reconcile his brethren to God. It is a great thing, when the Mediator, who can pacify God towards us, is one of ourselves. By this sort of allurement the Jews might have been ensnared, so as to become ever attached to the Levitical priesthood, had not the Apostle anticipated this, and showed that the Son of God not only excelled in glory, but that he was also endued with equal kindness and compassion towards us.

It is, then, on this subject that he speaks, when he says that he was *tried by our infirmities,* that he might condole with us. As to the word sympathy, (συμπαθεία,) I am not disposed to indulge in refinements; for frivolous, no less than curious, is this question, "Is Christ now subject to our sorrows?" It was not, indeed, the Apostle's object to weary us with such subtleties and vain speculations, but only to teach us that we have not to go far to seek a Mediator, since Christ of his own accord extends his hand to us, that we have no reason to dread the majesty of

---

77 In the Apostle's time there were many called high priests, such as the heads of the Levitical courses; but "the great high priest" meant him who alone had the privilege of entering into the holy of holies, that is, the high priest, as distinguished from all the rest. — *Ed.*

Chapter 4

Christ since he is our brother, and that there is no cause to fear, lest he, as one unacquainted with evils, should not be touched by any feelings of humanity, so as to bring us help, since he took upon him our infirmities, in order that he might be more inclined to succor us.[78]

Then the whole discourse of the Apostle refers to what is apprehended by faith, for he does not speak of what Christ is in himself, but shows what he is to us. By the *likeness*, he understands that of nature, by which he intimates that Christ has put on our flesh, and also its feelings or affections, so that he not only paroled himself to be real man, but had also been taught by his own experience to help the miserable; not because the Son of God had need of such a training, but because we could not otherwise comprehend the care he feels for our salvation. Whenever, then, we labor under the infirmities of our flesh, let us remember that the Son of God experienced the same, in order that he might by his power raise us up, so that we may not be overwhelmed by them.

But it may be asked, What does he mean by *infirmities?* The word is indeed taken in various senses. Some understand by it cold and heat; hunger and other wants of the body; and also contempt, poverty, and other things of this mind, as in many places in the writings of Paul, especially in 2 Corinthians xii. 10. But their opinion is more correct who include, together with external evils, the feelings of the souls such as fear, sorrow, the dread of death, and similar things.[79]

And doubtless the restriction, *without sin*, would not have been added, except he had been speaking of the inward feelings, which in us are always sinful on account of the depravity of our nature; but in Christ, who possessed the highest rectitude and perfect purity, they were free from everything vicious. Poverty, indeed, and diseases, and those things which are without

---

78 Calvin has followed the Vulg. In rendering this clause, "who cannot sympathize (*compati*) with our infirmities." Our version is that of Eramus and Beza. The meaning may thus be given, "Who cannot feel for us in our infirmities." — *Ed.*

79 The word "infirmities" is often used metonymically for things which we are too weak to bear, even trials and temptations. Christ, our high priest, feels for us in all those straits and difficulties, whatever they be, which meet us in our course, and make us feel and know our weaknesses. — *Ed.*

us, are not to be counted as sinful. Since, therefore, he speaks of infirmities akin to sin, there is no doubt but that he refers to the feelings or affections of the mind, to which our nature is liable, and that on account of its infirmity. For the condition of the angels is in this respect better than ours; for they sorrow not, nor fear, nor are they harassed by variety of cares, nor by the dread of death. These infirmities Christ of his own accord undertook, and he willingly contended with them, not only that he might attain a victory over them for us, but also that we may feel assured that he is present with us whenever we are tried by them.

Thus he not only really became a man, but he also assumed all the qualities of human nature. There is, however, a limitation added, *without sin;* for we must ever remember this difference between Christ's feelings or affections and ours, that his feelings were always regulated according to the strict rule of justice, while ours flow from a turbid fountain, and always partake of the nature of their source, for they are turbulent and unbridled.[80]

16. *Let us therefore come boldly,* or, *with confidence, etc.* He draws this conclusion, — that an access to God is open to all who come to him relying on Christ the Mediator; nay, he exhorts the faithful to venture without any hesitation to present themselves before God. And the chief benefit of divine teaching is a sure confidence in calling on God, as, on the other hand,

---

80 The common idea of what is here said is, that Christ though tried and tempted, was not yet guilty of sin, or did not fall into sin. That he had no sin, that he was without sin, is what we plainly learn from 2 Corinthians v. 21; 1 John iii. 5, etc.; but is this what is taught here? The clause, I conceive, may be thus rendered, —

"But was in all things tried in like manner except sin;"

that is, with the exception that he had no innate sin to contend with. The last words are literally, "in likeness with the exclusion of sin," which seems to import that it was a likeness with the exclusion of sin. But if the words "except (or without) sin" do not qualify "likeness," they must be connected with "tried" or tempted, and thus rendered, —

"But was in like manner tried in all things without sin;"

that is, without sinning, or falling into sin. The difference is, that in the one sense Christ had no inward sin to contend with, and that in the other he withstood temptation without falling into sin. Both senses are true, and either of them will suit this passage. — *Ed.*

the whole of religion falls to the ground, and is lost when this certainty is taken away from consciences.

It is hence obvious to conclude, that under the Papacy the light of the Gospel is extinct, for miserable men are bidden to doubt whether God is propitious to them or is angry with them. They indeed say that God is to be sought; but the way by which it is possible to come to him is not pointed out, and the gate is barred by which alone men can enter. They confess in words that Christ is a Mediator, but in reality they make the power of his priesthood of none effect, and deprive him of his honor.

For we must hold this principle, — that Christ is not really known as a Mediator except all doubt as to our access to God is removed; otherwise the conclusion here drawn would not stand, "We have a high priest Who is willing to help us; therefore we may come bold and without any hesitation to the throne of grace." And were we indeed fully persuaded that Christ is of his own accord stretching forth his hand to us, who of us would not come in perfect confidence?[81] It is then true what I said, that its power is taken away from Christ's priesthood whenever men have doubts, and are anxiously seeking for mediators, as though that one were not sufficient, in whose patronage all they who really trust, as the Apostle here directs them, have the assurance that their prayers are heard.

The ground of this assurance is, that the throne of God is not arrayed in naked majesty to confound us, but is adorned with a new name, even that of *grace*, which ought ever to be remembered whenever we shun the presence of God. For the glory of God, when we contemplate it alone, can produce no other effect than to fill us with despair; so awful is his throne. The Apostle, then, that he might remedy our diffidence, and free our minds from all fear and trembling, adorns it with "grace," and gives it a name which can allure us by its sweetness, as though he had said, "Since God has affirmed to his throne as it were the banner of 'grace' and of his paternal love towards us, there are no reasons why his majesty should drive us away."[82]

---

81 "Confidence," that is, of being heard. — *Ed.*

82 The "throne of grace" is evidently in opposition to the throne of judgment, which especially belongs to a king. Some of the Greek fathers regarded this as the throne of Christ; but most commentators consider it to be God's throne, as Christ is here represent-

The import of the whole is, that we are to call upon God without fear, since we know that he is propitious to us, and that this may be done is owing to the benefit conferred on us by Christ, as we find from Ephesians iii. 12; for when Christ receives us under his protection and patronage, he covers with his goodness the majesty of God, which would otherwise be terrible to us, so that nothing appears there but grace and paternal favor.

That we may obtain mercy, etc. This is not added without great reason; it is for the purpose of encouraging as it were by name those who feel the need of mercy, lest any one should be cast down by the sense of his misery, and close up his way by his own diffidence. This expression, "that we may obtain mercy", contains especially this most delightful truth, that all who, relying on the advocacy of Christ, pray to God, are certain to obtain mercy; yet on the other hand the Apostle indirectly, or by implication, holds out a threatening to all who take not this way, and intimates that God will be inexorable to them, because they disregard the only true way of being reconciled to him.

He adds, *To help in time of need,* or, for a seasonable help; that is, if we desire to obtain all things necessary for our salvation.[83] Now, this seasonableness refers to the time of calling, according to those words of Isaiah, which Paul accommodates

---

ed as a priest and as access to God is ever described as being through Christ. See Ephesians ii. 18. — *Ed.*

83 Calvin's version is, "and find grace for a seasonable help;" which according to his explanation, means a help during the season or period of "today." Doddridge has, "for our seasonable assistance," — Macknight, "for the purpose of seasonable help," — and Stuart, "and find favor so as to be assisted in time of need." Our version seems the best, "and find grace to help in the time of need." The address is to those exposed to trials and persecutions; and the seasonable or opportune help was such as their peculiar circumstances and wants required. The word εὔκαιρον, is in the Sept. put for "due season," or in its time, in Psalm civ. 27. The idea of Calvin is that some of the fathers, but is not suitable to this passage.

"Mercy" is compassion, and "grace" is favor or benefit received; it means sometimes favor entertained, but here the effect of favor — a benefit, and this benefit was to be a help in time of need. — *Ed.*

to the preaching of the Gospel, "Behold, now is the accepted time," etc., (Isaiah xlix. 8; 2 Corinthians vi. 2;) for the Apostle refers to that "today," during which God speaks to us. If we defer hearing until tomorrow, when God is speaking to us today, the unseasonable night will come, when what now may be done can no longer be done; and we shall in vain knock when the door is closed.

CHAPTER 5

HEBREWS V. 1-6

1. For every high priest taken from among men is ordained for men in things *pertaining* to God, that he may offer both gifts and sacrifices for sins:
2. Who can have compassion on the ignorant, and on them that are out of the way; for that he himself also is compassed with infirmity.
3. And by reason hereof he ought, as for the people, so also for himself, to offer for sins.
4. And no man taketh this honor unto himself, but he that is called of God, as *was* Aaron.
5. So also Christ glorified not himself to be made an high priest; but he that said unto him, Thou art my Son, to day have I begotten thee.
6. As he saith also in another *place*, Thou *art* a priest for ever after the order of Melchisedec.

1. *For every high priest, etc.* He compares Christ with the Levitical priests, and he teaches us what is the likeness and the difference between them; and the object of the whole discourse is, to show what Christ's office really is, and also to prove that whatever was ordained under the law was ordained on his account. Hence the Apostle passes on at last to show that the ancient priesthood was abolished.

He first says that the priests were *taken from among men;* secondly, that they did not act a private part but for the whole people; thirdly, that they were not to come empty to appease God, but furnished with sacrifices; fourthly, that they were not to be exempt from human infirmities, that they might more readily succor the distressed; and lastly, that they were not presumptuously to rush into this office, and that then only was the honor legitimate when they were chosen and approved by God. We shall consider briefly each of these points.

We must first, however, expose the ignorance of those who apply these things to our time, as though there was at this day the same need of priests to offer sacrifices; at the same time there is no necessity for a long refutation. For what can be more evident than that the reality found in Christ is compared with its types, which, being prior in time, have now ceased? But this will appear more fully from the context. How extremely ridiculous then are they who seek by this passage to establish and support the sacrifice of the mass! I now return to the words of the Apostle.

Taken from among men, etc. This he says of the priests. It hence follows that it was necessary for Christ to be a real man; for as we are very far from God, we stand in a manner before him in the person of our priest, which could not be, were he not one of us. Hence, that the Son of God has a nature in common with us, does not diminish his dignity, but commends it the more to us; for he is fitted to reconcile us to God, because he is man. Therefore Paul, in order to prove that he is a Mediator, expressly calls him man; for had he been taken from among angels or any other beings, we could not by him be united to God, as he could not react down to us.

For men, etc. This is the *second* clause; the priest was not privately a minister for himself, but was appointed for the common good of the people. But it is of great consequence to notice this, so that we may know that the salvation of us all is connected with and revolves on the priesthood of Christ. The benefit is expressed in these words, *ordains those things which pertain to God*. They may, indeed, be explained in two ways, as the verb καθίσταται has a passive as well as an active sense. They who take it passively give this version, "is ordained in those things," etc.; and thus they would have the preposition *in* to be understood; I approve more of the other rendering, that the high priest takes care of or ordains the things pertaining to God; for the construction flows better, and the sense is fuller.[84] But still in either way, what the Apostle had in view is the same, namely,

---

84 The former view is what is commonly taken, "is appointed;" and it comports with the subject in hand — the appointment of the

that we have no intercourse with God, except there be a priest; for, as we are unholy, what have we to do with holy things? We are in a word alienated from God and his service until a priest interposes and undertakes our cause.

That he may offer both gifts, etc. The *third* thing he mentions respecting a priest is the offering of gifts. There are however here two things, gifts and sacrifices; the first word includes, as I think, various kinds of sacrifices, and is therefore a general term; but the second denotes especially the sacrifices of expiation. Still the meaning is, that the priest without a sacrifice is no peacemaker between God and man, for without a sacrifice sins are not atoned for, nor is the wrath of God pacified. Hence, whenever reconciliation between God and man takes place, this pledge must ever necessarily precede. Thus we see that angels are by no means capable of obtaining for us God's favor, because they have no sacrifice. The same must be thought of Prophets and Apostles. Christ alone then is he, who having taken away sins by his own sacrifice, can reconcile God to us.

2. *Who can, etc.* This *fourth* point has some affinity to the first, and yet it may be distinguished from it; for the Apostle before taught us that mankind are united to God in the person of one man, as all men partake of the same flesh and nature; but now he refers to another thing, and that is, that the priest ought to be kind and gentle to sinners, because he partakes of their infirmities. The word which the Apostle uses, μετριοπαθεῖν is differently explained both by Greek and Latin interpreters.[85] I,

---

    priest, as it appears evident from what follows in verses 5 and 6. — *Ed.*

85 "The classic or philosophic use of the word μετριοπαθεῖν, may be briefly explained. The Stoics maintained that a man should be ἀπαθής, i.e., not subject to passions, such as anger, fear, hope, joy, etc. The Platonists on the other hand averred that a wise man should μετριοπαθής, moderate in his affections, and not ἀπαθής. The leading sense, then, or the word μετριοπαθεῖν, is to be moderate in our feelings or passions." — Stuart.

    But this is not exactly its meaning here. Schleusner, quoting the Greek Lexicographers, shows that it was used in the sense of being indulgent, or of acting kindly and forgivingly, or forebearingly; and this seems to be its meaning in this passage. The sentence is rendered by Macknight, "Being able to have a right measure of compassion on the ignorant and erring." It may be

however, think that it simply means one capable of sympathy. All the things which are here said of the Levitical priests do not indeed apply to Christ; for Christ we know was exempt from every contagion of sin; he therefore differed from others in this respect, that he had no necessity of offering a sacrifice for himself. But it is enough for us to know that he bare our infirmities, though free from sin and undefiled. Then, as to the ancient and Levitical priests, the Apostle says, that they were subject to human infirmity, and that they made atonement also for their own sins, that they might not only be kind to others when gone astray, but also condole or sympathize with them. This part ought to be so far applied to Christ as to include that exception which he mentioned before, that is, that he bare our infirmities, being yet without sin. At the same time, though ever free from sin, yet that experience of infirmities before described is alone abundantly sufficient to incline him to help us, to make him merciful and ready to pardon, to render him solicitous for us in our miseries. The sum of what is said is, that Christ is a brother to us, not only on account of unity as to flesh and nature, but also by becoming a partaker of our infirmities, so that he is led, and as it were formed, to show forbearance and kindness. The participle, δυνάμενος is more forcible than in our common tongue, *qui possit*, "who can," for it expresses aptness or fitness. *The ignorant* and those *out of the way*, or erring, he has named instead of sinners, according to what is done in Hebrew; for שגגה, *shegage*, means every kind of error or offense, as I shall have presently an occasion to explain.

4. *And no man, etc.* There is to be noticed in this verse partly a likeness and partly a difference. What makes an office lawful is the call of God; so that no one can rightly and orderly perform it without being made fit for it by God. Christ and Aaron had this in common, that God called them both; but they differed in this, that Christ succeeded by a new and different way and was made a perpetual priest. It is hence evident that Aaron's priesthood was temporary, for it was to cease. We see the object of the Apostle; it was to defend the right of Christ's priesthood; and he did this by showing that God was its author. But this

---

rendered, "Being capable of duly feeling for the ignorant and the erring," or the deceived, that is by sin. See as to the ignorant Leviticus v. 17-19; and as to the deceived by passions or interest, see Leviticus vi. 1-7 — *Ed.*

would not have been sufficient, unless it was made evident that an end was to be put to the old in order that a room might be obtained for this. And this point he proves by directing our attention to the terms on which Aaron was appointed, for we are not to extend them further than God's decree; and he will presently make it evident how long God had designed this order to continue. Christ then is a lawful priest, for he was appointed by God's authority. What is to be said of Aaron and his successors? That they had as much right as was granted them by the Lord, but not so much as men according to their own fancy concede to them.

But though this has been said with reference to what is here handled, yet we may hence draw a general truth, — that no government is to be set up in the Church by the will of men, but that we are to wait for the command of God, and also that we ought to follow a certain rule in electing ministers, so that no one may intrude according to his own humor. Both these things ought to be distinctly noticed for the Apostle here speaks not of persons only, but also of the office itself; nay, he denies that the office which men appoint without God's command is lawful and divine. For as it appertains to God only to rule his Church, so he claims this right as his own, that is, to prescribe the way and manner of administration. I hence deem it as indisputable, that the Papal priesthood is spurious; for it has been framed in the workshop of men. God nowhere commands a sacrifice to be offered now to him for the expiation of sins; nowhere does he command priests to be appointed for such a purpose. While then the Pope ordains his priests for the purpose of sacrificing, the Apostle denies that they are to be counted lawful priests; they cannot therefore be such, except by some new privilege they exalt themselves above Christ, for he dared not of himself to take upon him this honor, but waited for the command of the Father.

This also ought to be held good as to persons, that no individual is of himself to seize on this honor without public authority. I speak now of offices divinely appointed. At the same time it may sometimes be, that one, not called by God, is yet to be tolerated, however little he may be approved, provided the office itself be divine and approved by God; for many often creep in through ambition or some bad motives, whose call has no evidence; and yet they are not to be immediately rejected, especially when this cannot be done by the public decision of the Church. For during two hundred years before the coming of Christ the foulest corruptions prevailed with respect to the priesthood, yet the right of honor, proceeding from the calling of God, still continued as to the office itself; and the men themselves were tolerated, because the freedom of the Church was subverted. It hence appears that the greatest defect is the character of the office itself, that is, when men of themselves invent what God has never commanded. The less endurable then are those Romish sacrificers, who prattle of nothing but their own titles, that they may be counted sacred, while yet they have chosen themselves without any authority from God.

5. *Thou art my Son, etc.* This passage may seem to be far-fetched; for though Christ was begotten of God the Father, he was not on this account made also a priest. But if we consider the end for which Christ was manifested to the world, it will plainly appear that this character necessarily belongs to him. We must however bear especially in mind what we said on the first chapter; that the begetting of Christ, of which the Psalmist speaks, was a testimony which the Father rendered to him before men. Therefore the mutual relation between the Father and the Son is not what is here intended; but regard is rather had to men to whom he was manifested. Now, what sort of Son did God manifest to us? One indued with no honor, with no power? Nay, one who was to be a Mediator between himself and man; his begetting then included his priesthood.[86]

---

86 This passage, "Thou art my Son," etc., in this place, is only adduced to show that Christ was the Son of God: Christ did not honor or magnify or exalt himself, (for so δοξάζω means here,) but he who said to him, "Thou art my son," etc., did honor or exalt him. This is the meaning of the sentence. The verse may thus be rendered, —

5. So also Christ, himself he did not exalt to be a high priest, but he who had said to him, "My son art thou, I have this day begotten thee."

It is the same as though he had said, "Christ did not make himself a high priest but God." And the reason why he speaks of God as having said "My Son," etc., seems to be this, — to show that he who made him king (for the reference in Psalm 2 is to his appointment as a king) made him also a high priest. And this is confirmed by the next quotation from Psalm 110; for in the first

6 *As he saith in another place,* or, *elsewhere, etc.* Here is expressed more clearly what the Apostle intended. This is a remarkable passage, and indeed the whole Psalm from which it is taken; for there is scarcely anywhere a clearer prophecy respecting Christ's eternal priesthood and his kingdom. And yet the Jews try all means to evade it, in order that they might obscure the glory of Christ; but they cannot succeed. They apply it to David, as though he was the person whom God bade to sit on his right hand; but this is an instance of extreme effrontery; for we know that it was not lawful for kings to exercise the priesthood. On this account, Uzziah, that is, for the sole crime of intermeddling with an office that did not belong to him, so provoked God that he was smitten with leprosy. (2 Chronicles xxvi. 18.) It is therefore certain that neither David nor any one of the kings is intended here.

If they raise this objection and say, that princes are sometimes called כהנים *cohenim*, priests, I indeed allow it, but I deny that the word can be so understood here. For the comparison here made leaves nothing doubtful: Melchisedec was God's priest; and the Psalmist testifies that that king whom God has set on his right hand would be a כהן, *cohen*, according to the order of Melchisedec. Who does not see that this is to be understood of the priesthood? For as it was a rare and almost a singular thing for the same person to be a priest and a king, at least an unusual thing among God's people, hence he sets forth Melchisedec as the type of the Messiah, as though he had said, "The royal dignity will not prevent him to exercise the priesthood also, for a type of such a thing has been already presented in Melchisedec." And indeed all among the Jews, possessed of any modesty, have conceded that the Messiah is the person here spoken of, and that his priesthood is what is commended.

What is in Greek, κατὰ τάξιν *according to the order*, is in Hebrew, על-דברתי *ol-deberti*, and means the same, and may be rendered, "according to the way" or manner: and hereby is confirmed what I have already said, that as it was an unusual thing among the people of God for the same person to bear the office of a king and of a priest, an ancient example was brought forward, by which the Messiah was represented. The rest the Apostle himself will more minutely set forth in what follows.

---

verse he is spoken of as a king, and then in verse 4 his priesthood is mentioned. — *Ed.*

HEBREWS V. 7-11

7. Who in the days of his flesh, when he had offered up prayers and supplications with strong crying and tears unto him that was able to save him from death, and was heard in that he feared;
8. Though he were a Son, yet learned he obedience by the things which he suffered;
9. And being made perfect, he became the author of eternal salvation unto all them that obey him;
10. Called of God an high priest after the order of Melchisedec.
11. Of whom we have many things to say, and hard to be uttered, seeing ye are dull of hearing.

7. *Who in the days, etc.* As the form and beauty of Christ is especially disfigured by the cross, while men do not consider the end for which he humbled himself, the Apostle again teaches us what he had before briefly referred to, that his wonderful goodness shines forth especially in this respect, that he for our good subjected himself to our infirmities. It hence appears that our faith is thus confirmed, and that his honor is not diminished for having borne our evils.

He points out two causes why it behooved Christ to suffer, the proximate and the ultimate. The proximate was, that he might learn obedience; and the ultimate, that he might be thus consecrated a priest for our salutation.

The days of his flesh no doubt mean his life in this world. It hence follows, that the word *flesh* does not signify what is material, but a condition, according to what is said in 1 Corinthians xv. 50, "Flesh and blood shall not inherit the kingdom of God." Rave then do those fanatical men who dream that Christ is now divested of his flesh, because it is here intimated that he has outlived the days of his flesh for it is one thing to be a real man, though endued with a blessed immortality; it is another thing to be liable to those human sorrows and infirmities, which Christ sustained as long as he was in this world, but has now laid aside, having been received into heaven.

Let us now look into the subject. Christ who was a Son, who sought relief from the Father and was heard, yet suffered death, that thus he might be taught to obey. There is in every word a singular importance. By *days of the flesh* he intimates that the time of our miseries is limited, which brings no small alleviation. And doubtless hard were our condition, and by no means tolerable, if no end of suffering were set before us. The three things which follow bring us also no small consolations; Christ was a Son, whom his own dignity exempted from the common lot of men, and yet he subjected himself to that lot for our sakes: who now of us mortals can dare refuse the same condition? Another argument may be added, — though we may be pressed down by adversity, yet we are not excluded from the number of God's children, since we see him going before us who was by nature his only Son; for that we are counted his children is owing only to the gift of adoption by which he admits us into a union with him, who alone lays claim to this honor in his own right.

When he had offered up prayers, etc. The second thing he mentions respecting Christ is, that he, as it became him, sought a remedy that he might be delivered from evils; and he said this that no one might think that Christ had an iron heart which felt nothing; for we ought always to consider why a thing is said. Had Christ been touched by no sorrow, no consolation could arise to us from his sufferings; but when we hear that he also endured the bitterest agonies of mind, the likeness becomes then evident to us. Christ, he says, did not undergo death and other evils because he disregarded them or was pressed down by no feeling of distress, but he prayed with tears, by which he testified the extreme anguish of his soul.[87] Then by *tears* and *strong crying* the Apostle meant to express the intensity of his grief, for it is usual to show it by outward symptoms; nor do I doubt but that he refers to that prayer which the Evangelists mention,

---

87 "Prayers and supplications" are nearly of the same meaning; the first word means a request, a petition, strictly a prayer; and the last an earnest or humble entreaty. The last word is found only here in the New Testament; once in the Septuagint, in Job xli. 3; and once in the Apocrypha, 2 Macc. ix. 18. Hesychius, as quoted by Schleusner, gives παράκλησις, request, entreaty, as its meaning: it comes from ἱκέτης, a suppliant. The word ἱκετηρία, which is here used means first an olive branch wrapped in wool, carried by suppliants as a symbol of entreaty and hence used often in the sense of entreaty and supplication. — *Ed.*

"Father, if it be possible, let this cup pass from me," (Matthew xxvi. 42; Luke xxii. 42;) and also to another, "My God, my God, why hast thou forsaken me?" (Matthew xxvii. 46.) For in the second instance mention is made by the evangelists of strong crying; and in the first it is not possible to believe that his eyes were dry, since drops of blood, through excessive grief, flowed from his body. It is indeed certain that he was reduced to great straits; and being overwhelmed with real sorrows, he earnestly prayed his Father to bring him help.[88]

And what application is to be made of this? Even this, that whenever our evils press upon us and overwhelm us, we may call to mind the Son of God who labored under the same; and since he has gone before us there is no reason for us to faint. We are at the same time reminded that deliverance from evils can be found from no other but from God alone, and what better guidance can we have as to prayer than the example of Christ? He betook himself immediately to the Father. And thus the Apostle indicates what ought to be done by us when he says that he offered prayers to him who was able to deliver him from death; for by these words he intimates that he rightly prayed, because he fled to God the only Deliverer. His *tears* and *crying* recommend to us ardor and earnestness in prayer, for we ought not to pray to God formally, but with ardent desires.

And was heard, etc. Some render the following words, "on account of his reverence" or fears but I wholly differ from them. In the first place he puts the word alone εὐλαθείας without the possessive "his"; and then there is the preposition ἀπὸ "from,"

---

[88] Stuart on this passage very justly observes, "If Jesus died as a common virtuous suffered, and merely as a martyr to the truth, without any vicarious suffering laid upon him, then is his death a most unaccountable event in respect to the manner of his behavior while suffering it; and it must be admitted that multitudes of humble, sinful, meek and very imperfect disciples of Christianity have surpassed their Master in the fortitude, and collected firmness and calm complacency which are requisite to triumph over the pangs of a dying hour. But who can well believe this? Or who can regard Jesus as a simple sufferer in the ordinary way upon the cross, and explain the mysteries of his dreadful horror before and during the hours of crucifixion?"

What is referred to is certainly inexplicable, except we admit what is often and in various ways plainly taught us in God's word, that Christ died for our sins. — *Ed.*

not ὑπὲρ "on account of," or any other signifying a cause or a reason. As, then, εὐλάθεια means for the most part fear or anxiety, I doubt not but that the Apostle means that Christ was heard from that which he feared, so that he was not overwhelmed by his evils or swallowed up by death. For in this contest the Son of God had to engage, not because he was tried by unbelief, the source of all our fears, but because he sustained as a man in our flesh the judgment of God, the terror of which could not have been overcome without an arduous effort. Chrysostom interprets it of Christ's dignity, which the Father in a manner reverenced; but this cannot be admitted. Others render it "piety." But the explanation I have given is much more suitable, and requires no long arguments in its favor.[89]

Now he added this third particular, lest we should think that Christ's prayers were rejected, because he was not immediately delivered from his evils; for at no time was God's mercy and aid wanting to him. And hence we may conclude that God often hears our prayers, even when that is in no way made evident. For though it belongs not to us to prescribe to him as it were a fixed rule, nor does it become him to grant whatsoever requests we may conceive in our minds or express with our tongues, yet he shows that he grants our prayers in everything necessary for our salvation. So when we seem apparently to be repulsed, we obtain far more than if he fully granted our requests.

But how was Christ heard from what he feared, as he underwent the death which he dreaded? To this I reply, that we must consider what it was that he feared; why was it that he dreaded death except that he saw in it the curse of God, and that he had to wrestle with the guilt of all iniquities, and also with hell itself? Hence was his trepidation and anxiety; for extremely terrible is God's judgment. He then obtained what he prayed for, when he came forth a conqueror from the pains of death, when he was sustained by the saving hand of the Father, when

---

89 The idea of the effect of hearing, that is deliverance, is no doubt included in εἰσακουσθείς, "having been heard," as it is sometimes in the corresponding word in Hebrew; so that Stuart is justified in the rendering it delivered, — "and being delivered from that which he feared." It is rendered the same by Macknight, "and being delivered from fear." Both Beza and Grotius render the last word fear; and this is its meaning as used in the Septuagint. — Ed

after a short conflict he gained a glorious victory over Satan, sin, and hell. Thus it often happens that we ask this or that, but not for a right end; yet God, not granting what we ask, at the same time finds out himself a way to succor us.

8. *Yet learned he obedience, etc.* The proximate end of Christ's sufferings was thus to habituate himself to obedience; not that he was driven to this by force, or that he had need of being thus exercised, as the case is with oxen or horses when their ferocity is to be tamed, for he was abundantly willing to render to his Father the obedience which he owed. But this was done from a regard to our benefit, that he might exhibit to us an instance and an example of subjection even to death itself. It may at the same time be truly said that Christ by his death learned fully what it was to obey God, since he was then led in a special manner to deny himself; for renouncing his own will, he so far gave himself up to his Father that of his own accord and willingly he underwent that death which he greatly dreaded. The meaning then is that Christ was by his sufferings taught how far God ought to be submitted to and obeyed.

It is then but right that we also should by his example be taught and prepared by various sorrows, and at length by death itself, to render obedience to God; nay, much more necessary is this in our case, for we have a disposition contumacious and ungovernable until the Lord subdues us by such exercises to bear his yoke. This benefit, which arises from the cross, ought to allay its bitterness in our hearts; for what can be more desirable than to be made obedient to God? But this cannot be effected but by the cross, for in prosperity we exult as with loose reins; nay, in most cases, when the yoke is shaken off, the wantonness of the flesh breaks forth into excesses. But when restraint is put on our will, when we seek to please God, in this act only does our obedience show itself; nay, it is an illustrious proof of perfect obedience when we choose the death to which God may call us, though we dread it, rather than the life which we naturally desire.

9. *And being made perfect,* or *sanctified, etc.* Here is the ultimate or the remoter end, as they call it, why it was necessary for Christ to suffer: it was that he might thus become initiated into his priesthood, as though the Apostle had said that the enduring of the cross and death were to Christ a solemn kind of consecration, by which he intimates that all his sufferings had a regard to our salvation. It hence follows, that they are so far from being prejudicial to his dignity that they are on the contrary his glory; for if salvation be highly esteemed by us, how honorably ought we to think of its cause or author? For he speaks not here of Christ only as an example, but he ascends higher, even that he by his obedience has blotted out our transgressions. He became then the cause of salvation, because he obtained righteousness for us before God, having removed the disobedience of Adam by an act of an opposite kind, even obedience.

Sanctified suits the passage better than "made perfect." The Greek word τελειωθείς means both; but as he speaks here of the priesthood, he fitly and suitably mentions sanctification. And so Christ himself speaks in another place, "For their sakes I sanctify myself." (John xvii. 19.) It hence appears that this is to be properly applied to his human nature, in which he performed the office of a priest, and in which he also suffered.[90]

To all them that obey him. If then we desire that Christ's obedience should be profitable to us, we must imitate him; for the Apostle means that its benefit shall come to none but to those who obey. But by saying this he recommends faith to us; for he becomes not ours, nor his blessings, except as far as we receive them and him by faith. He seems at the same time to have adopted a universal term, *all,* for this end, that he might show that no one is precluded from salvation who is but teachable and becomes obedient to the Gospel of Christ.

10. *Called of God,* or *named by God, etc.* As it was necessary that he should pursue more at large the comparison between Christ and Melchisedec, on which he had briefly touched, and that the

---

[90] The word τελειωθείς, means here the same as in chapter ii. 10. Stuart gives it the same meaning here as in the former passage, "Then when exalted to glory," etc.; but this does not comport with what follows, for it was not his exaltation to glory that qualified him to be "the author (or the causer or effecter) of eternal salvation," but his perfect or complete work in suffering, by his having completely and perfectly performed the work of atonement. And that his suffering in obedience to God's will, even his vicarious suffering, is meant here, appears also from the following reference to his being a priest after the order of Melchisedec. The meaning then seems to be, that Christ having fully completed his work as a priest, and that by suffering, became thereby the author of eternal salvation. — *Ed*

mind of the Jews should be stirred up to greater attention, he so passes to a digression that he still retails his argument.

11. He therefore makes a preface by saying that he had *many things* to say, but that they were to prepare themselves lest these things should be said in vain. He reminds them that they were *hard* or difficult things; not indeed to repel them, but to stimulate them to greater attention. For as things that are easily understood render us slothful, so we become more keenly bent on hearing when anything obscure is set before us. He however states that the cause of the difficulty was not in the subject but in themselves. And indeed the Lord speaks to us so clearly and without any obscurity, that his word is rightly called our light; but its brightness become dim through our darkness.[91] This happens partly through our dullness and partly through our sloth; for though we are very dull to understand the truth of God, yet there is to be added to this vice the depravity of our affections, for we apply our minds to vanity rather than to God's truth. We are also continually impeded either by our perverseness, or by the cares of the world, or by the lusts of our flesh. *Of whom* does not refer to Christ, but to Melchisedec; yet he is not referred to as a private man, but as the type of Christ, and in a manner personating him.

---

91 The literal rendering is "Of whom we have many a word to say, and hardly explainable," or hard to be explained. This hardness of explanation was however owing to their dullness of comprehension, as Calvin justly observes. "Hard to be uttered" of our version is not correct; nor is "hard to be understood" of Doddridge right. Macknight gives the true meaning, "difficult to be explained." Beza's is the same. The reason is added "Since dull (or sluggish) ye are become in ears," or in hearings. To be dull in ears is to be inattentive; but to be sluggish in ears seems to mean stupidity, slowness of comprehension. The latter is evidently meant here; that is, a tardiness or slowness in understanding. To hear with the ear is in the language of Scripture to understand. (Matthew xi. 15; John viii. 43; 1 Corinthians xiv. 2.) Hence to be sluggish in ears is to be slow or tardy in understanding the Word of God. Stuart therefore gives the sense, "Since ye are dull of apprehension." — *Ed.*

HEBREWS V. 12-14

12. For when for the time ye ought to be teachers, ye have need that one teach you again which *be* the first principles of the oracles of God; and are become such as have need of milk, and not of strong meat.
13. For every one that useth milk *is* unskillful in the word of righteousness: for he is a babe.
14. But strong meat belongeth to them that are of full age, *even* those who by reason of use have their senses exercised to discern both good and evil.

12. *For when for the time ye ought, etc.* This reproof contains in it very sharp goads to rouse the Jews from their sloth. He says that it was unreasonable and disgraceful that they should still continue in the elements, in the first rudiments of knowledge, while they ought to have been teachers. "You ought," he says, "to have been the instructors of others, but ye are not even disciples capable of comprehending an ordinary truth; for ye do not as yet understand the first rudiments of Christianity." That he might, however, make them the more ashamed of themselves, he mentions the "first principles," or the elements of the beginning of God's words, as though he had said, You do not know the alphabet. We must, indeed, learn through life; for he alone is truly wise who owns that he is very far from perfect knowledge; but we ought still to profit so much by learning as not to continue always in the first principles. Nor are we to act in such a way, that what is said by Isaiah should be verified in us,

"There shall be to you a precept on precept, a precept on precept," *etc.* (Isaiah xxviii. 10;)

but we ought, on the contrary, so to exert ourselves, that our progress may correspond to *the time* allowed us.

Doubtless, not only years, but days also, must be accounted for; so that every one ought to strive to make progress; but few there are who summon themselves to an account as to past time, or who show any concern for the future. We are, therefore, justly punished for our sloth, for most of us remain in elements fitted for children. We are further reminded, that it is the duty of every one to impart the knowledge he has to his brethren; so that no one is to retain what he knows to himself, but to communicate it to the edification of others.⁹²

Such as have need of milk. Paul uses the same metaphor in 1 Corinthians iii. 2; and he reproaches the Corinthians with the same fault with what is mentioned here, at least with one that is very similar; for he says, that they were carnal and could not bear solid food. Milk then means an elementary doctrine suitable to the ignorant. Peter takes the word in another sense, when he bids us to desire the milk that is without deceit, (1 Peter ii. 2;) for there is a twofold childhood, that is, as to wickedness, and as to understanding; and so Paul tells us, "Be not children in understanding, but in wickedness." (1 Corinthians xiv. 20.) They then who are so tender that they cannot receive the higher doctrine, are by way of reproach called children.

For the right application of doctrines is to join us together, so that we may grow to a perfect manhood, to the measure of full age, and that we should not be like children, tossed here and there, and carried about by every wind of doctrine. (Ephesians iv. 14.) We must indeed show some indulgence to those who have not yet known much of Christ, if they are not capable as yet of receiving *solid food,* but he who has had time to grow, if he till continues a child, is not entitled to any excuse. We indeed see that Isaiah brands the reprobate with this mark, that they were like children newly weaned from the breasts. (Isaiah xxviii. 9.) The doctrine of Christ does indeed minister milk to babes as well as strong meat to adults; but as the babe is nourished by the milk of its nurse, not that it may ever depend on the breast, but that it may by degrees grow and take stronger food; so also at first we must suck milk from Scripture, so that we may

---

92 Our version of this clause is very literal and compact, and sufficiently plain, "For when for the time ye ought to be teachers." Its elegance and conciseness are not retained either by Macknight or by Stuart. What is implied in the words, "for the time," is sufficiently evident without being expressed. As to the following sentence, "Ye have need," etc., some difficulty has been found in the construction. I render it as follows, "Ye have again need of this — that some one should teach you the first principles of the oracles of God." I take τίνα to be accusative before "teach." The word "oracles" is used by Peter in the same sense, as designating the doctrines of the Gospels, 1 Peter iv. 11. — *Ed*

afterwards feed on its bread. The Apostle yet so distinguishes between milk and strong food, that he still understands sound doctrine by both, but the ignorant begin with the one, and they who are well-taught are strengthened by the other.

13. *For every one who uses milk,* or, *who partakes of milk, etc.* He means those who from tenderness or weakness as yet refuse solid doctrine; for otherwise he who is grown up is not averse to milk. But he reproves here an infancy in understanding, such as constrains God even to prattle with us. He then says, that babes are not fit to receive the *word of righteousness,* understanding by righteousness the perfection of which he will presently speak.[93] For the Apostle does not here, as I think, refer to the question, how we are justified before God, but takes the word in a simpler sense, as denoting that completeness of knowledge which leads to perfection, which office Paul ascribes to the Gospel in his epistle to the Colossians, i. 28; as though he had said, that those who indulge themselves in their ignorance preclude themselves from a real knowledge of Christ, and that the doctrine of the Gospel is unfruitful in them, because they never reach the goal, nor come even near it.

14. *Of full age,* or *perfect, etc.* He calls those perfect who are adults; he mentions them in opposition to babes, as it is done in 1 Corinthians ii. 6; xiv. 20; Ephesians iv. 13. For the middle and manly age is the full age of human life; but he calls those by a figure men in Christ; who are spiritual. And such he would have all Christians to be, such as have attained by continual practice a habit to *discern between good and evil.* For he cannot have been otherwise taught aright in the truth, except we are fortified by his protection against all the falsehoods and delusions of Satan; for on this account it is called the sword of the Spirit. And Paul points out this benefit conferred by sound doctrine when

---

[93] This is the view of Grotius and others, but some regard "the word of righteousness" as a paraphrase for the Gospel; and Stuart renders it, "the word of salvation." Dr. Owen says that the Gospel is called "the word of righteousness," because it reveals the righteousness of God, Romans i. 17. It may also be so called, because it reveals and contains the truth, the full truth, partly revealed previously. The word "righteousness" has this meaning both in the Old and New Testaments. See Psalm iii. 4; Isaiah xlv. 19, 23; and Matthew xxi. 23, 2 Corinthians xi. 15. "The ministers of righteousness" in the last text are opposed to false ministers. — Ed.

he says, "That we may not be carried about by every wind of doctrine." (Ephesians iv. 14.) And truly what sort of faith is that which doubts, being suspended between truth and falsehood? Is it not in danger of coming to nothing every moment?

But not satisfied to mention in one word the mind, he mentions all the *senses*, in order to show that we are ever to strive until we be in every way furnished by God's word, and be so armed for battle, that Satan may by no means steal upon us with his fallacies.[94]

It hence appears what sort of Christianity there is under the Papacy, where not only the grossest ignorance is commended under the name of simplicity, but where the people are also most rigidly prevented from seeking real knowledge; nay, it is easy to judge by what spirit they are influenced, who hardly allow that to be touched which the Apostle commands us to handle continually, who imagine that a laudable neglect which the Apostle here so severely reproves, who take away the word of God, the only rule of discerning rightly, which discerning he declares to be necessary for all Christians! But among those who are freed from this diabolical prohibition and enjoy the liberty of learning, there is yet often no less indifference both as to hearing and reading. When thus we exercise not our powers, we are stupidly ignorant and void of all discernment.

---

94 The word for "senses" means literally the organs of the senses, such as the eyes, the ears, etc., but here as signifying the senses themselves, as seeing, hearing, tasting, and smelling, by means of which those grown up are enabled by long experience to know what is good and wholesome for them, and also what is bad and injurious. By this comparison, which is here carried out fully, he intimates that the grown up in Christian truth attain by the habit of exercising all the senses or faculties of their minds, a capacity to distinguish between good and evil, between truth and error, in religion.

The doctrine of reserve cannot be drawn from this passage; for though the Apostle says that they were not capable, owing to their sloth, or taking strong food, he yet lays it before them. — *Ed.*

CHAPTER 6

HEBREWS VI. 1-2

1. Therefore leaving the principles of the doctrine of Christ, let us go on unto perfection; not laying again the foundation of repentance from dead works, and of faith toward God,
2. Of the doctrine of baptisms, and of laying on of hands, and of resurrection of the dead, and of eternal judgment.

1. *Therefore, leaving, etc.* To his reproof he joins this exhortation, — that leaving first principles they were to proceed forward to the goal. For by *the word of beginning* he understands the first rudiments, taught to the ignorant when received into the Church. Now, he bids them to leave these rudiments, not that the faithful are ever to forget them, but that they are not to remain in them; and this idea appears more clear from what follows, the comparison of a *foundation;* for in building a house we must never leave the foundation; and yet to be always engaged in laying it, would be ridiculous. For as the foundation is laid for the sake of what is built on it, he who is occupied in laying it and proceeds not to the superstruction, wearies himself with foolish and useless labor. In short, as the builder must begin with the foundation, so must he go on with his work that the house may be built. Similar is the case as to Christianity; we have the first principles as the foundation, but the higher doctrine ought immediately to follow which is to complete the building. They then act most unreasonably who remain in the first elements, for they propose to themselves no end, as though a builder spent all his labor on the foundation, and neglected to build up the house. So then he would have our faith to be at first so founded as afterwards to rise upwards, until by daily progress it be at length completed.[95]

Of repentance from dead works, etc. He here refers to a catechism commonly used. It is hence a probable conjecture that this Epistle was written, not immediately after the promulgation of the Gospel, but when they had some kind of polity established in the Churches; such as this, that the catechumen made a confession of his faith before he was admitted to baptism. And there were certain primary points on which the pastor questioned the catechumen, as it appears from the various testimonies of the fathers; there was an examination had especially on the creed called the Apostles' Creed. This was the first entrance, as it were, into the church to those who were adults and enlisted under Christ, as they were before alienated from faith in him. This custom the Apostle mentions, because there was a short time fixed for catechumens, during which they were taught the doctrine of religion, as a master instructs his children in the alphabet, in order that he may afterwards advance them to higher things.

But let us examine what he says. He mentions *repentance* and *faith*, which include the fullness of the Gospel; for what else does Christ command his Apostles to preach, but repentance and faith? When, therefore, Paul wished to show that he had faithfully performed his duty, he alleged his care and assiduity in teaching these two things. It seems then (as it may be said) unreasonable that the Apostle should bid repentance and faith to be omitted, when we ought to make progress in both through the whole course of our life. But when he adds, *from dead works,* he intimates that he speaks of first repentance; for though every sin is a dead work, either as it leads to death, or as it proceeds from the spiritual death of the soul; yet the faithful, already born again of the Spirit of God, cannot be said properly to repent from dead works. Regeneration is not indeed made perfect in them; but because of the seed of new life which is in them, however small it may be, this at least may be said of them that they cannot be deemed dead before God. The Apostle then does not include in general the whole of repentance, the practice of which ought to continue to the end; but he refers only to the beginning of repentance, when they who were lately and for

---

95 See Appendix S.

the first time consecrated to the faith, commenced a new life. So also the word, *faith,* means that brief summary of godly doctrine, commonly called the Articles of Faith.

To these are added, *the resurrection of the dead and eternal judgment.* These are some of the highest mysteries of celestial wisdom; nay, the very end of all religion, which we ought to bear in mind through the whole course of our life. But as the very same truth is taught in one way to the ignorant, and in another way to those who have made some proficiency, the Apostle seems here to refer to the common mode of questioning, "Dost thou believe the resurrection of the dead? Dost thou believe eternal life?" These things were suitable to children, and that only once; therefore to turn back to them again was nothing else but to retrograde.

2. *Of the doctrine of baptisms, etc.* Some read them separately, "of baptisms and of doctrine;" but I prefer to connect them, though I explain them differently from others; for I regard the words as being in apposition, as grammarians say, according to this form, "Not laying again the foundation of repentance, of faith in God, of the resurrection of the dead, which is the doctrine of baptisms and of the laying on of hands." If therefore these two clauses, the doctrine of baptisms and of the laying on of hands, be included in a parenthesis, the passage would run better; for except you read them as in apposition, there would be the absurdity of a repetition. For what is the doctrine of baptism but what he mentions here, faith in God, repentance, judgment, and the like?

Chrysostom thinks that he uses "baptisms" in the plural number, because they who returned to first principles, in a measure abrogated their first baptism: but I cannot agree with him, for the doctrine had no reference to many baptisms, but by baptisms are meant the solemn rites, or the stated days of baptizing.

With baptism he connects the *laying on of hands;* for as there were two sorts of catechumens, so there were two rites. There were heathens who came not to baptism until they made a profession of their faith. Then as to these, the catechizing was wont to precede baptism.[96] But the children of the faithful, as they were adopted from the womb, and belonged to the body of the

---

96 Calvin has followed some of the fathers in his exposition of these two clauses, who refer to a state of things which did not exist in the Church for a considerable time after the Apostolic age.

Church by right of the promise, were baptized in infancy; but after the time of infancy, they having been instructed in the faith, presented themselves as catechumens, which as to them took place after baptism; but another symbol was then added, the laying on of hands.

This one passage abundantly testifies that this rite had its beginning from the Apostles, which afterwards, however, was turned into superstition, as the world almost always degenerates into corruptions, even with regard to the best institutions. They have indeed contrived the fiction, that it is a sacrament by which the spirit of regeneration is conferred, a dogma by which they have mutilated baptism for what was peculiar to it, they transferred to the imposition of hands. Let us then know, that it was instituted by its first founders that it might be an appointed rite for prayer, as Augustine calls it. The profession of faith which youth made, after having passed the time of childhood, they indeed intended to confirm by this symbol, but they thought of nothing less than to destroy the efficacy of baptism. Wherefore the pure institution at this day ought to be retained, but the superstition ought to be removed. And this passage

---

What is here said comports with the time of the Apostles, and with that only more particularly. "Baptisms," being in the plural number, have been a knotty point to many; but there is an especial reason for this in an Epistle to the Hebrews; some of them had no doubt been baptized by John, such were afterwards baptized only in the name of Christ, Acts xix. 5, but those who not so baptized, were doubtless baptized in the name of Trinity. "The laying on of hands" on the baptized was an Apostolic practice, by which the miraculous gift of tongues was bestowed. Acts viii. 15-17; xix. 6.

To understand the different things mentioned in the first two verses, we must consider the particulars stated in the 4th and the 5th verses; they are explanatory of each other. The penitent were "the enlightened;" "faith towards God" was "the heavenly gift;" the baptized, who had hands laid on them, were those who were "made partakers of the Holy Ghost;" the prospect and promise of a "resurrection," was "the good word of God;" and "eternal judgment," when believed made them to feel "the powers (or the powerful influences) of the word to come." Thus the two passages illustrate one another. Such is the meaning which Schleusner gives δυνάμεις in this passage, which Scott and Bloomfield have adopted. — *Ed*

tends to confirm pedobaptism; for why should the same doctrine be called as to some baptism, but as to others the imposition of hands, except that the latter after having received baptism were taught in the faith, so that nothing remained for them but the laying on of hands?

HEBREWS VI. 3-6

3. And this will we do, if God permit.
4. For *it is* impossible for those who were once enlightened, and have tasted of the heavenly gift, and were made partakers of the Holy Ghost,
5. And have tasted the good word of God, and the powers of the world to come,
6. If they shall fall away, to renew them again unto repentance; seeing they crucify to themselves the Son of God afresh, and put *him* to an open shame.

3. *This will we do, etc.* A dreadful denunciation follows; but the Apostle thus fulminated, lest the Jews should indulge their own supineness, and trifle with the favor of God; as though he had said, "There ought not in this case it to be any delay; for there will not always be the opportunity for making progress; it is not in man's power to bound at once, whenever he pleases, from the starting point to the goal; but progress in our course is the special gift of God."

4. *For it is impossible, etc.* This passage has given occasion to many to repudiate this Epistle, especially as the Novatians armed themselves with it to deny pardon to the fallen. Hence those of the Western Church, in particular, refused the authority of this Epistle, because the sect of Novatus annoyed them; and they were not sufficiently conversant in the truth so as to be equal to refute it by argument. But when the design of the Apostle is understood, it then appears evident that there is nothing here which countenances so delirious an error. Some who hold sacred the authority of the Epistle, while they attempt to dissipate this absurdity, yet do nothing but evade it. For some take "impossible" in the sense of rare or difficult, which is wholly different from its meaning. Many confine it to that repentance by which the catechumens in the ancient Church were wont to

Chapter 6

be prepared for baptism, as though indeed the Apostles prescribed fasting, or such things to the baptized. And then what great thing would the Apostle have said, by denying that repentance, the appendage of baptism, could be repeated? He threatens with the severest vengeance of God all those who would cast away the grace which had been once received; what weight would the sentence have had to shake the secure and the wavering with terror, if he only reminded them that there was no longer room for their first repentance? For this would extend to every kind of offense. What then is to be said? Since the Lord gives the hope of mercy to all without exception, it is wholly unreasonable that any one for any cause whatever should be precluded.

The knot of the question is in the word, *fall away*. Whosoever then understands its meaning, can easily extricate himself from every difficulty. But it must be noticed, that there is a twofold falling away, one particular, and the other general. He who has in anything, or in any ways offended, has fallen away from his state as a Christian; therefore all sins are so many fallings. But the Apostle speaks not here of theft, or perjury, or murder, or drunkenness, or adultery; but he refers to a total defection or falling away from the Gospel, when a sinner offends not God in some one thing, but entirely renounces his grace.

And that this may be better understood, let us suppose a contrast between the gifts of God, which he has mentioned, and this falling away. For he falls away who forsakes the word of God, who extinguishes its light, who deprives himself of the taste of the heavens or gift, who relinquishes the participation of the Spirit. Now this is wholly to renounce God. We now see whom he excluded from the hope of pardon, even the apostates who alienated themselves from the Gospel of Christ, which they had previously embraced, and from the grace of God; and this happens to no one but to him who sins against the Holy Spirit. For he who violates the second table of the Law, or transgresses the first through ignorance, is not guilty of this defection; nor does God surely deprive any of his grace in such a way as to leave them none remaining except the reprobate.

If any one asks why the Apostle makes mention here of such apostasy while he is addressing believers, who were far off from a perfidy so heinous; to this I answer, that the danger was pointed out by him in time, that they might be on their guard.

And this ought to be observed; for when we turn aside from the right way, we not only excuse to others our vices, but we also impose on ourselves. Satan stealthily creeps on us, and by degrees allures us by clandestine arts, so that when we go astray we know not that we are going astray. Thus gradually we slide, until at length we rush headlong into ruin. We may observe this daily in many. Therefore the Apostle does not without reason forewarn all the disciples of Christ to beware in time; for a continued torpor commonly ends in lethargy, which is followed by alienation of mind.

But we must notice in passing the names by which he signalizes the knowledge of the Gospel. He calls it *illumination;* it hence follows that men are blind, until Christ, the light of the world, enlightens them. He calls it *a tasting of the heavenly gift;* intimating that the things which Christ confers on us are above nature and the world, and that they are yet tasted by faith. He calls it the *participation* of the Spirit; for he it is who distributes to every one, as he wills, all the light and knowledge which he can have; for without him no one can say that Jesus is the Lord, (1 Corinthians xii. 3;) he opens for us the eyes of our minds, and reveals to us the secret things of God. He calls it a *tasting of the good word of God;* by which he means, that the will of God is therein revealed, not in any sort of way, but in such a way as sweetly to delight us; in short, by this title is pointed out the difference between the Law and the Gospel; for that has nothing but severity and condemnation, but this is a sweet testimony of God's love and fatherly kindness towards us. And lastly, he calls it a *tasting of the powers of the world to come;* by which he intimates, that we are admitted by faith as it were into the kingdom of heaven, so that we see in spirit that blessed immortality which is hid from our senses.[97]

Let us then know, that the Gospel cannot be otherwise rightly known than by the illumination of the Spirit, and that being thus drawn away from the world, we are raised up to heaven, and that knowing the goodness of God we rely on his word.

But here arises a new question, how can it be that he who has once made such a progress should afterwards fall away? For God, it may be said, calls none effectually but the elect, and Paul testifies that they are really his sons who are led by his Spirit, (Romans viii. 14;) and he teaches us, that it is a sure

---

97 See Appendix T.

pledge of adoption when Christ makes us partakers of his Spirit. The elect are also beyond the danger of finally falling away; for the Father who gave them to be preserved by Christ his Son is greater than all, and Christ promises to watch over them all so that none may perish. To all this I answer, That God indeed favors none but the elect alone with the Spirit of regeneration, and that by this they are distinguished from the reprobate; for they are renewed after his image and receive the earnest of the Spirit in hope of the future inheritance, and by the same Spirit the Gospel is sealed in their hearts. But I cannot admit that all this is any reason why he should not grant the reprobate also some taste of his grace, why he should not irradiate their minds with some sparks of his light, why he should not give them some perception of his goodness, and in some sort engrave his word on their hearts. Otherwise, where would be the temporal faith mentioned by Mark iv. 17? There is therefore some knowledge even in the reprobate, which afterwards vanishes away, either because it did not strike roots sufficiently deep, or because it withers, being choked up.[98]

And by this bridle the Lord keeps us in fear and humility; and we certainly see how prone human nature is otherwise to security and foolish confidence. At the same time our solicitude ought to be such as not to disturb the peace of conscience. For the Lord strengthens faith in us, while he subdues our flesh: and hence he would have faith to remain and rest tranquilly as in a safe haven; but he exercises the flesh with various conflicts, that it may not grow wanton through idleness.

6. *To renew them again into repentance, etc.* Though this seems hard, yet there is no reason to charge God with cruelty when any one suffers only the punishment of his own defection; nor is this inconsistent with other parts of Scripture, where God's mercy is offered to sinners as soon as they sigh for it, (Ezekiel xviii. 27;) for repentance is required, which he never truly feels who has once wholly fallen away from the Gospel; for such are deprived, as they deserve, of God's Spirit and given up to a reprobate mind, so that being the slaves of the devil they rush headlong into destruction. Thus it happens that they cease not to add sin to sin, until being wholly hardened they despise God, or like men in despair, express madly their hatred to him. The end of all apostates is, that they are either smitten with stupor,

---

98 See Appendix U.

and fear nothing, or curse God their judge, because they cannot escape from him.⁹⁹

In short, the Apostle warns us, that repentance is not at the will of man, but that it is given by God to those only who have not wholly fallen away from the faith. It is a warning very necessary to us, lest by often delaying until tomorrow, we should alienate ourselves more and more from God. The ungodly indeed deceive themselves by such sayings as this, — that it will be sufficient for them to repent of their wicked life at their last breath. But when they come to die, the dire torments of conscience which they suffer, prove to them that the conversion of man is not an ordinary work. As then the Lord promises pardon to none but to those who repent of their iniquity, it is no wonder that they perish who either through despair or contempt, rush on in their obstinacy into destruction. But when any one rises up again after falling, we may hence conclude that he had not been guilty of defection, however grievously he may have sinned.

Crucifying again, etc. He also adds this to defend God's severity against the calumnies of men; for it would be wholly unbecoming, that God by pardoning apostates should expose his own Son to contempt. They are then wholly unworthy to obtain mercy. But the reason why he says, that Christ would thus be

---

99 Some render the verb "renew" actively, in this way, — "For it is impossible as to those who have been once enlightened, and have tasted of the heavenly gift, and have been made partakers of holy spirit, and have tasted the good word of God and the powers of the world to come, and have fallen away, to renew them again unto repentance, since they crucify again as to themselves to Son of God, and expose him to open shame."

This is more consistent with the foregoing, for the Apostle speaks of teaching. It is as though he had said "It is impossible for us as teachers;" as they had no commission. To "renew" may be rendered to "restore." It is only found here, but is used by the Sept. for a verb which means renewing in the sense of restoring. See Psalm ciii. 5; civ. 30; Lamentations v. 21. Josephus applies it to the renovation or restoration of the temple. The "crucifying" was what they did by falling away; for they thereby professed that he deserved to be crucified as an imposter, and thus counted his blood, as it is said in chapter x. 29, "unholy," as the blood of a malefactor; and they thus also exhibited him as an object of public contempt. — *Ed.*

crucified again, is, because we die with him for the very purpose of living afterwards a new life; when therefore any return as it were unto death, they have need of another sacrifice, as we shall find in the tenth chapter. Crucifying *for themselves* means as far as in them lies. For this would be the case, and Christ would be slandered as it were triumphantly, were it allowed men to return to him after having fallen away and forsaken him.

HEBREWS VI. 7-10

7. For the earth which drinketh in the rain that cometh oft upon it, and bringeth forth herbs meet for them by whom it is dressed, receiveth blessing from God:
8. But that which beareth thorns and briers *is* rejected, and *is* nigh unto cursing; whose end *is* to be burned.
9. But, beloved, we are persuaded better things of you, and things that accompany salvation, though we thus speak.
10. For God *is* not unrighteous to forget your work and labor of love, which ye have shewed toward his name, in that ye have ministered to the saints, and do minister.

7. *For the earth, etc.* This is a similitude most appropriate to excite a desire to make progress in due time, for as the earth cannot bring forth a good crop in harvest except it causes the seed as soon as it is sown to germinate, so if we desire to bring forth good fruit, as soon as the Lord sows his word, it ought to strike roots in us without delay; for it cannot be expected to fructify, if it be either choked or perish. But as the similitude is very suitable, so it must be wisely applied to the design of the Apostle.

The earth, he says, which by sucking in the rain immediately produces a blade suitable to the seed sown, at length by God's blessing produces a ripe crop; so they who receive the seed of the Gospel into their hearts and bring forth genuine shoots, will always make progress until they produce ripe fruit. On the contrary, the earth, which after culture and irrigation brings, forth nothing but thorns, affords no hope of a harvest; nay, the more that grows which is its natural produce, the more hopeless is the case. Hence the only remedy the husbandman has is to burn up the noxious and useless weeds. So they who destroy the seed of the Gospel either by their indifference or by corrupt affections, so as to manifest no sign of good progress in their life, clearly show themselves to be reprobates, from whom no harvest can be expected.

The Apostle then not only speaks here of the fruit of the Gospel, but also exhorts us promptly and gladly to embrace it, and he further tells us, that the blade appears presently after the seed is sown, and that growing follows the daily irrigations. Some render βοτάνην εὔθετὸν "a seasonable shoot," others, "a shoot meet;" either meaning suits the place; the first refers to time, the second to quality.[100] The allegorical meanings with which interpreters have here amused themselves, I pass by, as they are quite foreign to the object of the writer.

9. *But we are persuaded, etc.* As the preceding sentences were like thunderbolts, by which readers might have been struck dead, it was needful to mitigate this severity. He therefore says now, that he did not speak in this strain, as though he entertained such an opinion of them. And doubtless whosoever wishes to do good by teaching, ought so to treat his disciples as ever to add encouragement to them rather than to diminish it, for there is nothing that can alienate us more from attending to the truth than to see that we are deemed to be past hope. The Apostle then testifies that he thus warned the Jews, because he had a good hope of them, and was anxious to lead them to salvation. We hence conclude, that not only the reprobate ought to be reproved severely and with sharp earnestness, but also the elect themselves, even those whom we deem to be the children of God.

10. *For God is not unrighteous, etc.* These words signify as much as though he had said, that from good beginnings he hoped for a good end.

---

100 The word βοτάνη here means everything the earth produces service for food. It only occurs here in the New Testament, but is commonly used by the Sept. for עשב, which has the same extensive meaning: fruit or fruits would be its best rendering here. The word εὔθετος is also found in Luke ix. 62; xiv. 34; and it means fit, meet, suitable, or useful; and the last is the meaning given it here by Grotius, Schleusner, Stuart, Bloomfield, and others. It is indeed true that it is used in the Sept. in the sense of seasonable. See Psalm xxxii. 6 — *Ed*

But here a difficulty arises, because he seems to say that God is bound by the services of men: "I am persuaded," he says, "as to your salvation, because God cannot forget your works." He seems thus to build salvation on works, and to make God a debtor to them. And the sophists, who oppose the merits of works to the grace of God, make much of this sentence, "God is not unrighteous." For they hence conclude that it would be unjust for him not to render for works the reward of eternal salvation. To this I briefly reply that the Apostle does not here speak avowedly of the cause of our salvation, and that therefore no opinion can be formed from this passage as to the merits of works, nor can it be hence determined what is due to works. The Scripture shows everywhere that there is no other fountain of salvation but the gratuitous mercy of God: and that God everywhere promises reward to works, this depends on that gratuitous promise, by which he adopts us as his children, and reconciles us to himself by not imputing our sins. Reward then is reserved for works, not through merit, but the free bounty of God alone; and yet even this free reward of works does not take place, except we be first received into favor through the kind mediation of Christ.

We hence conclude, that God does not pay us a debt, but performs what he has of himself freely promised, and thus performs it, inasmuch as he pardons us and our works; nay, he looks not so much on our works as on his own grace in our works. It is on this account that he forgets not our works, because he recognizes himself and the work of his Spirit in them. And this is to be *righteous,* as the Apostle says, for he cannot deny himself. This passage, then, corresponds with that saying of Paul, "He who has begun in you a good work will perfect it." (Philippians i. 6.) For what can God find in us to induce him to love us, except what he has first conferred on us? In short, the sophists are mistaken in imagining a mutual relation between God's righteousness and the merits of our works, since God on the contrary so regards himself and his own gifts, that he carries on to the end what of his own goodwill he has begun in us, without any inducement from anything we do; nay, God is righteous in recompensing works, because he is true and faithful: and he has made himself a debtor to us, not by receiving anything from us; but as Augustine says, by freely promising all things.[101]

And labor of love, etc. By this he intimates that we are not to spare labor, if we desire to perform duty towards our neighbors; for they are not only to be helped by money, but also by counsel, by labor, and in various other ways. Great sedulity, then, must be exercised, many troubles must be undergone, and sometimes many dangers must be encountered. Thus let him who would engage in the duties of love, prepare himself for a life of labor.[102]

He mentions in proof of their love, that they had *ministered* and were still *ministering* to the *saints*. We are hence reminded, that we are not to neglect to serve our brethren. By mentioning the *saints*, he means not that we are debtors to them alone; for our love ought to expand and be manifested towards all mankind; but as the household of faith are especially recommended to us, peculiar attention is to be paid to them; for as love, when moved to do good, has partly a regard to God, and partly to our common nature, the nearer any one is to God, the more worthy he is of being assisted by us. In short, when we acknowledge any one as a child of God, we ought to embrace him with brotherly love.

By saying that they *had ministered* and were *still ministering*, he commended their perseverance; which in this particular was very necessary; for there is nothing to which we are more prone than to weariness in well-doing. Hence it is, that though many are found ready enough to help their brethren, yet the virtue of constancy is so rare, that a large portion soon relax as though

---

101 Nothing can exceed the clearness and the truth of the preceding remarks.

The word ἄδικος, unrighteousness, is rendered by many, unmerciful or unkind. But the reason for such a meaning is this: There are three kinds, we may say, of righteousness — that of the law, of love, and of promise. To act according to the law is to be righteous; to comply with what love requires, that is, to be kind and charitable, is to be righteous, and hence almsgiving is called righteousness has often the meaning of faithfulness or mercy. See 1 John i. 9. Therefore the meaning here is, that God is not so unrighteous as not to fulfill his promise. Hence the notion of merit is at once shown to be groundless. — *Ed*

102 See Appendix X.

their warmth had cooled. But what ought constantly to stimulate us is even this one expression used by the apostle, that the love shown to the saints is shown *towards the name* of the Lord; for he intimates that God holds himself indebted to us for whatever good we do to our neighbors, according to that saying,

> "What ye have done to one of the least of these, ye have done to me," (Matthew xxv. 40;)

and there is also another,

> "He that giveth to the poor lendeth to the Lord." (Proverbs xix. 17.)

HEBREWS VI. 11-15

11. And we desire that every one of you do shew the same diligence to the full assurance of hope unto the end:
12. That ye be not slothful, but followers of them who through faith and patience inherit the promises.
13. For when God made promise to Abraham, because he could swear by no greater, he sware by himself,
14. Saying, Surely blessing I will bless thee, and multiplying I will multiply thee.
15. And so, after he had patiently endured, he obtained the promise.

11. *And we desire, etc.* As he blended with exhortation, lest he should altogether grieve their minds; so he now freely reminds them of what was still wanting in them, lest his courtesy should appear to have in it any flattery. "You have made," he says, "your love evident by many acts of kindness; it remains, however, that your faith should correspond with it; you have sedulously labored not to be wanting in your duties to men; but with no less earnestness it behooves you to make progress in faith, so as to manifest before God its unwavering and full certainty."

Now, by these words the Apostle shows that there are two parts in Christianity which correspond with the two tables of the Law. Therefore, he who separates the one from the other, has nothing but what is mutilated and mangled. And hence it appears what sort of teachers they are who make no mention of faith, and enjoin only the duty of honesty and uprightness towards men; nay, it is a profane philosophy, that dwells only on the outward mask of righteousness, if indeed it deserves to be called philosophy; for it so unreasonably performs its own duties, that it robs God, to whom the preeminence belongs, of his own rights. Let us then remember, that the life of a Christian is not complete in all its parts, unless we attend to faith as well as to love.

To the full assurance of hope, or, *to the certainty of hope,* etc. As they who professed the Christian faith were distracted by various opinions, or were as yet entangled in many superstitions, he bids them to be so fixed in firm faith, as no longer to vacillate nor be driven here and there, suspended between alternate winds of doubts. This injunction is, however, applicable to all; for, as the truth of God is unchangeably fixed, so faith, which relies on him, when it is true, ought to be certain, surmounting every doubt. It is a full assurance, πληροφορία,[103] an undoubting persuasion, when the godly mind settles it with itself, that it is not right to call in question what God, who cannot deceive or lie, has spoken.

The word hope, is here to be taken for faith, because of its affinity to it. The Apostle, however, seems to have designedly used it, because he was speaking of perseverance. And we may hence conclude how far short of faith is that general knowledge which the ungodly and the devils have in common; for they also believe that God is just and true, yet they derive hence no good hope, for they do not lay hold on his paternal favor in Christ. Let us then know that true faith is ever connected with hope.

---

103 This noun and the verb from which it comes, are peculiar to the new testament, but the latter is once used in the Sept., Ecclesiastes viii. 11. The metaphor is taken from a ship in full sail, or from a tree fully laden with fruit. Fullness or perfection is the general idea. It is applied to knowledge in Colossians ii. 2, and to faith in Hebrew x. 22. It is also found once more in 1 Thessalonians i. 5, and is applied to the assurance with which the gospel was preached. It may be rendered certainly, or assurance, or full assurance. As a passive participle it means to be fully persuaded in Romans iv. 21, and in xiv. 5. See Appendix Y. — *Ed.*

He said *to the end,* or perfection; and he said this, that they might know that they had not yet reached the goal, and were therefore to think of further progress. He mentioned diligence, that they might know that they were not to sit down idly, but to strive in earnest. For it is not a small thing to ascend above the heavens, especially for these who hardly creep on the ground, and when innumerable obstacles are in the way. There is indeed, nothing more difficult than to keep our thoughts fixed on things in heaven, when the whole power of our nature inclines downwards, and when Satan or numberless devices draw us back to the earth. hence it is, that he bids us to beware of sloth or effeminacy.

12. *But followers,* or *imitators, etc.* To sloth he opposes imitation; it is then the same thing as though he said, that there was need of constant alacrity of mind; but it had far more weight, when he reminded them, that the fathers were not made partakers of the promises except through the unconquerable firmness of faith; for examples convey to us a more impressive idea of things. When a naked truth is set before us, it does not so much affect us, as when we see what is required of us fulfilled in the person of Abraham. But Abraham's example is referred to, not because it is the only one, but because it is more illustrious than that of any other. For though Abraham had this faith in common with all the godly; yet it is not without reason that he is called the father of the faithful. It is, then, no wonder that the Apostle selected him from all the rest, and turned towards him the eyes of his readers as to the clearest mirror of faith.

Faith and patience, etc. What is meant is, a firm faith, which has patience as its companion. For faith is what is, chiefly required; but as many who make at first a marvelous display of faith, soon fail, he shows, that the true evidence of that faith which is not fleeting and evanescent, is endurance. By saying that the *promises* were obtained by *faith,* he takes away the notion of merits; and still more clearly by saying, that they came by "inheritance"; for we are in no other way made heirs but by the right of adoption.[104]

---

104 The word for "patience" is properly long-suffering, or forbearance, Romans ii. 4; but it is used here in the same sense of patient expectation, as the participle clearly means in verse 15.

As to "inherit," the present, as Grotius says, is used for the past tense — "who inherited," or rather, "became heirs to the

13. *For when God made a promise to Abraham, etc.* His object was to prove, that the grace of God is offered to us in vain, except we receive the promise by faith, and constantly cherish it in the bosom of our heart. And he proves it by this argument, that when God promised a countless offspring to Abraham, it seemed a thing incredible; Sarah had been through life barren; both had reached a sterile old age, when they were nearer the grave than to a conjugal bed; there was no vigor to beget children, when Sarah's womb, which had been barren through the prime of life, was now become dead. Who could believe that a nation would proceed from them, equaling the stars in number, and like the sand of the sea? It was, indeed, contrary to all reason. Yet Abraham looked for this and feared no disappointment, because he relied on the Word of God.[105] We must, then, notice the circumstance as to time, that the Apostle's reasoning may appear evident; and what he subjoins refers to this — that he was made partaker of this blessing, but that it was after he had waited for what no one could have thought would ever come to pass. In this way ought glory to be given to God; we must quietly hope for what he does not as yet show to our senses, but hides from us and for a long time defers, in order that our patience may be exercised.

Why God did *swear by himself* we shall presently see. The manner of swearing, *Except blessing I will bless thee*, we have explained what it means in the third chapter: God's name is not here expressed, but must be understood, for except he performs what he promises, he testifies that he is not to he counted true and faithful.

---

    promises." They did not really possess them, as we find in chapter xi. 13, but heired them, as we may say; they died in faith and became entitled to them. The word "promises" is used here as well as in chapter xi.; for many things were included in what God had promised to the fathers, but chiefly the Messiah and the heavenly inheritance. — *Ed.*

105 It is said, that having "patiently endured" or rather waited, "he obtained the promise," that is, of a numerous posterity, the particular thing previously referred to. After having waited for twenty-five years, (see Genesis xii. 1-4, and Genesis xvii. 1-16,) a son was given him; and this beginning of the fulfilled promise was a pledge of its full accomplishment. This case is brought forward as an example of waiting faith. — *Ed.*

HEBREWS VI. 16-20

16. For men verily swear by the greater: and an oath for confirmation *is* to them an end of all strife.
17. Wherein God, willing more abundantly to shew unto the heirs of promise the immutability of his counsel, confirmed *it* by an oath:
18. That by two immutable things, in which *it was* impossible for God to lie, we might have a strong consolation, who have fled for refuge to lay hold upon the hope set before us:
19. Which *hope* we have as an anchor of the soul, both sure and steadfast, and which entereth into that within the veil;
20. Whither the forerunner is for us entered, *even* Jesus, made an high priest for ever after the order of Melchisedec.

16. *For men, etc.* It is an argument from the less to the greater; if credit is given to man, who is by nature false, when he swears, and for this reason, because he confirms what he says by God's name, how much more credit is due to God, who is eternal truth, when he swears by himself?

Now he mentions several things to commend this declaration; and first he says that men *swear by the greater;* by which he means that they who are wanting in due authority borrow it from another. He adds that there is so much reverence in an oath that it suffices for confirmation, and puts an end to all disputes where the testimonies of men and other proofs are wanting. Then is not he a sufficient witness for himself whom all appeal to as a witness? Is he not to obtain credit for what he says, who, by his authority, removes all doubts among others? If God's name, pronounced by man's tongue, possesses so much superiority, how much more weight ought it to have, when God himself swears by his own name? Thus much as to the main point.

But here in passing, two things are to be noticed, — that we are to swear by God's name when necessity requires, and that Christians are allowed to make an oath, because it is a lawful remedy for removing contentions. God in express words bids us to swear by his name; if other names are blended with it, the oath is profaned. For this there are especially three reasons: when there is no way of bringing the truth to light, it is not right, for the sake of verifying it, to have recourse to any but to God, who is himself eternal truth; and then, since he alone knows the heart, his own office is taken from him, when in things hidden, of which men can form no opinion, we appeal to any other judge; and thirdly, because in swearing we not only appeal to him as a witness, but also call upon him as an avenger of perjury in case we speak falsely. It is no wonder, then, that he is so greatly displeased with those who swear by another name, for his own honor is thus disparaged. And that there are different forms often used in Scripture, makes nothing against this truth; for they did not swear by heaven or earth, as though they ascribed any divine power to them, or attributed to them the least portion of divinity, but by this indirect protestation, so to speak, they had a regard to the one true God. There are indeed various kinds of protestations; but the chief one is, when we refer to God as a judge and directly appeal to his judgment-seat; another is, when we name things especially dear to us as our life, or our head, or anything of this kind; and the third is, when we call creatures as witnesses before God. But in all these ways we swear properly by no other than by God. hence they betray their impiety no less than their ignorance, who contend that it is lawful to connect dead saints with God so as to attribute to them the right of punishing.

Further, this passage teaches us, as it has been said, that an oath may be lawfully used by Christians; and this ought to be particularly observed, on account of fanatical men who are disposed to abrogate the practice of solemn swearing which God has prescribed in his Law. For certainly the Apostle speaks here of the custom of swearing as of a holy practice, and approved by God. Moreover, he does not say of it as having been formerly in use, but as of a thing still practiced. Let it then be employed as a help to find out the truth when other proofs are wanting.

17. *God, willing, etc.* See how kindly God as a gracious Father accommodates himself to our slowness to believe; as he sees that we rest not on his simple word, that he might more fully impress it on our hearts he adds an oath. Hence also it appears how much it concerns us to know that there is such a certainty respecting his goodwill towards us, that there is no longer any occasion for wavering or for trembling. For when God forbids his name to be taken in vain or on a slight occasion, and denounces the severest vengeance on all who rashly abuse it, when he commands reverence to be rendered to his majesty, he thus teaches us that he holds his name in the highest esteem and honor. The certainty of salvation is then a necessary thing; for he who forbids to swear without reason has been pleased to swear for the sake of rendering it certain. And we may hence also conclude what great account he makes of our salvation; for in order to secure it, he not only pardons our unbelief, but giving up as it were his own right, and yielding to us far more than what we could claim, he kindly provides a remedy for it.

Unto the heirs of promise, etc. He seems especially to point out the Jews; for though the heirship came at length to the Gentiles, yet the former were the first lawful heirs, and the latter, being aliens, were made the second heirs, and that beyond the right of nature. So Peter, addressing the Jews in his first sermon, says,

> "To you and to your children is the promise made, and to those who are afar of, whom the Lord shall call." (Acts ii. 39.)

He left indeed a place for adventitious heirs, but he sets the Jews in the first rank, according to what he also says in the third chapter, "Ye are the children of the fathers and of the covenant," etc. (Acts iii. 25.) So also in this place the Apostle, in order to make the Jews more ready to receive the covenant, shows that it was for their sakes chiefly it was confirmed by an oath. At the same time this declaration belongs at this day to us also, for we have entered into the place quitted by them through unbelief

Observe that what is testified to us in the Gospel is called the *counsel* of God, that no one may doubt but that this truth proceeds from the very inmost thoughts of God. Believers ought therefore to be fully persuaded that whenever they hear the voice of the Gospel, the secret counsel of God, which lay hid in him, is proclaimed to them, and that hence is made known to them what he has decreed respecting our salvation before the creation of the world.

18. *That by two immutable things, etc.* What God says as well as what he swears is immutable. (Psalm xii. 6; Numb. xxiii. 19.) It may be with men far otherwise; for their vanity is such that there cannot be much firmness in their word. But the word of God is in various ways extolled; it is pure and without any dross, like gold seven times purified. Even Balaam, though an enemy, was yet constrained to bring this testimony,

"God is not like the sons of men that he should lie, neither like men that he should repent: has he then said, and shall he not do it? Has he spoken, and shall he not make it good?" (Numbers xxiii. 19.)

The word of God, then, is a sure truth, and in itself authoritative, (αὐτόπιστος self-worthy of trust.) But when an oath is added it is an overplus added to a full measure. We have, then, this strong consolation, that God, who cannot deceive when he speaks, being not content with making a promise, has confirmed it by an oath.[106]

Who have fled for refuge, etc. By these words he intimates that we do not truly trust in God except when we forsake every other protection and flee for refuge to his sure promise, and feel assured that it is our only safe asylum. Hence by the word flee is set forth our poverty and our need; for we flee not to God except

---

106 The "two immutable things," says most, are the promise and the oath. But some of late, such as Stuart, have disputed this interpretation; and they hold that they are two oaths, — the first was made to Abraham respecting a Son (the Messiah) in whom all nations should be blessed; and the second refers to Christ's priesthood, recorded in Psalm cx. 4. This is the clearly to go out of the passage for its interpretation. The case of the fathers, and especially Abraham, in verses 12, 13, 14 and 15, was introduced for the sake of illustration. And having mentioned God's oath with regard to Abraham, he proceeds in verse 16 to state the use of an oath among men, and evidently reverting to the promise of eternal life implied in "the hope" mentioned in verse 11, he says that God confirmed that promise, called here God's "counsel," by an oath; and the oath specially referred to seems to have been that respecting the priesthood of his Son, more than once mentioned before and at the end of this chapter; for upon his priesthood in an especial manner depended the promise of eternal life. The "counsel" of God means his revealed counsel or gracious purpose, his promise of eternal life to those who believe. In establishing a priesthood by an oath, he confirmed this promise, for its accomplishment depended on that priesthood. To call two oaths two immutable things is nothing so apposite as to call so the promise and the oath by which the priesthood was established. — *Ed.*

when constrained. But when he adds *the hope set before us,* he intimates that we have not far to go to seek the aid we want, for God himself of his own free will meets us and puts as it were in our hand what we are to hope for; it is *set before us.* But as by this truth he designed to encourage the Jews to embrace the Gospel in which salvation was offered to them; so also he thus deprived the unbelieving, who rejected the favor presented to them, of every excuse. And doubtless this might have been more truly said after the promulgation of the Gospel than under the Law: "There is now no reason for you to say, 'Who shall ascent into heaven? Or, Who shall descend into the deep? Or, Who shall pass over the sea? For nigh is the word, it is in thy mouth and in thy heart.'"[107] (Deuteronomy xxx. 12; Romans x. 6.)

But there is a metonymy in the word *hope,* for the effect is put for the cause; and I understand by it the promise on which our hope leans or relies, for I cannot agree with those who take *hope* here for the thing hoped for — by no means: and this also must be added, that the Apostle speaks not of a naked promise, suspended as it were in the air, but of that which is received by faith; or, if you prefer a short expression, the hope here means the promise apprehended by faith. By the word *laying hold,* as well as by *hope,* he denotes firmness.

19. *As an anchor, etc.* It is a striking likeness when he compares faith leaning on God's word to an anchor; for doubtless, as long as we sojourn in this world, we stand not on firm ground,

---

107 The "strong consolation" is rendered by Theophylact "strong encouragement;" nor is it unsuitable here. The influence of the "two immutable things" was no other than to give strong encouragement to those who believed: the tendency was to confirm them in the faith. Stuart gives it the meaning of "persuasion," and renders the passage thus, "So that by two immutable things, concerning which is impossible for God to lie, we, who have sought for refuge, might be strongly persuaded to hold fast the hope that is set before us." The great objection to this is the separation of "fleeing" from the latter part of the sentence, which I find is done by none; and to seek for refuge, or to flee for refuge, is not the meaning of καταφυγόντες, but merely to flee; and to construe it by itself gives no meaning. We are hence under the necessity of construing it with what follows, "That we might have a strong consolation (or encouragement) who have fled to lay hold on the hope set before us." So Beza substantially, and Doddridge, and Macknight. — *Ed*

but are tossed here and there as it were in the midst of the sea, and that indeed very turbulent; for Satan is incessantly stirring up innumerable storms, which would immediately upset and sink our vessel, were we not to cast our anchor fast in the deep. For nowhere a haven appears to our eyes, but wherever we look water alone is in view; yea, waves also arise and threaten us; but as the anchor is cast through the waters into a dark and unseen place, and while it lies hid there, keeps the vessel beaten by the waves from being overwhelmed; so must our hope be fixed on the invisible God. There is this difference, — the anchor is cast downwards into the sea, for it has the earth as its bottom; but our hope rises upwards and soars aloft, for in the world it finds nothing on which it can stand, nor ought it to cleave to created things, but to rest on God alone. As the cable also by which the anchor is suspended joins the vessel with the earth through a long and dark intermediate space, so the truth of God is a bond to connect us with himself, so that no distance of place and no darkness can prevent us from cleaving to him. Thus when united to God, though we must struggle with continual storms, we are yet beyond the peril of shipwreck. Hence he says, that this anchor is *sure* and *steadfast,* or safe and firm.[108] It may indeed be that by the violence of the waves the anchor may be plucked off, or the cable be broken, or the beaten ship be torn to pieces. This happens on the sea; but the power of God to sustain us is wholly different, and so also is the strength of hope and the firmness of his word.

Which entereth into that, or *those things, etc.* As we have said, until faith reaches to God, it finds nothing but what is unstable and evanescent; it is hence necessary for it to penetrate even into heaven. But as the Apostle is speaking to the Jews, he alludes to the ancient Tabernacle, and says, that they ought not to abide

---

108 "Safe," that is safely fixed; and "firm," that is strong, so as not to be bent nor broken, as Parens says. Stuart seems to have inverted the proper meaning of the words, as he applies ἀσφαλῶ to the anchor as having been made of good materials, and θεβαίαν as signifying that it is firmly fixed. The first word means what cannot fall, be subverted, or overthrown, and must therefore refer to what is safely fixed; and the other means firm, stable, constant, enduring. So Schleusner renders the words, "*tutam ac firmam,*" safe and firm; and he quotes Phavorinus as giving the meaning of the first word ἕδραιος, steadfast. — *Ed*

Chapter 6

in those things which are seen, but to penetrate into the inmost recesses, which lie hid within the veil, as though he had said, that all the external and ancient figures and shadows were to be passed over, in order that faith might be fixed on Christ alone.

And carefully ought this reasoning to be observed, — that as Christ has entered into heaven, so faith ought to be directed there also: for we are hence taught that faith should look nowhere else. And doubtless it is in vain for man to seek God in his own majesty, for it is too far removed from them; but Christ stretches forth his hand to us, that he may lead us to heaven. And this was shadowed forth formerly under the Law; for the high priest entered the holy of holies, not in his own name only, but also in that of the people, inasmuch as he bare in a manner the twelve tribes on his breast and on his shoulders; for as a memorial for them twelve stones were wrought on the breastplate, and on the two onyx stones on his shoulders were engraved their names, so that in the person of one man all entered into the sanctuary together. Rightly then does the Apostle speak, when he reminds them that our high priest has entered into heaven; for he has not entered only for himself, but also for us. There is therefore no reason to fear that access to heaven will be closed up against our faith, as it is never disjoined from Christ. And as it becomes us to follow Christ who is gone before, he is therefore called our *Forerunner*, or precursor.[109]

---

109 Calvin's version is "Where our precursor Jesus has entered." The πρόδρομος is one who goes before to prepare the way for those who follow him. It is used in the Sept. to designate the first ripe grapes and the first ripe figs. Numbers xiii. 20; Isaiah xxviii. 4. These were the precursors for us (or, in our behalf) Jesus has entered." He has not only gone to prepare a place for his people; but he is also their leader whom they are to follow; and where he has entered they shall also enter. His entrance is a pledge of their entrance. — *Ed*

CHAPTER 7

HEBREWS VII. 1-3

1. For this Melchisedec, king of Salem, priest of the most high God, who met Abraham returning from the slaughter of the kings, and blessed him;
2. To whom also Abraham gave a tenth part of all; first being by interpretation King of righteousness, and after that also King of Salem, which is, King of peace;
3. Without father, without mother, without descent, having neither beginning of days, nor end of life; but made like unto the Son of God; abideth a priest continually.

1. *For this Melchisedec, etc.* He has hitherto been stimulating the Jews by exhortations, that they might attentively consider the comparison between Christ and Melchisedec. At the end of the last chapter, that he might return from his digression to his subject, he quoted again the passage from the Psalms; and now he enters fully into what he had before slightly referred to; for he enumerates particularly the things connected with Melchisedec, in which he resembled Christ. It is indeed no wonder that he dwells so minutely on this subject. It was doubtless no common thing that in a country abounding in the corruptions of so many superstitions, a man was found who preserved the pure worship of God; for on one side he was nigh to Sodom and Gomorrah, and on the other to the Canaanites, so that he was on every side encompassed by ungodly men. Besides, the whole world was so fallen into impiety, that it is very probable that God was nowhere faithfully worshipped except in the family of Abraham; for his father and his grandfather, who ought to have retained true religion, had long before degenerated into idolatry. It was therefore a memorable fact, that there was still a king who not only retained true religion, but also performed himself the office of a priest. And it was doubtless necessary that in him who was to be a type of the Son of God all things excellent should be found: and that Christ was shadowed forth by this type is evident from the Psalm referred to; for David did not say without reason, "Thou art a priest forever after the order Melchisedec;" no, but on the contrary, by these words a sublime mystery was recommended to the Church.

Let us now consider each of those particulars in which the Apostle makes Christ like Melchisedec.[110]

The first likeness is in the name; for it was not without a mystery that he was called *the King of righteousness*. For though this honor is ascribed to kings who rule with moderation and in equity, yet this belongs really to Christ alone, who not only exercises authority justly as others do, but also communicates to us the righteous of God, partly when he makes us to be counted righteous by a gratuitous reconciliation, and partly when he renews us by his Spirit, that we may lead a godly and holy life. He is then called the King of righteousness, because of what he effects in diffusing righteousness on all his people.[111] It hence follows, that out of his kingdom nothing but sin reigns among

---

110 The passage reads better, and the meaning appears more evident, when we consider *was* as understood in the first verse, as Calvin does. The first part refers to what he did as to Abraham: and the second, to what he was as a type of Christ.

Now this Melchisedec, king of Salem, was a priest of the most high God; who met Abraham returning from the overthrow of the kings, and blessed him; to whom Abraham also divided the tenth of all: being first indeed, by interpretation, King of righteousness, and then also King of Salem, which is, King of Peace; without father, without mother, without decent, having no beginning of days or end of life, but

By saying that he "blessed" Abraham, we are to render that he prayed God to bless him, as we find it explained in Genesis xiv. 19.

111 It is not as a king, but as a priest that Christ is our righteousness. Therefore strictly speaking, as a king, he administers righteousness, or acts righteously. "The king of righteousness," may be rendered, as Stuart does, a righteous king. See Psalm xlv. 7 — *Ed.*

men. And therefore Zechariah, when he introduces him, as by the solemn decree of God, into the possession of his kingdom, thus extols him, —

"Rejoice, O daughter of Sion, Behold thy righteous King cometh to thee," (Zechariah ii. 10;)

intimating that the righteousness, which is otherwise wanting to us, is brought to us by the coming of Christ.

The second likeness which the Apostle states is as to the kingdom of *peace*. This peace indeed is the fruit of that righteousness which he has mentioned. It hence follows that wherever Christ's kingdom extends, there peace ought to be, as we find in Isaiah 2 and 9, and in other places. But as peace among the Hebrews means also a prosperous and happy state, it may be so taken here: yet I prefer to understand it here of that inward peace which tranquilizes the conscience and renders it confident before God. And the excellency of this blessing cannot be sufficiently estimated, unless you consider on the other hand, how miserable a thing it is to be tormented by constant inquietude; which must necessarily be the case until we have our consciences pacified by being reconciled to God through Christ.

3. *Without father, etc.* I prefer this rendering to that of "unknown father;" for the Apostle meant to express something more emphatic than that the family of Melchisedec was obscure or unknown. Nor does this objection disturb me, that the reality does not correspond with the figure or type, because Christ has a Father in heaven, and had a mother on earth; for the Apostle immediately explains his meaning by adding *without descent*, or kindred. He then exempts Melchisedec from what is common to others, a descent by birth; by which he means that he is eternal, so that his beginning from men was not to be sought after. It is indeed certain that he descended from parents; but the Apostle does not speak of him here in his private capacity; on the contrary, he sets him forth as a type of Christ. He therefore allows himself to see nothing in him but what Scripture contains. For in treating of things respecting Christ, such reverence ought to be observed as not to know anything but what is written in the Word of the Lord. Now, as the Holy Spirit in mentioning this king, the most illustrious of his age, is wholly silent as to his

birth, and makes afterwards no record of his death, is not this the same thing as though eternity was to be ascribed to him? And what was shadowed forth in Melchisedec is really exhibited in Christ. It behooves us then to be satisfied with this moderate view, that while Scripture sets forth to us Melchisedec as one who had never been born and never died, it shows to us as in a mirror, that Christ has neither a beginning nor an end.[112]

But we hence also learn how much reverence and sobriety is required as to the spiritual mysteries of God: for what is not found read in Scripture the Apostle is not only willing to be ignorant of, but also would have us to seek to know. And surely it is not lawful for us to allege anything of Christ from our own thoughts. And Melchisedec is not to be considered here, as they say, in his private capacity, but as a sacred type of Christ; nor ought we to think that it was accidentally or inadvertently omitted that no kindred is ascribed to him, and that nothing is said of his death; but on the contrary, that this was done designedly by the Spirit, in order to give us an idea of one above the common order of men. There seems therefore to be no probability in the conjecture of those who say that Melchisedec was Shem the son of Noah; for if we make him to be some known individual, we destroy this third likeness between Melchisedec and Christ.

Made like, or *assimilated, etc.* Not as far as what was typified required; for we must always bear in mind that there is but an analogy between the thing signified and the sign; for they make themselves ridiculous who imagine that he came down from heaven, in order that there might be a perfect similarity. It is enough that we see in him the lineaments of Christ, as the form of the living man may be seen in his picture, while yet the man himself is very different from what represents him.[113] It seems

---

112 Some regard what is said of Melchisedec being without father, etc., as meaning that he was so in his office as a king and priest, there being no account of a predecessor or of a successor to him; but this view cannot be taken on account of these words, "without mother, without descent," etc., Calvin gives the explanation commonly received. — *Ed.*

113 Our version "made like," etc., is objected to by Stuart; and he renders it, "being like," alleging that the Apostle's object is to show, not that Melchisedec was "made like" to Christ as a priest, but the contrary, according to Psalm cx. 4. But the object here seems to be different: he shows why it is that there is no record

not to be worth one's while to refute the delirious notions of those who dream that Christ himself, or the holy Spirit, or an angel, appeared at that time; unless indeed one thought it to be the duty of a right-minded man to dispute with Postillus and such fanatics; for that impostor asserts that he is Melchisedec with no less supercilious folly than those mad spirits of old, mentioned by Jerome, who pretended that they were Christ.

HEBREWS VII. 4-10

4. Now consider how great this man *was,* unto whom even the patriarch Abraham gave the tenth of the spoils.
5. And verily they that are of the sons of Levi, who receive the office of the priesthood, have a commandment to take tithes of the people according to the law, that is, of their brethren, though they come out of the loins of Abraham:
6. But he whose descent is not counted from them received tithes of Abraham, and blessed him that had the promises.
7. And without all contradiction the less is blessed of the better.
8. And here men that die receive tithes; but there he *receiveth them,* of whom it is witnessed that he liveth.
9. And as I may so say, Levi also, who receiveth tithes, payed tithes in Abraham.
10. For he was yet in the loins of his father, when Melchisedec met him.

4. *Now consider, etc.* This is the fourth comparison between Christ and Melchisedec, that Abraham presented tithes to him. But though tithes were instituted for several reasons, yet the Apostle here refers only to what serves his present purpose. One reason why tithes were paid to the Levites was, because they were the children of Abraham, to whose seed the land was promised. It was, then, by a hereditary right that a portion of the land was

---

of Melchisedec's office as to its beginning or end; it was that he might be made a fit type to represent the Son of God. — *Ed.*

allotted to them; for as they were not allowed to possess land, a compensation was made to them in tithes. There was also another reason, — that as they were occupied in the service of God and the public ministry of the Church, it was right that they should be supported at the public cost of the people. Then the rest of the Israelites owed them tithes as a remuneration for their work. But these reasons bear not at all on the present subject; therefore, the Apostle passes them by. The only reason now alleged is, that as the people offered the tithes as a sacred tribute to God, the Levites only received them. It hence appears that it was no small honor that God in a manner substituted them for himself. Then Abraham, being one of the chief sergeants of God and a prophet, having offered tithes to Melchisedec the priest, thereby confessed that Melchisedec excelled him in dignity. If, then, the *patriarch* Abraham owned him more honourable than himself, his dignity must have been singular and extraordinary. The word *patriarch* is mentioned for the sake of setting forth his dignity; for it was in the highest degree honourable to him to have been called a father in the Church of God.

Then the argument is this, — Abraham, who excelled all others, was yet inferior to Melchisedec; then Melchisedec had the highest place of honor, and is to be regarded as superior to all the sons of Levi. The first part is proved, for what Abraham owed to God he gave to Melchisedec: then by paying him the tenth he confessed himself to be inferior.

5. *And verily they, etc.* It would be more suitable to render the words thus, "because they are the sons of Levi." The Apostle indeed does not assign it as a reason that they received tithes because they were the sons of Levi; but he is comparing the whole tribe with Melchisedec in this way. Though God granted to the Levites the right of requiring tithes from the people, and thus set them above all the Israelites, yet they have all descended from the same parent; and Abraham, the father of them all, paid tithes to a priest of another race: then all the descendants of Abraham are inferior to this priest. Thus the right conferred on the Levites was particular as to the rest of their brethren; yet Melchisedec, without exception, occupies the highest place, so that all are inferior to him. Some think that the tenths of tenths are intended, which the Levites paid to the higher priests; but there is no reason thus to confine the general declaration. The view, then, I have given is the most probable.

6. *Blessed him,* *etc.* This is the fifth comparison between Christ and Melchisedec. The Apostle assumes it as an admitted principle that the less is blessed by the greater; and then he adds that Melchisedec blessed Abraham: hence the conclusion is that the less was Abraham. But for the sake of strengthening his argument he again raises the dignity of Abraham; for the more glorious Abraham is made, the higher the dignity of Melchisedec appears. For this purpose he says that Abraham had the *promises;* by which he means that he was the first of the holy race with whom God made the covenant of eternal life. It was not indeed a common honor that God chose him from all the rest that he might deposit with him the privilege of adoption and the testimony of his love. But all this was no hindrance that he should not submit himself in all his preeminence to the priesthood of Melchisedec. We hence see how great he was to whom Abraham gave place in these two things, — that he suffered himself to be blessed by him, and that he offered him tithes as to God's vicegerent.

7. *The less is,* [114] *etc.* Let us first know what the word *blessed* means here. It means indeed a solemn praying by which he who is invested with some high and public honor, recommends to God men in private stations and under his ministry. Another way of blessing is when we pray for one another; which is commonly done by all the godly. But this blessing mentioned by the Apostle was a symbol of greater authority. Thus Isaac blessed his son Jacob, and Jacob himself blessed his grandsons, Ephraim and Manasseh. (Genesis xxvii. 27; xlviii. 15.) This was not done mutually, for the son could not do the like to the father; but a higher authority was required for such a blessing as this. And this appears more evident still from Numbers vi. 23, where a command is given to the priest to bless the people, and then a promise is immediately added, that they would be blessed whom they blessed. It hence appears that the blessing of the priest depended on this, — that it was not so much man's blessing as that of God. For as the priest in offering sacrifices represented Christ, so in blessing the people he was nothing

---

[114] The words are in the neuter gender, "what is less blessed by the greater." This is an idiom; the neuter is put for the masculine, as πᾶν is used for all men in John vi. 37, and πᾶν μωρὰ for foolish men in 1 Corinthians i. 27. The meaning is, "the inferior is blessed by his superior." — *Ed*

more than a minister and legate of the supreme God. In the same sense ought to be understood what Luke records when he says, that Christ lifted up his hands and blessed the Apostles. (Luke xxiv. 50.) The practice of lifting up the hands he no doubt borrowed from the priests, in order to show that he was the person by whom God the Father blesses us. Of this blessing mention is also made in Psalm cxvi. 17; cxviii. 1

Let us now apply this idea to what the apostle treats of: The blessing of the priest, while it is a divine work is also an evidence of a higher honor; then Melchisedec, in blessing Abraham, assumed to himself a higher dignity. This he did, not presumptuously, but according to his right as a priest: then he was more eminent than Abraham. Yet Abraham was he with whom God was pleased to make the covenant of salvation; though, then, he was superior to all others, yet he was surpassed by Melchisedec.[115]

8. *Of whom it is witnessed that he liveth.* He takes the silence respecting his death, as I have said, as an evidence of his life. This would not indeed hold as to others, but as to Melchisedec it ought rightly to be so regarded, inasmuch as he was a type of Christ. For as the spiritual kingdom and priesthood of Christ are spoken of here, there is no place left for human conjectures; nor is it lawful for us to seek to know anything farther than what we read in Scripture. But we are not hence to conclude that the man who met Abraham is yet alive, as some have childishly thought, for this is to be applied to the other person whom he represented, even the Son of God. And by these words the Apostle intended to show, that the dignity of Melchisedec's priesthood was to be perpetual, while that of the Levites was temporary.[116]

---

[115] There are three kinds of blessing mentioned in Scripture, — prayer for a blessing, Matthew v. 44; prophetic blessing, as in the case of the patriarchs, chapter xi. 20, 21; and sacerdotal blessing, as recorded in Numbers vi. 23-27. The latter is what is meant here. It was a blessing announced in the name of the Lord, or a prayer offered in his name, and by his authority. — *Ed.*

[116] Critics often make a difficulty where is none. The obvious meaning of this verse is given by Calvin, — continual succession, owing to death, betokened the unenduring character of the Levitical priesthood; but the perpetuity of that Melchisedec is proved by this, that he lives. To live often means to be perpetual; and to die

For he thus reasons, — those to whom the Law assigns tithes are dying men; by which it was indicated that the priesthood would some time be abrogated, as their life came to an end: but the Scripture makes no mention of the death of Melchisedec, when it relates that tithes were paid to him; so the authority of his priesthood is limited by no time, but on the contrary there is given an indication of perpetuity. And this is added for this purpose, lest a posterior law, as it is usual, should seem to take away from the authority of a former law. For it might have been otherwise objected and said, that the right which Melchisedec formerly possessed is now void and null, because God had introduced another law by Moses, by which he transferred the right to the Levites. But the Apostle anticipates this objection by saying, that tithes were paid to the Levites only for a time, because they did not live; but that Melchisedec, because he is immortal, retains even to the end what was once given to him by God.

9. *Levi also, etc.* He advances farther, and says, that even Levi himself, who was then *in the loins of Abraham*, was not exempt from the same subordination; for Abraham, by paying tithes, made himself and his posterity inferior to the priesthood of Melchisedec.[117] But here one, on the other hand, may say, that in the same way Judas also of whose seed Christ was born, paid tithes. But this knot can be easily untied, when one considers two things which are settled beyond all dispute among Christians: first, Christ is not to be counted simply as one of the sons of Abraham, but is to be exempted by a peculiar privilege from the common order of men; and this is what he himself said, "If he is the son of David, then does David call him his Lord?" (Matthew xxii. 45;) secondly, since Melchisedec is a type of Christ, it is by no means reasonable that the one should be set in opposition to the other; for we must remember that common saying, that what is subordinate is not in opposition: hence the

---

intimates what is evanescent. The Levites were dying men, which showed the character of their office, Melchisedec is represented as not dying, which betokens that his office as a priest is perpetual. — *Ed.*

117 Our version is "For he was yet," etc., ἔτι, here is not yet, but even, as in Luke i. 15, or then, as rendered by Stuart; "For he was even (or then) in the loins of his father when Melchisedec met him."
— *Ed*

type, which comes short of the reality, ought by no means to be opposed to it, nor can it be, for such is the conflict of equals.

These five particulars, mentioned by the Apostle, complete the comparison between Christ and Melchisedec, and thus is dissipated the gloss of those who seek to show that the chief likeness between them is in offering of bread and wine. We see that the Apostle carefully, and even scrupulously, examines here each of these points; he mentions the name of the man, the seat of his kingdom, the perpetuity of his life, his right to tithes, and his benediction.

There is, forsooth! in these things, less importance than in the oblation! Shall we say that the Spirit of God, through forgetfulness, omitted this, so that he dwelt on minor things, and left unnoticed the chief thing, and what was most necessary for his purpose? I marvel the more that so many of the ancient doctors of the Church were so led away by this notion, that they dwelt only on the offering of bread and wine. And thus they spoke, "Christ is a priest according to the order of Melchisedec; and Melchisedec offered bread and wine; then the sacrifice of bread and wine is suitable to the priesthood of Christ." The Apostle will hereafter speak largely of the ancient sacrifices; but of this new sacrifice of bread and wine he says not a word. Whence then did ecclesiastical writers derive this notion? Doubtless, as one error usually leads to another, having of themselves imagined a sacrifice in Christ's Supper without any command from him, and thus adulterated the Supper by adding a sacrifice, they afterwards endeavored to find out plausible arguments here and there in order to disguise and cover their error. This offering of bread and wine pleased them, and was instantly laid hold on without any discretion. For who can concede that these men were more intelligent than the Spirit of God? Yet if we receive what they teach, we must condemn God's Spirit for inadvertence in having omitted a matter so important, especially as the question is avowedly handled!

I hence conclude, that the ancients invented a sacrifice, of which Moses had never thought; for Melchisedec offered bread and wine, not to God, but on the contrary to Abraham and his companions. These are the words, "Melchisedec, king of Salem, went out to meet him, and brought forth bread and wine; and the same was priest to the most high God, and blessed him." (Genesis xiv. 18.) The first thing mentioned was a royal act; he refreshed those wearied after the battle and their journey with sustenance; the blessing was the act of a priest. If then his offering had anything mystical in it, the completion of it is to be found in Christ, when he fed the hungry and those wearied with fatigue. But the Papists are extremely ridiculous, who though they deny that there is bread and wine in the Mass, yet prattle about the sacrifice of bread and wine.

HEBREWS VII. 11-14

> 11. If therefore perfection were by the Levitical priesthood, (for under it the people received the law,) what further need *was there* that another priest should rise after the order of Melchisedec, and not be called after the order of Aaron?
> 12. For the priesthood being changed, there is made of necessity a change also of the law.
> 13. For he of whom these things are spoken pertaineth to another tribe, of which no man gave attendance at the altar.
> 14. For *it is* evident that our Lord sprang out of Juda; of which tribe Moses spake nothing concerning priesthood.

11. *If therefore perfection,* or, moreover if perfection,[118] *etc.* From the same testimony the Apostle concludes, that the old covenant was abrogated by the coming of Christ. He has hitherto spoken of the office and person of the priest; but as God had instituted a priesthood for the purpose of ratifying the Law, the former being abolished, the latter necessarily ceases. That this may be better understood, we must bear in mind the general truth, — That no covenant between God and man is in force and ratified, except it rests on a priesthood. Hence the Apostle says, that the Law was introduced among the ancient people under the Levitical priesthood; by which he intimates, that it not only

---

118 The particles Εἰ μὲν οὖν, are rendered by Elsner, "but if," — by Doddridge, "now if," — by Stuart, "moreover if," and by Macknight, "moreover, if indeed;" and all these consider that there is here a commencement from what has preceded. — *Ed*

prevailed during the time of the Law, but that it was instituted, as we have said for the sake of confirming the Law.

He now reasons thus, If the ministry of the Church was perfect under the order of Aaron, why was it necessary to return to another order? For in perfection nothing can be changed. It then follows, that the ministry of the Law was not perfect, for that new order was to be introduced of which David speaks.[119]

For under it the people received the Law, etc. This parenthesis is inserted in order that we may know that the Law was annexed to the priesthood. The Apostle had in view to prove that in the Law of Moses there was no ultimate end at which we ought to stop. This he proves by the abrogation of the priesthoods and in this way: Had the authority of the ancient priesthood been such as to be sufficient fully to establish the Law, God would have never introduced in its place another and a different priesthood. Now, as some might doubt whether the abolition of the Law followed the abolition of the priesthood, he says that the Law was not only brought in under it, but that it was also by it established.[120]

12. *For the priesthood being changed,* or, *transferred, etc.* As the authority of the Law and the priesthood is the same, Christ became not only a priest, but also a Lawgiver; so that the right of Aaron, as well as of Moses, was transferred to him. The sum of the whole is, that the ministry of Moses was no less temporary than that of Aaron; and hence both were annulled by the coming of Christ, for the one could not stand without the other. By the word *Law*, we understand what peculiarly belonged to Moses; for the Law contains the rule of life, and the gratuitous

---

119 "Perfection," or completion, rather than consummation is no doubt the best word τελείωσις. To render it "perfect expiation," as Schleusner does, is not to render the word, but to explain it. The imperfection of the Levitical priesthood was doubtless its capacity really to make an atonement for sin, as its work was ceremonial and typical: but it was enough for the present purpose merely to say that it was not perfect, as it failed to answer the great end of establishing a priesthood. And the Apostle grounds its deficiency, or imperfect character, on the fact that a priest of another order had been promised. This was an argument which the Jews could not resist, as it was founded on the Scriptures, which they themselves acknowledged as divine. — Ed

120 See Appendix Z.

covenant of life; and in it we find everywhere many remarkable sentences by which we are instructed as to faith, and as to the fear of God. None of these were abolished by Christ, but only that part which regarded the ancient priesthood.

For Christ is here compared with Moses; whatever then they had in common, is not to be taken to the account, but only the things in which they differ. They in common offer God's mercy to us, prescribe the rule of a holy and godly life, teach us the true worship of God, and exhort us to exercise faith and patience, and all the duties of godliness. But Moses was different from Christ in this respect, that while the love of the Gospel was not as yet made known, he kept the people under veils, set forth the knowledge of Christ by types and shadows, and, in short, accommodated himself to the capacity of ignorant people, and did not rise higher than to puerile elements. We must then remember, that the Law is that part of the ministration which Moses had as peculiarly his own, and different from that of Christ. That law, as it was subordinate to the ancient priesthood, was abolished when the priesthood was abolished. And Christ, being made a priest, was invested also with the authority of a legislator, that he might be the teacher and interpreter of the new covenant. At the same time, the word Law is applied, though not in its strict sense, to the Gospel; but this impropriety of language is so far from having anything harsh in it, that on account of the contrast it adds beauty to the sentence, as we find in the seventh chapter of the Epistle to the Romans

Moreover, the impiety of the Pope is extremely arrogant, who has inserted this article in his decretals, that he himself is now invested with the same authority as Aaron formerly had, because the Law and also the priesthood have been transferred to him. We see what the Apostle says; he maintains that ceremonies have ceased since the time when Christ came forth with command to proclaim the new covenant. It is then absurd hence to conclude, that anything has been transferred to the ministers of Christ; for Christ himself is alone contrasted here with Moses and Aaron. Under what pretext then can Antichrist arrogate to himself any such authority? I do not indeed speak now for the sake of disproving so gross an arrogance; but it is worth while to remind readers of this sacrilegious audacity, that they may know that this notorious servant of the servants of Christ wholly disregards the honor of his Master, and boldly mangles the Scriptures, that he may have some cloak for his own tyranny.

13. For he of whom these things are spoken, or, *said*,[121] *etc.* As the Apostle was speaking to them who confessed Jesus the Son of Mary to be the Christ, he proves that an end was put to the ancient priesthood, because the new Priest, who had been set in the place of the old, was of another tribe, and not of Levi; for according to the Law the honor of the priesthood was to continue, by a special privilege, in that tribe. But he says that it was *evident* that Christ was born of the tribe of Judah, for it was then a fact commonly known. As then they acknowledged that he was the Christ, it was also necessary that they should be persuaded that he was the son of David; for he who had been promised could derive his origin from no other.

HEBREWS VII. 15-22

15. And it is yet far more evident: for that after the similitude of Melchisedec there ariseth another priest,
16. Who is made, not after the law of a carnal commandment, but after the power of an endless life.
17. For he testifieth, Thou *art* a priest for ever after the order of Melchisedec.
18. For there is verily a disannulling of the commandment going before for the weakness and unprofitableness thereof.
19. For the law made nothing perfect, but the bringing in of a better hope *did*; by the which we draw nigh unto God.
20. And inasmuch as not without an oath *he was made priest*:

---

121 Calvin renders "for", γὰρ, "doubtless — certe," and Stuart, "now;" but it may better be rendered here, "for," as a reason is given for a change in "the law" respecting the priesthood. The γὰρ in the former verse may be rendered "indeed," or "wherefore" as by Macknight. In the 11th verse, the Apostle proves the imperfection or defectiveness of the Levitical priesthood, by the promise of another priest after the order of Melchisedec for Christ was not of the tribe specified by the Law. — Ed

21. (For those priests were made without an oath; but
this with an oath by him that said unto him, The Lord
sware and will not repent, Thou *art* a priest for ever
after the order of Melchisedec:)
22. By so much was Jesus made a surety of a better
testament.

15. *And it is yet far more evident, etc.* He proves by another argument, that the Law is abolished. He reasoned before as to the person of the priest, but now as to the nature of the priesthood, and the reason for which it was appointed. The ancient priesthood, he says, had to do with external rites; but in Christ's priesthood there is nothing but what is spiritual. It hence appears, that the former was evanescent and temporary; but that the latter was to be perpetual.

16. *Carnal commandment, etc.* It was called *carnal*, because it refers to things corporal, that is, to external rites. We know how Aaron and his sons were initiated into their office. What was fulfilled in Christ by the hidden and celestial power of the Spirit, was shadowed forth under the Law by ointment, various vestments, the sprinkling of blood, and other earthly ceremonies. Now this kind of institution was suitable to the nature of the priesthood; it hence follows, that the priesthood itself was liable to change. At the same time, as we shall hereafter see, the priesthood was not so carnal, but that it was still spiritual; but the Apostle here refers only to the difference between Christ and Aaron. However spiritual then might have been the meaning of these shadows, they were yet but shadows in themselves; and as they were made up of the elements of this world, they may justly be called earthly.

After the power of an endless life, or, of an indissoluble life. As Christ is a perpetual priest, it was necessary, that he should be different from Aaron as to the manner of his appointment; and so it was, for it was not Moses, a mortal man, who consecrated him, but the Holy Spirit, and that not with oil, nor with the blood of goats, nor with the outward pomp of vestments, but with celestial power, which the Apostle here sets in opposition to weak elements. We hence see how the eternity of his priesthood was exhibited in Christ.

17. *Thou art a priest forever, etc.* It is on the single word *forever*, that the Apostle lays stress in this passage; for he confirms what he said of an *indissoluble life*. He then shows that Christ differs from the whole race of Levi, because he is made a priest for ever.[122]

But here it may be objected, as the Jews also do, that the word, לעולם, *laoulam*, does not always mean eternity, but the extent of one age, or, at farthest, a long time; and it is added, that when Moses speaks of the ancient sacrifices, he often uses this expression, "This ordinance shall be forever." (Exodus xii. 17, and xix. 9.) To this I answer that whenever the sacrifices of the Law are mentioned, "forever" is to be confined to the time of the Law; nor ought this to be deemed strange; for by the coming of Christ a certain renovation of the world was effected. Whenever, then, Moses speaks of his own ministration, he extends the longest time no farther than to Christ. It must yet be also observed, that "forever" is applied to the ancient sacrifices, not with regard to the external ceremony, but on account of their mystical signification. On the present occasion, however, this reason ought to be sufficient, that Moses and his ministrations were for ever; that is, until the coming of the kingdom of Christ, under whom the world was renovated. Now when Christ is come, and a perpetual priesthood is given to him, we can find no end to his age, so that it cannot terminate after a certain period of time. So when applied to him, the word ought to be understood in the sense of eternity; for by the context we are always to judge of the meaning of the word, לעולם, *laoulam*

18. *For there is verily a disannulling,* or *abrogation, etc.* As the Apostle's discourse depends on this hinge, that the Law together with the priesthood had come to an end, he explains the reason why it ought to have been abolished, even because it was weak and unprofitable. And he speaks thus in reference to the ceremonies, which had nothing substantial in them, nor in themselves anything available to salvation; for the promise of favor annexed to them, and what Moses everywhere testifies that God would be pacified by sacrifices and that sins would be

---

122 This paragraph extends from the 11th verse to the end of the 17th. The "law" parenthetically referred to in the 11th, seems not to be the Mosaic Law generally, as too commonly supposed, but the law respecting the Levitical priesthood, as it appears evident from the 12th and the following verses, for what is spoken of is Christ as being a priest not in succession from Aaron, but according to the order of Melchisedec. See Appendix A2. — Ed.

expiated, did not properly belong to sacrifices, but were only adventitious to them. For as all types had a reference to Christ, so from him they derived all their virtue and effect; nay, of themselves they availed nothing or effected nothing; but their whole efficacy depended on Christ alone

But as the Jews foolishly set up these in opposition to Christ, the Apostle, referring to this notion, shows the difference between these things and Christ. For as soon as they are separated from Christ, there is nothing left in them, but the weakness of which he speaks; in a word, there is no benefit to be found in the ancient ceremonies, except as they refer to Christ; for in this way they so made the Jews acquainted with God's grace, that they in a manner kept them in expectation of it. Let us then remember that the Law is useless, when separated from Christ. And he also confirms the same truth by calling it the *commandment going before;* for it is a well-known and common saying, that former laws are abrogated by the latter. The Law had been promulgated long before David; but he was in possession of his kingdom when he proclaimed this prophecy respecting the appointment of a new priest; this new Law then annulled the former.

19. *For the Law made nothing perfect, etc.* As he had spoken rather harshly of the Law, he now mitigates or, as it were, corrects that asperity; for he concedes to it some utility, as it had pointed out the way which leads at length to salvation. It was, however, of such a kind as to be far short of perfection. The Apostle then reasons thus: The Law was only a beginning; then something more perfect was necessarily, to follow; for it is not fit that God's children should always continue in childish elements. By the word *bringing in,* or introduction, he means a certain preparation made by the Law, as children are taught in those elements which smooth the way to what is higher. But as the preposition ἐπὶ denotes a consequence, when one thing follows another; it ought, as I think, to be thus rendered, "but added was an introduction into a better hope." For he mentions two introductions, according to my view; the first by Melchisedec as a type; and the second by the Law, which was in time later. Moreover, by *Law* he designates the Levitical priesthood, which was superadded to the priesthood of Melchisedec.

By a *better hope* is to be understood the condition of the faithful under the reign of Christ; but he had in view the fathers, who could not be satisfied with the state in which they were then, but aspired to higher things. Hence that saying, "Many kings and prophets desired to see the things which ye see." (Luke x. 24.) They were therefore led by the hand of the Law as a schoolmaster, that they might advance farther.[123]

By the which we draw nigh, etc. There is to be understood here an implied contrast between us and the fathers; for in honor and privilege we excel them, as God has communicated to us a full knowledge of himself, but he appeared to them as it were afar off and obscurely. And there is an allusion here made to the tabernacle or the temple; for the people stood afar off in the court, nor was there a nearer access to the sanctuary opened to any one except to the priests; and into the interior sanctuary the highest priest only entered; but now, the tabernacle being removed, God admits us into a familiar approach to himself, which the fathers were not permitted to have. Then he who still holds to the shadows of the Law, or seeks to restore them, not only obscures the glory of Christ, but also deprives us of an immense benefit; for he puts God at a great distance from us, to approach whom there is a liberty granted to us by the Gospel. And whosoever continues in the Law, knowingly and willingly deprives himself of the privilege of approaching nigh to God.

20. *And inasmuch as not without an oath, etc.* Here is another argument, why the Law ought to give place to the Gospel; for God has set Christ's priesthood above that of Aaron, since in honor to the former he was pleased to make an oath. For when he appointed the ancient priests, he introduced no oath; but it is said of Christ, the Lord swore; which was doubtless done for the sake of honoring him. We see the end for which he again quotes the Psalmist, even that we may know, that more honor through God's oath was given to Christ than to any others. But we must bear in mind this truth, that a priest is made that he may be the surety of a covenant. The Apostle hence concludes, that the covenant which God has made by Christ with us, is far more excellent than the old covenant of which Moses was the interpreter.

---

123 Calvin is peculiar in his view of this verse. He considered the Law to be "an introduction to a better hope." Many agree with our version, such as Beza, Doddridge, Macknight, Stuart, etc. But there are those who render "introduction" in connection with "disannulling." See Appendix B2. — *Ed.*

HEBREWS VII. 23-28

23. And they truly were many priests, because they were not suffered to continue by reason of death:
24. But this *man*, because he continueth ever, hath an unchangeable priesthood.
25. Wherefore he is able also to save them to the uttermost that come unto God by him, seeing he ever liveth to make intercession for them.
26. For such an high priest became us, *who is* holy, harmless, undefiled, separate from sinners, and made higher than the heavens;
27. Who needeth not daily, as those high priests, to offer up sacrifice, first for his own sins, and then for the people's: for this he did once, when he offered up himself.
28. For the law maketh men high priests which have infirmity; but the word of the oath, which was since the law, *maketh* the Son, who is consecrated for evermore.

23. *And they truly, etc.* He had already touched on this comparison; but as the subject deserved more attention, he unfolds it more fully, though the point discussed is different from what it was before; for then he concluded that the ancient priesthood was to come to an end because they who exercised it were mortal; but now he simply shows that Christ remains perpetually a priest. This he does by an argument taken from things unequal; the ancient priests were many, for death put an end to their priesthood; but there is no death to prevent Christ from discharging his office. Then he alone is a perpetual priest. Thus a different cause produces different effects.

25. *Wherefore he is able to save, etc.* This is the fruit of an eternal priesthood, even our salvation, if indeed we gather this fruit by faith as we ought to do. For where death is or a change, you will there seek salvation in vain; hence they who cleave to the ancient priesthood, can never attain salvation. When he says, *them that come unto God,* or who approach God, by this phrase he points out the faithful who alone enjoy the salvation procured by Christ; but he yet at the same time indicates what faith ought to regard in a mediator. The chief good of man is to be united to his God, with whom is the fountain of life and of all blessings; but their own unworthiness drives all away from any access to him. Then the peculiar office of a mediator is to bring us help in this respect, and to stretch out his hand to us that he may lead us to heaven. And he ever alludes to the ancient shadows of the Law; for though the high priest carried the names of the twelve tribes on his shoulders and symbols on his breast, yet he alone entered the sanctuary, while the people stood in the court. But now by relying on Christ the Mediator we enter by faith into heaven, for there is no longer any veil intervening, but God appears to us openly, and lovingly invites us to a familiar access.[124]

Seeing he ever liveth, etc. What sort of pledge and how great is this of love towards us! Christ liveth for us, not for himself! That he was received into a blessed immortality to reign in heaven, this has taken place, as the Apostle declares, for our sake. Then the life, and the kingdom, and the glory of Christ are all destined for our salvation as to their object; nor has Christ any thing, which may not be applied to our benefit; for he has been given to us by the Father once for all on this condition, that all his should be ours. He at the same time teaches us by what Christ is doing, that he is performing his office as a priest; for it belongs to a priest to *intercede* for the people, that they may

---

124 Calvin's version of the former part of the verse is, "Hence he is also able to save for ever those who through him draw nigh to God." Instead of "to the uttermost" of our version, we have here "forever," according to the Vulg. Macknight renders the phrase the same and Stuart "always." But the original, εἰς τὸ παντελὲς, do not refer to time, but to what is fully or perfectly done. It is so taken by Erasmus, Beza, Capellus and Schleusner. There is another difference, whether to connect the words with "able" or with "save." Most join them with "save," "he is able also fully (or, for ever) able to save." When we consider what the subject is — the perfection of Christ as a priest, and not the character of his salvation. We must see that the latter is the right view, and that the passage ought to have been thus rendered, — "And hence he is fully (or perfectly) able to save those who through him come to God." And the words which follow may be deemed as affording a reason for this, "always living in order to intercede for them," or, "to interpose in their behalf."

However, there is not much difference in the meaning, whether the word "fully" or perfectly be connected with "able" or with "save;" the same truth is essentially conveyed. — *Ed.*

obtain favor with God. This is what Christ is ever doing, for it was for this purpose that he rose again from the dead. Then of right, for his continual intercession, he claims for himself the office of the priesthood.

26. *For such an high priest, etc.* He reasons from what is necessarily connected with the subject. These conditions, or qualifications, as they commonly say, are of necessity required in a priest — that he should be just, harmless, and pure from every spot. This honor belongs to Christ alone. Then what was required for the real discharge of the office was wanting in the priests of the law. It hence follows, that there was no perfection in the Levitical priesthood; nor was it indeed in itself legitimate, unless it was subservient to that of Christ; and, doubtless, the external ornaments of the high priest indicated this defect; for why were those costly and splendid vestments used with which God commanded Aaron to be adorned while performing holy rites, except that they were symbols of a holiness and excellency far exceeding all human virtues? Now, these types were introduced, because the reality did not exist. It then appears that Christ alone is the fully qualified priest.

Separate from sinners, etc. This clause includes all the rest. For there was some holiness, and harmlessness, and purity in Aaron, but only a small measure; for he and his sons were defiled with many spots; but Christ, exempt from the common lot of men, is alone free from every sin; hence in him alone is found real holiness and innocency. For he is not said to be separate from us, because he repels us from his society, but because he has this excellency above us all, that he is free from every uncleanness.[125]

---

125 Christ as a priest was "holy" with regard to God; "harmless," or innocent, or guileless, according to Chrysostom, with respect to men; "undefiled" as to himself, morally so, as the priests under the law were so ceremonially; "separate," or separated "from sinners" removed from their society to another place, and "exalted higher than the heavens." There is an allusion to the Levitical high priest, especially in the three last words, and a contrast in the two last; the Levitical high priest continued among sinners, Christ is removed from them; the former entered into the holy of holies, the latter has entered into a place higher that the heavens, even the heavens of heavens. How immeasurable is the superiority of our high priest! — *Ed.*

And we hence conclude, that all prayers, which are not supported by Christ's intercession, are rejected.

It may, however, be asked as to angels, whether they are separate from sinners? And if so, what prevents them from discharging the offices of the priesthood, and from being our mediators with God? To this there is an easy reply: — No one is a lawful priest, except he is appointed by God's command; and God has nowhere conferred this honor on angels. It would then be a sacrilegious usurpation, were they, without being called, to intrude into the office; besides, it is necessary, as we shall presently see at the beginning of the next chapter, that the Mediator between God and men should himself be a man. At the same time the last thing mentioned here by the Apostle is abundantly sufficient as an answer to the question; for no one can unite us to God but he who reaches to God; and this is not the privilege of angels, for they are not said to have been *made higher than the heavens*. It then belongs to Christ alone to conciliate God to us, as he has ascended above all the heavens. Now, these words mean the same as though Christ were said to have been placed above all orders of creatures, so that he stands eminent above all angels.

27. *Who needeth not, etc.* He pursues the contrast between Christ and the Levitical priests; and he points out especially two defects, so to speak, in the ancient priesthood, by which it appears that it was not perfect. And here, indeed, he only touches briefly on the subject; but he afterwards explains every particular more at large, and particularly that which refers to the daily sacrifices, as the main question was respecting these. It is briefly also that I will now touch on the several points. One of the defects of the ancient priesthood was, that the high priest offered sacrifices for his own sins; how then could he have pacified God for others, who had God justly displeased with himself? Then they were by no means equal to the work of expiating for sins. The other defect was, that they offered various sacrifices daily; it hence follows, that there was no real expiation; for sins remain when purgation is repeated. The case with Christ was wholly different; for he himself needed no sacrifice, as he was sprinkled with no spot of sin; and such was the sacrifice, that it was alone sufficient to the end of the world, for he offered himself.[126]

---

126 See Appendix C2.

28. *For the law, etc.* From the defects of men he draws his conclusion as to the weakness of the priesthood, as though he had said, "Since the law makes no real priests, the defect must by some other means be remedied; and it is remedied by the *word of the oath;* for Christ was made a priest, being not of the common order of men, but the Son of God, subject to no defect, but adorned and endowed with the highest perfection." He again reminds us, that the *oath* was posterior to the law, in order to show that God, being not satisfied with the priesthood of the law, designed to constitute a better priesthood; for in the institutions of God what succeeds advances the former to a better state, or it abolishes what was designed to exist only for a time.

CHAPTER 8

HEBREWS VIII. 1-6

1. Now of the things which we have spoken *this is* the sum: We have such an high priest, who is set on the right hand of the throne of the Majesty in the heavens;
2. A minister of the sanctuary, and of the true tabernacle, which the Lord pitched, and not man.
3. For every high priest is ordained to offer gifts and sacrifices: wherefore *it is* of necessity that this man have somewhat also to offer.
4. For if he were on earth, he should not be a priest, seeing that there are priests that offer gifts according to the law:
5. Who serve unto the example and shadow of heavenly things, as Moses was admonished of God when he was about to make the tabernacle: for, See, saith he, *that* thou make all things according to the pattern shewed to thee in the mount.
6. But now hath he obtained a more excellent ministry, by how much also he is the mediator of a better covenant, which was established upon better promises.

1. *Now of the things, etc.* That readers might know the subject he handles, he reminds them that his object is to prove that Christ's priesthood, by which that of the law had been abolished, is spiritual. He, indeed, proceeds with the same argument; but as he contends with various reasonings, he introduced this admonition, that he might keep his readers attentive to what he had in view.

He has already shown that Christ is a high priest; he now contends that his priesthood is celestial. It hence follows, that by his coming the priesthood established by Moses under the law was made void, for it was earthly. and as Christ suffered in the humble condition of his flesh, and having taken the form of a servant, made himself of no reputation in the world, (Philippians ii. 7;) the Apostle reminds us of his ascension, by which was removed not only the reproach of the cross, but also of that abject and mean condition which he had assumed together with our flesh; for it is by the power of the Spirit which gloriously appeared in the resurrection and the ascension of Christ, that the dignity of his priesthood is to be estimated. He then reasons thus — "Since Christ has ascended to the right hand of God, that he might reign gloriously in heaven, he is not the minister of the earthly but of the heavenly sanctuary.[127]

2. *Of the sanctuary,* or, literally, *of holy things, etc.* The word is to be taken, as being in the neuter gender; and the Apostle explains himself by saying, *of the true tabernacle.* [128]

But it may be asked, whether the tabernacle built by Moses was a false one, and presumptuously constructed, for there is an implied contrast in the words? To this I answer, that to us mentioned here is not set in opposition to what is false, but only to what is typical; as we find in John i. 17, "The law was given by Moses, but grace and truth came by Jesus Christ." Then the old tabernacle was not the empty inventions of man, but the

---

127 See Appendix D2.

128 It is better to take "holy things" as designating the holy duties of the priest, afterwards specified when the offering of gifts and sacrifices is mentioned, than as signifying "the sanctuary." Christ is a priest and a minister in sacred things, and a minister in the true tabernacle. He has holy things to do, and he does them, not in the shadowy and typical tabernacle, but in that which is real and celestial.

We find, that the word in the next chapter means the holiest place, accompanied as here with the article, chapter ix. 8-12, and without the article, the holy place or the sanctuary, chapter ix. 2. So then if this meaning be taken, the rendering here ought to be, "the minister of the holiest;" and then "tabernacle" is used as including the whole building, as in chapter ix. 2. But the context here seems to favor the former meaning. The version of Doddridge is, "A minister of holy things." — *Ed.*

effigy of the heavenly tabernacle. As, however, a shadow differs from the substance, and the sign from the thing signified, the Apostle denies it to have been the true tabernacle, as though he had said, that it was only a shadow.

Which the Lord pitched, or, *fixed, etc.* What does the Apostle mean by locating Christ's priesthood in heaven? For doubtless he suffered on earth, and by an earthly blood he atoned for our sins, for he derived his origin from the seed of Abraham; the sacrifice of his death was visible; and lastly, that he might offer himself to the Father, it was necessary for him to descend from heaven to the earth, and as man to become exposed to the sorrows of this mortal life, and at length to death itself. To all this I reply, that whatever of an earthly kind appears at first sight to be in Christ, it is to be viewed spiritually by the eye of faith. Thus his flesh, which proceeded from the seed of Abraham, since it was the temple of God, possessed a vivifying power; yea, the death of Christ became the life of the world, which is certainly above nature. The Apostle therefore does not refer to what belongs peculiarly to human nature, but to the hidden power of the Spirit; and hence it is, that the death of Christ has nothing earthly in it. When therefore we speak of Christ, let us learn to raise up all our thoughts to the kingdom of God, so that no doubt may remain in us.

Nearly to the same purpose is the language of Paul in 2 Corinthians v. 1; he calls God the builder of this tabernacle, in order to set forth its stability and perpetuity; for, on the other hand, what is built by men's hands, is unstable, and at last sure to perish. But he says this, because redemption was truly a divine work, attained by the death of Christ; and in this the power of Christ manifested itself in a wonderful manner.

3. *For every high priest, etc.* The Apostle intends to show, that Christ's priesthood cannot coexist with the Levitical priesthood. He proves it in this way, — "The Law appointed priests to offer sacrifices to God; it hence appears that the priesthood is an empty name without a sacrifice. But Christ had no sacrifice, such as was offered under the Law; it hence follows, that his priesthood is not earthly or carnal, but one of a more excellent character."

Let us now examine every clause. The first thing that deserves notice, is that which he teaches that no priest is appointed except to offer gifts; it is hence evident, that no favor from

God can be obtained for men except through the interposition of a sacrifice. Hence, that our prayers may be heard, they must be founded on a sacrifice; their audacity, therefore, is altogether pernicious and fatal, who pass by Christ and forget his death, and yet rush into the presence of God. Now, if we wish to pray in a profitable manner, we must learn ever to set before us the death of Christ, which alone sanctifies our prayers. For God will never hear us unless he is reconciled; but he must be first pacified, for our sins cause him to be displeased with us. Sacrifice must necessarily precede, in order that there may be any benefit from prayer.

We may hence further conclude, that no one either among men or angels is qualified for pacifying God, for all are without any sacrifice of their own which they can offer to appease God. And hereby is abundantly exposed the effrontery of the Papists who make Apostles and martyrs to share with Christ as mediators in the work of intercession; for in vain do they assign them such an office, except they supply them with sacrifices.[129]

4. *For if he were on earth, etc.* It is now beyond dispute that Christ is a high priest; but as the office of a judge does not exist without laws and statutes, so the office of sacrificing must be connected with Christ as a priest: yet he has no earthly or visible sacrifice; he cannot then be a priest on earth. We must always hold this truth that when the Apostle speaks of the death of Christ, he regards not the external action, but the spiritual benefit. He suffered death as men do, but as a priest he atoned for the sins of the world in a divine manner; there was an external shedding of blood, but there was also an internal and spiritual purgation; in a word, he died on earth, but the virtue and efficacy of his death proceeded from heaven.

What immediately follows some render thus, "He could not be a priest of the number of those who offer gifts according to the Law." But the words of the Apostle mean another thing; and therefore I prefer this rendering, "He could not be a priest as long as there are priests who," etc. For he intends to show one of these two things, either that Christ is no priest, while the priesthood of the Law continued, as he had no sacrifice, or that

---

129 "This man" of our version, in the latter clause of the verse, should be either "he," or "this high priest," in contrast with the high priest at the beginning of the verse. Such is the rendering of Macknight and Stuart. — *Ed.*

the sacrifices of the law ceased as soon as Christ appeared. The first of these is against all reason, for it is an act of impiety to deprive Christ of his priesthood. It then remains for us to confess, that the Levitical order is now abolished.

5. *Who serve unto the example, etc.* The verb λατρεύειν to serve, I take here to mean the performing of sacred rites; and so ἐν or ἐπὶ is to be understood. This is certainly more appropriate than the rendering given by some, "Who serve the shadow and example of heavenly things; and the construction in Greek will admit naturally of the meaning I have proposed. In short, he teaches us that the true worship of God consists not in the ceremonies of the Law, and that hence the Levitical priests, while exercising their functions, had nothing but a shadow and a copy, which is inferior to the prototype, for this is the meaning of the word ὑποδείγμα, exemplar. And he thus anticipates what might have been raised as an objection; for he shows that the worship of God, according to the ancient sacrifices, was not superfluous, because it referred to what was higher, even to heavenly realities.[130]

---

130 Our version of this clause is hardly intelligible. Calvin's rendering with a little addition would convey a clear meaning. "Who do service in that which is the exemplar and shadow of celestial things." Stuart considers "tabernacle" as being understood. We have the words, "who serve the tabernacle," in chapter xiii. 10, that is, "who do the service belonging to the tabernacle," or, "who attend on the tabernacle." So the literal rendering here is, "who serve the model and shadow of celestial things," which means, "who do the service belonging to the model and shadows of celestial things." The tabernacle no doubt is what is meant; and it is called a "model," or likeness, because it emblematically represented, or exhibited things heavenly, and a "shadow," because it was not the substance or the reality. Stuart seems to have unwisely combined the two words, "a mere copy;" for the two ideas they convey are not thus so clearly seen.

But to "serve," or to do service, includes what was done by the people as well as by the priests. Those who offered the sacrifices, as well as the priests through whom they offered the sacrifices, or performed the services belonging to the tabernacle; the latter are meant here, and the former or both in chapter x. 2; xiii. 10. To serve the Lord, and to offer sacrifices to him, are in Exodus represented as the same; see chapter viii. 1; x. 7, 26. — *Ed.*

As Moses was admonished by God, etc. This passage is found in Exodus xxv. 40; and the apostle adduces it here on purpose, so that he might prove that the whole service, according to the Law, was nothing more than a picture as it were, designed to shadow forth what is found spiritually in Christ. God commanded that all the parts of the tabernacle should correspond with the original pattern, which had been shown to Moses on the mount. And if the form of the tabernacle had a reference to something else, then the same must have been the case as to the rituals and the priesthood; it hence follows that there was nothing real in them.

This is a remarkable passage, for it contains three things entitled to special notice.

First, we hence learn that the ancient rituals were not without reason appointed, as though God did by them engage the attention of the people as with the diversions of children; and that the form of the tabernacle was not an empty thing, intended only to allure and attract the eyes by its external splendor; for there was a real and spiritual meaning in all these things, since Moses was commanded to execute every thing according to the original pattern which was given from heaven. Extremely profane then must the opinion of those be, who hold that the ceremonies were only enjoined that they might serve as means to restrain the wantonness of the people, that they might not seek after the foreign rites of heathens. There is indeed something in this, but it is far from being all; they omit what is much more important, that they were the means of retaining the people in their expectation of a Mediator.

There is, however, no reason that we should be here overcurious, so as to seek in every nail and minute things some sublime mystery, as Hesychius did and many of the ancient writers, who anxiously toiled in this work; for while they sought refinedly to philosophize on things unknown to them, they childishly blundered, and by their foolish trifling made themselves ridiculous. We ought therefore to exercise moderation in this respect, which we shall do if we seek only to know what has been revealed to us respecting Christ.

Secondly, we are here taught that all those modes of worship are false and spurious, which men allow themselves by their own wit to invent, and beyond God's command; for since God gives this direction, that all things are to be done according to his own rule, it is not lawful for us to do anything different from it; for these two forms of expression, "see that thou do all things according to the patterns," and, "See that thou do nothing beyond the pattern," amount to the same thing. Then by enforcing the rule delivered by himself, he prohibits us to depart from it even in the least thing. For this reason all the modes of worship taught by men fall to the ground, and also those things called sacraments which have not proceeded from God.

Thirdly, let us hence learn that there are no true symbols of religion but those which conform to what Christ requires. We must then take heed, lest we, while seeking to adapt our own inventions to Christ, transfigure him, as the Papists do, so that he should not be at all like himself; for it does not belong to us to devise anything as we please, but to God alone it belongs to show us what to do; it is to be "according to the pattern" showed to us.

6. *But now has he obtained a more excellent ministry, etc.* As he had before inferred the excellency of the covenant from the dignity of the priesthood, so also now he maintains that Christ's priesthood is more excellent than that of Aaron, because he is the interpreter and Mediator of a better covenant. Both were necessary, for the Jews were to be led away from the superstitious observance of rituals, by which they were prevented from advancing directly forward to the attainment of the real and pure truth of the Gospel. The Apostle says now that it was but right that Moses and Aaron should give way to Christ as to one more excellent, because the gospel is a more excellent covenant than the Law, and also because the death of Christ was a nobler sacrifice than the victims under the Law.

But what he adds is not without some difficulty, — that the covenant of the Gospel was proclaimed on better promises;[131] for it is certain that the fathers who lived under the Law had

---

[131] Instead of "proclaimed," it is "established" in our version, and in that of Doddridge, and Macknight, and of Stuart, "sanctioned." The verb means what is set as a law; that is, firmly and irrevocably fixed. It was a covenant firmly set or founded on more excellent promises. What these are, we learn in the following verses.

This verse is connected with the fourth; and the fifth is to be put in a parenthesis. The reasoning is, — Though he is no priest on earth, yet he has a higher ministry, inasmuch as the covenant of which he is the Mediator is far superior to that of priests on

the same hope of eternal life set before them as we have, as they had the grace of adoption in common with us, then faith must have rested on the same promises. But the comparison made by the Apostle refers to the form rather than to the substance; for though God promised to them the same salvation which he at this day promises to us, yet neither the manner nor the character of the revelation is the same or equal to what we enjoy. If anyone wishes to know more on this subject, let him read the 4th and 5th chapter of the Epistle to the Galatians and my Institutes.

HEBREWS VIII. 7-13

7. For if that first *covenant* had been faultless, then should no place have been sought for the second.
8. For finding fault with them, he saith, Behold, the days come, saith the Lord, when I will make a new covenant with the house of Israel and with the house of Judah:
9. Not according to the covenant that I made with their fathers in the day when I took them by the hand to lead them out of the land of Egypt; because they continued not in my covenant, and I regarded them not, saith the Lord.
10. For this *is* the covenant that I will make with the house of Israel after those days, saith the Lord; I will put my laws into their mind, and write them in their hearts: and I will be to them a God, and they shall be to me a people:
11. And they shall not teach every man his neighbor, and every man his brother, saying, Know the Lord: for all shall know me, from the least to the greatest.
12. For I will be merciful to their unrighteousness, and their sins and their iniquities will I remember no more.
13. In that he saith, A new *covenant*, he hath made the first old. Now that which decayeth and waxeth old *is* ready to vanish away.

---

earth; that is, the Levitical priests. Then he proceeds to the end of the chapter with the covenant, and shows its superiority. — *Ed.*

7. *For if that first, etc.* He confirms what he had said of the excellency of the covenant which God has made with us through Christ; and he confirms it on this ground, because the covenant of the Law was neither valid nor permanent; for if nothing was wanting in it, why was another substituted for it? But another has been substituted; and from this it is evident that the old covenant was not in every respect perfect. To prove this he adduces the testimony of Jeremiah, which we shall presently examine.

But it seems hardly consistent to say, that after having said that no place would have been sought for the second covenant, had the first been faultless, he should then say that the people were at fault, and that for this cause the new covenant was introduced as a remedy; and thus it appears unjust, that if the blame was in the people it should be transferred to God's covenant. Then the argument seems not valid, for though God might have a hundred times blamed the people, yet the covenant could not on that account be deemed faulty. The answer to this objection may be easily given. Though the crime of violating the covenant was justly imputed to the people, who had through their own perfidy departed from God, yet the weakness of the covenant is also pointed out, because it was not written in their hearts. Then, to render it perfect and valid, God declares that it needed an amendment. It was not, therefore, without reason that the Apostle contended that a place was to be sought for a second.[132]

8. *Behold, the days come, etc.* (Jeremiah xxxi. 31-34.) The Prophet speaks of future time; he arraigns the people of perfidy, because they continued not faithful after having received the Law. The Law, then, was the covenant which was broken, as God complains, by the people. To remedy this evil, he promised a new and a different covenant, the fulfillment of which prophecy was the abrogation of the old covenant.

---

132 This apparent inconsistency is avoided by some by rendering the 8th verse differently, "But finding fault," that is, with the first covenant, "he" Chrysostom, Beza, Doddridge, our own version, as well as Calvin and the Vulgate, connect "them" with "finding fault with," and more correctly too; for the Israelites are blamed in the very passage that is quoted. There was a double fault or defect, which is explained in Romans viii. 3, "For what the law could not do, in that it was weak through the flesh," etc. This double fault or weakness more fully sets forth the excellency of the new covenant. —*Ed.*

But it may be said, the Apostle seems unreasonably to turn this prophecy to suit his own purpose; for here the question is respecting ceremonies, but the Prophet speaks of the whole Law: what has it to do with ceremonies, when God inscribes on the heart the rule of a godly and holy life, delivered by the voice and teaching of men? To this I reply that the argument is applied from the whole to a part. There is no doubt but that the Prophet includes the whole dispensation of Moses when he says, "I have made with you a covenant which you have not kept." Besides, the Law was in a manner clothed with ceremonies; now when the body is dead, what is the use of garments? It is a common saying that the accessory is of the same character with his principal. No wonder, then, that the ceremonies, which are nothing more than appendages to the old covenant, should come to an end, together with the whole dispensation of Moses. Nor is it unusual with the Apostles, when they speak of ceremonies, to discuss the general question respecting the whole Law. Though, then, the prophet Jeremiah extends wider than to ceremonies, yet as it includes them under the name of the old covenant, it may be fitly applied to the present subject.

Now, by the *days* which the prophet mentions, all agree that Christ's kingdom is signified; it hence follows, that the old covenant was changed by the coming of Christ. And he names *the house of Israel and the house of Judah,* because the posterity of Abraham had been divided into two kingdoms. So the promise is to gather again all the elect together into one body, however separated they may have been formerly.

9. *Not according to the covenant, etc.* Here is expressed the difference between the covenant which then existed and the new one which he caused them to expect. The Prophet might have otherwise said only: "I will renew the covenant which through your fault has come to nothing;" but he now expressly declares that it would be one unlike the former. By saying that the covenant was made in the day when he laid holds on their hand to rescue them from bondage, he enhanced the sin of defection by thus reminding them of so great a benefit. At the same time he did not accuse one age only of ingratitude; but as these very men who had been delivered immediately fell away, and as their posterity after their example continually relapsed, hence the whole nation had become covenant-breakers.

By saying that he *disregarded* them or cared not for them, he intimates that it would profit them nothing to have been once adopted as his people, unless he succored them by this new kind of remedy. At the same time the Prophet expresses in Hebrew something more; but this has little to do with the present question.[133]

10 *For this is the covenant that I will make, etc.* There are two main parts in this covenant; the first regards the gratuitous remission of sins; and the other, the inward renovation of the heart; there is a third which depends on the second, and that is the illumination of the mind as to the knowledge of God. There are here many things most deserving of notice.

The first is, that God calls us to himself without effect as long as he speaks to us in no other way than by the voice of man. He indeed teaches us and commands what is right but he speaks to the deaf; for when we seem to hear anything, our ears are only struck by an empty sound; and the heart, full of depravity and perverseness, rejects every wholesome doctrine. In short, the word of God never penetrates into our hearts, for they are iron and stone until they are softened by him; nay, they have engraven on them a contrary law, for perverse passions rule within, which lead us to rebellion. In vain then does God proclaim his Law by the voice of man, unless he writes it by his Spirit on our hearts, that is, unless he forms and prepares us for obedience. It hence appears of what avail is freewill and the uprightness of nature before God regenerates us. We will indeed and choose freely; but our will is carried away by a sort of insane impulse to resist God. Thus it comes that the Law is ruinous and fatal to us as long as it remains written only on tables of stone, as Paul also teaches us. (2 Corinthians iii. 3.) In short, we then only obediently embrace what God commands, when by his Spirit he changes and corrects the natural pravity of our hearts; otherwise he finds nothing in us but corrupt affections and a heart wholly given up to evil. The declaration indeed is clear, that a new covenant is made according to which God engraves his laws on our hearts, for otherwise it would be in vain and of no effect.[134]

---

133 See Appendix E2.

134 The Apostle adopts here the Septuagint version. The Hebrew is "I will put my law in their inmost part, and on their heart will I

The second particular refers to the gratuitous pardon of sins. Though they have sinned, saith the Lord, yet I will pardon them. This part is also most necessary; for God never so forms us for obedience to his righteousness, but that many corrupt affections of the flesh still remain; nay, it is only in part that the viciousness of our nature is corrected; so that evil lusts break out now and then. And hence is that contest of which Paul complains, when the godly do not obey God as they ought, but in various ways offend. (Romans vii. 13.) Whatever desire then there may be in us to live righteously, we are still guilty of eternal death before God, because our life is ever very far from the perfection which the Law requires. There would then be no stability in the covenant, except God gratuitously forgave our sins. But it is the peculiar privilege of the faithful who have once embraced the covenant offered to them in Christ, that they feel assured that God is propitious to them; nor is the sin to which they are liable, a hindrance to them, for they have the promise of pardon.

And it must be observed that this pardon is promised to them, not for one day only, but to the very end of life, so that they have a daily reconciliation with God. For this favor is extended to the whole of Christ's kingdom, as Paul abundantly proves in the fifth chapter of his second Epistle to the Corinthians. And doubtless this is the only true asylum of our faith, to which if we flee not, constant despair must be our lot. For we are all of us guilty; nor can we be otherwise released then by fleeing to God's mercy, which alone can pardon us.

And they shall be to me, etc. It is the fruit of the covenant, that God chooses us for his people, and assures us that he will be the guardian of our salvation. This is indeed the meaning of these words, *And I will be to them a God;* for he is not the God of the dead, nor does he take us under his protection, but that he may make us partakers of righteousness and of life, so that David justly exclaims, "Blessed are the people to whom the Lord is God (Psalm cxliv. 15.) There is further no doubt but that this truth belongs also to us; for though the Israelites had the first place, and are the proper and legitimate heirs of the covenant,

---

write (or engrave) it." The word "law" and "heart", are put here in the plural number, and the "inmost part" is rendered "mind." These changes are according to the peculiar character of the two languages. — *Ed.*

yet their prerogative does not hinder us from having also a title to it. In short, however far and wide the kingdom of Christ extends, this covenant of salvation is of the same extent.

But it may be asked, whether there was under the Law a sure and certain promise of salvation, whether the fathers had the gift of the Spirit, whether they enjoyed God's paternal favor through the remission of sins? Yes, it is evident that they worshipped God with a sincere heart and a pure conscience, and that they walked in his commandments, and this could not have been the case except they had been inwardly taught by the Spirit; and it is also evident, that whenever they thought of their sins, they were raised up by the assurance of a gratuitous pardon. And yet the Apostle, by referring the prophecy of Jeremiah to the coming of Christ, seems to rob them of these blessings. To this I reply, that he does not expressly deny that God formerly wrote his Law on their hearts and pardoned their sins, but he makes a comparison between the less and the greater. As then the Father has put forth more fully the power of his Spirit under the kingdom of Christ, and has poured forth more abundantly his mercy on mankind, this exuberance renders insignificant the small portion of grace which he had been pleased to bestow on the fathers. We also see that the promises were then obscure and intricate, so that they shone only like the moon and stars in comparison with the clear light of the Gospel which shines brightly on us.

If it be objected and said, that the faith and obedience of Abraham so excelled, that hardly any such an example can at this day be found in the whole world; my answer is this, that the question here is not about persons, but that reference is made to the economical condition of the Church. Besides, whatever spiritual gifts the fathers obtained, they were accidental as it were to their age; for it was necessary for them to direct their eyes to Christ in order to become possessed of them. Hence it was not without reason that the Apostle, in comparing the Gospel with the Law, took away from the latter what is peculiar to the former. There is yet no reason why God should not have extended the grace of the new covenant to the fathers. This is the true solution of the question.

11. *And they shall not teach, etc.* We have said that the third point is as it were a part of the second, included in these words, *I will put my laws in their mind*; for it is the work of the Spirit of

God to illuminate our minds, so that we may know what the will of God is, and also to bend our hearts to obedience. For the right knowledge of God is a wisdom which far surpasses the comprehension of man's understanding; therefore, to attain it no one is able except through the secret revelation of the Spirit. Hence Isaiah, in speaking of the restoration of the Church, says, that all God's children would be his disciples or scholars. (Isaiah xxviii. 16.) The meaning of our Prophet is the same when he introduces God as saying, *They shall know me.* For God does not promise what is in our own power, but what he alone can perform for us. In short, these words of the Prophet are the same as though he had said, that our minds are blind and destitute of all right understanding until they are illuminated by the Spirit of God. Thus God is rightly known by those alone to whom he has been pleased by a special favor to reveal himself.

By saying, *From the least to the greatest,* he first intimates that God's grace would be poured on all ranks of men, so that no class would be without it. He, secondly, reminds us that no rude and ignorant men are precluded from this heavenly wisdom, and that the great and the noble cannot attain it by their own acuteness or by the help of learning. Thus God connects the meanest and the lowest with the highest, so that their ignorance is no impediment to the one, nor can the other ascend so high by their own acumen; but the one Spirit is equally the teacher of them all.

Fanatical men take hence the occasion to do away with public preaching, as though it were of no use in Christ's kingdom; but their madness may be easily exposed. Their objection is this: "After the coming of Christ every one is to teach his neighbor; away then with the external ministry, that a place may be given to the internal inspiration of God." But they pass by this, that the Prophet does not wholly deny that they would teach one another, but his words are these, *They shall not teach, saying, Know the Lord;* as though he had said, "Ignorance shall not as heretofore so possess the minds of men as not to know who God is." But we know that the use of teaching is twofold; first, that they who are wholly ignorant may learn the first elements; and secondly, that those who are initiated may make progress. As then Christians, as long as they live, ought to make progress, it cannot surely be said, that any one is so wise that he needs not to be taught; so that no small part of our wisdom is a teachable spirit. And what is the way of making progress if we desire to be the disciples of Christ? This is shown to us by Paul when he says, that Christ gave pastors and teachers. (Ephesians iv. 11.) It hence appears that nothing less was thought of by the Prophet than to rob the Church of such a benefit.[135] His only object was to show that God would make himself known to small and great, according to what was also predicted by Joel ii. 28. It ought also in passing to be noticed, that this light of sacred knowledge is promised peculiarly to the Church; hence this passage belongs to none but to the household of faith.[136]

13. *In that he saith, A new, etc.* From the fact of one covenant being established, he infers the subversion of the other; and by calling it the old covenant, he assumes that it was to be abrogated; for what is old tends to a decay.[137] Besides, as the new is substituted, it must be that the former has come to an end; for the second, as it has been said, is of another character. But if the

---

135 It is a sufficient answer to the fanatics here alluded to, that their conclusion from his text militates against the practice of the apostolic Church as established by Christ himself, he having sent apostles, evangelists, pastors and teachers. — *Ed.*

136 The 12th verse is passed over. It differs in words, though not in substance, both from the Hebrew and the Sept. It is indeed the latter version with the addition of these words, "and their iniquities." The nouns are in the singular number in Hebrew, "unrighteousness" and "sin." When the Apostle quotes again the passage in chapter x. 17, he leaves out "unrighteousness," and mentions only "sins and iniquities." There is also a shade of difference as to the first verb. In Hebrew remission or forgiveness is its meaning, but here the idea is mercy. The Apostle no doubt considered that the truth was essentially conveyed in the Greek version. — *Ed.*

137 This verse may be thus rendered, —
"By saying, 'a new covenant,' he has made ancient the first: now what is ancient and becomes old is nigh a dissolution (or disappearing.)"
It is said to be ancient in contrast with the new; and old or aged is afterwards added to be ancient in order to show its weak and feeble character, being like an old man tottering on the brink of the grave, who, when buried, disappears from among the living. It is supposed that there is here an intimation of the dissolution of the whole Jewish polity, which soon afterwards took place. — *Ed.*

whole dispensation of Moses, as far as it was opposed to the dispensation of Christ, has passed away, then the ceremonies also must have ceased.

CHAPTER 9

HEBREWS IX. 1-5

1. Then verily the first *covenant* had also ordinances of divine service, and a worldly sanctuary.
2. For there was a tabernacle made; the first, wherein *was* the candlestick, and the table, and the shewbread; which is called the sanctuary.
3. And after the second veil, the tabernacle which is called the Holiest of all;
4. Which had the golden censer, and the ark of the covenant overlaid round about with gold, wherein *was* the golden pot that had manna, and Aaron's rod that budded, and the tables of the covenant;
5. And over it the cherubims of glory shadowing the mercyseat; of which we cannot now speak particularly.

1 *Then verily the first, etc*[138] After having spoken generally of the abrogation of the old covenant, he now refers specially to the ceremonies. His object is to show that there was nothing practiced then to which Christ's coming has not put an end. He says first, that under the old covenant there was a specific form of divine worship, and that it was peculiarly adapted to that time. It will hereafter appear by the comparison what kind of things were those rituals prescribed under the Law.

---

138 Rather, "Yet even the first," etc. It is connected with the last verse of the preceding chapter; as though he had said, — "Though the covenant is become antiquated, yet it had many things divinely appointed connected with it." Μὲν οὖν mean "yet," or however. See Art. viii. 4. Macknight has "Now verily;" and Stuart, "Moreover." — *Ed*

Some copies read, πρώτη σκηνὴ the first tabernacle; but I suspect that there is a mistake as to the word "tabernacle;" nor do I doubt but that some unlearned reader, not finding a noun to the adjective, and in his ignorance applying to the tabernacle what had been said of the covenant, unwisely added the word σκηνὴ tabernacle. I indeed greatly wonder that the mistake had so prevailed, that it is found in the Greek copies almost universally.[139] But necessity constrains me to follow the ancient reading. For the Apostle, as I have said, had been speaking of the old covenant; he now comes to ceremonies, which were additions, as it were, to it. He then intimates that all the rites of the Mosaic Law were a part of the old covenant, and that they partook of the same ancientness, and were therefore to perish.

Many take the word λατρείας as an accusative plural. I agree with those who connect the two words together, δικαιώματα λατρείας for institutes or rites, which the Hebrews call חוקים, and the Greeks have rendered by the word δικαιώματα ordinances. The sense is, that the whole form or manner of worshipping God was annexed to the old covenant, and that it consisted of sacrifices, ablutions, and other symbols, together with the sanctuary. And he calls it a *worldly sanctuary*, because there was no heavenly truth or reality in those rites; for though the sanctuary was the effigy of the original pattern which had been shown to Moses; yet an effigy or image is a different thing from the reality, and especially when they are compared, as here, as things opposed to each other. Hence the sanctuary in itself was indeed earthly, and is rightly classed among the elements of the world, it was yet heavenly as to what it signified.[140]

---

139 It has since been discovered that it is not found in many of the best MSS., and is dismissed from the text by Griesbach and all modern critics. The noun understood is evidently "covenant," spoken of in the preceding chapter. — *Ed*.

140 Many, such as Grotius, Beza, etc., consider that "ordinances" and "services" (not service) are distinct, and both in the objective case, and render the words "rituals, services, and a wordly sanctuary." And if the sequel is duly examined, it will be found that this is the right construction. The Apostle, according to the manner of the prophet, reverses the order, and speaks distinctly of these three particulars, — first, "the wordly sanctuary" — the tabernacle in verses 2, 3, 4, and 5; secondly, "the services" in verses 6 and 7; and thirdly, "the rituals" in verse 10, where the word

2. *For there was a tabernacle, etc.* As the Apostle here touches but lightly on the structure of the tabernacle, that he might not be detained beyond what his subject required; so will I also designedly abstain from any refined explanation of it. It is then sufficient for our present purpose to consider the tabernacle in its three parts, — the first was the court of the people; the middle was commonly called the sanctuary; and the last was the inner sanctuary, which they called, by way of eminence, *the holy of holies.* [141]

As to the first sanctuary, which was contiguous to the court of the people, he says that there were the *candlestick* and *the table* on which the *shew-bread* was set: he calls this place, in the plural number, the holies. Then, after this is mentioned, the most secret place, which they called the holy of holies, still more remote from the view of the people, and it was even hid from the priests who ministered in the first sanctuary; for as by a veil the sanctuary was closed up to the people, so another veil kept the priests from the holy of holies. There, the Apostle says, was the θυμιατήριον by which name I understand the altar of incense, or fumigation, rather than the censer;[142] then *the ark of the covenant,* with its covering, *the two cherubim, the golden pot* filled with *manna, the rod of Aaron, and the two tables.* Thus far the Apostle proceeds in describing the tabernacle.

But he says that the pot in which Moses had deposited the manna, and Aaron's rod which had budded, were in the ark with the two tables; but this seems inconsistent with sacred his-

---

"ordinances" again occur. There can therefore be hardly a doubt as to the construction of the first verse. The sanctuary is called worldly in contrast with what is heavenly or divine, not made with hands: see verse 11. — *Ed.*

141 See Appendix F2.

142 This is evidently a mistake, for the altar of incense was in the sanctuary — the first tabernacle. See Exodus xxx. 1-6. The word is used in the Sept., for "censer," 2 Chronicles xxvi. 19. There were many censors made, as it is supposed, of brass; for they were daily used in the sanctuary for incense; but this golden censor was probably used only on the day of expiation, when the chief priest entered the holiest place; and the probability is, though there is no account of this in the Old Testament, that it was laid up or deposited, as Stuart suggests, in the holy of holies. — *Ed.*

tory, which in 1 King s viii. 9, relates that there was nothing in the ark but the two tables. But it is easy to reconcile these two passages: God had commanded the pot and Aaron's rod to be laid up before the testimony; it is hence probable that they were deposited in the ark, together with the tables. But when the Temple was built, these things were arranged in a different order, and certain history relates it as a thing new that the ark had nothing else but the two tables.[143]

5. *Of which we cannot now, etc.* As nothing can satisfy, curious men, the apostle cuts off every occasion for refinements unsuitable to his present purpose, and lest a longer discussion of these things should break off the thread of his argument. If, therefore, any one should disregard the Apostle's example, and dwell more minutely on the subject, he would be acting very unreasonably. There might be, indeed, an occasion for doing this elsewhere; but it is now better to attend to the subject of which he treats: it may further be said, that to philosophize beyond just limits, which some do, is not only useless, but also dangerous. There are some things which are not obscure and fitted for the edification of faith; but discretion and sobriety ought to be observed, lest we seek to be wise above what God has been pleased to reveal.

HEBREWS IX. 6-12

6. Now when these things were thus ordained, the priests went always into the first tabernacle, accomplishing the service *of God*
7. But into the second *went* the high priest alone once every year, not without blood, which he offered for himself, and *for* the errors of the people:
8. The Holy Ghost this signifying, that the way into the holiest of all was not yet made manifest, while as the first tabernacle was yet standing:

---

143 Stuart observes, "Our author is speaking of the tabernacle, and not of the temple; still less of the second temple, which must have lacked even the tables of testimony. The probability is, that the ark, during its many removals, and in particular during its captivity by the Philistines, was deprived of those sacred deposits; for we hear no more concerning them." — *Ed.*

9. *Which was* a figure for the time then present, in which were offered both gifts and sacrifices, that could not make him that did the service perfect, as pertaining to the conscience;
10. *Which stood* only in meats and drinks, and divers washings, and carnal ordinances, imposed *on them* until the time of reformation.
11. But Christ being come an high priest of good things to come, by a greater and more perfect tabernacle, not made with hands, that is to say, not of this building;
12. Neither by the blood of goats and calves, but by his own blood he entered in once into the holy place, having obtained eternal redemption *for us*

6. *Now, when these things were thus ordained, etc.* Omitting other things, he undertakes to handle the chief point in dispute: he says that the priests who performed sacred rites were wont to enter the first tabernacle daily, but that the chief priest entered the holy of holies only yearly with the appointed sacrifice. He hence concludes, that while the tabernacle under the Law was standing, the sanctuary was closed up, and that only through that being removed could the way be open for us to the kingdom of God. We see that the very form of the ancient tabernacle reminded the Jews that they were to look for something else. Then foolishly did they act who, by retaining the shadows of the Law, willfully obstructed their own way.

He mentions πρώτην σκηνὴν the first tabernacle, in ver. 2, in a different sense from what it has here, for here it means the first sanctuary, but there the whole tabernacle; for he sets it in opposition to the spiritual sanctuary of Christ, which he presently mentions. He contends that this had fallen for our great benefit, for through its fall a more familiar access to God has been obtained for us.

7. *For himself and for the errors of the people,* or for his own and the ignorances of the people. As the verb שגג, *shegag,* means in Hebrew to err, to mistake, so שגגה, *shegage,* derived from it, properly denotes error, or mistake; but yet it is generally taken for any kind of sin; and doubtless we never sin except when deceived by the allurements of Satan. The Apostle does not understand by it mere ignorance, as they say, but, on the contrary, he includes also voluntary sins; but as I have already said, no sin is free from error or ignorance; for however knowingly and willfully any one may sin, yet it must be that he is blinded by his lust, so that he does not judge rightly, or rather he forgets himself and God; for men never deliberately rush headlong into ruin, but being entangled in the deceptions of Satan, they lose the power of judging rightly.[144]

9. *Which was a figure, etc.* The word παραθολὴ, used here, signifies, as I think, the same thing with ἀντίτυπος, antitype; for he means that that tabernacle was a second pattern which corresponded with the first. For the portrait of a man ought to be so like the man himself, that when seen, it ought immediately to remind us of him whom it represents. He says further, that it was a *figure,* or likeness, *for the time then present,* that is, as long as the external observance was in force; and he says this in order to confine its use and duration to the time of the Law; for it means the same with what he afterwards adds, that all the ceremonies were imposed until the time of reformation; nor is it any objection that he uses the present tense in saying, *gifts are offered;* for as he had to do with the Jews, he speaks by way of concession, as though he were one of those who sacrificed. *Gifts* and *sacrifices* differ, as the first is a general term, and the other is particular.

That could not make him that did the service perfect as pertaining to the conscience; that is, they did not reach the soul so as to confer true holiness. I do not reject the words, *make perfect,* and yet I prefer the term *sanctify,* as being more suitable to the context. But that readers may better understand the meaning of the Apostle, let the contrast between the flesh and the conscience

---

144 It is said that the high priest entered the holiest place "once every year," that is, on one day, the day of expiation, every year; but on that day he went in at least three times. See Leviticus xvi. 12-15; and probably four times, according to the Jewish tradition; and one of the times, as supposed by Stuart, was for the purpose of bringing out the golden censer.

The word rendered "errors," literally means "ignorances," and so some render it "sins of ignorance;" but it is used in the Apocrypha as designating sins in general; and Grotius refers to Tob. iii. 3; Judith v. 20; Sirach xxiii. 2, 1 Macc. xiii. 39. And that it means sins of all kinds is evident from the account given in Leviticus 16 of the atonement made on the annual man, says Estius, "is ignorant; and all sins proceed from error in judgement." Hence it seems, sins were called ignorances. — *Ed.*

be noticed; he denies that worshippers could be spiritually and inwardly cleansed by the sacrifices of the Law. It is added as a reason, that all these rites were of the flesh or carnal. What then does he allow them to be? It is commonly supposed, that they were useful only as means of training to men, conducive to virtue and decorum. But they who thus think do not sufficiently consider the promises which are added. This gloss, therefore, ought to be wholly repudiated. Absurdly and ignorantly too do they interpret *the ordinances of the flesh,* as being such as cleansed or sanctified only the body; for the Apostle understands by these words that they were earthly symbols, which did not reach the soul; for though they were true testimonies of perfect holiness, yet they by no means contained it in themselves, nor could they convey it to men; for the faithful were by such helps led, as it were, by the hand to Christ, that they might obtain from him what was wanting in the symbols.

Were any one to ask why the Apostle speaks with so little respect and even with contempt of Sacraments divinely instituted, and extenuates their efficacy? This he does, because he separates them from Christ; and we know that when viewed in themselves they are but beggarly elements, as Paul calls them. (Galatians iv. 9.)

10. *Until the time of reformation, etc.* Here he alludes to the prophecy of Jeremiah. (Jeremiah xxxi. 31.) The new covenant succeeded the old as a reformation. He expressly mentions *meats* and *drinks,* and other things of minor importance, because by these trifling observances a more certain opinion may be formed how far short was the Law of the perfection of the Gospel.[145]

11. *But Christ being come, etc.* He now sets before us the reality of the things under the Law, that it may turn our eyes from them to itself; for he who believes that the things then shadowed forth under the Law have been really found in Christ, will no longer cleave to the shadows, but will embrace the substance and the genuine reality.

But the particulars of the comparison between Christ and the ancient high priest, ought to be carefully noticed. He had said that the high priest alone entered the sanctuary once a year with blood to expiate sins. Christ is in this life the ancient high priests for he alone possesses the dignity and the office

---

145 See Appendix G2.

of a high priest; but he differs from him in this respect, that he brings with him eternal blessings which secure a perpetuity to his priesthood. Secondly, there is this likeness between the ancient high priest and ours, that both entered the holy of holies through the sanctuary; but they differ in this, that Christ alone entered into heaven through the temple of his own body. That the holy of holies was once every year opened to the high priest to make the appointed expiation — this obscurely prefigured the one true sacrifice of Christ. To enter once then was common to both, but to the earthly it was every year, while it was to the heavenly forever, even to the end of the world. The offering of blood was common to both; but there was a great difference as to the blood; for Christ offered, not the blood of beasts, but his own blood. Expiation was common to both; but that according to the Law, as it was inefficacious, was repeated every year; but the expiation made by Christ is always effectual and is the cause of eternal salvation to us. Thus, there is great importance almost in every word. Some render the words, "But Christ standing by," or asking; but the meaning of the Apostle is not thus expressed; for he intimates that when the Levitical priests had for the prefixed time performed their office, Christ came in their place, according to what we found in the seventh chapter.

Of good things to come, etc. Take these for eternal things; for as μέλλων καιρός, time to come, is set in opposition to the present τῷ ἐνεστηκότι; so future blessings are to the present. The meaning is, that we are led by Christ's priesthood into the celestial kingdom of God, and that we are made partakers of spiritual righteousness and of eternal life, so that it is not right to desire anything better. Christ alone, then, has that by which he can retain and satisfy us in himself.[146]

By a greater and more perfect tabernacle, etc. Though this passage is variously explained, yet I have no doubt but that he means the body of Christ; for as there was formerly an access for the Levitical high priest to the holy of holies through the sanctuary, so Christ through his own body entered into the glory of heaven; for as he had put on our flesh and in it suffered, he obtained for himself this privilege, that he should appear before

---

146 "Good things (or blessings) to come," may have a reference to the blessings promised in the Old Testament as the blessings of the kingdom of Christ, included in "the eternal redemption" mentioned in the next verse. — *Ed.*

God as a Mediator for us. In the first place, the word sanctuary is fitly and suitably applied to the body of Christ, for it is the temple in which the whole majesty of God dwells. He is further said to have made a way for us by his body to ascend into heaven, because in that body he consecrated himself to God, he became in it sanctified to be our true righteousness, he prepared himself in it to offer a sacrifice; in a word, he made himself in it of no reputation, and suffered the death of the cross; therefore, the Father highly exalted him and gave him a name above every name, that every knee should bow to him. (Philippians ii. 8-10.) He then entered into heaven through his own body, because on this account it is that he now sits at the Father's right hand; he for this reason intercedes for us in heaven, because he had put on our flesh, and consecrated it as a temple to God the Father, and in it sanctified himself to obtain for us an eternal righteousness, having made an expiation for our sins.[147]

It may however seem strange, that he denies the body of Christ to be *of this building;* for doubtless he proceeded from

---

[147] There is no other view that is satisfactory. The idea that has been by some suggested, that the "better tabernacle" is the visible heaven through which he entered into the heaven of heavens, has no evidence in its support. Some of the Ancients, such as Ambrose, and also Doddridge and Scott consider heaven as intended, as in chapter viii. 2, (but "tabernacle" in that passage means the whole structure, especially the holy of holies.) According to this view διὰ is rendered in — "in a greater and more perfect tabernacle." But Chrysostom, Theophylact, Grotius, Beza, etc., agree with Calvin in regarding Christ's human nature as signified by the "tabernacle;" and what confirms this exposition is what we find in chapter x. 5, 10, and 20. "Not made with hands," and "not of this creation," for no objection; for Christ's body was supernaturally formed; and the contrast is with the material tabernacle, a human structure, made by men and made of earthly materials. It is, however, better to connect "tabernacle" with the preceding than with the following words, —

But Christ, having come the high priest of the good things to come by means of a better and more perfect tabernacle, not made with hands, that is, not of this creation, has entered once for all into the holiest, not indeed with (or by) the blood of goats and calves but (or by) his own blood, having obtained an eternal redemption.

"Creation" here means the world; it was not made of worldy materials. See verse 1. — *Ed.*

the seed of Abraham, and was liable to sufferings and to death. To this I reply, that he speaks not here of his material body, or of what belongs to the body as such, but of the spiritual efficacy which emanates from it to us. For as far as Christ's flesh is quickening, and is a heavenly food to nourish souls, as far as his blood is a spiritual drink and has a cleansing power, we are not to imagine anything earthly or material as being in them. And then we must remember that this is said in allusion to the ancient tabernacle, which was made of wood, brass, skins, silver, and gold, which were all dead things; but the power of God made the flesh of Christ to be a living and spiritual temple.

12. *Neither by the blood of goats, etc.* All these things tend to show that the things of Christ so far excel the shadows of the Law, that they justly reduce them all to nothing. For what is the value of Christ's blood, if it be deemed no better than the blood of beasts? What sort of expiation was made by his death, if the purgations according to the Law be still retained? As soon then as Christ came forth with the efficacious influence of his death, all the typical observances must necessarily have ceased.

HEBREWS IX. 13-17

13. For if the blood of bulls and of goats, and the ashes of an heifer sprinkling the unclean, sanctifieth to the purifying of the flesh:
14. How much more shall the blood of Christ, who through the eternal Spirit offered himself without spot to God, purge your conscience from dead works to serve the living God?
15. And for this cause he is the mediator of the new testament, that by means of death, for the redemption of the transgressions *that were* under the first testament, they which are called might receive the promise of eternal inheritance.
16. For where a testament *is*, there must also of necessity be the death of the testator.
17. For a testament *is* of force after men are dead: otherwise it is of no strength at all while the testator liveth.

13. *For if the blood of bulls, etc.* This passage has given to many all occasion to go astray, because they did not consider that sacraments are spoken of, which had a spiritual import. The cleansing of the flesh they leave explained of what avails among men, as the heathens had their expiations to blot out the infamy of crimes. But this explanation is indeed very heathenish; for wrong is done to God's promises, if we restrict the effect to civil matters only. Often does this declaration occur in the writings of Moses, that iniquity was expiated when a sacrifice was duly offered. This is no doubt the spiritual teaching of faith. Besides, all the sacrifices were destined for this end, that they might lead men to Christ; as the eternal salvation of the soul is through Christ, so these were true witnesses of this salvation.

What then does the Apostle mean when he speaks of the purgations of the flesh? He means what is symbolical or sacramental, as follows, — If the blood of beasts was a true symbol of purgation, so that it cleansed in a sacramental manner, how much more shall Christ who is himself the truth, not only bear witness to a purgation by an external rite, but also really perform this for consciences? The argument then is from the signs to the thing signified; for the effect by a long time preceded the reality of the signs.

14. *Who through the eternal Spirit, etc.* He now clearly shows how Christ's death is to be estimated, not by the external act, but by the power of the Spirit. For Christ suffered as man; but that death becomes saving to us through the efficacious power of the Spirit; for a sacrifice, which was to be an eternal expiation, was a work more than human. And he calls the Spirit *eternal* for this reason, that we may know that the reconciliation, of which he is the worker or effecter, is eternal.[148] By saying, *without spot,*

---

[148] Some as Grotius and Schleusner, take "the eternal Spirit" as meaning the same thing as "endless life" in chapter vii. 16, — "who having (or in) an eternal spirit," or life, etc.; they give the sense of "in" to διὰ. The comparison they represent to be between perishable victims and the sacrifice of Christ, who possesses a spirit or life that is eternal.

Others, as Junius and Beza, consider Christ's divine nature as signified by "the eternal Spirit." Beza says, that it was the Deity united to humanity that consecrated the whole sacrifice and endued it with vivifying power. The view of Stuart can hardly be comprehended.

or unblamable, though he alludes to the victims under the Law, which were not to have a blemish or defect, he yet means, that Christ alone was the lawful victim and capable of appeasing God; for there was always in others something that might be justly deemed wanting; and hence he said before that the covenant of the Law was not ἀμεμπτον, blameless.

From dead works, etc. Understand by these either such works as produce death, or such as are the fruits or effects of death; for as the life of the soul is our union with God, so they who are alienated from him through sin may be justly deemed to be dead.

To serve the living God. This, we must observe, is the end of our purgation; for we are not washed by Christ, that we may plunge ourselves again into new filth, but that our purity may serve to glorify God. Besides, he teaches us, that nothing can proceed from us that can be pleasing to God until we are purified by the blood of Christ; for as we are all enemies to God before our reconciliation, so he regards as abominable all our works; hence the beginning of acceptable service is reconciliation. And then, as no work is so pure and so free from stains, that it can of itself please God, it is necessary that the purgation through the blood of Christ should intervene, which alone can efface all stains. And there is a striking contrast between the living God and dead works.

15. *And for this cause he is Mediator of the New Testament, etc.* He concludes that there is no more need of another priest, for Christ fulfills the office under the New Testament; for he claims not for Christ the honor of a Mediator, so that others may at

---

But the explanation most commonly adopted is that given here by Calvin that the Holy Spirit is meant, whose aid and influence are often mentioned in connection with Christ; see Matthew xii. 28; Acts i. 2; x. 38. Some MSS and fathers have "holy" instead of "eternal," but the greatest number and the best have the last word. Dr. Owen, Doddridge and Scott take this view. Why the Spirit is called "eternal" is not very evident. It may have been for the purpose of showing that the Spirit mentioned before in verse 8 is the same Spirit, he being eternal, and thus in order to prove that the offering of Christ was according to the divine will. God is said to be eternal in Romans xvi. 26, where a reference is made to the past and the present dispensation, with the view, as it seems, to show that he is the author of both. But perhaps the explanation of Calvin is the most suitable. — *Ed.*

the same time remain as such with him; but he maintains that all others were repudiated when Christ undertook the office. But that he might more fully confirm this fact, he mentions how he commenced to discharge his office of a Mediator; even through death intervening. Since this is found alone in Christ, being wanting in all others, it follows that he alone can be justly deemed a Mediator.[149]

He further records the virtue and efficacy of his death by saying that he paid the price for sins under the *first covenant* or testament, which could not be blotted out by the blood of beasts; by which words he was seeking draw away the Jews from the Law to Christ. For, if the Law was so weak that all the remedies it applied for expiating sins did by no means accomplish what they represented, who could rest in it as in a safe harbor? This one thing, then, ought to have been enough to stimulate them to seek for something better than the law; for they could not but be in perpetual anxiety. On the other hand, when we come to Christ, as we obtain in him a full redemption, there is nothing which can any more distress us. Then, in these words he shows that the Law is weak, that the Jews might no longer recumb on it; and he teaches them to rely on Christ, for in him is found whatever can be desired for pacifying consciences.

Now, if any one asks, whether sins under the Law where remitted to the fathers, we must bear in mind the solution already stated, — that they were remitted, but remitted through Christ. Then notwithstanding their external expiations, they were always held guilty. For this reason Paul says, that the Law was a handwriting against us. (Colossians ii. 14.) For when the sinner came forward and openly confessed that he was guilty before God, and acknowledged by sacrificing an innocent an-

---

149 Here begins a new subject, that the covenant, or it may be viewed as the resumption of what is found in chapter viii. 6, 7. "For this cause," or for this reason, refers, as it seems, to what follows, "in order that," ὅπως, etc. —

And for this reason is he the Mediator of a new covenant, in order that death being undergone for the redemption of transgressions under the first covenant, they who were called might receive the promise of the eternal inheritance.

As in Romans iii. 25, 26, the reference is to the retrospective effect of Christ's expiatory sacrifice. Hence "are called" is not correct; and the participle is in the past tense. To "receive the promise," means to enjoy its fulfillment. — *Ed.*

imal that he was worthy of eternal death, what did he obtain by his victim, except that he sealed his own death as it were by this handwriting? In short, even then they only reposed in the remission of sins, when they looked to Christ. But if only a regard to Christ took away sins, they could never have been freed from them, had they continued to rest in the Law. David indeed declares, that blessed is the man to whom sins are not imputed, (Psalm xxxii. 2;) but that he might be a partaker of this blessedness, it was necessary for him to leave the Law, and to have his eyes fixed on Christ; for if he rested in the Law, he could never have been freed from guilt.

They who are called, etc. The object of the divine covenant is, that having been adopted as children, we may at length be made heirs of eternal life. The Apostle teaches us that we obtain this by Christ. It is hence evident, that in him is the fulfillment of the covenant. But the *promise of the inheritance* is to be taken for the promised inheritance, as though he had said, "The promise of eternal life is not otherwise made to us to be enjoined, than through the death of Christ." Life, indeed, was formerly promised to the fathers, and the same has been the inheritance of God's children from the beginning, but we do not otherwise enter into the possession of it, than through the blood of Christ previously shed.

But he speaks of the *called,* that he might the more influence the Jews who were made partakers of this calling; for it is a singular favor, when we have the gift of the knowledge of Christ bestowed on us. We ought then to take the more heed, lest we neglect so valuable a treasure, and our thoughts should wander elsewhere. Some regard the *called* to be the elect, but incorrectly in my judgment; for the Apostle teaches here the same thing as we find in Romans iii. 25, that righteousness and salvation have been procured by the blood of Christ, but that we become partakers of them by faith.

16. *For where a testament is, etc.* Even this one passage is a sufficient proof, that this Epistle was not written in Hebrew; for ברית, *berit,* means in Hebrew a covenant, but not a testament; but in Greek, διαθήκη, includes both ideas; and the Apostle, alluding to its secondary meaning, holds that the promises should not have been otherwise ratified and valid, had they not been sealed by the death of Christ. And this he proves by referring to what is usually the case as to wills or testaments, the effect of which is suspended until the death of those whose wills they are.

The Apostle may yet seem to rest on too weak an argument, so that what he says may be easily disproved. For it may be said, that God made no testament or will under the Law; but it was a covenant that he made with the ancient people. Thus, neither from the fact nor from the name, can it be concluded that Christ's death was necessary. For if he infers from the fact, that Christ ought to have died, because a testament is not ratified except by the death of the testator, the answer may be this, that ברית, *berit*, the word ever used by Moses, is a covenant made between those who are alive, and we cannot think otherwise of the fact itself. Now, as to the word used, he simply alluded, as I have already said, to the two meanings it has in Greek; he therefore dwells chiefly on the thing in itself. Nor is it any objection to say, that it was a covenant that God made with his people; for that very covenant bore some likeness to a testament, for it was ratified by blood.[150]

We must ever hold this truth, that no symbols have ever been adopted by God unnecessarily or unsuitably. And God in establishing the covenant of the law made use of blood. Then it was not such a contract, as they say, between the living, as did not require death. Besides, what rightly belongs to a testament is, that it begins to take effect after death. If we consider that the Apostle reasons from the thing itself, and not from the word, and if we bear in mind that he avowedly takes as granted what I have already stated, that nothing has been instituted in vain by God, there will be no great difficulty.

If anyone objects and says, that the heathens ratified covenants according to the other meaning by sacrifices; this indeed I admit to be true; but God did not borrow the rite of sacrificing from the practice of the heathens; on the contrary, all the heathen sacrifices were corruptions, which had derived their origin from the institutions of God. We must then return to the same point, that the covenant of God which was made with blood, may be fitly compared to a testament, as it is of the same kind and character.

---

150 See Appendix H2.

HEBREWS IX. 18-23

18. Whereupon neither the first *testament* was dedicated without blood.
19. For when Moses had spoken every precept to all the people according to the law, he took the blood of calves and of goats, with water, and scarlet wool, and hyssop, and sprinkled both the book, and all the people,
20. Saying, This *is* the blood of the testament which God hath enjoined unto you.
21. Moreover he sprinkled with blood both the tabernacle, and all the vessels of the ministry.
22. And almost all things are by the law purged with blood; and without shedding of blood is no remission.
23. *It was* therefore necessary that the patterns of things in the heavens should be purified with these; but the heavenly things themselves with better sacrifices than these.

18. *Whereupon neither the first, etc.* It hence appears that the fact is what is mainly urged, and that it is not a question about the word, though the Apostle turned to his own purpose a word presented to his attention in that language in which he wrote, as though one, while speaking of God's covenant, which is often called in Greek μαρτυρία, a testimony, were to recommend it among other things under that title. And doubtless that is a testimony, μαρτυρία, to which angels from heaven has borne witness, and of which there have been so many illustrious witnesses on earth, even all the holy Prophets, Apostles, and a vast number of martyrs, and of which at last the Son of God himself became a surety. No one in such a discourse would deem any such thing as unreasonable. And yet the Hebrew word, תעודה, *toude*, will admit of no such meaning as a covenant; but as nothing is advanced but what is consistent with the thing itself, no scrupulous regard is to be paid to the meaning of a word.

The Apostle then says, that the old testament or covenant was *dedicated with blood.* He hence concludes, that men were even then reminded, that it could not be valid and efficacious except death intervened. For though the blood of beasts was then shed, yet, he denies that it availed to confine an everlasting covenant. That this may appear more clearly, we must notice the custom of sprinkling which he quotes from Moses. He first teaches us that the covenant was dedicated or consecrated, not that it had in itself anything profane; but as there is nothing so holy that men by their uncleanness will not defile, except God prevents it by making a renewal of all things, therefore the dedication was made on account of men, who alone wanted it.

He afterwards adds, that the *tabernacle and all the vessels*, and also the very *book* of the law, were *sprinkled;* by which rite the people were then taught, that God could not be sought or looked to for salvation, nor rightly worshipped, except faith in every case looked to an intervening blood. For the majesty of God is justly to be dreaded by us, and the way to his presence is nothing to us but a dangerous labyrinth, until we know that he is pacified towards us through the blood of Christ, and that this blood affords to us a free access. All kinds of worship are then faulty and impure until Christ cleanses them by the sprinkling of his blood.[151]

---

151 It is worthy of notice that the Apostle mentions here several things which are not particularly by Moses in Exodus xxiv. 3-8, where the account is given; and yet what is there stated sufficiently warrants the particulars mentioned here. The blood of "goats" is not mentioned, and yet burnt offerings are said to have been offered, and goats were so offered; see Leviticus i. 10. Moses says nothing of "scarlet wool and hyssop;" but he mentions "sprinkling," and this was commonly done thereby; see Leviticus xiv. 51. "Blood" only is mentioned by Moses; but we find that when sprinkled, "water" was often connected with it. See Leviticus xiv. 52; Numbers xix. 18 The main difficulty is respecting "the book" being sprinkled, which is not stated by Moses. But as the altar was sprinkled, there was the same reason for sprinkling the book, though that is not expressly mentioned. However, it is evident that this was the general opinion among the Jews, for otherwise the Apostle would not have mentioned it in an Epistle especially addressed to them.

Then the "tabernacle," it was not expressly mentioned that it was sprinkled with blood when consecrated; and this was some time after the covenant was made. The setting up of the tabernacle is mentioned in Exodus xl. 17-33. In the previous verses, 9 and 10, there is a direction given to anoint the tabernacle, and all its vessels, and also to hallow them and to anoint the alter, and to sanctify it. The hallowing or sanctifying was no doubt done by sprinkling them with blood. See as a proof of this Exodus xxix.

For the tabernacle was a sort of visible image of God; and as the *vessels* for ministering were destined for his service, so they were symbols of true worship. But since none of these were for salvation to the people, we hence reasonably conclude, that where Christ does not appear with his blood, we have nothing to do with God. So doctrine itself, however unchangeable may be the will of God, cannot be efficacious for our benefit, unless it be dedicated by blood, as is plainly set forth in this verse.

I know that others give a different interpretation; for they consider the tabernacle to be the body of the Church, and vessels the faithful, whose ministry God employs; but what I have stated is much more appropriate. For whenever God was to be called upon, they turned themselves to the sanctuary; and it was a common way of speaking to say that they stood before the Lord when they appeared in the temple.

20. *Saying, This is the blood of the testament,*[152] *etc.* If that was the blood of the testament, then neither the testament was without blood ratified, nor the blood without the testament available for expiation. It is hence necessary that both should be united; and we see that before the explanation of the Law, no symbol was added, for what would a sacrament be except the word preceded it? Hence a symbol is a kind of appendage to the word. And mark, this word was not whispered like a magic incantation, but pronounced with a clear voice, as it was destined for the people, according to what the words of the covenant express, *which God hath enjoined unto you.*[153] Perverted, then, are

---

21. We hence perceive how well acquainted the writer must have been with the Jewish rituals. — Ed.

152 Both Calvin and our verse retain the word "testament" as derived from verse 17; but as that verse and the preceding are to be viewed as parenthetic, the word "covenant" is the term used by Moses. The latter is the word adopted by Beza, Doddridge, Macknight, and Stuart, "This is the blood of the covenant," etc. — Ed.

153 The Apostle here follows neither the Hebrew nor the Septuagint. The Hebrew is "which the Lord (Jehovah) hath made with you;" and the Septuagint, "Which the Lord hath covenanted (διέθετο) with you." And instead of "Behold the blood of the covenant," (the same in both) we have here, "This is the blood of the covenant." But though the words are different, yet the meaning is

the sacraments, and it is a wicked corruption when there is no explanation of the commandment given, which is as it were the very soul of the sacrament. Hence the Papists, who take away the true understanding of things from signs, retain only dead elements.

This passage reminds us that the promises of God are then only profitable to us when they are confirmed by the blood of Christ. For what Paul testifies in 2 Corinthians i. 20, that all God's promises are yea and amen in Christ — this happens when his blood like a seal is engraven on our hearts, or when we not only hear God speaking, but also see Christ offering himself as a pledge for those things which are spoken. If this thought only came to our minds, that what we read is not written so much with ink as with the blood of Christ, that when the Gospel is preached, his sacred blood distills together with the voice, there would be far greater attention as well as reverence on our part. A symbol of this was the sprinkling mentioned by Moses!

At the same time there is more stated here than what is expressed by Moses; for he does not mention that the book and the people were sprinkled, nor does he name the *goats*, nor the *scarlet wool*, nor the *hyssop*. As to the book, that it was sprinkled cannot be clearly shown, yet the probability is that it was, for Moses is said to have produced it after he had sacrificed; and he did this when he bound the people to God by a solemn compact. With regard to the rest, the Apostle seems to have blended together various kinds of expiations, the reason for which was the same. Nor indeed was there anything unsuitable in this, since he was speaking of the general subject Or purgation under the Old Testament, which was done by means of blood. Now as to the sprinkling made by hyssop and scarlet wool, it is evident that it represented the mystical sprinkling made by the Spirit. We know that the hyssop possesses a singular power to cleanse and to purify; so Christ employs his Spirit to sprinkle us in order to wash us by his own blood when he leads us to true repentance, when he purifies us from the depraved lusts of our flesh, when he imbues us with the precious gift of his own righteousness. For it was not in vain that God had instituted this rite. David also alluded to this when he said,

---

essentially the same, — the main things regarded by the Apostles in their quotations. — *Ed*

"Thou wilt sprinkle me, O Lord, with hyssop, and I shall be cleansed." (Psalm li. 7.)

These remarks will be sufficient for those who wish to be sober-minded in their speculations.

22. *And almost all things, etc.* By saying *almost* he seems to imply that some things were otherwise purified. And doubtless they often washed themselves and other unclean things with water. But even water itself derived its power to cleanse from the sacrifices; so that the Apostle at length truly declares that without blood there was no remission.[154] Then uncleanness was imputed until it was expiated by a sacrifice. And as without Christ there is no purity nor salvation, so nothing without blood can be either pure or saving; for Christ is never to be separated from the sacrifice of his death. But the Apostle meant only to say that this symbol was almost always made use of. But if at any time the purgation was not so made, it was nevertheless through blood, since all the rites derived their efficacy in a manner from the general expiation. For the people were not each of them sprinkled, (for how could so small a portion of blood be sufficient for so large a multitude?) yet the purgation extended to all. Hence the particle *almost* signifies the same as though he had said, that the use of this rite was so common that they seldom omitted it in purgations. For what Chrysostom says, that unfitness is thus denoted, because these were only figures under the Law, is inconsistent with the Apostle's design.

No remission, etc. Thus men are prevented from appearing before God; for as he is justly displeased with them all, there is no ground for them to promise themselves any favor until he is pacified. But there is but one way of pacification, and that is by an expiation made by blood: hence no pardon of sins can be hoped for unless we bring blood, and this is done when we flee by faith to the death of Christ.

23. *The patterns,* or *exemplars, etc.* Lest any one should object and say that the blood by which the old testament was dedicated was different from that of a testator, the Apostle meets this objection, and says that it was no wonder that the tabernacle

---

154 Metals were purified by fire, and clothes by being washed in water, (Numbers xxxi. 22-24;) but these were purifications not accompanied with remission of sins. So that what is said here is literally true. — *Ed.*

which was earthly was consecrated by the sacrificing of beasts; for there was an analogy and a likeness between the purification and the things purified. But the heavenly pattern or exemplar of which he now speaks was to be consecrated in a very different way; there was here no need of goats or of calves. It hence follows that the death of the testator was necessary.

The meaning then is this, — as under the Law there were only earthly images of spiritual things, so the rite of expiation was also, so to speak, carnal and figurative; but as the heavenly pattern allows of nothing earthly, so it requires another blood than that of beasts, such as may correspond with its excellency. Thus the death of the testator is necessary, in order that the testament may be really consecrated.

He calls the kingdom of Christ *heavenly things*,[155] for it is spiritual and possesses a full revelation of the truth. *Better sacrifices* he mentions instead of "a better sacrifice," for it was only one; but he uses the plural number for the sake of the antithesis or contrast.

---

155 By making "heavenly things" to mean things in heaven above, and not in the kingdom of heaven on earth, commentators have been under the necessity of altering the sense of the word "purified." The tabernacle represented the whole kingdom of Christ, both on earth and in heaven. The sanctuary and the court, where the alter of burnt offering was, represented what Christ has done and is doing on earth; and the holy of holies was a representation of Christ's kingdom in heaven. The victims were slain in the court without the vail; the shedding of blood was the atonement, but its sprinkling was its purifying and sanctifying effects. All the heavenly things in the Church on earth require purifying by the sprinkling of the blood of the atoning sacrifice once offered by Christ; and it is to this the reference is made here. And having provided means for purification, he as the high priest, by virtue of his sacrifice, entered into the holiest, heavenly things on earth, for the Church here below, in order to prepare it for the holiest above. "In the heavens" may probably refer to two parts of Christ's kingdom, the one in heaven and the other on earth; and latter, as things which require a sacrifice; and then in the following verse the former part is alluded to, the kingdom above, even heaven, represented by the holy of holies. — *Ed.*

HEBREWS IX. 24-28

24. For Christ is not entered into the holy places made with hands, *which are* the figures of the true; but into heaven itself, now to appear in the presence of God for us:
25. Nor yet that he should offer himself often, as the high priest entereth into the holy place every year with blood of others;
26. For then must he often have suffered since the foundation of the world: but now once in the end of the world hath he appeared to put away sin by the sacrifice of himself.
27. And as it is appointed unto men once to die, but after this the judgment:
28. So Christ was once offered to bear the sins of many; and unto them that look for him shall he appear the second time without sin unto salvation.

24. *For Christ is not entered, etc.* This is a confirmation of the former verse. He had spoken of the true sanctuary, even the heavenly; he now adds that Christ entered there. It hence follows that a suitable confirmation is required. *The holy places* he takes for the sanctuary; he says that it is *not made with hands*, because it ought not to be classed with the created things which are subject to decay; for he does not mean here the *heaven* we see, and in which the stars shine, but the glorious kingdom of God which is above all the heavens. He calls the old sanctuary the ἀντίτυπον, the antitype of the true, that is, of the spiritual; for all the external figures represented as in a mirror what would have otherwise been above our corporeal senses. Greek writers sometimes use the same word in speaking of our sacraments, and wisely too and suitably, for every sacrament is a visible image of what is invisible.

Now to appear, etc. So formerly the Levitical priest stood before God in the name of the people, but typically; for in Christ is found the reality and the full accomplishment of what was typified. The ark was indeed a symbol of the divine presence; But it is Christ who really presents himself before God, and stands there to obtain favor for us, so that now there is no reason why we should flee from God's tribunal, since we have so kind an advocate, through whose faithfulness and protection we are made secure and safe. Christ was indeed our advocate when he was on earth; but it was a further concession made to our infirmity that he ascended into heaven to undertake there the office of an advocate. So that whenever mention is made of his ascension into heaven, this benefit ought ever to come to our minds, that he appears there before God to defend us by his advocacy. Foolishly, then, and unreasonably the question is asked by some, has he not always appeared there? For the Apostle speaks here only of his intercession, for the sake of which he entered the heavenly sanctuary.

25. *Nor yet that he should offer himself often, etc.* How, then, is he a priest, one may say, if he offers no sacrifices? To this I reply that it is not requited of a priest that he should be continually sacrificing; for even under the Law there were days appointed for the chief sacrifices every year; they had also their hours daily morning and evening. But as that only true sacrifice which Christ offered once for all is ever efficacious, and thus perpetual in its effects, it is no wonder that on its virtue, which never fails, Christ's eternal priesthood should be sustained. And here again he shows how and in what things Christ differs from the Levitical priest. Of the sanctuary he had spoken before; but he notices one difference as to the kind of sacrifice, for Christ offered himself and not an animal; and he adds another; that he repeated not his sacrifice, as under the Law, for the repetition there was frequent and even incessant.

26. *For then must he often have suffered, etc.* He shows how great an absurdity follows, if we do not count it enough that an expiation has been made by the one sacrifice of Christ. For he hence concludes that he must have died often; for death is connected with sacrifices. How this latter supposition is most unreasonable; it then follows that the virtue of the one sacrifice is eternal and extends to all ages. And he says *since the foundation of the world,* or from the beginning of the world[156] for in all

---

156 This sentence is not to be taken strictly in its literal meaning; for the world was founded and all things were set in due order before sin entered into it. The phrase is used in a similar way in Luke xi. 50. It is a popular mode of speaking intelligible to common readers though not suitable to over-nice and hair-splitting critics.

ages from the beginning there were sins which needed expiation. Except then the sacrifice of Christ was efficacious, no one of the fathers would have obtained salvation; for as they were exposed to God's wrath, a remedy for deliverance would have failed them, had not Christ by suffering once suffered so much as was necessary to reconcile men to God from the beginning of the world even to the end. Except then we look for many deaths, we must be satisfied with the one true sacrifice.

And hence it is evident how frivolous is the distinction, in the acuteness of which the Papists take so much delight; for they say that the sacrifice of Christ on the cross was bloody, but that the sacrifice of the mass which they pretend to offer daily to God, is unbloody. Were this subtle evasion adopted, then the Spirit of God would be accused of inadvertence, having not thought of such a thing; for the Apostle assumes it here as an admitted truth, that there is no sacrifice without death. I care nothing that ancient writers have spoken thus; for it is not in the power of men to invent sacrifices as they please. Here stands a truth declared by the Holy Spirit, that sins are not expiated by a sacrifice except blood be shed. Therefore the notion, that Christ is often offered, is a device of the devil.

But now once in the end of the world, etc. He calls that the end of the world or the consummation of the ages, which Paul calls "the fullness of time," (Galatians iv. 4;) for it was the maturity of that time which God had determined in his eternal purpose; and thus cut off is every occasion for men's curiosity, that they may not dare to inquire why it was no sooner, or why in that age rather than in another. For it behooves us to acquiesce in God's secret purpose, the reason for which appears clear to him, though it may not be evident to us. In short, the Apostle intimates that Christ's death was in due time, as he was sent into the world for this end by the Father, in whose power is the lawful right to regulate all things as well as time, and who ordains

---

The truth implied, as Beza observes, is, that sins since the beginning of the world have alone have been expiated by the blood of Christ, the virtue of which extends to all sins, past and future. The effects of his sufferings being perpetual and the same as to all ages, from the beginning to the end of the world, there was no necessity of having them repeated. As to their retrospective influence, see verse 15, and Romans iii. 25, 26 — *Ed.*

their succession with consummate wisdom, though often hid from us

This consummation is also set in opposition to the imperfection of past time; for God so held his ancient people in suspense, that it might have been easily concluded that things had not yet reached a fixed state. Hence Paul declares that the end of the ages had come upon us, (1 Corinthians x. 11;) by which he means that the kingdom of Christ contained the accomplishment of all things. But since it was the fullness of time when Christ appeared to expiate sins, they are guilty of offering him an atrocious insult, who seek to renew his sacrifice, as though all things were not completed by his death. He then appeared once for all; for had he done so once or twice, there must have been something defective in the first oblation; but this is inconsistent with fullness.

To put away, or *to destroy sin, etc.*[157] This agrees with Daniel's prophecy, in which the sealing up and the abolition of sins are promised, and in which it is also declared that there would be an end to sacrifices, (Daniel ix. 24-27;) for to what purpose are expiations when sins are destroyed? But this destruction is then only effected, when sins are not imputed to those who flee to the sacrifice of Christ; for though pardon is to be sought daily, as we daily provoke God's wrath; yet as we are reconciled to God in no other way than by the one death of Christ, sin is rightly said to be put away or destroyed by it.

27. *And as it is appointed, etc.* The meaning is this: since we patiently wait after death for the day of judgment, it being the common lot of nature which it is not right to struggle against; why should there be less patience in waiting for the second coming of Christ? For if a long interval of time does not diminish, as to men, the hope of a happy resurrection, how unreasonable would it be to render less honor to Christ? But less would it be,

---

157 Literally it is "for the abolishing of sin," as Doddridge renders it. The word occurs only in one other place, chapter vii. 18, and is rendered "disannulling;" and Macknight gives it that meaning here, taking "sin" in the sense of sin-offering, "He hath been manifested to abolish sin-offering by the sacrifice of himself." But this is inconsistent with the drift of the passage. To remove or abolish sin is doubtless what is meant. To "take away sin," is the version of Beza; and "to remove the punishment due to sin," is that of Stuart. — *Ed.*

were we to call upon him to undergo a second death, when he had once died. Were any one to object and say, that some had died twice, such as Lazarus, and not *once;* the answer would be this, — that the Apostle speaks here of the ordinary lot of men; but they are to be excepted from this condition, who shall by an instantaneous change put off corruption, (1 Corinthians xv. 51;) for he includes none but those who wait for a long time in the dust for the redemption of their bodies.

28. *The second time without sin, etc.* The Apostle urges this one thing, — that we ought not to be disquieted by vain and impure longings for new kinds of expiations, for the death of Christ is abundantly sufficient for us. Hence he says, that he once appeared and made a sacrifice to abolish sins, and that at his second coming he will make openly manifest the efficacy of his death, so that sin will have no more power to hurt us.[158]

To *bear,* or, take away sins, is to free from guilt by his satisfaction those who have sinned. He says the sins of *many,* that is, of all, as in Romans v. 15. It is yet certain that all receive no benefit from the death of Christ; but this happens, because their unbelief prevents them. At the same time this question is not to be discussed here, for the Apostle is not speaking of the few or of the many to whom the death of Christ may be available; but he simply means that he died for others and not for himself; and therefore he opposes many to one.[159]

But what does he mean by saying that Christ will *appear without sin?* Some say, without a propitiation or an expiatory sacrifice for sin, as the word sin is taken in Romans viii. 3; 2 Corinthians v. 21; and in many places in the writings of Moses; but in my judgment he intended to express something more suit-

---

158 "Was once offered," προσενεχθείς, — Grotius regarded this participle as having a reflective sense, "having once for all offered up himself;" and so does Stuart. The first aorist passive has often this sense. "By whom was he offered?" asks Theophylact; he answers, "by himself, he being a high priest." This amounts to the same thing. — *Ed*

159 "We are told that οἱ πολλοὶ is often equivalent to πάντες. It is not however quite certain that the Apostle here meant to express πάντων; the verse concludes with the mention of those who 'wait for him' i.e., who wait for Christ's second coming in humble hope of receiving their reward; and these manifestly are not the whole human race." — Bp. Middleton, quoted by Bloomfield. — *Ed*

able to his present purpose, namely, that Christ at his coming will make it known how truly and really he had taken away sins, so that there would be no need of any other sacrifice to pacify God; as though he had said, "When we come to the tribunal of Christ, we shall find that there was nothing wanting in his death."¹⁶⁰

And to the same effect is what he immediately adds, *unto salvation to them who look,* or wait *for him.* Others render the sentence differently, "To them who look for him unto salvation;" But the other meaning is the most appropriate; for he means that those shall find complete salvation who recumb with quiet minds on the death of Christ; for this looking for or wanting has a reference to the subject discussed. The Scripture indeed does elsewhere ascribe this in common to believers, that they look for the coming of the Lord, in order to distinguish them from the ungodly, by whom his coming is dreaded, (1 Thessalonians i. 10;) but as the Apostle now contends that we ought to acquiesce in the one true sacrifice of Christ, he calls it the looking for Christ, when we are satisfied with his redemption alone, and seek no other remedies or helps.¹⁶¹

---

160 Schleusner and Stuart consider "without sin" to mean "without sin-offering" without any sacrifice for sin. Doddridge and Scott take its meaning to be "without being in the likeness of sinful flesh," or, without that humiliating form in which he atoned for sin. Some have said, "without sin" being imputed to him. The construction which the passage seems to afford is this, "without bearing sin." The previous clause is that, to bear or to suffer for, he having made the first time a full and complete expiation.

To "bear sins," is not, as some say, to take them away, in allusion to the scape goat, but to endure the punishment due to them, to make an atonement for them. See 1 Peter ii. 24; where the same word to "bear," in connection with "sins," is used; and where it clearly means to bear the penalty of sin; the end of the verse is, "with whose stripes we are healed." — *Ed.*

161 Most commentators adopt the same view, as conveyed in our version, connecting "salvation" with appearing, such as Beza, Grotius, Doddridge, Scott and Stuart. — *Ed.*

CHAPTER 10

HEBREWS X. 1-4

1. For the law having a shadow of good things to come, *and* not the very image of the things, can never with those sacrifices which they offered year by year continually make the comers thereunto perfect.
2. For then would they not have ceased to be offered? because that the worshippers once purged should have had no more conscience of sins.
3. But in those *sacrifices there is* a remembrance again *made* of sins every year.
4. For *it is* not possible that the blood of bulls and of goats should take away sins.

1. *For the Law having a shadow, etc.* He has borrowed this similitude from the pictorial art; for a shadow here is in a sense different from what it has in Colossians ii. 17; where he calls the ancient rites or ceremonies shadows, because they did not possess the real substance of what they represented. But he now says that they were like rude lineaments, which shadow forth the perfect picture; for painters, before they introduce the living colors by the pencil, are wont to mark out the outlines of what they intend to represent. This indistinct representation is called by the Greeks σκιαγραφία, which you might call in Latin, *"umbratilem"*, shadowy. The Greeks had also the εἰκών, the full likeness. Hence also "eiconia" are called images (*imagines*) in Latin, which represent to the life the form of men or of animals or of places.

The difference then which the Apostle makes between the Law and the Gospel is this, — that under the Law was shadowed forth only in rude and imperfect lines what is under the Gospel set forth in living colors and graphically distinct. He thus confirms again what he had previously said, that the Law was not useless, nor its ceremonies unprofitable. For though there was not in them the image of heavenly things, finished, as they say, by the last touch of the artist; yet the representation, such as it was, was of no small benefit to the fathers; but still our condition is much more favorable. We must however observe, that the things which were shown to them at a distance are the same with those which are now set before our eyes. Hence to both the same Christ is exhibited, the same righteousness, sanctification, and salvation; and the difference only is in the manner of painting or setting them forth.

Of good things to come, etc. These, I think, are eternal things. I indeed allow that the kingdom of Christ, which is now present with us, was formerly announced as future; but the Apostle's words mean that we have a lively image of future blessings. He then understands that spiritual pattern, the full fruition of which is deferred to the resurrection and the future world. At the same time I confess again that these good things began to be revealed at the beginning of the kingdom of Christ; but what he now treats of is this, that they are not only future blessings as to the Old Testament, but also with respect to us, who still hope for them.

Which they offered year by year, etc. He speaks especially of the yearly sacrifice, mentioned in Leviticus 16, though all the sacrifices are here included under one kind. Now he reasons thus: When there is no longer any consciousness of sin, there is then no need of sacrifice; but under the Law the offering of the same sacrifice was often repeated; then no satisfaction was given to God, nor was guilt removed nor were consciences appeased; were it otherwise there would have been made an end of sacrificing. We must further carefully observe, that he calls those the same sacrifices which were appointed for a similar purpose; for a better notion may be formed of them by the design for which God instituted them, than by the different beasts which were offered.

And this one thing is abundantly sufficient to confute and expose the subtlety of the Papists, by which they seem to themselves ingeniously to evade an absurdity in defending the sacrifice of the mass; for when it is objected to them that the repetition of the sacrifice is superfluous, since the virtue of that sacrifice which Christ offered is perpetual, they immediately reply that the sacrifice in the mass is not different but the same. This is their answer. But what, on the contrary, does the Apostle say? He expressly denies that the sacrifice which is repeatedly offered, though the same, is efficacious or capable of making an atonement. Now, though the Papists should cry out a thousand times that the sacrifice which Christ once offered is the same with, and not different from what they make daily, I shall still always contend, according to the express words of the Apostle, that since the offerings of Christ availed to pacify God, not only an end was put to former sacrifices, but that it is also impious to repeat the sacrifice. It is hence quite evident that the offering of Christ in the mass is sacrilegious.[162]

3. *A remembrance again*, etc. Though the Gospel is a message of reconciliation with God, yet it is necessary that we should daily remember our sins; but what the Apostle means is, that sins were brought to remembrance that guilt might be removed by the means of the sacrifice then offered. It is not, then, any

---

162 No remark is made on the second verse. Doddridge and Beza read the first clause without negative οὐκ and not as a question, according to the Vulg. And the Syr. Versions, "Otherwise they would have ceased to be offered." Most MSS. favor our present reading. There is no real difference in the meaning.

The words, "no more conscience of sins," are rendered by Beza, "no more conscious of sins;" by Doddridge, "no more consciousness of sins;" and by Stuart, "no longer conscious of sins." The true meaning is no doubt thus conveyed. We meet with two other instances of conscience, συνειδήσης, being followed by what may be called the genitive case of the object, "conscience of the idol," i.e., as to the idol, 1 Corinthians viii. 7, — "conscience of God," i.e., as to God, or towards God, 1 Peter ii. 19. And here, "conscience of sins," must mean conscience with reference to sins, i.e., conviction of sins, a conscience apprehensive of what sins deserve. It is a word, says Parkhurst, which "is rarely found in the ancient heathen writers;" but it occurs often in the New Testament, though not but once in the Sept., Ecclesiastes x. 20. Its common meaning is conscience, and not consciousness, though it may be so rendered here, consistently with the real meaning of the passage. Michaelis in his Introduction to the New Testament, is referred to by Parkhurst, as having produced two instances, one from Philo, and the other from Diod. Siculus, in which it means "consciousness." — Ed

kind of remembrance that is here meant, but that which might lead to such a confession of guilt before God, as rendered a sacrifice necessary for its removal.

Such is the sacrifice of the mass with the Papists; for they pretend that by it the grace of God is applied to us in order that sins may be blotted out. But since the Apostle concludes that the sacrifices of the Law were weak, because they were every year repeated in order to obtain pardon, for the very same reason it may be concluded that the sacrifice of Christ was weak, if it must be daily offered, in order that its virtue may be applied to us. With whatever masks, then, they may cover their mass, they can never escape the charge of an atrocious blasphemy against Christ.

4. *For it is not possible, etc.* He confirms the former sentiment with the same reason which he had adduced before, that the blood of beasts could not cleanse souls from sin. The Jews, indeed, had in this a symbol and a pledge of the real cleansing; but it was with reference to another, even as the blood of the calf represented the blood of Christ. But the Apostle is speaking here of the efficacy of the blood of beasts in itself. He therefore justly takes away from it the power of cleansing. There is also to be understood a contrast which is not expressed, as though he had said, "It is no wonder that the ancient sacrifices were insufficient, so that they were to be offered continually, for they had nothing in them but the blood of beasts, which could not reach the conscience; but far otherwise is the power of Christ's blood: It is not then right to measure the offering which he has made by the former sacrifices."

HEBREWS X. 5-10

5. Wherefore when he cometh into the world, he saith, Sacrifice and offering thou wouldest not, but a body hast thou prepared me:
6. In burnt offerings and *sacrifices* for sin thou hast had no pleasure.
7. Then said I, Lo, I come (in the volume of the book it is written of me,) to do thy will, O God.

8. Above when he said, Sacrifice and offering and burnt offerings and *offering* for sin thou wouldest not, neither hadst pleasure *therein*; which are offered by the law;
9. Then said he, Lo, I come to do thy will, O God. He taketh away the first, that he may establish the second.
10. By the which will we are sanctified through the offering of the body of Jesus Christ once *for all*

5. *Wherefore, when he cometh, etc.* This entering into the world was the manifestation of Christ in the flesh; for when he put on man's nature that he might be a Redeemer to the world and appeared to men, he is said to have then come into the world, as elsewhere he is said to have descended from heaven. (John vi. 41.) And yet the fortieth Psalm, which he quotes, seems to be improperly applied to Christ, for what is found there by no means suits his character, such as, "My iniquities have laid hold on me," except we consider that Christ willingly took on himself the sins of his members. The whole of what is said, no doubt, rightly accords with David; but as it is well known that David was a type of Christ, there is nothing unreasonable in transferring to Christ what David declared respecting himself, and especially when mention is made of abolishing the ceremonies of the Law, as the case is in this passage. Yet all do not consider that the words have this meaning, for they think that sacrifices are not here expressly repudiated, but that the superstitious notion which had generally prevailed, that the whole worship of God consisted in them, is what is condemned; and if it be so, it may be said that this testimony has little to do with the present question. It behoves us, then, to examine this passage more minutely, that it may appear evident whether the apostle has fitly adduced it.

Everywhere in the Prophets sentences of this kind occur, that sacrifices do not please God, that they are not required by him, that he sets no value on them; nay, on the contrary, that they are an abomination to him. But then the blame was not in the sacrifices themselves, but what was adventitious to them was referred to; for as hypocrites, while obstinate in their impiety, still sought to pacify God with sacrifices, they were in this manner reproved. The Prophets, then, rejected sacrifices, not as they were instituted by God, but as they were vitiated by wicked men, and profaned through unclean consciences. But here the reason is different, for he is not condemning sacrifices offered in hypocrisy, or otherwise not rightly performed through the depravity and wickedness of men; but he denies that they are required of the faithful and sincere worshippers of God; for he speaks of himself who offered them with a clean heart and pure hands, and yet he says that they did not please God.

Were any one to except and say that they were not accepted on their own account or for their own worthiness, but for the sake of something else, I should still say that unsuitable to this place is an argument of this kind; for then would men be called back to spiritual worship, when ascribing too much to external ceremonies; then the Holy Spirit would be considered as declaring that ceremonies are nothing with God, when by men's error they are too highly exalted.

David, being under the Law, ought not surely to have neglected the rite of sacrificing. He ought, I allow, to have worshipped God with sincerity of heart; but it was not lawful for him to omit what God had commanded, and he had the command to sacrifice in common with all the rest. We hence conclude that he looked farther than to his own age, when he said, *Sacrifice thou wouldest not*. It was, indeed, in some respects true, even in David's time, that God regarded not sacrifices; but as they were yet all held under the yoke of the schoolmaster, David could not perform the worship of God in a complete manner, unless when clothed, so to speak, in a form of this kind. We must, then, necessarily come to the kingdom of Christ, in order that the truth of God's unwillingness to receive sacrifice may fully appear. There is a similar passage in Psalm xvi. 10, "Thou wilt not suffer thine holy one to see corruption;" for though God delivered David for a time from corruption, yet this was not fully accomplished except in Christ.

There is no small importance in this, that when he professes that he would do the *will* of God, he assigns no place to sacrifices; for we hence conclude that without them there may be a perfect obedience to God, which could not be true were not the Law annulled. I do not, however, deny but that David in this place, as well as in Psalm li. 16, so extenuated external sacrifices as to prefer to them that which is the main thing; but there is no doubt but that in both places he cast his eyes on the kingdom of Christ. And thus the Apostle is a witness, that Christ is justly introduced as the speaker in this Psalm, in which not even the lowest place among God's commandments is allowed to sacrifices, which God had yet strictly required under the Law.

But a body hast thou prepared me, etc. The words of David are different, "An ear hast thou bored for me," a phrase which some think has been borrowed from an ancient rite or custom of the Law, (Exodus xxi. 6;) for if any one set no value on the liberty granted at the jubilee, and wished to be under perpetual servitude, his ear was bored with an awl. The meaning, as they thinks was this, "Thou shalt have me, O Lord, as a servant forever." I, however, take another view, regarding it as intimating docility and obedience; for we are deaf until God opens our ears, that is, until he corrects the stubbornness that cleaves to us. There is at the same time an implied contrast between the promiscuous and vulgar mass, (to whom the sacrifices were like phantoms without any power,) and David, to whom God had discovered their spiritual and legitimate use and application.

But the Apostle followed the Greek translators when he said, "A body hast thou prepared;" for in quoting these words the Apostles were not so scrupulous, provided they perverted not Scripture to their own purpose. We must always have a regard to the end for which they quote passages, for they are very careful as to the main object, so as not to turn Scripture to another meaning; but as to words and other things, which bear not on the subject in hand, they use great freedom.[163]

7. *In the volume or chapter of the book, etc. Volume* is properly the meaning of the Hebrew word; for we know that books were formerly rolled up in the form of a cylinder. There is also nothing unreasonable in understanding *book* as meaning the Law, which prescribes to all God's children the rule of a holy life; though it seems to me a more suitable view to consider him as saying, that he deemed himself to be in the catalogue of those who render themselves obedient to God. The Law, indeed, bids us all to obey God; but David means, that he was numbered among those who are called to obey God; and then he testifies that he obeyed his vocation, by adding, *I come to do thy will;* and this peculiarly belongs to Christ. For though all the saints aspire after the righteousness of God, yet it is Christ alone who was fully competent to do God's will.

---

163 This is no doubt true; but here the identity of meaning is difficult to be made out. See Appendix I2. — *Ed.*

This passage, however, ought to stimulate us all to render prompt obedience to God; for Christ is a pattern of perfect obedience for this end, that all who are his may contend with one another in imitating him, that they may together respond to the call of God, and that their life may exemplify this saying, *Lo, I come.* To the same purpose is what follows, *It is written,* that is, that we should do the will of God, according to what is said elsewhere, that the end of our election is, to be holy and unblamable in his sight. (Colossians i. 22.)

9. *He taketh away, etc.* See now why and for what purpose this passage was quoted, even that we may know that the full and perfect righteousness under the kingdom of Christ stands in no need of the sacrifices of the Law; for when they are removed, the will of God is set up as a perfect rule. It hence follows, that the sacrifices of beasts were to be removed by the priesthood of Christ, as they had nothing in common with it. For there was no reason, as we have said, for him to reject the sacrifices on account of an accidental blame; for he is not dealing with hypocrites, nor does he condemn the superstition of perverted worship; but he denies that the usual sacrifices are required of a pious man rightly instructed, and he testifies that without sacrifices God is fully and perfectly obeyed.

10. *By the which will, etc.* After having accommodated to his subject David's testimony, he now takes the occasion to turn some of the words to his own purpose, but more for the sake of ornament than of explanation. David professed, not so much in his own person as in that of Christ, that he was ready to do the will of God. This is to be extended to all the members of Christ; for Paul's doctrine is general, when he says, "This is the will of God, even your sanctification, that every one of you abstain from uncleanness". (1 Thessalonians iv. 3.) But as it was a supereminent example of obedience in Christ to offer himself to the death of the cross, and as it was for this especially that he put on the form of a servant, the Apostle says, that Christ by offering himself fulfilled the command of his Father, and that we have been thus *sanctified.* [164] When he adds, *through the offering of the*

---

164 "Sanctified," here, as in chapter ii. 11, includes the idea of expiation; it is to be sanctified, or cleansed from guilt, rather than from pollution, because it is said to be by the offering of the body of Christ, which was especially an expiation for sins, as it appears from what follows; and the main object of the quotation after-

body, etc., he alludes to that part of the Psalm, where he says, "A body hast thou prepared for me," at least as it is found in Greek. He thus intimates that Christ found in himself what could appease God, so that he had no need of external aids. For if the Levitical priests had a fit body, the sacrifices of beasts would have been superfluous. But Christ alone was sufficient, and was by himself capable of performing whatever God required.

HEBREWS X. 11-18

11. And every priest standeth daily ministering and offering oftentimes the same sacrifices, which can never take away sins:
12. But this man, after he had offered one sacrifice for sins for ever, sat down on the right hand of God;
13. From henceforth expecting till his enemies be made his footstool.
14. For by one offering he hath perfected for ever them that are sanctified.
15. *Whereof* the Holy Ghost also is a witness to us: for after that he had said before,
16. This *is* the covenant that I will make with them after those days, saith the Lord, I will put my laws into their hearts, and in their minds will I write them;
17. And their sins and iniquities will I remember no more.

---

wards made was to show that by his death remission of sins is obtained.

"By the which will," or, by which will, is commonly taken to mean, "By the accomplishing of which will;" or ἐν may be taken as in chapter iv. 11, in the sense of κατὰ, "according to which will we are cleansed (that is, from guilt) through the offering of the body of Christ once made."

"Will" here does not mean the act of willing, but the object of the will, that which God wills, approves and is pleased with, and is set in opposition to the legal sacrifices. And as there is a οἱ in many good copies after ἐσμὲν, some have rendered the verse thus, "By which will we are cleansed who are cleansed by the offering of the body of Christ once made." Thus "the will," or what pleased God, is first opposed to the sacrifices, and then identified with the offering of Christ's body. — *Ed*

18. Now where remission of these *is, there is* no more offering for sin.

11. *And every priest, etc.* Here is the conclusion of the whole argument, — that the practice of daily sacrificing is inconsistent with and wholly foreign to the priesthood of Christ; and that hence after his coming the Levitical priests whose custom and settled practice was daily to offer, were deposed from their office; for the character of things which are contrary is, that when one thing is set up, the other falls to the ground. He has hitherto labored enough, and more than enough, in defending the priesthood of Christ; the conclusion then is, that the ancient priesthood, which is inconsistent with this, has ceased; for all the saints find a full consecration in the one offering of Christ. At the same time the word τετελείωκεν, which I render "has consecrated," may yet be rendered "has perfected;" but I prefer the former meaning, because he treats here of sacred things.[165]

By saying, *them who are sanctified*, he includes all the children of God; and he reminds us that the grace of sanctification is sought elsewhere in vain.

But lest men should imagine that Christ is now idle in heaven, he repeats again that he *sat down at God's right hand;* by which phrase is denoted, as we have seen elsewhere, his dominion and power. There is therefore no reason for us to fear, that he will suffer the efficacy of his death to be destroyed or to lie buried; for he lives for this end, that by his power he may fill heaven and earth. He then reminds us in the words of the Psalm how long this state of things is to be, even until Christ shall lay prostrate all his enemies. If then our faith seeks Christ sitting on God's right hand, and recumbs quietly on him as there sitting, we shall at length enjoy the fruit of his victory; yea, when our foes, Satan, sin, death, and the whole world are vanquished, and when corruption of our flesh is cast off, we shall triumph for ever together with our head.

15. *The Holy Ghost also is a witness, etc.*[166] This testimony from Jeremiah is not adduced the second time without reason or superfluously. He quoted it before for a different purpose, even

---

165 See Appendix K2.

166 "Now testify to us does also the Holy Spirit;" such may be the rendering of the words. The δὲ is translated "And," by Macknight,

to show that it was necessary for the Old Testament to be abrogated, because another, a new one, had been promised, and for this end, to amend the weakness of the old.[167] But he has now another thing in view; for he takes his stand on these words alone, *Their iniquities will I remember no more;* and hence he concludes, that there is no more need of a sacrifice since sins are blotted out.[168]

This inference may indeed seem not to be well founded; for though formerly there were innumerable promises as to the remission of sins under the Law and in the prophets, yet the Church ceased not to offer sacrifices; hence remission of sins does not exclude sacrifices. But if you consider each particular more closely, you will find that the fathers also had the same promises as to the remission of sins, under the Law, as we have at this day; relying on them, they called on God, and rejoiced

---

and "Morever," by Stuart, but "Now" seems the most suitable. — *Ed*

[167] The quotation as made here affords a remarkable instance of what Calvin has previously said, that the Apostles were not very scrupulous in the use of words, but attended to the meaning. The words have been before quoted in chapter viii. 10-12. There we have "into their mind — καρδίας," here, "into their minds — διανοιῶν;" and in the 12th verse in chapter viii., and the 17th in this chapter, are in words wholly different, though in meaning essentially the same. We need not wonder then that there is sometimes a variety in quotations made from the Old Testament, since the Apostle varies in a quotation when given the second time by himself. — *Ed*

[168] This quotation clearly shows the meaning of the word "sanctified." The sanctified, or those atoned for, or expiated, were made perfect by having their sins perfectly and completely forgiven them. The sufficiently of Christ's sacrifice for taking away sins, for a full and complete remission, is the subject throughout, and not the effect of that sacrifice in the work of sanctification. The chapter begins with sins as to the conscience; and here the words of Jeremiah are referred to, not for the purpose of showing that the new covenant provides for the renovation of the heart, (though it includes that too.) but of proving that it secures the free and full remission of sins, procured, as stated before, by the one sacrifice of Christ, once offered and perpetually efficacious. — *Ed*.

in the pardon they obtained. And yet the Prophet, as though he had adduced something new and unheard of before, promises that there would be no remembrance of sins before God under the new covenant. Hence we may conclude, that sins are now remitted in a way different from what they were formerly; but this difference is not in the promise, nor in faith, but in the very price by which remissions is procured. God then does not now remember sins, because an expiation has been made once for all; otherwise what is said by the Prophet would have been to no purpose, that the benefit of the New Testament was to be this — that God would no more remember sins.

Now, since we have come to the close of the discussion respecting the priesthood of Christ, readers must be brief reminded, that the sacrifices of the Law are not more effectually proved here to have been abolished, than the sacrifice of the mass practiced by the Papists is proved to be a vain fiction.

They maintain that their mass is a sacrifice for expiating the sins of the living and of the dead; but the Apostle denies that there is now any place for a sacrifice, even since the time in which the prophecy of Jeremiah has been fulfilled.

They try to make an evasion by saying, that it is not a new sacrifice, or different from that of Christ, but the same; on the contrary, the Apostle contends that the same sacrifice ought not to be repeated, and declares that Christ's sacrifice is only one, and that it was offered for all; and, further, he often claims for Christ alone the honor of being a priest, so that no one was fit to offer him but himself alone.

The Papists have another evasion, and call their sacrifice bloodless; but the Apostle affirms it as a truth without exception, that death is necessary in order to make a sacrifice.

The Papists attempt to evade again by saying, that the mass is the application of the one sacrifice which Christ has made; but the Apostle teaches us on the contrary, that the sacrifices of the Law were abolished by Christ's death for this reason, because in them a remembrance of sins was made; it hence appears evident, that this kind of application which they have devised has ceased.

In short, let the Papists twist themselves into any forms they please, they can never escape from the plain arguments of the Apostle, by which it appears clear that their mass abounds in impieties; for first, according to the Apostle's testimony, Christ alone was fit to offer himself; in the mass he is offered by other hands; — secondly, the Apostle asserts that Christ's sacrifice was not only one, but was also once offered, so that it is impious to repeat it; but in the mass, however they may prate about the sacrifice, yet it is evidently made every day, and they themselves confess it; — thirdly, the Apostle acknowledges no sacrifice without blood and death; they then chatter in vain, that the sacrifice they offer is bloodless; — fourthly, the Apostle in speaking of obtaining pardon for sins, bids us to flee to that one sacrifice which Christ offered on the cross, and makes this distinction between us and the fathers, that the rite of continually sacrificing was done away by the coming of Christ; but the Papists, in order to make the death of Christ efficacious, require daily applications by means of a sacrifice; so that they calling themselves Christians, differ nothing from the Jews except in the external symbol.

HEBREWS X. 19-23

19. Having therefore, brethren, boldness to enter into the holiest by the blood of Jesus,
20. By a new and living way, which he hath consecrated for us, through the veil, that is to say, his flesh;
21. And *having* an high priest over the house of God;
22. Let us draw near with a true heart in full assurance of faith, having our hearts sprinkled from an evil conscience, and our bodies washed with pure water.
23. Let us hold fast the profession of *our* faith without wavering; (for he *is* faithful that promised;)

19. *Having therefore, brethren, etc.* He states the conclusion or the sum of his previous doctrine, to which he then fitly subjoins a serious exhortation, and denounces a severe threatening on those who had renounced the grace of Christ. Now, the sum of what he had said is, that all the ceremonies by which an access under the Law was open to the sanctuary, have their real fulfillment in Christ, so that to him who has Christ, the use of them is superfluous and useless To set this forth more fully, he allegorically describes the access which Christ has opened to us; for he compares heaven to the old sanctuary, and sets forth the things which have been spiritually accomplished in Christ in typical expressions. Allegories do indeed sometimes obscure rather than illustrate a subject; but when the Apostle transfers to Christ the ancient figures of the Law, there is no small elegance in what he says, and no small light is attained; and he did this, that we may recognize as now really exhibited in him whatever the Law shadowed forth. But as there is great weight almost in every word, so we must remember that there is here to be understood a contrast, — the truth or reality as seen in Christ, and the abolition of the ancient types.

He says first, that we have *boldness to enter into the holiest.* This privilege was never granted to the fathers under the Law, for the people were forbidden to enter the visible sanctuary, though the high priest bore the names of the tribes on his shoulders, and twelve stones as a memorial of them on his breast. But now the case is very different, for not only symbolically, but in reality an entrance into heaven is made open to us through the favor of Christ, for he has made us a royal priesthood.[169]

He adds, *by the blood of Jesus,* because the door of the sanctuary was not opened for the periodical entrance of the high priest, except through the intervention of blood. But he afterwards marks the difference between this blood and that of beasts; for the blood of beasts, as it soon turns to corruption, could not long retain its efficacy; but the blood of Christ, which is subject to no corruption, but flows ever as a pure stream, is sufficient for us even to the end of the world. It is no wonder that beasts slain in sacrifice had no power to quicken, as they were dead; but Christ who arose from the dead to bestow life on us, communicates his own life to us. It is a perpetual consecration of the way, because the blood of Christ is always in a manner distilling before the presence of the Father, in order to irrigate heaven and earth.

20. *Through the veil, etc.* As the veil covered the recesses of the sanctuary and yet afforded entrance there, so the divinity,

---

169 Macknight makes this "entrance" to be death! As though the Apostle was speaking of what was future, while in verse 22, with which the contents of this verse and the following are connected, he says, "let us draw near;" that is, we who have this entrance, even "the new and living way." Possessing such a privilege, they were to draw nigh. It is clearly an entrance and a way which believers now possess. — *Ed.*

though hid in the flesh of Christ, yet leads us even into heaven; nor can any one find God except he to whom the man Christ becomes the door and the way. Thus we are reminded, that Christ's glory is not to be estimated according to the external appearance of his flesh; nor is his flesh to be despised, because it conceals as a veil the majesty of God, while it is also that which conducts us to the enjoyment of all the good things of God.

21. *And having a high priest, etc.* Whatever he has previously said of the abrogation of the ancient priesthood, it behoves us now to bear in mind, for Christ could not be a priest without having the former priests divested of their office, as it was another order. He then intimates that all those things which Christ had changed at his coming ought to be relinquished; and God has set him over his whole house for this end, — that every one who seeks a place in the Church, may submit to Christ and choose him, and no other, as his leader and ruler.[170]

22. *Let us draw near with a true heart, etc.* As he shows that in Christ and his sacrifice there is nothing but what is spiritual or heavenly, so he would have what we bring on our part to correspond. The Jews formerly cleansed themselves by various washings to prepare themselves for the service of God. It is no wonder that the rites for cleansing were carnal, since the worship of God itself, involved in shadows, as yet partook in a manner of what was carnal. For the priest, being a mortal, was chosen from among sinners to perform for a time sacred things; he was, indeed, adorned with precious vestments, but yet they were those of this world, that he might stand in the presence of God; he only came near the work of the covenant; and to sanctify his entrance, he borrowed for a sacrifice a brute animal either from herd or the flock. But in Christ all these things are far superior; He himself is not only pure and innocent, but is also the fountain of all holiness and righteousness, and was constituted a priest by a heavenly oracle, not for the short period of a mortal life, but perpetually. To sanction his appointment an oath was interposed. He came forth adorned with all the gifts of the Holy Spirit in the highest perfection; he propitiated God by his own blood, and reconciled him to men; he ascended up above all the heavens to appear before God as our Mediator.

Now, on our part, nothing is to be brought but what corresponds with all this, as there ought to be a mutual agreement or

---

170 See Appendix L2.

concord between the priest and the people. Away then with all the external washings of the flesh, and cease let the whole apparatus of ceremonies; for the Apostle sets a *true heart,* and the certainty of faith, and a cleansing from all vices, in opposition to these external rites. And hence we learn what must be the frame of our minds in order that we may enjoy the benefits conferred by Christ; for there is no coming to him without an upright or a true heart, and a sure faith, and a pure conscience.

Now, a *true* or sincere heart is opposed to a heart that is hypocritical and deceitful.[171] By the term *full assurance,* πληροφορία the Apostle points out the nature of faith, and at the same time reminds us, that the grace of Christ cannot be received except by those who possess a fixed and unhesitating conviction. The *sprinkling of the heart from an evil conscience* takes place, either when we are, by obtaining pardon, deemed pure before God, or when the heart, cleansed from all corrupt affections, is not stimulated by the goads of the flesh. I am disposed to include both these things.[172] What follows, *our bodies washed with pure water,* is generally understood of baptism; but it seems to me

---

[171] This true, sincere, or upright heart, freed from vice and pollution, was symbolized by the washing at the end of the verse. Without washing the priests were not allowed to minister, and were threatened with death, Exodus xxx. 19-21; and when any of them touched an unclean thing, he was not allowed to eat of holy things until he washed himself, see xii. 6 [sic]. Washing the body was a most important thing, as it symbolized the inward washing of the heart, which alone makes us true, or sincere, or faithful to God.

We have here two things — a sincere heart, and assurance of faith: the last is then set forth by sprinkling, a word borrowed for Levitical rites; and the first by the washing of the body as under the law. — *Ed.*

[172] Πονηρὸς means רע in Hebrew, the evil of sin wicked, and also the effect of sin, miserable It seems to be in the latter sense here; a miserable conscience is one oppressed with guilt. So Grotius and Stuart regard the meaning. It is the same as "consciousness of sin" in verse 2. What seems to be meant is an accusing or guilty conscience, laboring under the pressure of conscious sin. But Doddridge and Scott, like Calvin, combine the two ideas of guilt and pollution; though washing, afterwards mentioned, appears more appropriately to refer to the latter; and forgiveness is what is most commonly connected with the blood of Christ. — *Ed*

more probable that the Apostle alludes to the ancient ceremonies of the Law; and so by water he designates the Spirit of God, according to what is said by Ezekiel, "I will sprinkle clean water upon you." (Ezekiel xxxvi. 25.) The meaning is, that we are made partakers of Christ, if we come to him, sanctified in body and soul; and yet that this sanctification is not what consists in a visible parade of ceremonies, but that it is from faith, pure conscience, and that cleanness of soul and body which flows from, and is effected by, the Spirit of God. So Paul exhorts the faithful to cleanse themselves from all filthiness of flesh and spirit, since they had been adopted by God as his children.[173] (2 Corinthians vii. 1.)

23. *Let us hold fast, etc.* As he exhorts here the Jews to persevere, he mentions hope rather than faith; for as hope is born of faith, so it is fed and sustained by it to the last. He requires also *profession* or confession, for it is not true faith except it shows itself before men. And he seems indirectly to touch the dissimulation of those who paid too much attention, in order to please their own nation, to the ceremonies of the Law. He therefore bids them not only to believe with the heart, but also to show and to profess how much they honored Christ.

But we ought carefully to notice the reason which he subjoins, *for he is faithful that promised.* For we hence first learn, that our faith rests on this foundation, that God is true, that is, true to his promise, which his word contains; for that we may believe, the voice or word of God must precede; but it is not every kind of word that is capable of producing faith; a promise alone is that on which faith recumbs. And so from this passage we may learn the mutual relation between the faith of men and the promise of God; for except God promises, no one can believe.[174]

---

173 See Appendix M2.

174 Our version has "faith," but it should be "hope," as found in almost all copies. "Profession of hope" is a Hebraism for professed hope, or the hope we profess. He mentioned "faith" in the preceding verse, and now "hope" as being its daughter, and as that which especially sustained them under their trials. — *Ed.*

HEBREWS X. 24-27

24. And let us consider one another to provoke unto love and to good works:
25. Not forsaking the assembling of ourselves together, as the manner of some *is*; but exhorting *one another*: and so much the more, as ye see the day approaching.
26. For if we sin willfully after that we have received the knowledge of the truth, there remaineth no more sacrifice for sins,
27. But a certain fearful looking for of judgment and fiery indignation, which shall devour the adversaries.

24. *And let us consider one another, etc.* I doubt not but that he addresses the Jews especially in this exhortation. It is well-known how great was the arrogance of that nation; being the posterity of Abraham, they boasted that they alone, to the exclusion of all others, had been chosen by the Lord to inherit the covenant of eternal life. Inflated by such a privilege, they despised other nations, and wished to be thought as being alone in the Church of God; nay, they superciliously arrogated to themselves the name of being The Church. It was necessary for the Apostles to labor much to correct this pride; and this, in my judgment, is what the Apostle is doing here, in order that the Jews might not bear it ill that the Gentiles were associated with them and united as one body in the Church.

And first, indeed, he says, *Let us consider one another*; for God was then gathering a Church both from the Jews and from the Gentiles, between whom there had always been a great discord, so that their union was like the combination of fire and water. Hence the Jews recoiled from this, for they thought it a great indignity that the Gentiles, should be made equal with them. To this goad of wicked emulation which pricked them, the Apostle sets up another in opposition to it, even that of *love;* or the word παροξυσμὸς, which he uses, signifies the ardor of contention. Then that the Jews might not be inflamed with envy, and be led into contention, the Apostle exhorts them to a godly emulation, even to stimulate one another to love.[175]

---

175 The words literally are, "And let us observe (or take notice of) one another for the instigation of love and of good works;" that

25. *Not forsaking the assembling of ourselves together, etc.* This confirms the view that has been given. The composition of the Greek word ought to be noticed; for ἐπι signifies an addition; then ἐπισυναγωγὴ, assembling together, means a congregation increased by additions. The wall of partition having been pulled down, God was then gathering those as his children who had been aliens from the Church; so the Gentiles were a new and unwonted addition to the Church. This the Jews regarded as a reproach to them, so that many made a secession from the Church, thinking that such a mixture afforded them a just excuse; nor could they be easily induced to surrender their own right; and further, they considered the right of adoption as peculiar, and as belonging exclusively to themselves. The Apostle, therefore, warns them, lest this equality should provoke them to forsake the Church; and that he might not seem to warn them for no reason, he mentions that this neglect was common to many.[176]

We now understand the design of the apostle, and what was the necessity that constrained him to give this exhortation. We may at the same time gather from this passage a general doctrine:

---

is, "Let us notice the state and circumstances of each other for the purpose of stimulating love and acts of kindness and benevolence, its proper fruits." Love is the principle, and good or benevolent works are what it produces.

"And let us attentively consider one another in order to the quickening of love and good works." — Macknight.

"Let us moreover attentively regard one another for the sake of exciting to love and good works." — Stuart.

The idea of emulation seems not to be included in the words. The meaning of the exhortation is, to take opportunity which circumstances afforded, to promote love and the exercise of benevolence. As an instance of the want of love, he notices in the next verse their neglect of meeting together for divine worship; and by not meeting together they had no opportunity of doing the good work admonishing and exhorting one another. — *Ed.*

176 Another view is commonly given of the cause of this neglect; it was the dread of persecution, according to Doddridge; and Scott says, that it was either "timidity or lukewarmness." As the Apostle had previously mentioned "love" the probability is that the main cause was coldness and indifference; and the cause of such a neglect is still for the most part the same. — *Ed.*

It is an evil which prevails everywhere among mankind, that every one sets himself above others, and especially that those who seem in anything to excel cannot well endure their inferiors to be on an equality with themselves. And then there is so much morosity almost in all, that individuals would gladly make churches for themselves if they could; for they find it so difficult to accommodate themselves to the ways and habits of others. The rich envy one another; and hardly one in a hundred can be found among the rich, who allows to the poor the name and rank of brethren. Unless similarity of habits or some allurements or advantages draw us together, it is very difficult even to maintain a continual concord among ourselves. Extremely needed, therefore, by us all is the admonition to be stimulated to love and not to envy, and not to separate from those whom God has joined to us, but to embrace with brotherly kindness all those who are united to us in faith. And surely it behoves us the more earnestly to cultivate unity, as the more eagerly watchful Satan is, either to tear us by any means from the Church, or stealthily to seduce us from it. And such would be the happy effect, were no one to please himself too much, and were all of us to preserve this one object, mutually to provoke one another to love, and to allow no emulation among ourselves, but that of doing "good works". For doubtless the contempt of the brethren, moroseness, envy, immoderate estimate of ourselves, and other sinful impulses, clearly show that our love is either very cold, or does not at all exist.

Having said, "Not forsaking the assembling together," he adds, *But exhorting* one another; by which he intimates that all the godly ought by all means possible to exert themselves in the work of gathering together the Church on every side; for we are called by the Lord on this condition, that every one should afterwards strive to lead others to the truth, to restore the wandering to the right way, to extend a helping hand to the fallen, to win over those who are without. But if we ought to bestow so much labor on those who are yet aliens to the flock of Christ, how much more diligence is required in exhorting the brethren whom God has already joined to us?

As the manner of some is, etc. It hence appears that the origin of all schisms was, that proud men, despising others, pleased themselves too much. But when we hear that there were faithless men even in the age of the Apostles, who departed from the

Church, we ought to be less shocked and disturbed by similar instances of defection which we may see in the present day. It is indeed no light offense when men who had given some evidence of piety and professed the same faith with us, fall away from the living God; but as it is no new thing, we ought, as I have already said, to be less disturbed by such an event. But the Apostle introduced this clause to show that he did not speak without a cause, but in order to apply a remedy to a disease that was making progress.

And so much the more, etc. Some think this passage to be of the same import with that of Paul,

> "It is time to awake out of sleep, for now is our salvation nearer than when we believed." (Romans xiii. 11.)

But I rather think that reference is here made to the last coming of Christ, the expectation of which ought especially to rouse us to the practice of a holy life as well as to careful and diligent efforts in the work of gathering together the Church. For to what end did Christ come except to collect us all into one body from that dispersion in which we are now wandering? Therefore, the nearer his coming is, the more we ought to labor that the scattered may be assembled and united together, that there may be one fold and one shepherd (John x. 16.)

Were any one to ask, how could the Apostle say that those who were as yet afar off from the manifestation of Christ, saw the day near and just at hand? I would answer, that from the beginning of the kingdom of Christ the Church was so constituted that the faithful ought to have considered the Judge as coming soon; nor were they indeed deceived by a false notion, when they were prepared to receive Christ almost every moment; for such was the condition of the Church from the time the Gospel was promulgated, that the whole of that period might truly and properly be called the last. They then who have been dead many ages ago lived in the last days no less than we. Laughed at is our simplicity in this respect by the worldly-wise and scoffers, who deem as fabulous all that we believe respecting the resurrection of the flesh and the last judgment; but that our faith may not fail through their mockery, the Holy Spirit reminds us that a thousand years are before God as one day, (2 Peter iii. 8;) so that whenever we think of the eternity of the celestial kingdom no time ought to appear long to us. And further, since Christ, after having completed all things necessary for our salvation, has ascended into heaven, it is but reasonable that we who are continually looking for his second manifestation should regard every day as though it were the last.[177]

26. *For if we sin willfully,* or *voluntarily etc.* He shows how severe a vengeance of God awaits all those who fall away from the grace of Christ; for being without that one true salvation, they are now as it were given up to an inevitable destruction. With this testimony *Novatus* and his sect formerly armed themselves, in order to take away the hope of pardon from all indiscriminately who had fallen after baptism. They who were not able to refute his calumny chose rather to deny the authority of this Epistle than to subscribe to so great an absurdity. But the true meaning of the passage, unaided by any help from any other part, is quite sufficient of itself to expose the effrontery of *Novatus*

Those who *sin,* mentioned by the Apostle, are not such as offend in any way, but such as forsake the Church, and wholly alienate themselves from Christ. For he speaks not here of this or of that sin, but he condemns by name those who willfully renounced fellowship with the Church. But there is a vast difference between particular fallings and a complete defection of this kind, by which we entirely fall away from the grace of Christ. And as this cannot be the case with any one except he has been already enlightened, he says, *If we sin willfully, after*

---

177 "As ye see drawing nigh the day;" so are the words literally. The day of judgment, say some; the day of Jerusalem's destruction, say other. Dodddridge introduces both in his paraphrase; and Scott and Bloomfield regard the day of judgment as intended; but Stuart is in favor of the opinion that the destruction of Jerusalem is what is referred to, and so Hammond and Mede.

The word "day" is applied to both. The day of judgment is called "that day," (Jude 6;) and the destruction of Jerusalem is called the Son of man's day, "his day," (Luke xvii. 24) And both these days must have been well known to the Hebrews to whom Paul was writing. The reference, then, might have been well thus made to either without any addition. But the sentence itself seems to favor the opinion that the day of Jerusalem is intended; "as ye see," he says; which denotes that there were things in the circumstances of the times which clearly betokened the approaching ruin of that city and nation. — *Ed.*

that we have received the knowledge of the truth; as though he had said, "If we knowingly and willingly renounce the grace which we had obtained." It is now evident how widely apart is this doctrine from the error of *Novatus*

And that the Apostle here refers only to apostates, is clear from the whole passage; for what he treats of is this, that those who had been once received into the Church ought not to forsake it, as some were wont to do. He now declares that there remained for such no sacrifice for sin, because they had willfully sinned after having received the knowledge of the truth. But as to sinners who fall in any other way, Christ offers himself daily to them, so that they are to seek no other sacrifice for expiating their sins. He denies, then, that any sacrifice remains for them who renounce the death of Christ, which is not done by any offense except by a total renunciation of the faith.

This severity of God is indeed dreadful, but it is set forth for the purpose of inspiring terror. He cannot, however, be accused of cruelty; for as the death of Christ is the only remedy by which we can be delivered from eternal death, are not they who destroy as far as they can its virtue and benefit worthy of being left to despair? God invites to daily reconciliation those who abide in Christ; they are daily washed by the blood of Christ, their sins are daily expiated by his perpetual sacrifice. As salvation is not to be sought except in him, there is no need to wonder that all those who willfully forsake him are deprived of every hope of pardon: this is the import of the adverb ἔτι, more. But Christ's sacrifice is efficacious to the godly even to death, though they often sin; nay, it retains ever its efficacy, for this very reason, because they cannot be free from sin as long as they dwell in the flesh. The Apostle then refers to those alone who wickedly forsake Christ, and thus deprive themselves of the benefit of his death.

The clause, "after having received the knowledge of the truth," was added for the purpose of aggravating their ingratitude; for he who willingly and with deliberate impiety extinguishes the light of God kindled in his heart has nothing to allege as an excuse before God. Let us then learn not only to receive with reverence and prompt docility of mind the truth offered to us, but also firmly to persevere in the knowledge of it, so that we may not suffer the terrible punishment of those who despise it.[178]

27. *But a certain fearful looking for, etc.* He means the torment of an evil conscience which the ungodly feel, who not only have no grace, but who also know that having tasted grace they have lost it forever through their own fault; such must not only be pricked and bitten, but also tormented and lacerated in a dreadful manner. Hence it is that they war rebelliously against God, for they cannot endure so strict a Judge. They indeed try in every way to remove the sense of God's wrath, but all in vain; for when God allows them a short respite, he soon draws them before his tribunal, and harasses them with the torments which they especially shun.

He adds, *fiery indignation,* or the heat of fire; by which he means, as I think, a vehement impulse or a violent ardor. The word *fire* is a common metaphor; for as the ungodly are now in a heat through dread of divine wrath, so they shall then burn through the same feeling. Nor is it unknown to me, that the sophists have refinedly speculated as to this fire; but I have no regard of their glosses, since it is evident that it is the same mode of speaking as when Scripture connects fire with worm. (Isaiah lxvi. 24.) But no man doubts but that worm is used metaphorically to designate that dreadful torment of conscience by which the ungodly are gnawed.[179]

Which shall devour the adversaries. It shall so devour them as to destroy, but not to consume them; for it will be inextinguish-

---

178 See Appendix N2.

179 It is πυρὸς ζῶλος, "heat of fire;" which means hot or burning fire; the genitive here, as in some other instances, is the main subject. See chapter iii. 13, note. The language is still borrowed from the Old Testament: God often destroyed the rebellious among the Israelites with fire — a symbol of the dreadful punishment of the wicked hereafter. See Leviticus x. 2; Numbers xvi. 35. The word ζῶλος is properly heat, but is used in a variety of senses; heat of emulation — "envy," Acts xiii. 45; — of wrath — "indignation" Acts v. 17; — of concern, good and bad — "zeal," Romans x. 2, and Philippians iii. 6; — of suspicion as to love — "jealousy," 2 Corinthians xi. 2; — and of affection — "love," 2 Corinthians xi. 2. It is the context that determines the character of this heat. Here is has evidently its literal meaning, as being connected with fire, only the noun is used for the adjective. — *Ed*

able. And thus he reminds us, that they are all to be counted the enemies of Christ who have refused to hold the place granted them among the faithful; for there is no intermediate state, as they who depart from the Church give themselves up to Satan.

HEBREWS X. 28-31

28. He that despised Moses' law died without mercy under two or three witnesses:
29. Of how much sorer punishment, suppose ye, shall he be thought worthy, who hath trodden under foot the Son of God, and hath counted the blood of the covenant, wherewith he was sanctified, an unholy thing, and hath done despite unto the Spirit of grace?
30. For we know him that hath said, Vengeance *belongeth* unto me, I will recompense, saith the Lord. And again, The Lord shall judge his people.
31. *It is* a fearful thing to fall into the hands of the living God.

28. *He that despised, etc.* This is an argument from the less to the greater; for if it was a capital offense to violate the law of Moses, how much heavier punishment does the rejection of the gospel deserve, a sin which involves so many and so heinous impieties! This reasoning was indeed most fitted to impress the Jews; for so severe a punishment on apostates under the Law was neither new to them, nor could it appear unjustly rigorous. They ought then to have acknowledged that vengeance just, however severe, by which God now sanctions the majesty of his Gospel[180]

Hereby is also confirmed what I have already said, that the Apostle speaks not of particular sins, but of the entire denial of Christ; for the Law did not punish all kinds of transgressions with death, but apostasy, that is, when any one wholly renounced religion; for the Apostle referred to a passage in

---

180 "Despised" of our version ought to have been "rejected," as Calvin renders the word, for the renouncing of the Law is what is meant. Followed by "commandment" in Mark vii. 9, it is rendered "reject," and "cast off" when followed by "faith" in 1 Timothy v. 12; and "cast off" would be very suitable here. — *Ed.*

Deuteronomy xvii. 2-7,[181] where we find, that if any one violated God's covenant by worshipping foreign gods, he was to be brought outside of the gate and stoned to death.

Now, though the Law proceeded from God, and Moses was not its author, but its minister, yet the Apostle calls it the law of Moses, because it had been given through him: this was said in order to amplify the more the dignity of the Gospel, which has been delivered to us by the Son of God.

Under two or three witnesses, etc. This bears not on the present subject; but it was a part of the civil law of Moses that two or three witnesses were required to prove the accused guilty. However, we hence learn what sort of crime the Apostle meant; for had not this been added, an opening would have been left for many false conjectures. But now it is beyond all dispute that he speaks of apostasy. At the same time that equity ought to be observed which almost all statesmen have adopted, that no one is to be condemned without being proved guilty by the testimony of two witnesses.[182]

29. *Who has trodden under foot the Son of God, etc.* There is this likeness between apostates under the Law and under the Gospel, that both perish without mercy; but the kind of death is different; for the Apostle denounces on the despisers of Christ not only the deaths of the body, but eternal perdition. And therefore he says that a sorer punishment awaits them. And he designates the desertion of Christianity by three things; for he

---

181 Both Doddridge and Stuart refer to Numbers xv. 30, 31, but incorrectly, as there the specific sin of apostasy is not mentioned, nor is there mention made of witnesses. Besides, it is not the presumptuous or willful sin there referred to, that is here intended, but the sin of apostasy, when it is the result of a free choice, without any outward constraining power as under violent persecution. — *Ed.*

182 "Neither the king nor the Senate," says Grotius, "had the power to pardon." It is to be observed that God delegated the power to execute apostates to the rulers of Israel: but we find here that he has under the Gospel resumed that power and holds it in his own hands; the execution of the vengeance belongs alone to him, and the punishment will be everlasting perdition. Then to assume such a power now is a most impious presumption, whether done by civil or ecclesiastical rulers. To put apostates or heretics to death, receives no sanction from the Gospel, and is wholly alien to its spirit. — *Ed.*

says that thus the Son of God is trodden under foot, that his blood is counted an unholy thing, and that despite is done to the Spirit of grace. Now, it is a more heinous thing to tread under foot than to despise or reject; and the dignity of Christ is far different from that of Moses; and further, he does not simply set the Gospel in opposition to the Law, but the person of Christ and of the Holy Spirit to the person of Moses.

The blood of the covenant, etc. He enhances ingratitude by a comparison with the benefits. It is the greatest indignity to count the blood of Christ unholy, by which our holiness is effected; this is done by those who depart from the faith. For our faith looks not on the naked doctrine, but on the blood by which our salvation has been ratified. He calls it the blood of the *covenant*, because then only were the promises made sure to us when this pledge was added. But he points out the manner of this confirmation by saying that we are *sanctified*; for the blood shed would avail us nothing, except we were sprinkled with it by the Holy Spirit; and hence come our expiation and sanctification. The apostle at the same time alludes to the ancient rite of sprinkling, which availed not to real sanctification, but was only its shadow or image.[183]

The Spirit of grace. He calls it the Spirit of grace from the effects produced; for it is by the Spirit and through his influence that we receive the grace offered to us in Christ. For he it is who enlightens our minds by faith, who seals the adoption of God on our hearts, who regenerates us unto newness of life, who grafts us into the body of Christ, that he may live in us and we in him. He is therefore rightly called the Spirit of grace, by whom

---

183 The words "covenant," and "sanctified," and "unclean" or "unholy," are derived from the old dispensation. "The blood of the covenant" was the blood shed on the cross; and the reference to it is not as sprinkled for the ratifying of the covenant, but as the blood of atonement, as "the blood of the New Testament, or rather covenant, "shed for many for the remission of sins," Matthew xxvi. 28. Then "sanctified" has the same meaning here as in verse 10 and in chapter ii. 11, expiated or atoned for; "by which he has expiated." He who professes the Christian faith, professes to believe in the atoning sacrifice of Christ, that Christ shed his blood for many for the remission of sins. As to "unholy," or rather unclean, such was the blood of a malefactor or impostor, and as such Christ was counted by the Jews and by every Jew who returned to Judaism. — *Ed.*

Christ becomes ours with all his blessings. But to do despite to him, or to treat him with scorn, by whom we are endowed with so many benefits, is an impiety extremely wicked. Hence learn that all who willfully render useless his grace, by which they had been favored, act disdainfully towards the Spirit of God.

It is therefore no wonder that God so severely visits blasphemies of this kind; it is no wonder that he shows himself inexorable towards those who tread under foot Christ the Mediator, who alone reconciles us to himself; it is no wonder that he closes up the way of salvation against those who spurn the Holy Spirit, the only true guide.[184]

30. *For we know him that hath said, etc.* Both the passages are taken from Deuteronomy xxxii. 35, 36. But as Moses there promises that God would take vengeance for the wrongs done to his people, it seems that the words are improperly and constrainedly applied to the vengeance referred to here; for what does the Apostle speak of? Even that the impiety of those who despised God would not be unpunished. Paul also in Romans xii. 19, knowing the true sense of the passage, accommodates it to another purpose; for having in view to exhort us to patience, he bids us to give place to God to take vengeance, because this office belongs to him; and this he proves by the testimony of Moses. But there is no reason why we should not turn a special declaration to a universal truth. Though then the design of Moses was to console the faithful, as they would have God as the avenger of wrongs done to them; yet we may always conclude from his words that it is the peculiar office of God to take vengeance on the ungodly. Nor does he pervert his testimony who hence proves that the contempt of God will not be unpunished;

---

184 Most strangely does Schleusner paraphrase this clause, "contumaciously repudiating the divine favor." The case here contemplated is the same with that in chapter vi. 4-6. The Holy Spirit is there so distinctly mentioned that it is impossible to turn or change the plain meaning of the passage; and to be "partakers of the Holy Spirit" was no doubt to be in that age. Here he is mentioned only as the holy Spirit of grace, i.e., the bestower of grace, or it may be taken as meaning "the gracious" or benevolent "Spirit;" as "God of all grace" in 1 Peter v. 10, may mean either the author and giver of every grace, or the most gracious God, though the former meaning is most consistent with the context

for he is a righteous judge who claims to himself the office of taking vengeance.

At the same time the Apostle might here also reason from the less to the greater, and in this manner: "God says that he will not suffer his people to be injured with impunity, and declares that he will surely be their avenger: If he suffers not wrongs done to men to be unpunished, will he not avenge his own? Has he so little or no care and concern for his own glory, as to connive at and pass by indignities offered to him?" But the former view is more simple and natural, — that the Apostle only shows that God will not be mocked with impunity, since it is his peculiar office to render to the ungodly what they have deserved.[185]

The Lord shall judge his people. Here another and a greater difficulty arises; for the meaning of Moses seems not to agree with what here intended. The Apostle seems to have quoted this passage as though Moses had used the word punish, and not judge; but as it immediately follows by way of explanation, "He will be merciful to his saints," it appears evident that to judge here is to act as a governor, according to its frequent meaning in the Hebrew; but this seems to have little to do with the present subject. Nevertheless he who weighs well all things will find that this passage is fitly and suitably adduced here; for God cannot govern the Church without purifying it, and without restoring to order the confusion that may be in it. Therefore this governing ought justly to be dreaded by hypocrites, who will then be punished for usurping a place among the faithful, and for perfidiously using the sacred name of God, when the master of the family undertakes himself the care of setting in order his own house. It is in this sense that God is said to arise to judge his people, that is, when he separates the truly godly from hypocrites, (Psalm i. 4;) and in Psalm cxxv. 5,@/footnote@ where the Prophet speaks of exterminating hypocrites, that they might no more dare to boast that they were of the Church, because God bore with them; he promises peace to Israel after having executed his judgment.

---

185 The quotation is literally neither from the Hebrew nor from the Sept., but is the same as quoted in Romans xii. 19; which seems to show that Paul is the Author of both epistles. The Hebrew is, "Mine is vengeance and recompense;" and the Sept., "In the day vengeance will I recompense." The sense is the same, though the words are different. — *Ed.*

It was not then unreasonably that the apostle reminded them that God presided over his Church and omitted nothing necessary for its rightful government, in order that they might all learn carefully to keep themselves under his power, and remember that they had to render an account to their judge.[186]

He hence concludes that *it is a fearful thing to fall into the hands of the living God.* A mortal man, however incensed he may be, cannot carry his vengeance beyond death; but God's power is not bounded by so narrow limits; besides, we often escape from men, but we cannot escape from God's judgment. Who soever then considers that he has to do with God, must (except he be extremely stupid) really tremble and quake; nay, such an apprehension of God must necessarily absorb the whole man, so that no sorrows, or torments can be compared with it. In short, whenever our flesh allures us or we flatter ourselves by any means in our sins, this admonition alone ought to be sufficient to arouse us, that "it is a fearful thing to fall into to hands of the living God;" for his wrath is furnished with dreadful punishments which are to be forever.

However, the saying of David, when he exclaimed, that it was better to fall into Gods hands than into the hands of men, (2 Samuel xxiv. 14,) seems to be inconsistent with what is said here. But this apparent inconsistency vanishes, when we consider that David, relying confidently on God's mercy, chose him as his Judge rather than men; for though he knew that God was displeased with him, yet he felt confident that he would be reconciled to him; in himself, indeed, he was prostrate on the ground, but yet he was raised up by the promise of grace. As then he believed God not to be inexorable, there is no wonder that he dreaded his wrath less, than that of men; but the Apostle here speaks of God's wrath as being dreadful to the reprobate, who being destitute of the hope of pardon, expect nothing but extreme severity, as they have already closed up against themselves the door of grace. And we know that God is set forth in various ways according to the character of those whom he addresses; and this is what David means when he says, "With the merciful thou wilt be merciful, and with the froward thou wilt be froward." (Psalm xviii. 25-27.)

---

186 See Appendix O2.

HEBREWS X. 32-35

32. But call to remembrance the former days, in which, after ye were illuminated, ye endured a great fight of afflictions;
33. Partly, whilst ye were made a gazingstock both by reproaches and afflictions; and partly, whilst ye became companions of them that were so used.
34. For ye had compassion of me in my bonds, and took joyfully the spoiling of your goods, knowing in yourselves that ye have in heaven a better and an enduring substance.
35. Cast not away therefore your confidence, which hath great recompense of reward.

32. *But call to remembrance, etc.* In order to stimulate them, and to rouse their alacrity to go forward, he reminds them of the evidences of piety which they had previously manifested; for it is a shameful thing to begin well, and to faint in the middle of our course, and still more shameful to retrograde after having made great progress. The remembrance then of past warfare, if it had been carried on faithfully and diligently under the banner of Christ, is at length useful to us, not as a pretext for sloth, as though we had already served our time, but to render us more active in finishing the remaining part of our course. For Christ has not enlisted us on this condition, that we should after a few years ask for a discharge like soldiers who have served their time, but that we should pursue our warfare even to the end.

He further strengthens his exhortation by saying, that they had already performed great exploits at a time when they were as yet new recruits: the more shame then would it be to them, if now they fainted after having been long tried; for the word *enlightened* is to be limited to the time when they first enlisted under Christ, as though he had said, "As soon as ye were initiated into the faith of Christ, ye underwent hard and arduous contests; now practice ought to have rendered you stronger, so as to become more courageous." He, however, at the same time reminds them, that it was through God's favor that they believed, and not through their own strength; they were enlightened when immersed in darkness and without eyes to see, except light from above had shone upon them. Whenever then those things which we have done or suffered for Christ come to our minds, let them be to us so many goads to stir us on to higher attainments.[187]

33. *Partly, whilst ye were made, etc.* We see who they were whom he addresses, even those whose faith had been proved by no common trials, and yet he refrains not from exhorting them to greater things. Let no man therefore deceive himself by self-flattery as though he had reached the goal, or had no need of incentives from others.

Now he says, that they had been *made gazingstocks both by reproaches and afflictions,* or exposed to public shame by reproaches and distresses, as though they were exposed on a public theater.[188] We hence learn that the persecutions which they had sustained were remarkably severe. But we ought especially to notice the latter clause, when he says that they became *companions,* or associates of the godly in their persecutions; for as it is Christ's cause for which all the godly contend, and as it is what their contend for in common, whatever one of them suffers, all the rest ought to transfer, as it were, to themselves; and this is what ought by all means to be done by us, unless we would separate ourselves from Christ himself.[189]

---

187 "A great fight of affliction," is rendered by Doddridge, "a great contest of sufferings;" by Macknight. "a great combat of afflictions;" and by Stuart, "a great contest with sufferings." The last word may be deemed as the genitive case of the object, "a great contest as to sufferings;" or the word πολλὴν, may be rendered, "long contest as to sufferings." Doddridge remarks that contest ὑπομέω is used to show the courage displayed. But "endure," is in the case not the proper word, but "sustain," If "endure" be retained, then we must give its secondary sense to ἄθλησιν, toil, labor, struggle; and so Schleusner does, "Ye endured the great toil of sufferings," or, a great struggle with sufferings. — Ed

188 The words may be rendered, "When ye were publicly exposed to reproaches and afflictions," or, to revilings and persecutions. They were reproached with bad names, or reviled, and also oppressed and persecuted. — Ed.

189 The latter clause of this verse is rendered the same as in our version by Beza and Macknight, while Grotius, Doddridge, Stuart and Bloomfield, give in effect this rendering, "when ye became partakers (i.e., in sympathy, and in their losses) with those who

34. *And took joyfully,* [190] *etc.* There is no doubt but as they were men who had feelings, the loss of their goods caused them grief; but yet their sorrow was such as did not prevent the joy of which the Apostle speaks. As poverty is deemed an evil, the plunder of their goods considered in itself touched them with grief; but as they looked higher, they found a cause for joy, which allayed whatever grief they felt. It is indeed thus necessary that our thoughts should be drawn away from the world, by looking at the heavenly recompense; nor do I say any other thing but what all the godly find to be the case by experience. And no doubt we joyfully embrace what we are persuaded will end in our salvation; and this persuasion the children of God doubtless have respecting the conflicts which they undertake for the glory of Christ. Hence carnal feelings never so prevail in overwhelming them with grief, but that with their minds raised up to heaven they emerge into spiritual joy.

And this is proved by what he subjoins, *knowing that ye have in heaven a better and an enduring substance.* Joyfully then did they endure the plundering of their goods, not because they were glad to find themselves plundered; but as their minds were fixed on the recompense, they easily forgot the grief occasioned by their present calamity. And indeed wherever there is a lively perception of heavenly things, the world with all its allure-

---

were so treated." It signifies, says Grotius, that they sympathized with their brethren in their calamities, and also succored them as far as they could by praying for them, and administering to their wants. In Matthew xxiii. 30, κοινωνοὶ αὐτῶν is rendered, "partakers with them," or sharers with them; and so it might be rendered here, "sharers with those who were so treated," i.e., sharers in reproach and suffering. — *Ed.*

190 The preceding clause is literally "For ye sympathized with my bonds." There is a different reading, "For ye sympathized with the prisoners — δεσμίοις. The authority as to MSS. is nearly equal; and there is nothing decisive in the context. A similar phrase is in chapter iv. 15. "who cannot sympathize with our infirmities." Grotius, Hammond and Stuart, are in the text as it is, and also Bishop Jebb, and Bloomfield.

There is here a clear instance of an inverted order as to the subjects previously mentioned which often occur in the Prophets, and in other parts of Scripture. The last subject in the previous verse is here first referred to, and then the first. — *Ed.*

ments is not so relished, that either poverty or shame can overwhelm our minds with grief. If then we wish to bear anything for Christ with patience and resigned minds, let us accustom ourselves to a frequent meditation on that felicity, in comparison with which all the good things of the world are nothing but refuse. Nor are we to pass by these words, "knowing that ye have";[191] for except one be fully persuaded that the inheritance which God has promised to his children belongs to him, all his knowledge will be cold and useless.

35. *Cast not away, therefore, etc.* He shows what especially makes us strong to persevere, even the retaining of confidence; for when that is lost, we lose the recompense set before us. It hence appears that confidence is the foundation of a godly and holy life. By mentioning *reward*, he diminishes nothing from the gratuitous promise of Salvation; for the faithful know that their labor is not vain in the Lord in such a way that they still rest on God's mercy alone. But it has been often stated elsewhere how reward is not incompatible with the gratuitous imputation of righteousness.

HEBREWS X. 36-39

36. For ye have need of patience, that, after ye have done the will of God, ye might receive the promise.
37. For yet a little while, and he that shall come will come, and will not tarry.
38. Now the just shall live by faith: but if *any man* draw back, my soul shall have no pleasure in him.
39. But we are not of them who draw back unto perdition; but of them that believe to the saving of the soul.

---

191 Calvin leaves out ἐν ἑαυτοῖς, as the Vulg. does. The ἐν is deemed by most spurious, but most retain ἑαυτοῖς, though they do not connect it as in our version, with "knowing," and render the clause thus, "knowing that you have for yourselves in heaven a better and an enduring substance," or property or possession. The word for "substance" occurs only here, except in the plural number in Acts ii. 45. It occurs often in the Sept., and stands for words in Hebrew, which signify substance, wealth, riches, possessions. — *Ed*

36. *For ye have need of patience, etc.* He says that patience is necessary, not only because we have to endure to the end, but as Satan has innumerable arts by which he harasses us; and hence except we possess extraordinary patience, we shall a thousand times be broken down before we come to the half of our course. The inheritance of eternal life is indeed certain to us, but as life is like a race, we ought to go on towards the goal. But in our way there are many hindrances and difficulties, which not only delay us, but which would also stop our course altogether, except we had great firmness of mind to pass through them. Satan craftily suggests every kind of trouble in order to discourage us. In short, Christians will never advance two paces without fainting, except they are sustained by patience.[192] This then is the only way or means by which we can firmly and constantly advance; we shall not otherwise obey God, nor even enjoy the promised inheritance, which is here by metonymy called the "promise".

37. *For yet a little while,* or, *for yet a very little time, etc.* That it may not be grievous to us to endure, he reminds us that the time will not be long. There is indeed nothing that avails more to sustain our minds, should they at any time become faint, than the hope of a speedy and near termination. As a general holds forth to his soldiers the prospect that the war will soon end, provided they hold out a little longer; so the Apostle reminds us that the Lord will shortly come to deliver us from all evils, provided our minds faint not through want of firmness.

And in order that this consolation might have more assurance and authority, he adduces the testimony of the Prophet Habakkuk. (Habakkuk ii. 4.) But as he follows the Greek version, he departs somewhat from the words of the Prophet. I will first briefly explain what the Prophet says, and then we shall compare it with what the Apostle relates here.

When the Prophet had spoken of the dreadful overthrow of his own nation, being terrified by his prophecy, he had nothing to do but to quit as it were the world, and to betake himself to

---

192 Or, "patient waiting," as rendered by Erasmus and Stuart, and not "perseverance," as rendered by Macknight. They were to suffer patiently their trials, looking forward to their termination; and in order to encourage them patiently to endure, he reminds them in the next verse that it will only be for a very short time. — Ed.

his watchtower; and his watchtower was the Word of God, by which he was raised as it were into heaven. Being thus placed in this station, he was bidden to write a new prophecy, which brought to the godly the hope of salvation. Yet as men are naturally unreasonable, and are so hasty in their wishes that they always think God tardy, whatever haste he may make, he told them that the promise would come without delay; at the same time he added, "If it tarries, wait for it." By which he meant, that what God promises will never come so soon, but that it seems to us to tarry, according to an old proverb, "Even speed is delay to desire." Then follow these words, "Behold, his soul that is lifted up is not upright in him; but the just shall live by his faith." By these words he intimates that the ungodly, however they may be fortified by defenses, should not be able to stand, for there is no life of security but by faith. Let the unbelieving then fortify themselves as they please, they can find nothing in the whole world but what is fading, so that they must ever be subject to trembling; but their faith will never disappoint the godly, because it rests on God. This is the meaning of the Prophet.

Now the Apostle applies to God what Habakkuk said of the promise; but as God by fulfilling his promises in a manner shows what he is, as to the subject itself there is not much difference; nay, the Lord comes whenever he puts forth his hand to help us. The Apostle follows the Prophet in saying, That it would be shortly; because God defers not his help longer than it is expedient; for he does not by delaying time deceive us as men are wont to do; but he knows his own time which he suffers not to pass by without coming to our aid at the moment required. Now he says, *He that cometh will come, and will not tarry.* Here are two clauses: by the first we are taught that God will come to our aid, for he has promised; and by the second, that he will do so in due time, not later than he ought.[193]

---

[193] It is evident from the manner in which the quotation is made, that the Apostle meant only to adapt to his own purpose the passage in Habakkuk; he does not quote it in the order in which it is found there, nor literally from the Hebrew, nor wholly so from the Sept. What is said in Habakkuk of the vision, he applies here to the Lord. Surely, such a use of a passage is legitimate.

The coming of Christ mentioned here, according to Mede, was his coming to destroy Jerusalem, and to put an end to the Jewish polity. If "the approaching day," in verse 25, be considered to be

38. *Now the just, etc.* He means that patience is born of faith; and this is true, for we shall never be able to carry on our contests unless we are sustained by faith, even as, on the other hand, John truly declares, that our victory over the world is by faith. (1 John v. 4.) It is by faith that we ascend on high; that we leap over all the perils of this present life, and all its miseries and troubles; that we possess a quiet standing in the midst of storms and tempests. Then the Apostle announced this truth, that all who are counted just before God do not live otherwise than by faith. And the future tense of the verb *live*, betokens the perpetuity of this life. Let readers consult on this subject Romans i. 17, and Galatians iii. 11, where this passage is quoted.

But if any man draw back, etc. This is the rendering of עפלה elation, as used by the Prophet, for the words are, "Where there shall be elation or munition, the soul of that man shall not continue right in him." The Apostle gives here the Greek version, which partly agrees with the words of the Prophet, and partly differs from them. For this drawing back differs but little, if anything, from that elation or pride with which the ungodly are inflated, since their refractory opposition to God proceeds from that false confidence with which they are inebriated; for hence it is that they renounce his authority and promise themselves a quiet state, free from all evil. They may be said, then, to draw back, when they set up defenses of this kind, by which they drive away every fear of God and reverence for his name. And thus by this expression is intimated the power of faith no less than the character of impiety; for pride is impiety, because it renders not to God the honor due to him, by rendering man obedient to him. From self-security, insolence, and contempt, it comes that as long as it is well with the wicked, they dare, as one has said, to insult the clouds. But since nothing is more contrary to faith than this drawing back, for the true character of faith is, that it draws a man unto submission to God when drawn back by his own sinful nature.

The other clause, "He will not please my soul," or as I have rendered it more fully, "My soul shall not delight in him," is to

---

that event then the same event is most probably referred to here. Besides, he speaks here of the enmity of the unbelieving Jews; and as our Savior represented the destruction of Jerusalem as a blessing to his people, it becomes still more probable that Christ's coming to destroy that nation is intended. — *Ed.*

be taken as the expression of the Apostle's feeling; for it was not his purpose to quote exactly the words of the Prophet, but only to refer to the passage to invite readers to a closer examination of it.[194]

39. *But we are not of them which draw back, etc.* The Apostle made a free use of the Greek version, which was most suitable to the doctrine which he was discussing; and he now wisely applies it. He had before warned them, lest by forsaking the Church they should alienate themselves from the faith and the grace of Christ; he now teaches them that they had been called for this end, that they might not draw back. And he again sets faith and drawing back in opposition the one to the other, and also the preservation of the soul to its perdition.

Now let it be noticed that this truth belongs also to us, for we, whom God has favored with the light of the Gospel, ought

---

194 This verse, with the exception of the two clauses being inverted, and of my being not added to "faith," is literally the same with the Sept. But the last clause here and the first in Habakkuk, differs in words materially from the Hebrew, according to the received text. There are two MSS. which give עלפה instead of עפלה, a transposition of two letters. If not exactly in words. The Hebrew, then, would be as follows —

Behold the fainting! Not right is his soul within him;
But the righteousness by his faith shall he live.

The fainting i.e., as to faith and he who "draws back," or withdraws through fear, as the verb means, are descriptive of the same character. To persevere in expecting the fulfillment of a promise, is the subject in Habakkuk and also in this passage. And then, that the soul of the fainting is not right, is the same as to say that such a soul is not what God approves.

A theological dispute has arisen, though unnecessarily, from the construction of the last clause in this verse. The introduction of "any one," or any man, has been objected to, and that it ought to be "but if he," i.e., "the righteousness" draw back, etc. The probability is, that as "anyone" should not be ascribed to Beza, for Pagininus and others had done so before him. However, the doctrine of perseverance is in no way imperiled by leaving out "any one." The Bible is full of this mode of addressing Christians, and yet the Bible assures us that the sheep of Christ shall never perish. Warnings and admonitions are the very means which God employs to secure the final salvation of his people; and to conclude from such warnings that they may finally fall away, is by no means a legitimate argument. — *Ed.*

to acknowledge that we have been called in order that we may advance more and more in our obedience to God, and strive constantly to draw nearer to him. This is the real preservation of the soul, for by so doing we shall escape eternal perdition.

CHAPTER 11

HEBREWS XI. 1

1. Now faith is the substance of things hoped for, the evidence of things not seen.

1. *Now faith, etc.* Whoever made this the beginning of the eleventh chapter, has unwisely disjointed the context; for the object of the Apostle was to prove what he had already said -that there is need of patience.[195] He had quoted the testimony of Habakkuk, who says that the just lives by faith; he now shows what remained to be proved — that faith can be no more separated from patience than from itself. The order then of what he says is this, — "We shall not reach the goal of salvation except we have patience, for the Prophet declares that the just lives by faith; but faith directs us to things afar off which we do not as yet enjoy; it then necessarily includes patience." Therefore the minor proposition in the argument is this, *Faith is the substance of things hoped for, etc.* It is hence also evident, that greatly mistaken are they who think that an exact definition of faith is given here; for the Apostle does not speak here of the whole of what faith is, but selects that part of it which was suitable to his purpose, even that it has patience ever connected with it.[196] Let us now consider the words.

---

195 Griesbach makes the division at the thirty-eighth verse of the last chapter, and this is no doubt what the subject requires. — *Ed.*

196 "Faith is here generally described, not only as it justifies, but also as it acts towards God and lays hold on his promises, works, and blessings revealed in his word, past, present, and future." — *Pareus.*

He calls faith the *hypostasis,* the substance of things hoped for. We indeed know that what we hope for is not what we have as it were in hand, but what is as yet hid from us, or at least the enjoyment of which is delayed to another time. The Apostle now teaches us the same thing with what we find in Romans viii. 24; where it is said that what is hoped for is not seen, and hence the inference is drawn, that it is to be waited for in patience. So the Apostle here reminds us, that faith regards not present things, but such as are waited for. Nor is this kind of contradiction without its force and beauty: Faith, he says, is the hypostasis, the prop, or the foundation on which we plant our foot, — the prop of what? Of things absent, which are so far from being really possessed by us, that they are far beyond the reach of our understanding.

The same view is to be taken of the second clause, when he calls faith the *evidence* or demonstration of things *not seen;* for demonstration makes things to appear or to be seen; and it is commonly applied to what is subject to our senses.[197]

---

[197] The two words "substance" and "evidence" have been variously rendered, though the meaning continues materially the same: "substinance" and "demonstration" by Beza: "confident expectation" and "conviction" by Grotius and Doddridge: "confidence" and "evidence" by Macknight: "confidence" and "convincing evidence" by Stuart. When the primary meaning of words is suitable, there is no necessity of having recourse to what is secondary. The first word means properly a foundation, a basis, a prop, a support: and what can be more appropriate here? Faith is the basis or the prop (as Calvin renders it in his exposition) of things hoped for; that is, faith is the foundation of hope; it is the fulcrum on which hope rests. The other word is properly "demonstration" a proof supported by reasons — what is made clear and evident. Conviction is the result of demonstration. So, then, the meaning is this — faith sustains hope, and exhibits to view things unseen: it is the basis on which the objects of hope rest, and the demonstration or manifestation of what is not seen.

The word "substance" is derived from the Vulgate: though its etymological meaning corresponds with the original, yet its received meaning is quite different. The original word occurs five times in the New Testament, and is rendered "confidence" in 2 Corinthians ix. 4, xi. 17; Hebrews iii. 14, — "person" in Hebrew i. 3, — and here "substance;" but why not its more literal meaning, "foundation?"

Then these two things, though apparently inconsistent, do yet perfectly harmonize when we speak of faith; for the Spirit of God shows to us hidden things, the knowledge of which cannot reach our senses: Promised to us is eternal life, but it is promised to the dead; we are assured of a happy resurrection, but we are as yet involved in corruption; we are pronounced just, as yet sin dwells in us; we hear that we are happy, but we are as yet in the midst of many miseries; an abundance of all good things is promised to us, but still we often hunger and thirst; God proclaims that he will come quickly, but he seems deaf when we cry to him. What would become of us were we not supported by hope, and did not our minds emerge out of the midst of darkness above the world through the light of God's word and of his Spirit? Faith, then, is rightly said to be the subsistence or substance of things which are as yet the objects of hope and the evidence of things not seen. *Augustine* sometimes renders evidence "conviction," which I do not disapprove, for it faithfully expresses the Apostle's meaning: but I prefer "demonstration," as it is more literal.

HEBREWS XI. 2-4

2. For by it the elders obtained a good report.
3. Through faith we understand that the worlds were framed by the word of God, so that things which are seen were not made of things which do appear.
4. By faith Abel offered unto God a more excellent sacrifice than Cain, by which he obtained witness that he was righteous, God testifying of his gifts: and by it he being dead yet speaketh.

2. *For by it the elders,* [198] *etc.* He handles this subject to the end

---

The things "hoped for" include the promises; but the things "not seen," all that is revealed as to what is past and is to come, — the creation, the future destiny of man, etc. — *Ed*.

198 Macknight and Stuart render the word "ancients" and more suitably in our language. The word "elders" most commonly refers to age, but "ancients" to time: those meant here were such as lived before and under the Law. — *Ed*.

of the chapter — that the fathers obtained salvation and were accepted by God in no other way than by faith.

The Jews indeed had some reasons for paying great deference to the fathers; but a foolish admiration of the fathers had so prevailed among them, that it proved a great hindrance to a thorough surrender of themselves to Christ and to his government. It was occasioned either by ambition or superstition, or by both. For when they heard that they were the blessed and holy seed of Abraham, inflated with this distinction they fixed their eyes on men rather than on God. Then added to this was a false emulation; for they did not consider what was mainly worthy of imitation in their fathers. It thus happened that they became attached to the old ceremonies, as though the whole of religion and perfect holiness consisted in them. This error the Apostle exposes and condemns; and be shows what was the chief excellency of the fathers, in order that their posterity might understand how they might become really like them.

Let us then bear in mind that the main point and the very hinge on which the Apostle's argument turns is this, — That all the fathers from the beginning of the world, were approved by God in no other way than by being united to him by faith: and this he shows, that the Jews might know that by faith alone they could be bound together in holy unity with the fathers, and that as soon as they renounced faith, they became banished from the Church, and that they were then no longer the legitimate children of Abraham, but a degenerate race and bastards.[199]

3. *Through,* or by, *faith we understand,* [200] *etc.* This is a most striking proof of the last verse; for we differ nothing from the

---

[199] The verb rendered in our version "obtained a good report," is rendered by Calvin, "obtained a testimony;" by Beza, "were approved;" by Macknight "were born witness to;" and Stuart, "obtained commendation". It is better to retain the idea of a testimony, as a reference is made either to the written testimony of Scripture, or to some express testimony given by God, as in the case of Abel. As the verb is everywhere used in a good sense, as referring to a good testimony, "the good report" of our version, or "the honorable testimony" of Doddridge, seems to convey the right meaning. — *Ed.*

[200] That is "We, by faith in God's word which gives the record, understand, or know how the world was made." This the heathens did not know by the light of reason, and yet they might have

brute creation, if we understand not that the world has been created by God. To what end have men been endued with understanding and reason, except that they might acknowledge their Creator? But it is by faith alone we know that it was God who created the world. No wonder then that faith shone forth in the fathers above all other virtues.

But it may be here asked, Why does the Apostle assert that what even infidels acknowledge is only understood by faith? For the very appearance of heaven and earth constrains even the ungodly to acknowledge some Maker; and hence Paul condemns all for ingratitude, because they did not, after having known God, give him the honor due to him. (Romans i. 25.) And no doubt religion would not have so prevailed among all nations, had not men's minds been impressed with the convictions that God is the Creator of the world. It thus then appears that this knowledge which the Apostle ascribes to faith, exists without faith.

To this I reply, — that though there has been an opinion of this kind among heathens, that the world was made by God, it was yet very evanescent, for as soon as they formed a notion of

---

known this, as the Apostle declares in Romans i. 20. The reference here, according to this view, is to the fact, to the case as it was, but in the Romans to what ought to have been the case.

Why "worlds?" the same word, though in the plural number is rendered "world" in verse 36 and 1 Corinthians x. 11, and so here by Beza and others. The universe, the whole visible creation, is what is meant, as it appears from "seen" in the next clause: and the word αἰών, in the singular number, says Stuart, is not employed to designate the "world" that is the universe. It is said to be used plurally to express the various parts of which the world is composed. But the term "world" in our language comprehends the whole: it means the whole visible creation.

The verb "framed," is rendered "compacted" by Beza — "adjusted" by Doddridge — "produced" by Macknight — and "formed" by Stuart. Calvin has "fitted" or joined together, *aptata*, the word used by the Vulgate. It is justly said by Leigh, that the verb properly means to compact or knit together disjointed parts, either of a body or a building. But it is used also in the sense of adjusting, fitting, preparing, setting in order, and perfecting, or completing. It is most commonly used in the sense of making perfect or complete. But we may render the words "the world was set in order by the word of God." — *Ed.*

some God, they became instantly vain in their imaginations, so that they groped in the dark, having in their thoughts a mere shadow of some uncertain deity, and not the knowledge of the true God. Besides, as it was only a transient opinion that flit in their minds, it was far from being anything like knowledge. We may further add, that they assigned to fortune or chance the supremacy in the government of the world, and they made no mention of God's providence which alone rules everything. Men's minds therefore are wholly blind, so that they see not the light of nature which shines forth in created things, until being irradiated by God's Spirit, they begin to understand by faith what otherwise they cannot comprehend. Hence most correctly does the Apostle ascribe such an understanding to faith; for they who have faith do not entertain a slight opinion as to God being the Creator of the world, but they have a deep conviction fixed in their minds and behold the true God. And further, they understand the power of his word, not only as manifested instantaneously in creating the world, but also as put forth continually in its preservation; nor is it his power only that they understand, but also his goodness, and wisdom, and justice. And hence they are led to worship, love, and honor him.

Not made of things which do appear. As to this clause, all interpreters seem to me to have been mistaken; and the mistake has arisen from separating the preposition from the participle φαινομένων. They give this rendering, "So that visible things were made from things which do not appear." But from such words hardly any sense can be elicited, at least a very jejune sense; and further, the text does not admit of such a meaning, for then the words must have been, ἐκ μὴ φαινομένων: but the order adopted by the Apostle is different. If, then, the words were rendered literally, the meaning would be as follows, — "So that they became the visible of things not visible," or, not apparent. Thus the preposition would be joined to the participle to which it belongs. Besides, the words would then contain a very important truth, — that we have in this visible world, a conspicuous image of God; and thus the same truth is taught here, as in Romans i. 20, where it is said, that the invisible things of God are made known to us by the creation of the world, they being seen in his works. God has given us, throughout the whole framework of this world, clear evidences of his eternal wisdom, goodness, and power; and though he is in himself invisible, he in a manner becomes visible to us in his works.[201]

Correctly then is this world called the mirror of divinity; not that there is sufficient clearness for man to gain a full knowledge of God, by looking at the world, but that he has thus so far revealed himself, that the ignorance of the ungodly is without excuse. Now the faithful, to whom he has given eyes, see sparks of his glory, as it were, glittering in every created thing. The world was no doubt made, that it might be the theater of the divine glory.

---

[201] Moderns no less than the ancients differ from Calvin as to this clause; and yet his explanation is more suited to the passage, and especially to εἰς τὸ which means properly, to the end that, or, in order to, denoting the object or final cause. But there is no authority for making ἐκ and φαινομένων one word as he proposes: yet if the transposition of μὴ be admitted, which both ancient and modern critics allow, the meaning advocated by Calvin may still be defended: "in order that of things not apparent there might be things visible;" the things not apparent or visible being the power, wisdom and goodness of God, in exact harmony with Romans i. 20, where God's power and divinity are said to be "invisible things" — τὰ ἀόρατα: they are things not apparent.

Again, the verb κατηρτίσθαι denotes not creation, but the fitting or adjusting, or setting in order of things previously created: it seems to designate the work done, not as described in the first verse of Genesis, but in the following verses: so that the object or design of this adjustment or arrangement is what is expressed in this clause; it was, that there might be visible things as evidence or manifestations of things invisible.

It may be further said, that the world is said to have been set in order by the word of God: and so it is recorded in Genesis: but this word or fiat is not mentioned in the first verse of that book, in which the heavens and the earth are said to have been created. It hence appears that the reference here is to the setting in order of this world, and not to the first creation of its materials; and if so, the second clause cannot refer to the creation of the world out of nothing, as it is necessarily connected with what the first clause contains.

"Faith" then refers here, if this view must be taken, not to the fact that the world was made by God, which even heathens admitted, but to the design of God in creation, the manifestation of his own glory. "The heavens," says the Psalmist "declare the glory of God," etc. — Ed.

4. By faith Abel offered, *etc.* The Apostle's object in this chapter is to show, that however excellent were the works of the saints, it was from faith they derived their value, their worthiness, and all their excellences; and hence follows what he has already intimated, that the fathers pleased God by faith alone.

Now he commends faith here on two accounts, — it renders obedience to God, for it attempts and undertakes nothing, but what is according to the rule of God's word, — and it relies on God's promises, and thus it gains the value and worth which belongs to works from his grace alone. Hence, wherever the word faith is found in this chapter, we must bear in mind, that the Apostle speaks of it, in order that the Jews might regard no other rule than God's word, and might also depend alone on his promises.

He says, first, that Abel's *sacrifice* was for no other reason preferable to that of his brother, except that it was sanctified by faith:[202] for surely the fat of brute animals did not smell so sweetly, that it could, by its odor, pacify God. The Scripture indeed shows plainly, why God accepted his sacrifice, for Moses's words are these, "God had respect to Abel, and to his gifts." It is hence obvious to conclude, that his sacrifice was accepted, because he himself was graciously accepted. But how did he obtain this favor, except that his heart was purified by faith.

God testifying, etc. He confirms what I have already stated, that no works, coming from us can please God, until we ourselves are received into favor, or to speak more briefly, that no works are deemed just before God, but those of a just man: for

---

[202] "Abel's offering was more acceptable than that of Cain, because he had faith." — Grotius.

The word "sacrifice," θυσία, means properly an offered victim, but sometimes anything offered to God. Indeed Abel's sacrifice is called in Genesis iv. 4, an offering. The word πλείων is literally more, but is used in the sense of more in number, quantity or excellency. The last is evidently the meaning here; for Abel's offering, according to the account given, was not in the number or quantity, but in quality. Then a better or a more excellent sacrifice, and not a fuller, as some have rendered it, is the right version. — *Ed*

he reasons thus, — God bore a testimony to Abel's gifts; then he had obtained the praise of being just before God.[203]

This doctrine is useful, and ought especially to be noticed, as we are not easily convinced of its truth; for when in any work, anything splendid appears, we are immediately rapt in admiration, and we think that it cannot possibly be disapproved of by God: but God, who regards only the inward purity of the heart, heeds not the outward masks of works. Let us then learn, that no right or good work can proceed from us, until we are justified before God.

By it he being dead, etc. To faith he also ascribes this, — that God testified that Abel was no less the object of his care after his death, than during his life: for when he says, that though dead, he still speaketh, he means, as Moses tells us, that God was moved by his violent death to take vengeance. When, therefore, Abel or his blood is said to speak, the words are to be understood figuratively. It was yet a singular evidence of God's love towards him, that he had a care for him when he was dead; and

---

203 What the Apostle evidently refers to are these words, "the Lord had respect to Abel and to his offering." He calls this "testifying." How this was done, we are not told. The divine approbation was in some way conveyed; there was respect had to Abel and to his offering, but not to Cain nor to his offering. The Apostle says here first, that Abel "obtained a testimony that he was righteous," and then he adds by way of explanation: God testifying of his gifts. It seems then that the approbation of his gifts was the testimony he received that he was righteous, this was evidently the meaning of the Apostle. Now the question is, how was this testimony as to that sacrifice. What was it? Such, we may reasonably conclude as was given in other recorded instances; it was by fire sent from heaven to consume the sacrifice. See Leviticus ix. 24; 1 Kings xviii. 38; 2 Chronicles vii. 1.

"By which," and "by it," are commonly referred to faith, but the passage would be plainer, by referring them to "the sacrifice." It was by the means or medium of the sacrifice, that the testimony was given, and it was on the account of it that Abel was put to death; "and through it, having died, he yet speaketh;" that is, though he died, owing to his sacrifice being approved, he yet speaketh, that is, by his example as a believer, say some, in the atonement; as a sufferer in behalf of the truth, say others. — *Ed.*

it hence appears, that he was one of God's saints, whose death is precious to him.[204]

HEBREWS XI. 5-6

5. By faith Enoch was translated that he should not see death; and was not found, because God had translated him: for before his translation he had this testimony, that he pleased God.
6. But without faith *it is* impossible to please *him*: for he that cometh to God must believe that he is, and *that* he is a rewarder of them that diligently seek him.

5. *By faith Enoch, etc.* He chose a few of the most ancient, that he might make a transition to Abraham and his posterity. He teaches us that through faith, it was that Enoch was translated.

But we ought especially to consider the reason why God in so unusual a manner removed him from the earth. The event was remarkable, and hence all may know how dear he was to God. Impiety and all kinds of corruptions then prevailed everywhere. Had he died as other men, it would have not occurred to any, that he was thus preserved from the prevailing contagion by God's providence; but, as he was taken away without dying, the hand of God from heaven, removing him as it were from the fire, was openly manifested. It was not to then an ordinary honor with which God had favored him. Moses indeed tells us, that he was a righteous man, and that he walked with God; but as righteousness begins with faith, it is justly ascribed to his faith, that he pleased God.[205]

---

204 Though this view has been taken by Grotius and many others, yet the one suggested above is what has been mostly adopted. It is Abel himself who here speaks as a man of faith; it is the voice of his blood that is referred to in chapter xii. 24. Instead of the received reading, the preponderance of copies is in favor of λαλεῖ — *Ed*

205 "He reasons thus: — He who pleases God is endued with faith; Enoch pleased God; then Enoch was endued with faith." — J. Capellus.

As to the subtle questions which the curious usually moot, it is better to pass them over, without taking much notice of them. They ask, what became of these two men, Enoch and Elijah? And then, that they may not appear merely to ask questions, they imagine that they are reserved for the last days of the Church, that they may then come forth into the world; and for this purpose the Revelation of John is referred to. Let us leave this airy philosophy to those light and vain minds, which cannot be satisfied with what is solid. Let it suffice us to know, that their translation was a sort of extraordinary death; nor let us doubt but that they were divested of their mortal and corruptible flesh, in order that they might, with the other members of Christ, be renewed into a blessed immortality.[206]

6. *But without faith, etc.* What is said here belongs to all the examples which the Apostle records in this chapter; but as there is in the passage some measure of obscurity, it is necessary to examine its meaning more closely.

But there is no better interpreter than the Apostle himself. The proof, then, which he immediately subjoins, may serve as an explanation. The reason he assigns why no one can please God without faith, is this, — because no one will ever come to God, except he believes that God is, and is also convinced that he is a remunerator to all who seek him. If access then to God is not opened, but by faith, it follows, that all who are without it, are the objects of God's displeasure. Hence the Apostle shows how faith obtains favor for us, even because faith is our teacher as to the true worship of God, and makes us certain as to his goodwill, so that we may not think that we seek him in vain.

---

[206] It is the Sept. that is followed by the Apostle. Instead of "he walked with God," we have here, "he pleased God;" and for, "he was not," the phrase is "he was not found." One part of the verse is nearly a literal quotation, "and he was not found, because God had translated him;" and this ought to be put parenthetically, for what follows is connected with the first clause, as it contains a reason for what is there asserted; Enoch was through faith translated, for he had a testimony that he pleased God; and to please God is an evidence of faith, as proved by the following verse.

Strange are the vagaries of learned men! Some of the German divines have attempted to prove that Enoch was not translated without dying. Though no words can express the event more clearly than those of the Apostle. This is an instance of what men will do to support a false system, when once fully imbibed. — *Ed.*

These two clauses ought not to be slightly passed over, — that we must believe that God is, and that we ought to feel assured that he is not sought in vain.[207]

It does not indeed seem a great matter, when the Apostle requires us to believe that God is; but when you more closely consider it, you will find that there is here a rich, profound, and sublime truth; for though almost all admit without disputing that God is, yet it is evident, that except the Lord retains us in the true and certain knowledge of himself, various doubts will ever creep in, and obliterate every thought of a Divine Being. To this vanity the disposition of man is no doubt prone, so that to forget God becomes an easy thing. At the same time the Apostle does not mean, that men ought to feel assured that there is some God, for he speaks only of the true God; nay, it will not be sufficient for you to form a notion of any God you please; but you must understand what sort of Being the true God is; for what will it profit us to devise and form an idol, and to ascribe to it the glory due to God?

We now then perceive what the Apostle means in the first clause; he denies that we can have an access to God, except we have the truth, that God is deeply fixed in our hearts, so as not to be led here and there by various opinions.

It is hence evident, that men in vain weary themselves in serving God, except they observe the right way, and that all religions are not only vain, but also pernicious, with which the true and certain knowledge of God is not connected; for all are prohibited from having any access to God, who do not distinguish and separate him from all idols; in short, there is no religion except where this truth reigns dominant. But if the true knowledge of God has its seat in our hearts it will not fail to lead us to honor and fear him; for God, without his majesty is not really known. Hence arises the desire to serve him, hence it

---

207 To "come to God," is very expressive, and is literally the word. To "approach to" by Doddridge, and "to worship," by Macknight, are no improvements, but otherwise. God is represented as sitting on the throne of grace; hence the idea of coming to him. Enoch walked with God, as though God was a friend and a companion; hence to come to him is the appropriate expression. Stuart says, that it is a metaphor derived from the practice of coming to the temple to worship, God being represented as there present.
— Ed.

comes that the whole life is so formed, that he is regarded as the end in all things

The second clause is that we ought to be fully persuaded that God is not sought in vain; and this persuasion includes the hope of salvation and eternal life, for no one will be in a suitable state of heart to seek God except a sense of the divine goodness be deeply felt, so as to look for salvation from him. We indeed flee from God, or wholly disregard him, when there is no hope of salvation. But let us bear in mind, that this is what must be really believed, and not held merely as a matter of opinions; for even the ungodly may sometimes entertain such a notion, and yet they do not come to God; and for this reason, because they have not a firm and fixed faith.[208] This then is the other part of faith by which we obtain favor with God, even when we feel assured that salvation is laid up for us in him.

But many shamefully pervert this clause; for they hence elicit the merits of works, and the conceit about deserving. And they reason thus: "We please God by faith, because we believe him to be a rewarder; then faith has respect to the merits of works." This error cannot be better exposed, than by considering how God is to be sought; while any one is wandering from the right way of seeking him,[209] he cannot be said to be engaged in the work. Now Scripture assigns this as the right way, — that a man, prostrate in himself, and smitten with the conviction that he deserves eternal death, and in self-despair, is to flee to Christ as the only asylum for salvation. Nowhere certainly can we find that we are to bring to God any merits of works to put us in a state of favor with him. Then he who understands that this is the only right way of seeking God, will be freed from every

---

208 "Certainly there is no true faith in the doctrine of salvation, unless it be attended with this magnetic force, by which it draws the soul to God." — Archb. Leighton

209 Calvin does not connect "diligently" with seeking, as in our version. Merely to seek, is what the verb means. It is rendered in Acts xv. 17, "to seek after," and so in Romans iii. 11, and carefully is added to it on chapter xii. 17. It is found often in the Sept. in the sense of seeking, and stands for a verb in Hebrew, which means simply to seek. See Deuteronomy iv. 29; Psalm xiv. 2; Jeremiah xxix. 13. Stuart's version is, "Who seek him?" and so is Beza's — Ed.

difficulty on the subject; for reward refers not to the worthiness or value of works but to faith.

Thus, these frigid glosses of the Sophists, such as, "by faith we please God, for we deserve when we intend to please," fall wholly to the ground. The Apostle's object was to carry us much higher, even that conscience might feel assured that it is not a vain thing to seek God; and this certainty or assurance far exceeds what we can of ourselves attain, especially when any one considers his own self. For it is not to be laid down as an abstract principle, that God is a rewarder to those who seek him; but every one of us ought individually to apply this doctrine to himself, so that we may know that we are regarded by God, that he has such a care for our salvation as never to be wanting to us, that our prayers are heard by him, that he will be to us a perpetual deliverer. But as none of these things come to us except through Christ, our faith must ever regard him and cleave to him alone.

From these two clauses, we may learn how, and why it is impossible for man to please God without faith; God justly regards us all as objects of his displeasure, as we are all by nature under his curse; and we have no remedy in our own power. It is hence necessary that God should anticipate us by his grace; and hence it comes, that we are brought to know that God is, and in such a way that no corrupt superstition can seduce us, and also that we become assured of a certain salvation from him.

Were any one to desire a fuller view of this subject, he should make his commencement here, — that we in vain attempt to try anything, except we look to God; for the only true end of life is to promote his glory; but this can never be done, unless there be first the true knowledge of him. Yet this is still but the half of faith, and will profit us but little, except confidence be added. Hence faith will only then be complete and secure us God's favor, when we shall feel a confidence that we shall not seek him in vain, and thus entertain the certainty of obtaining salvation from him. But no one, except he be blinded by presumption, and fascinated by self-love, can feel assured that God will be a rewarder of his merits. Hence this confidence of which we speak recumbs not on works, nor on man's own worthiness, but on the grace of God alone; and as grace is nowhere found but in Christ, it is on him alone that faith ought to be fixed.

HEBREWS XI. 7

7. By faith Noah, being warned of God of things not seen as yet, moved with fear, prepared an ark to the saving of his house; by the which he condemned the world, and became heir of the righteousness which is by faith.

7. *By faith Noah, etc.* It was a wonderful example of magnanimity, that when the whole world were promising themselves impunity, and securely and unrestrainedly indulging themselves in sinful pleasures, Noah alone paid regard to Gods vengeance though deferred for a considerable time, — that he greatly wearied himself for a hundred and twenty years in building the ark, — that he stood unshaken amidst the scoffs of so many ungodly men, — that he entertained no doubt but that he would be safe in the midst of the ruin of the whole world, — yea, that he felt sure of life as it were in the grave, even in the ark. It is briefly that I shall touch on the subject; each one can better for himself weigh all the circumstances.

The Apostle ascribes to faith the praise of so remarkable a fortitude. He has been hitherto speaking of the fathers who lived in the first age of the world; but it was a kind of regeneration when Noah and his family emerged from the deluge. It is hence evident that in all ages men have neither been approved by God, nor performed anything worthy of praise otherwise than by faith.

Let us now then see what are the things he presents to our consideration in the case of Noah. They are the following, — that having been warned of things to come, but not yet made visible, he feared, — that he built an ark, — that he condemned the world by building it, — and that he became the heir of that righteousness which is faith.[210]

---

210 This is a very clear statement of the case of Noah. Many learned critics have given a different view, among moderns, Stuart and Dr. Bloomfield. The word rendered very correctly in our version, "being moved with fear," they have rendered "with reverence" connecting it with "prepared." The only other instance in which it occurs, it has the meaning of fear or dread, as to the consequences, see Acts xxiii. 10. Besides, the whole tenor of the passage comports with this meaning: what was the warning? It was

What I have just mentioned is that which especially sets forth the power of faith; for the Apostle ever reminds us of this truth, that faith is the evidence of things not seen; and doubtless it is its peculiar office to behold in God's word the things which are hid, and far removed from our senses. When it was declared to Noah that there would be a deluge after one hundred and twenty years, first, the length of time might have removed every fear; secondly, the thing in itself seemed incredible; thirdly, he saw the ungodly heedlessly indulging in sinful pleasures; and lastly, the terrible announcement of a deluge might have appeared to him as intended only to terrify men. But Noah attended so much to God's word, that turning away his eyes from the appearance of things at that time, he feared the destruction which God had threatened, as though it was present. Hence the faith which he had in God's word prepared him to render obedience to God; and of this he afterwards gave a proof by building the ark.

But here a question is raised. Why does the Apostle make faith the cause of fear, since it has respect to promises of grace rather than to threatening? For Paul for this reason calls the Gospel, in which God's righteousness is offered to us for salvation, the word of faith. It seems then to have been improperly stated, that Noah was by faith led to fear. To this, I reply, that

---

that of a dreadful judgment; and how is judgment to be regarded, but with fear? Faith, as Calvin will tell us presently, regards judgments as well as promises. Men are exhorted to flee from the wrath to come: when they believe that there is a wrath to come, do not they fear? Doddridge and Scott coincide with Calvin.

The other difference is, as to δι ἧς, "by which," before "condemned." This is not so manifestly wrong as the other, yet the meaning which Calvin gives is the most obvious, and the most suitable. Stuart refers "which" to faith, while it ought evidently to be referred to the ark; Noah by building the ark which he did by faith, condemned the conduct of others in neglecting to provide for the coming destruction. His preparation, done by faith, condemned their neglect, which was owing to unbelief.

As to the word "heir," it means an heir in prospect, and an heir in possession, as in chapter i. 2. So it is evidently to be understood here. Noah became heir or possessor of the righteousness, which is by faith. The rendering of Stuart is nothing so expressive as the literal, "and obtained the justification which is by faith."
— *Ed.*

faith indeed properly springs from promises; it is founded on them, it rests on them. We hence say that Christ is the real object of faith, for through him our heavenly Father is reconciled to us, and by him all the promises of salvation are sealed and confirmed. Yet there is no reason why faith should not look to God and reverently receive whatever he may say; or if you prefer another way of stating the subject, it rightly belongs to faith to hear God whenever he speaks, and unhesitatingly to embrace whatsoever may proceed from his sacred mouth. Thus far it has regard to commands and threatening, as well as to gratuitous promises. But as no man is moved as he ought and as much as is needful, to obey God's commands, nor is sufficiently stirred up to deprecate his wrath, unless he has already laid hold on the promises of grace, so as to acknowledge him as a kind Father, and the author of salvation, — hence the Gospel is called the word of faith, the principal part being stated for the whole; and thus is set forth the mutual relation that there is between them both. Faith, then, though its most direct regard is to God's promises, yet looks on his threatening so far as it is necessary for it to be taught to fear and obey God.

Prepared an ark, etc. Here is pointed out that obedience which flows from faith as water from a fountain. The work of building the ark was long and laborious. It might have been haltered by the scoffs of the ungodly, and thus suspended a thousand times; nor is there a doubt but they mocked and derided the holy man on every side. That he then bore their wanton insults with an unshaken spirit, is a proof that his resolution to obey was not of an ordinary kind. But how was it that he so perseveringly obeyed God except that he had previously rested on the promise which gave him the hope of deliverance; and in this confidence he persevered even to the last; for he could not have had the courage willingly to undergo so many toils, nor could he have been able to overcome so many obstacles, nor could he have stood so firm in his purpose for so long a time, had he not beforehand possessed this confidence.

It hence appears that faith alone is the teacher of obedience; and we may on the contrary draw this conclusion, that it is unbelief that prevents us to obey God. And at this day the unbelief of the world exhibits itself dreadfully in this way, for there are a very few who obey God.

By the which he condemned the world, etc. It were strange to say that Noah's deliverance condemned the world, and the context will hardly allow faith to be meant; we must then understand this of the ark. And he is said on two accounts to have by the ark condemned the world; for by being so long occupied in building it, he took away every excuse from the wicked; — and the event which followed proved how just was the destruction of the world; for why was the ark made the means of deliverance to one family, except that the Lord thus spared a righteous man that he should not perish with the ungodly. Had he then not been preserved, the condemnation of the world would not have been so apparent. Noah then by obeying God's command condemned by his example the obstinate disobedience of the world: his wonderful deliverance from the midst of death, was an evidence that the world justly perished; for God would have doubtless saved it, had it not been unworthy of salvation

Of the righteousness which is by faith. This is the last thing in the character of Noah, which the Apostle reminds us to observe. Moses records that he was a righteous man: history does not expressly say that the cause and root of his righteousness was faith, but the Apostle declares that as arising from the facts of the case. And this is not only true, because no one ever devotes himself really and sincerely to God's service, but he who relies on the promises of his paternal kindness, and feels assured that his life is approved by him; but also on this account, because the life of no one, however holy it may be, when tried by the rule of God's law, can please him without pardon being granted. Then righteousness must necessarily recumb on faith.

HEBREWS XI. 8-12

8. By faith Abraham, when he was called to go out into a place which he should after receive for an inheritance, obeyed; and he went out, not knowing whither he went.
9. By faith he sojourned in the land of promise, as *in* a strange country, dwelling in tabernacles with Isaac and Jacob, the heirs with him of the same promise:
10. For he looked for a city which hath foundations, whose builder and maker *is* God.

11. Through faith also Sara herself received strength to conceive seed, and was delivered of a child when she was past age, because she judged him faithful who had promised.

12. Therefore sprang there even of one, and him as good as dead, *so many* as the stars of the sky in multitude, and as the sand which is by the sea shore innumerable.

8. *By faith Abraham, etc.* He comes now to Abraham, who is the chief father of God's church on earth, and in whose name the Jews gloried, as though by the distinction of being the holy race of Abraham alone, they were removed from the common order of men. But he now reminds them of what they ought to possess as the main thing, that they might be counted among his children. He therefore calls their attention to faith, for Abraham himself had no excellency which did not proceed from faith.

He first teaches us that faith was the cause why he immediately obeyed God when he was commanded to remove from his own country; and then that through the same faith it was that he went on without wavering, according to what he was called to do even to the end. By these two things, — his promptness in obeying, and his perseverance, was Abraham's faith most clearly proved.

When he was called, etc. The old Latin translator and Erasmus apply this to his name, which is extremely tame and frigid. On the contrary, I refer it to the oracle by which he was called from his own country. He indeed did in this way undergo a voluntary exile, while yet he did nothing but by God's command; and no doubt it is one of the chief things which belong to faith, not to move a step except God's word shows us the way, and as a lantern gives us light, according to what David says. (Psalm cxix. 105.) Let us then learn that it is a thing to be observed through life, that we are to undertake nothing to which God does not call us.

To go out into a place, [211] *etc.* To the command was added a promise, that God would give him a land for an inheritance. This

---

211 This is differently connected by Calvin, his version is "by faith Abraham, when he was called, obeyed, so that he went forth," etc. Bloomfield by supposing ὥστε understood before ἐξελθεῖν, seems to be of the same opinion. Beza renders the verb by a gerund, "abiendo," by departing. This construction is more agree-

promise he immediately embraced, and hastened as though he was sent to take possession of this land. It is a no ordinary trial of faith to give up what we have in hand, in order to seek what is afar off, and unknown to us. For when God commanded him to leave his own country, he did not point out the place where he intended him to live, but left him in suspense and perplexity of mind: "go", he said, "into the place that I will show thee." (Genesis xii. 1.) Why did he defer to point out the place, except that his faith might be more and more exercised? Besides, the love of his native land might not only have retarded the alacrity of Abraham, but also held him so bound to it, so as not to quit his home. His faith then was not of an ordinary kind, which thus broke through all hindrances and carried him where the Lord called him to go.

9. *By faith he sojourned, etc.* The second particular is, that having entered into the land, he was hardly received as a stranger and a sojourner. Where was the inheritance which he had expected? It might have indeed occurred instantly to his mind, that he had been deceived by God. Still greater was the disappointment, which the Apostle does not mention, when shortly after a famine drove him from the country, when he was compelled to flee to the land of Gerar; but the Apostle considered it enough to say, as a commendation to his faith, that he became a sojourner in the land of promise; for to be a sojourner seemed contrary to what had been promised. That Abraham then courageously sustained this trial was an instance of great fortitude; but it proceeded from faith alone.

With Isaac and Jacob, etc. He does not mean that they dwelt in the same tent, or lived at the same time; but he makes Abraham's son and grandson his companions, because they sojourned alike in the inheritance promised to them, and yet failed not in their faith, however long it was that God delayed the time; for the longer the delay the greater was the trial; but

---

able to the location of the words; the other introduces an unnatural transposition. Besides, the idea is somewhat different. There are thus two things in the verse stated more directly, as evidences and proofs of faith, — his departure from his own country, and his ignorance as to the country where he was going. His faith was such that he obeyed, so as to leave his own country, and also to go to a country, of which he knew nothing. — *Ed*

by setting up the shield of faith they repelled all the assaults of doubt and unbelief.[212]

10. *For he looked for*, etc. He gives a reason why he ascribes their patience to faith, even because they looked forward to heaven. This was indeed to see things invisible. It was no doubt a great thing to cherish in their hearts the assurance given them by God respecting the possession of the land until it was after some ages realized; yet as they did not confine their thoughts, no, not to that land, but penetrated even into heaven, it was still a clearer evidence of their faith.

He calls heaven a *city that has foundations*, because of its perpetuity; for in the world there is nothing but what is transitory and fading. It may indeed appear strange that he makes God the Maker of heavens as though he did not also create the earth; to this I answer, that as in earthly buildings, the hands of men make use of materials, the workmanship of God is not unfitly set in opposition to them. Now, whatever is formed by men is like its authors in instability; so also is the perpetuity of the heavenly life, it corresponds with the nature of God its founder.[213] Moreover, the Apostle teaches us that all weariness is relieved by expectation, so that we ought never to be weary in following God.

---

212 The preposition μετὰ may often be rendered "as well as." See Matthew ii. 3; Luke xi. 7, 1 Corinthians xvi. 11; "dwelling in tents, as well as Isaac and Jacob, co-heirs to the same promise." It means not here the same time, says Grotius, but parity as to what is stated. — *Ed*

213 The words, "builder and maker," are rendered by Calvin, "master builder and maker." The terms seem reversed. The first word means the maker or worker; and the second, the master-builder or planner. Beza's version is, "the maker, (artifex) and the founder, (conditor)." The order is, according to what is very common in Scripture, the effect mentioned first, then the cause, of the maker first, then the contriver. The last word, no doubt used in the sense of a worker or maker, but also in the sense of an architect or planner; but the former word means a skillful worker or artificer, but not a master-builder. In order, therefore, to give a sistant meaning to each, the sentence is to be thus rendered, — "Whose maker and planner is God;" he not only made it, but also planned and contrived it. — *Ed*.

11. *Through faith also, Sarah herself, etc.* That women may know that this truth belongs to them as well as to men, he adduces the example of Sarah; which he mentions in preference to that of others, because she was the mother of all the faithful.

But it may seem strange that her faith is commended, who was openly charged with unbelief; for she laughed at the word of the angel as though it were a fable; and it was not the laugh of wonder and admiration, for otherwise she would not have been so severely reproved by the angel. It must indeed be confessed, that her faith was blended with unbelief;[214] but as she cast aside her unbelief when reproved, her faith is acknowledged by God and commended. What then she rejected at first as being incredible, she afterwards as soon as she heard that it came from God, obediently received.

And hence we deduce a useful doctrine, — that when our faith in some things wavers or halts, it ceases not to be approved of God, provided we indulge not the spirit of unbelief. The meaning then is, that the miracle which God performed when Isaac was born, was the fruit of the faith of Abraham, and of his wife, by which they laid hold on the power of God.

Because she judged him faithful, etc. These reasons, by which the power and character of faith are set forth, ought to be carefully noticed. Were any one only to hear that Sarah brought forth a child through faith, all that is meant would not be conveyed to him, but the explanation which the Apostle adds removes every obscurity; for he declares that Sarah's faith was this, — that she counted God to be true to his word, that is, to what he had promised.

---

214 "The same thing is affirmed of Abraham, Genesis xvii. 17. The truth is the first annunciation, that a child would spring from them, occasioned both in his and Sarah's mind a feeling of incongruity, of impossibility, that the course of nature should be so reversed. Subsequent consideration brought both to a full belief in the reality of the promised blessing." — Stuart.

It is remarkable, that at the first announcement Abraham laughed, as Sarah did afterward; and not only so, but he also said, "O that Ishmael might live before thee!" evidently showing that he did not then believe the promise which had been made to him. In the following chapter, the 18th, the promise is repeated, when Sarah laughed. And in order to confirm them both, they were reminded of God's power, verse 14. Then faith overcame unbelief. — Ed.

There are two clauses to this declaration; for we hence learn first, that there is no faith without God's word, for of his faithfulness we cannot be convinced, until he has spoken. And this of itself is abundantly sufficient to confute the fiction of the sophists respecting implicit faith; for we must ever hold that there is a mutual relation between God's word and our faith. But as faith is founded chiefly, according to what has been already said, on the benevolence or kindness of God, it is not every word, though coming from his mouth, that is sufficient; but a promise is necessary as an evidence of his favor. Hence Sarah is said to have counted God faithful who had promised. True faith then is that which hears God speaking and rests on his promise.

12. *Therefore sprang there even of one, etc.* He now also reminds the Jews, that it was by faith that they were the descendants of Abraham; for he was as it were half dead,[215] and Sarah his wife, who had been barren in the flower of her age, was now sterile, being far advanced in years. Sooner then might oil be expected to flow from a stone, than a nation to proceed from them: and yet there sprang from them an innumerable multitude. If now the Jews are proud of their origin, let them consider what it was. Whatever they are, everything is doubtless to be ascribed to the faith of Abraham and Sarah. It hence follows, that they cannot retain and defend the position they have acquired in any other way than by faith.

---

215 Calvin renders ταῦτα adverbially "quidem," "and indeed dead;" Doddridge "in his repeat;" Macknight, "to these matters;" Stuart "as to these things." But the word is rendered in Luke vi. 23, "in the like manner;" and this would be the best rendering here. Abraham was like Sarah, "dead" as to the power of begetting children, — "Therefore even from one, and him in a like manner dead, there sprang so many as the stars," etc. — *Ed*

HEBREWS XI. 13-16

13. These all died in faith, not having received the promises, but having seen them afar off, and were persuaded of *them*, and embraced *them*, and confessed that they were strangers and pilgrims on the earth.[216]
14. For they that say such things declare plainly that they seek a country.
15. And truly, if they had been mindful of that *country* from whence they came out, they might have had opportunity to have returned.
16. But now they desire a better *country*, that is, an heavenly: wherefore God is not ashamed to be called their God: for he hath prepared for them a city.

13. *These all died in faith, etc.* He enhances by a comparison the faith of the patriarchs: for when they had only tasted of the promises, as though fully satisfied with their sweetness, they despised all that was in the world; and they never forgot the taste of them, however small it was either in life or in death.[217]

At the same time the expression *in faith,* is differently explained. Some understand simply this that they died in faith, because in this life they never enjoyed the promised blessings, as at this day also salvation is hid from us, being hoped for. But I rather assent to those who think that there is expressed here a difference between us and the fathers; and I give this explanation, — "Though God gave to the fathers only a taste of that grace which is largely poured on us, though he showed to them at a distance only an obscure representation of Christ, who is now set forth to us clearly before our eyes, yet they were satisfied and never fell away from their faith: how much greater reason then have we at this day to persevere? If we grow faint, we are doubly inexcusable". It is then an enhancing circumstance, that the fathers had a distant view of the spiritual kingdom of

---

216 Griesbach and most critics consider καὶ πεισθέντες as not genuine, and therefore exclude it from the text. — *Ed*

217 "These all" must be limited to Abraham, and those mentioned after him, for to them the promises had been made; and he speaks only of such. So Beza and Stuart. — *Ed*.

Christ, while we at this day have so near a view of it, and that they hailed the promises afar off, while we have them as it were quite near us; for if they nevertheless persevered even unto death, what sloth will it be to become wearied in faith, when the Lord sustains us by so many helps. Were any one to object and say, that they could not have believed without receiving the promises on which faith is necessarily founded: to this the answer is, that the expression is to be understood comparatively; for they were far from that high position to which God has raised us. Hence it is that though they had the same salvation promised them, yet they had not the promises so clearly revealed to them as they are to us under the kingdom of Christ; but they were content to behold them afar off.[218]

And confessed that they were strangers, etc. This confession was made by Jacob, when he answered Pharaoh, that the time of his pilgrimage was short compared with that of his fathers, and full of many sorrows. (Genesis xlvii. 9.) Since Jacob confessed himself a pilgrim in the land, which had been promised to him as a perpetual inheritance, it is quite evident that his mind was by no means fixed on this world, but that he raised it up above the heavens. Hence the Apostle concludes, that the fathers, by speaking thus, openly showed that they had a better country in heaven; for as they were pilgrims here, they had a country and an abiding habitation elsewhere.

---

218 Mention is made of "promises;" and then "heavenly country" is the only thing afterwards specified. Abraham, Isaac and Jacob had received many promises which were not fulfilled to them — a numerous seed, the land of Canaan, the Messiah, the resurrection (implied in the promise of being their God) and the heavenly country. There is no reason why all these should not form the "promises" which they saw afar and embraced, though the promise of the heavenly country is alone afterwards, expressly mentioned, it being as it were the completion of all the other promises, and suitably referred to after the acknowledgment they made of being strangers and sojourners on the earth. Their faith embraced all the promises, while it had a especial reference to the eternal inheritance, which though they entered into rest, as to their spirits, they have not yet attained, and which shall not be attained either by them, or by us, until Christ's second coming, when we shall together be introduced into the heavenly country. See a Note on the 39th and 40th verses. — *Ed.*

But if they in spirit amid dark clouds, took a flight into the celestial country, what ought we to do at this day? For Christ stretches forth his hand to us, as it were openly, from heaven, to raise us up to himself. If the land of Canaan did not engross their attention, how much more weaned from things below ought we to be, who have no promised habitation in this world?

15. *And truly if they had been mindful, etc.* He anticipates an objection that might have been made, — that they were strangers because they had left their own country. The apostle meets this objection, and says, that though they called themselves strangers, they yet did not think of Mesopotamia; for if they had a desire to return, they might have done so: but they had willingly banished themselves from it, nay, they had disowned it, as though it did not belong to them. By another country, then, they meant, that which is beyond this world.[219]

16. *Wherefore God is not ashamed, etc.* He refers to that passage, "I am the God of Abraham, the God of Isaac, and the God of Jacob." (Exodus iii. 6.) It is a singular honor when God makes men illustrious, by attaching his name to them; and designs thus to have himself distinguished from idols. This privilege, as the Apostle teaches us, depends also on faith; for when the holy fathers aspired to a celestial country, God on the other hand counted them as citizens. We are hence to conclude, that there is no place for us among God's children, except we renounce the world, and that there will be for us no inheritance in heaven, except we become pilgrims on earth; Moreover, the Apostle justly concludes from these words, — "I am the God of Abraham, of Isaac, and of Jacob," that they were heirs of heaven, since he who thus speaks is not the God of the dead, but of the living.

HEBREWS XI. 17-22

17. By faith Abraham, when he was tried, offered up Isaac: and he that had received the promises offered up his only begotten *son,*

18. Of whom it was said, That in Isaac shall thy seed be called:

---

219 "But now they desire," etc. The historical present is used here instead of the past tense — "But now they desired, etc." So Beza, Grotius, and others. — *Ed.*

19. Accounting that God *was* able to raise *him* up, even from the dead; from whence also he received him in a figure.
20. By faith Isaac blessed Jacob and Esau concerning things to come.
21. By faith Jacob, when he was a dying, blessed both the sons of Joseph; and worshipped, *leaning* upon the top of his staff.
22. By faith Joseph, when he died, made mention of the departing of the children of Israel; and gave commandment concerning his bones.

17. *By faith Abraham, etc.* He proceeds with the history of Abraham, and relates the offering up of his son; and it was a singular instance of firmness, so that there is hardly another like it to be found. Hence for the sake of enhancing it, he adds, *when he was tempted,* or tried. Abraham had indeed already proved what he was, by many trials; yet as this trial surpassed every other, so the Apostle would have it to be regarded above all his trials. It is then as though he had said, "The highest excellency of Abraham was the sacrificing of his son:" for God is said to have then in an especial manner tried him. And yet this act flowed from faith; then Abraham had nothing more excellent than faith, which brought forth such extraordinary fruit.

The word, *tempted* or *tried,* means no other thing than proved. What James says, that we are not tempted by God, is to be understood differently, (Jas. i. 13;) he means that God does not tempt us to do evil; for he testifies that this is really done by every man's own lust. At the same time he says not that God does not try our integrity and obedience, though God does not thus search us, as if he knew not otherwise what is hid in our hearts; nay, God wants no probation that he may know us; but when he brings us to the light, that we may by our works show what was before hid, he is said to try or prove us; and then that which is made openly manifest, is said to be made known to God. For it is a very usual and frequent mode of speaking in Scripture, that what is peculiar to men is ascribed to God.

The sacrificing of Isaac is to be estimated according to the purpose of the heart: for it was not owing to Abraham that he did not actually perform what he was commanded to do. His resolution to obey was then the same, as though he had actually sacrificed his son.

And offered up his only-begotten Son, etc. By these various circumstances, the Apostle intended to show, how great and how severe the trial of Abraham was; and there are still other things related by Moses, which had the same tendency. Abraham was commanded to take his own son, his only begotten and beloved son Isaac, to lead to the place, which was afterwards to be shown to him, and there to sacrifice him with his own hands. These tender words God seems to have designedly accumulated, that he might pierce the inmost heart of the holy man, as with so many wounds; and then that he might more severely try him, he commanded him to go a three-days' journey. How sharp, must we think, was his anguish to have continually before his eyes his own son, whom he had already resolved to put to a bloody death! As they were coming to the place, Isaac pierced his breast with yet a new wound, by asking him, "Where is the victim?" The death of a son, under any circumstances, must have been very grievous, a bloody death would have still caused a greater sorrow; but when he was bidden to slay his own, — that indeed must have been too dreadful for a father's heart to endure; and he must have been a thousand times disabled, had not faith raised up his heart above the world. It is not then without reason, that the apostle records that he was then *tried.*

It may, however, be asked, why is Isaac called the only begotten, for Ishmael was born before him and was still living. To this the answer is, that by God's express command he was driven from the family, so that he was accounted as one dead, at least, he held no place among Abraham's children.

And he that received the promises, etc. All the things we have hitherto related, however deeply they must have wounded the heart of Abraham, yet they were but slight wounds compared with this trial, when he was commanded, after having received the promises, to slay his son Isaac; for all the promises were founded on this declaration, "In Isaac shall thy seed be called," (Genesis xxi. 12;)[220] for when this foundation was taken away,

---

[220] The words literally are "In Isaac shall be called to thee a seed." But the Hebrew ב and the Greek ἐν, mean often by or through, or by the means of: and the Hebrew verb, to be called, as well as the Greek, may sometimes be rendered to be. Hence Macknight seems to have been right in his version of the clause, "By Isaac

no hope of blessing or of grace remained. Here nothing earthly was the matter at issue, but the eternal salvation of Abraham, yea, of the whole world. Into what straits must the holy man have been brought when it came to his mind, that the hope of eternal life was to be extinguished in the person of his son? And yet by faith he emerged above all these thoughts, so as to execute what he was commanded. Since it was a marvelous fortitude to struggle through so many and so great obstacles, justly is the highest praise awarded to faith, for it was by faith alone that Abraham continued invincibly.

But here arises no small difficulty, How is it that Abraham's faith is praised when it departs from the promise? For as obedience proceeds from faith, so faith from the promise; then when Abraham was without the promise, his faith must have necessarily fallen to the ground. But the death of Isaac, as it has been already said, must have been the death as it were of all the promises; for Isaac is not to be considered as a common man, but as one who had Christ included in him. This question, which would have been otherwise difficult to be solved, the Apostle explains by adding immediately, that Abraham ascribed this honor to God, that he was able to raise his son again from the dead. He then did not renounce the promise given to him, but extended its power and its truth beyond the life of his son; for he did not limit God's power to so narrow bounds as to tie it to Isaac when dead, or to extinguish it. Thus he retained the promise, because he bound not God's power to Isaac's life, but felt persuaded that it would be efficacious in his ashes when dead no less than in him while alive and breathing.

19. *From whence also, etc.* As though he said, "Nor did hope disappoint Abraham, for it was a sort of resurrection, when his son was so suddenly delivered from the midst of death. The word *figure,* which is here used, is variously explained. I take it simply as meaning likeness; for though Isaac did not really rise from the dead, yet he seemed to have in a manner risen, when he was suddenly and wonderfully rescued through the unex-

---

a seed shall be thee;" which is better than that of Stuart, "After Isaac shall thy seed be named," for this is less literal, and the meaning is not conveyed. — *Ed*

pected favor of God.[221] However, I do not dislike what some say, who think that our flesh, which is subject to death, is set forth in the ram which was substituted for Isaac. I also allow that to be true which some have taught, that this sacrifice was a representation of Christ. But I have now to state what the Apostle meant, not what may in truth be said; and the real meaning here, as I think, is, that Abraham did not receive his Son otherwise than if he had been restored from death to new life.

20. *By faith Isaac, etc.* It was also the work of faith to bless as to future things; for when the thing itself does not exist and the word only appears, faith must necessarily bear rule. But first we must notice of what avail is the blessing of which he speaks. For to *bless* often means to pray for a blessing. But the blessing of Isaac was very different; for it was as it were an introduction into the possession of the land, which God had promised to him and his posterity. And yet he had nothing in that land but the right of burial. Then strange seemed these high titles, "Let people serve thee, and tribes bow down to thee," (Genesis xxvii. 29;) for what dominion could he have given who himself was hardly a free man? We hence see that this blessing depended on faith; for Isaac had nothing which he could have bestowed on his children but the word of God.

It may, however, be doubted whether there was any faith in the blessing given to Esau, as he was a reprobate and rejected by God. The answer is easy, for faith mainly shone forth, when

---

[221] The meaning given by Stuart and some others is very far fetched, though said to be natural, that "Abraham believed that God could raise Isaac from the dead, because he had, as it were, obtained him from the dead, i.e., he was born of those who were dead as to these things." Hence the rendering given is "comparatively." Abraham had, as to his purpose, sacrificed him, so that he considered him as dead; and he received him back from the dead, not really, but in a way bearing a likeness to such a miracle. This sense is alone compatible with the former clause, which mentions Abraham's faith in God's power to raise his son from the dead; he believed that God was able to do this; and then it is added that Abraham had received back his son as though he had sacrificed him, and as though God had raised him from the dead. What actually took place bore a likeness to the way which he had anticipated. Costallio gives the meaning, "it was the same as though he had sacrificed him, and received him also in a manner he received him." — *Ed.*

he distinguished between the two twins born to him, so that he gave the first place to the younger; for following the oracle of God, he took away from the firstborn the ordinary right of nature. And on this depended the condition of the whole nation, that Jacob was chosen by God, and that this choice was sanctioned by the blessing of the father.

21. *By faith Jacob, etc.* It was the Apostle's object to attribute to faith whatever was worthy of remembrance in the history of the people: as, however, it would have been tedious to recount everything, he selected a few things out of many, such at this. For the tribe of Ephraim was so superior to the rest, that they in a manner did lie down under its shade; for the Scripture often includes the ten tribes under this name. And yet Ephraim was the younger of the two sons of Joseph, and when Jacob blessed him and his brother, they were both young. What did Jacob observe in the younger, to prefer him to the first born? Nay, when he did so, his eyes were dim with age, so that he could not see. Nor did he lay his right hand by chance on the head of Ephraim, but he crossed his hands, so that he moved his right hand to the left side. Besides, he assigned to them two portions, as though he was now the Lord of that land, from which famine had driven him away. There was nothing here agreeable to reason; but faith ruled supreme. If, then, the Jews wish to be anything, they should glory in nothing else, but in faith.

And worshipped on the top, etc. This is one of those places from which we may conclude that the points were not formerly used by the Hebrews; for the Greek translators could not have made such a mistake as to put staff here for a bed, if the mode of writing was then the same as now. No doubt Moses spoke of the head of his couch, when he said על ראש המטה, *ol rash emethe;* but the Greek translators rendered the words, "On the top of his staff" as though the last word was written, *mathaeh*. The Apostle hesitated not to apply to his purpose what was commonly received: he was indeed writing to the Jews; but they who were dispersed into various countries, had changed their own language for the Greek. And we know that the Apostles were not so scrupulous in this respect, as not to accommodate themselves to the unlearned, who had as yet need of milk; and in this there is no danger, provided readers are ever brought back to the pure and original text of Scripture. But, in reality, the difference is but little; for the main thing was, that Jacob worshipped, which was an evidence of his gratitude. He was therefore led by faith to submit himself to his son.[222]

22. *By faith Joseph, etc.* This is the last thing which Moses records respecting the patriarchs, and it deserves to be particularly noticed; for wealth, luxuries, and honors, made not the holy man to forget the promise, nor detained him in Egypt; and this was an evidence of no small faith. For whence had he so much greatness of mind, as to look down on whatever was elevated in the world, and to esteem as nothing whatever was precious in it, except that he had ascended up into heaven. In ordering his bones to be exported, he had no regard to himself, as though his grave in the land of Canaan would be sweeter or better than in Egypt; but his only object was to sharpen the desire of his own nation, that they might more earnestly aspire after redemption; he wished also to strengthen their faith, so that they might confidently hope that they would be at length delivered.

---

[222] Various have been the opinions on this clause. It is clear that the words here refer to a time different from that mentioned in Genesis xlvii. 31. They are connected in Genesis with the oath which Joseph made to his father to bury him in Canaan; but here with the blessing of his sons recorded in the following chapter, xlviii. 15, 16. These were two separate transactions, and the words only occur in the first; and it seems from the words of the Apostle, that the act and position of Jacob were also the same in the second instance.

The points are of no authority; and the Apostle adopted the Septuagint version, and thus sanctioned it: and there is no reason to dispute that sanction. David is said to worship upon his bed, (1 Kings i. 47;) but the word for bed there is different. All the difficulty here vanishes, if we throw aside as we ought to do, the points. The word for worship in Hebrew means to prostrate one's self on the ground, the humblest mode of adoration; but it is used also to designate merely an act of worship. See 1 Samuel i. 3; 2 Kings v. 5, 18. The reason why Jacob is said to have worshipped unable to adopt the usual posture. — *Ed.*

HEBREWS XI. 23-27

23. By faith Moses, when he was born, was hid three months of his parents, because they saw *he was* a proper child; and they were not afraid of the king's commandment.
24. By faith Moses, when he was come to years, refused to be called the son of Pharaoh's daughter;
25. Choosing rather to suffer affliction with the people of God, than to enjoy the pleasures of sin for a season;
26. Esteeming the reproach of Christ greater riches than the treasures in Egypt: for he had respect unto the recompense of the reward.
27. By faith he forsook Egypt, not fearing the wrath of the king: for he endured, as seeing him who is invisible.

23. *By faith Moses, etc.* There have been others, and those heathens, who from no fear of God, but only from a desire of propagating an offspring, preserved their own children at the peril of life; but the Apostle shows that the parents of Moses were inducted to save him for another reason, even for this, — that as God had promised to them, under their oppression, that there would come some time a deliverer, they relied confidently on that promise, and preferred the safety of the infant to their own.

But he seems to say what is contrary to the character of faith, when he says that they were induced to do this by the beauty of the child; for we know that Jesse was reproved, when he brought his sons to Samuel as each excelled in personal appearance; and doubtless God would not have us to regard what is externally attractive. To this I answer, that the parents of Moses were not charmed with beauty, so as to be induced by pity to save him, as the case is commonly with men; but that there was some mark, as it were, of future excellency imprinted on the child, which gave promise of something extraordinary. There is, then, no doubt but that by his very appearance they were inspired with the hope of an approaching deliverance; for they considered that the child was destined for the performance of great things.

Moreover, it ought to have had a great weight with the Jews, to hear that Moses, the minister of their redemption, had been in an extraordinary manner rescued from death by means of faith. We must, however, remark, that the faith here praised was very weak; for after having disregarded the fear of death, they ought to have brought up Moses; instead of doing so, they exposed him. It is hence evident that their faith in a short time not only wavered, but wholly failed; at least they neglected their duty when they cast forth the infant on the bank of the river. But it behoves us to be more encouraged when we hear that their faith, though weak, was yet so approved by God as to secure that life to Moses, on which depended the deliverance of the Church.

24. *By faith Moses, when he was come to years,* etc. The example of Moses ought to have been remembered by the Jews, more than that of any other; for through him they were delivered from bondage, and the covenant of God was renewed, with them, and the constitution of the Church established by the publication of the Law. But if faith is to be considered as the main thing in Moses, it would be very strange and unreasonable that he should draw them away to anything else. It hence follows that all they make a poor proficiency in the Law who are not guided by it to faith.

Let us now see what the things are for which he commends the faith of Moses. The first excellency he mentions is, that when grown up, he disregarded the adoption of Pharaoh's daughter. He refers to his age, for had he done this when a boy, it might have been imputed to his levity, or his ignorance; for as understanding and reason are not strong in children, they heedlessly rush headlong into any course of life; young people also are often carried here and there by unreflecting ardor. That we may then know that nothing was done thoughtlessly, and without a long deliberation, the Apostle says, that he was of mature age, which is also evident from history.[223]

---

[223] Literally it is "when he became great," that is, in age or in years: he was, as it appears from Acts vii. 23, about forty years of age. The word "great," both in Hebrew and Greek, has sometimes this meaning. "When arrived at mature age," by Stuart, is better than "when he was grown up," by Doddridge and Macknight.

It is said that he refused, that is by his conduct. He acted in such a way as to show that he rejected the honor of being adopted son of Pharoah's daughter. The verb means to deny, to renounce, to disown. He renounced the privilege offered to him. Others are

But he is said to have disregarded his adoption; for when he visited his brethren, when he tried to relieve them, when he avenged their wrongs, he fully proved that he preferred to return to his own nation, rather than to remain in the king's court: it was then the same as a voluntary rejection of it. This the Apostle ascribes to faith; for it would have been much better for him to remain in Egypt, had he not been persuaded of the blessing promised to the race of Abraham; and of this blessing, the only witness was God's promise; for he could see nothing of the kind with his eyes. It hence appears, that he beheld by faith what was far removed from his sight.

26 *Esteeming the reproach of Christ greater riches, etc.* This clause ought to be carefully noticed; for we here learn that we ought to shun as a deadly poison whatever cannot be enjoyed without offending God; for the *pleasures of sin* he calls all the allurements of the world which draw us away from God and our calling. But the comforts of our earthly life, which we are allowed by pure conscience, and God's permission to enjoy, are not included here. Let us then ever remember that we ought to know and understand what God allows us. There are indeed some things in themselves lawful, but the use of which is prohibited to us, owing to circumstances as to time, place, or other things. Hence as to all the blessings connected with the present life, what is ever to be regarded is, that they should be to us helps and aids to follow God and not hindrances. And he calls these pleasures of sin temporary or for *a time*, because they soon vanish away together with life itself.[224]

In opposition to these he sets the *reproach of Christ*, which all the godly ought willingly to undergo. For those whom God has chosen, he has also foreordained to be conformed to the image of his own son; not that he exercises them all by the same kind of reproaches or by the same cross, but that they are all to

---

said to "deny the power" of godliness, that is by their works. 2 Timothy iii. 5. — *Ed.*

224 This clause is rendered by Doddridge, "than to enjoy the temporary pleasures of sin:" by Macknight, "than to have the temporary fruition of sin," which is literal rendering; so Beza. Schleusner thinks the "sin" to have been that of idolatry: but the words seem rather to refer to the sin of indulgence in vain and demoralizing pursuits, too commonly prevalent in royal courts.— *Ed*

be so minded as not to decline to undertake the cross in common with Christ. Let every one then bear in mind, that as he is called to this fellowship he is to throw off all hindrances. Nor must we omit to say, that he reckons among the reproaches of Christ all the ignominious trials which the faithful have had to endure from the beginning of the world; for as they were the member of the same body, so they had nothing different from what we have. As all sorrows are indeed the rewards of sin, so they are also the fruits of the curse pronounced on the first man: but whatever wrongs we endure from the ungodly on account of Christ, these he regards as his own.[225] Hence Paul gloried that he made up what was wanting as to the sufferings of Christ. Were we rightly to consider this, it would not be so grievous and bitter for us to suffer for Christ.

He also explains more fully what he means in this clause by the *reproach of Christ*, by what he has previously declared when he said, that Moses chose to *suffer affliction with the people of God*. He could not have otherwise avowed himself as one of God's people, except he had made himself a companion to his own nation in their miseries. Since, then, this is the end, let us not separate ourselves from the body of the Church: whatever we suffer, let us know that it is consecrated on account of the head.

---

225 The "The reproach of Christ" is differently understood: —

The reproach of the anointed, that is the people of Israel, called God's anointed, Psalm cv. 15; Hebrews iii. 13. — Grotius.

The reproach like that of Christ: as Christ, though rich, became poor to redeem mankind, so Moses despised the treasures of Egypt, for the purpose of delivering Israel from bondage. A similar construction is found in 2 Corinthians i. 5. "The sufferings of Christ," that is, like those of Christ. — Stuart.

The reproach for Christ, that is, for avowing his expectation of him in common with the distressed people. Macknight, Scott, Bloomfield. For this opinion there is not a particle of evidence from the account we have in Exodus. The Egyptians knew nothing of the redeemer; they therefore could not have reproached the Israelites on his account.

The reproach of Christ's people, the word Christ being sometimes taken for his Church, 1 Corinthians xii. 12; and this seems to be the view of Calvin.

The second view is the most satisfactory, and is confirmed by chapter xiii. 13, "bearing his reproach," that is, a reproach like his. — *Ed.*

So on the other hand he calls those things the *treasures of Egypt*, which no one can otherwise possess than by renouncing and forsaking the Church.

For he had respect unto the recompense of the reward, or for he looked to the remuneration.[226] He proves by the description he gives, that the magnanimity of Moses' mind was owing to faith; for he had his eyes fixed on the promise of God. For he could not have hoped that it would be better for him to be with the people of Israel than with the Egyptians, had he not trusted in the promise and in nothing else.

But if any one hence concludes, that his faith did not recumb on God's mercy alone, because he had respect to the reward; to this I answer, that the question here is not respecting righteousness or the cause of salvation, but that the Apostle generally includes what belongs to faith. Then faith, as to righteousness before God, does not look on reward, but on the gratuitous goodness of God, not on our works but on Christ alone; but faith, apart from justification, since it extends generally to every word of God, has respect to the reward that is promised; yea, by faith we embrace whatever God promises: but he promises reward to works; then faith lays hold on this. But all this has no place in free justification, for no reward for works can be hoped for, except the imputation of gratuitous justification goes before

27. *By faith he forsook Egypt, etc.* This may be said of his first as well as of his second departure, that is, when he brought out the people with him. He then indeed left Egypt when he fled from the house of Pharaoh. Add to this, that his going out is recorded by the Apostle before he mentions the celebration of the Passover. He seems then to speak of the flight of Moses; nor is what he adds, that he *feared not the wrath of the king,* any

---

226 The words are very striking, "For he looked away," that is, from difficulties or present trials, "unto the retribution," the rendering of the recompose. What was the retribution? It was what corresponded with what he did by faith: he engaged by faith in the work of delivering his brethren from bondage. His retribution in this work was, no doubt, then undertaking for his own nation. What his faith in God's promise enabled him to look to, was the deliverance of his people, which was to be his retribution. In this respect he acted, though in a business infinitely inferior, on the same principle with the Savior, "who for the joy (of redeeming mankind) that was set before him, endured the cross," etc. Chapter xii. 2 — *Ed.*

objection to this, though Moses himself relates that he was constrained to do so by fear. For if we look at the beginning of his course he did not fear, that is, when he avowed himself to be the avenger of his people. However, when I consider all the circumstances, I am inclined to regard this as his second departure; for it was then that he bravely disregarded the fierce wrath of the king, being armed with such power by God's Spirit, that he often of his own accord defied the fury of that wild beast. It was doubtless an instance of the wonderful strength of faith, that he brought out a multitude untrained for war and burdened with many incumbrances, and yet hoped that a way would be opened to him by God's hand through innumerable difficulties. He saw a most powerful king in a furious rage, and he knew that he would not cease till he had tried his utmost. But as he knew that God had commanded him to depart, he committed the event to him, nor did he doubt but that he would in due time restrain all the assaults of the Egyptians.

As seeing him who is invisible. Nay, but he had seen God in the midst of the burning bush: this then seems to have been said improperly, and not very suitable to the present subject. I indeed allow, that Moses was strengthened in his faith by that vision, before he took in hand the glorious work of delivering the people; but I do not admit that it was such a view of God, as divested him of his bodily senses, and transferred him beyond the trials of this world. God at that time only showed him a certain symbol of his presence; but he was far from seeing God as he is. Now, the Apostle means, that Moses so endured, as though he was taken up to heaven, and had God only before his eyes; and as though he had nothing to do with men, was not exposed to the perils of this world and had no contests with Pharaoh. And yet, it is certain, that he was surrounded with so many difficulties, that he could not but think sometimes that God was far away from him, or at least, that the obstinacy of the king, furnished as it was with so many means of resistance, would at length overcome him.

In short, God appeared to Moses in such a way, as still to leave room for faith; and Moses, when beset by terrors on every side, turned all his thoughts to God. He was indeed assisted to do this, by the vision which we have mentioned; but yet he saw more in God than what that symbol intimated: for he understood his power, and that absorbed all his fears and dangers. Relying on God's promise, he felt assured that the people, though then oppressed by the tyranny of the Egyptians, were already, as it were, the lords of the promised land.[227]

We hence learn, that the true character of faith is to set God always before our eyes; secondly, that faith beholds higher and more hidden things in God than what our senses can perceive; and thirdly, that a view of God alone is sufficient to strengthen our weakness, so that we may become firmer than rocks to withstand all the assaults of Satan. It hence follows, that the weaker and the less resolute any one is, the less faith he has.

HEBREWS XI. 28-31

28. Through faith he kept the Passover, and the sprinkling of blood, lest he that destroyed the firstborn should touch them.
29. By faith they passed through the Red sea as by dry *land*: which the Egyptians assaying to do were drowned.
30. By faith the walls of Jericho fell down, after they were compassed about seven days.
31. By faith the harlot Rahab perished not with them that believed not, when she had received the spies with peace.

28. *Through faith he kept the Passover, etc.* This ought to have availed much to commend faith to the Jews; for they held this first sacrifice of the Passover in the highest esteem. But, he says, that it was kept by faith, not because the Paschal lamb was a type of Christ, but because its benefit did not appear, when he sprinkled the doorposts with blood: when therefore the effect was yet hid, it was necessarily looked for by faith. Nay, it might have seemed strange, that Moses should set a few drops

---

227 It is said that he "endured," rather persevered; for the reference is not to sufferings, but to trials and difficulties: he was made strong by faith in an invisible God to resist and surmount them all. "He was strengthened," Doddridge; "he courageously persevered," Macknight; "he continued steadfast," Stuart. The word is only found here. — *Ed.*

of blood, as a remedy, in opposition to God's vengeance; but being satisfied with God's word alone, that the people would be exempt from the scourge that was coming on the Egyptians, he did not hesitate. Hence the Apostle justly commends his faith in this respect.

They who explain that the Passover was by faith celebrated by Moses, because he had respect to Christ, say indeed what is true; but the Apostle here records simply his faith, because he acquiesced in God's word alone, when the effect did not appear: therefore out of place here are philosophical refinements. And the reason why he mentions Moses alone, as celebrating the Passover, seems to be this, that God through him instituted the Passover.[228]

29. *By faith they passed,* etc. It is certain, that many in that multitude were unbelieving; but the Lord granted to the faith of a few, that the whole multitude should pass through the Red Sea dry-shod. But in doing the same thing, there was a great difference between the Israelites and the Egyptians; while the former passed through safely, the latter coming after them were drowned. Whence was this difference, but that the Israelites had the word of God, and that the Egyptians were without it. The argument then derives its force from what happened to the contrary; hence, he says, that the *Egyptians were drowned.* That disastrous event was the punishment of their temerity, as on the other hand, the Israelites were preserved safe, because they relied on God's word, and refused not to march through the midst of the waters.

30. *By faith the walls of Jericho fell,* etc. As he had before taught us, that the yoke of bondage was by faith broken asunder, so now he tells us, that by the same faith the people gained the possession of the promised land. For at their first entrance the

---

228 Some render the words, "by faith he instituted the Passover." The verb is properly to make, but like עשה in Hebrew, it is used in a variety of senses. Doddridge has "celebrated;" Macknight, "appointed;" and Stuart, "observed." To make the Passover is, no doubt, to keep or observe it; for such is the meaning of the phrase, as it appears from Numbers 9: 10, 11. The word πάσχα is doubtless a Syriac term, and derived originally from the Hebrew פסח which means to pass over; though several of the Greek fathers derived it from πάσχειν, to suffer. It sometimes means the paschal feast, Luke xxii. 11, and sometimes the paschal Lamb, Mark xiv. 12; 1 Corinthians v. 7 — *Ed*

city Jericho stood in their way; it being fortified and almost impregnable, it impeded any farther progress, and they had no means to assail it. The Lord commanded all the men-of-war to go round it once every day, and on the seventh day seven times. It appeared to be a work childish and ridiculous; and yet they obeyed the divine command; nor did they do so in vain, for success according to the promise followed. It is evident, that the walls did not fall through the shout of men, or the sound of trumpets; but because the people believed that the Lord would do what he had promised.

We may also apply this event to our benefit and instruction: for it is not otherwise, than by faith, that we can be freed from the tyranny of the Devil, and be brought to liberty; and by the same faith, it is that we can put to flight our enemies, and that all the strongholds of hell can be demolished.

31. *By faith the harlot Rahab, etc.* Though at the first view, this example may seem, on account of the meanness of the person, hardly entitled to notice, and even unworthy of being recorded, yet it was not unsuitably, nor without reason, adduced by the Apostle. He has hitherto shown that the Patriarchs, whom the Jews most honored and venerated, did nothing worthy of praise except through faith; and that all the benefits conferred on us by God, even the most remarkable, have been the fruits of the same faith: but he now teaches us, that an alien woman, not only of a humble condition among her own people, but also a harlot, had been adopted into the body of the Church through faith.

It hence follows, that those who are most exalted, are of no account before God, unless they have faith; and that, on the other hand, those who are hardly allowed a place among the profane and the reprobate, are by faith introduced into the company of angels.

Moreover, James also bears testimony to the faith of Rahab, (James ii. 25,) and it may be easily concluded from sacred history, that she was endued with true faith; for she professed her full persuasion of what God had promised to the Israelites; and of those whom fear kept from entering the land, she asked pardon for herself and her friends, as though they were already conquerors; and in all this, she did not consider men, but God himself. The evidence of her faith was, that she received the spies at the peril of her life: then, by means of faith, she escaped safe from the ruin of her own city. She is mentioned as a *harlot*, in order to amplify the grace of God.

Some, indeed, render זונה, *zune*, a hostess, as though she kept a public house, or an inn; but as the word means a harlot everywhere in Scripture, there is no reason why we should explain it otherwise in this place. The Rabbis, thinking it strange and disgraceful to their nation, were it said, that the spies entered into the house of a harlot; have invented this forced meaning.[229] But such a fear was groundless; for in the history of Joshua, this word, harlot, is expressly added, in order that we may know that the spies came into the city Jericho clandestinely, and concealed themselves in a harlot's house. At the same time this must be understood of her past life; for faith is an evidence of repentance.

HEBREWS XI. 32-34

32. And what shall I more say? for the time would fail me to tell of Gedeon, and *of* Barak, and *of* Samson, and *of* Jephthae; *of* David also, and Samuel, and *of* the prophets:
33. Who through faith subdued kingdoms, wrought righteousness, obtained promises, stopped the mouths of lions,
34. Quenched the violence of fire, escaped the edge of the sword, out of weakness were made strong, waxed valiant in fight, turned to flight the armies of the aliens.

32. *And what shall I say more? etc.* As it was to be feared, that by referring to a few examples, he should appear to confine the praises of faith to a few men; he anticipates this, and says, that there would be no end if he was to dwell on every instance; for what he had said of a few extended to the whole Church of God.

---

229 And it has been adopted by many of the German divines, who seem in many instances to follow any vagary, Rabbinical or heathen, rather than the word of God. There is nothing in Scripture that countenances this notion. The word is never used in the sense of a hostess: and the ancient versions ever render the Hebrew word by πόρνη, a harlot. — *Ed*

He first refers to the time that intervened between Joshua and David, when the Lord raised up judges to govern the people; and such were the four he now mentions, *Gideon, Barak, Samson,* and *Jephthah.*

It seemed indeed strange in *Gideon,* with three hundred men to attack an immense host of enemies, and to shake pitchers appeared like a sham alarm. *Barak* was far inferior to his enemies, and was guided only by the counsel of a woman. *Samson* was a mere countryman, and had never used any other arms than the implements of husbandry: what could he do against such proved conquerors, by whose power the whole people had been subdued? Who would not at first have condemned the rashness of *Jephthah,* who avowed himself the avenger of a people already past hope? But as they all followed the guidance of God, and being animated by his promise, undertook what was commanded them, they have been honored with the testimony of the Holy Spirit.[230]

Then the Apostle ascribes all that was praiseworthy in them to faith; though there was not one of them whose faith did not halt. *Gideon* was slower to take up arms than what he ought to have been; nor did he venture without some hesitation to commit himself to God. *Barak* at first trembled, so that he was almost forced by the reproofs of Deborah. *Samson* being overcome by the blandishments of a concubine, inconsiderately betrayed the safety of the whole people. *Jephthah,* hasty in making a foolish vow, and too obstinate in performing it, marred the finest victory by the cruel death of his own daughter. Thus, in all the saints, something reprehensible is ever to be found; yet faith, though halting and imperfect, is still approved by God. There is, therefore, no reason why the faults we labor under should break us down, or dishearten us, provided we by faith go on in the race of our calling.

Of David, etc. Under David's name he includes all the pious kings, and to them he adds *Samuel* and the *Prophets.* He there-

---

230 The history of Gideon we have in Judges vi. 11, to the end of the 8th chapter: of Barak, in Judges iv. 6, to the end of the 5th: of Samson, in Judges xiii. 24, to the end of the 16th: and of Jephthah, in Judges xi. 1, to the end of the 12th chapter. Thus we see that the order of time in which they lived is not here observed, it being not necessary for the object of the Apostle. Barak was before Gideon, Jephthah before Samson, and Samuel before David. — *Ed.*

fore means in short to teach us, that the kingdom of Judah was founded in faith; and that it stood to the last by faith. The many victories of David, which he had gained over his enemies, were commonly known. Known also, was the uprightness of Samuel, and his consummate wisdom in governing the people. Known too were the great favors conferred by God on prophets and kings. The Apostle declares that there are none of these things which ought not to be ascribed to faith.

But it is to some only of these innumerable benefits of God that he refers, in order that the Jews might from them draw a general conclusion, — that as the Church has always been preserved by God's hand through faith, so at this day there is no other way by which we may know his kindness towards us.

It was by faith that David so many times returned home as a conqueror; that Hezekiah recovered from his sickness; that Daniel came forth safe and untouched from the lions' den, and that his friends walked in a burning furnace as cheerfully as on a pleasant meadow. Since all these things were done by faith, we must feel convinced, that in no other way than by faith is God's goodness and bounty to be communicated to us. And that clause ought especially to be noticed by us, where it is said that they *obtained the promises* by faith;[231] for though God continues faithful, were we all unbelieving, yet our unbelief makes the promises void, that is, ineffectual to us.

34. *Out of weakness were made strong, etc.* Chrysostom refers this to the restoration of the Jews from exile, in which they were like men without hope; I do not disapprove of its applications to Hezekiah. We might at the same time extend it wider, that the Lord, by his hand, raised on high his saints, whenever they were cast down; and brought help to their weakness, so as to endue them with full strength.

---

231 The previous sentence, "wrought righteousness," is differently understood. Some refer it to a righteous and upright course of life, and others to the conduct of rulers and judges. The latter is the most suitable meaning here; and the words may be rendered "executed justice." Samuel was an example of this.

To "obtain promises" is to receive the things promised. — *Ed.*

HEBREWS XI. 35-40

35. Women received their dead raised to life again: and others were tortured, not accepting deliverance; that they might obtain a better resurrection:
36. And others had trial of *cruel* mockings and scourgings, yea, moreover of bonds and imprisonment:
37. They were stoned, they were sawn asunder, were tempted, were slain with the sword: they wandered about in sheepskins and goatskins; being destitute, afflicted, tormented;
38. (Of whom the world was not worthy:) they wandered in deserts, and *in* mountains, and *in* dens and caves of the earth.
39. And these all, having obtained a good report through faith, received not the promise:
40. God having provided some better thing for us, that they without us should not be made perfect.

35. *Women received, etc.* He had already mentioned instances in which God had remunerated the faith of his servants, he now refers to examples of a different kind, — that saints, reduced to extreme miseries, struggled by faith so as to persevere invincible even to death. These instances at the first view widely differ: some triumphed gloriously over vanquished enemies, were preserved by the Lord through various miracles, and were rescued by means new and unusual from the midst of death; while others were shamefully treated, were despised by almost the whole world, were consumed by want, were so hated by all as to be compelled to hide themselves in the coverts of wild beasts, and lastly, were drawn forth to endure savage and cruel tortures: and these last seemed wholly destitute of God's aid, when he thus exposed them to the pride and the cruelty of the ungodly. They seem then to have been very differently treated from the former ones; and yet faith ruled in both, and was alike powerful in both; nay, in the latter its power shone forth in a much clearer light. For the victory of faith appears more splendid in the contempt of death than if life were extended to the fifth generation. It is a more glorious evidence of faith, and worthy of higher praise, when reproaches, want, and extreme troubles are borne with resignation and firmness, than when recovery from sickness is miraculously obtained, or any other benefit from God.

The sum of the whole is, that the fortitude of the saints, which has shone forth in all ages, was the work of faith; for our weakness is such that we are not capable of overcoming evils, except faith sustains us. But we hence learn, that all who really trust in God are endued with power sufficient to resist Satan in whatever way he may assail them, and especially that patience in enduring evils shall never be wanting to us, if faith be possessed; and that, therefore, we are proved guilty of unbelief when we faint under persecutions and the cross. For the nature of faith is the same now as in the days of the holy fathers whom the Apostle mentions. If, then, we imitate their faith, we shall never basely break down through sloth or listlessness.

Others were tortured, etc. As to this verb, ἐτυμπανίσθησαν, I have followed Erasmus, though others render it "imprisoned." But the simple meaning is, as I think, that they were stretched on a rack, as the skin of a drum, which is distended.[232] By saying that they were *tempted*, he seems to have spoken what was superfluous; and I doubt not but that the likeness of the words, ἐπρίσθησαν and ἐπειράσθησαν, was the reason that the word was added by some unskillful transcriber, and thus crept into the text, as also Erasmus has conjectured.[233] By *sheepskins* and

---

[232] The τύμπανον was, according to Schleusner, a machine on which the body was stretched; and then cudgels or rods, and whips were used. This appears from the account given in 2 Macc. 6: 19, 30. It is said that Eleasar, rather than transgress the Law, went of his own accord "to the torment" — ἐπὶ τὸ τύμπανον, and in the 30th verse mention is made of stripes or strokes — πληγαῖς, and of being lashed or whipped — μαστιγούμενος. This was to be tympanized or tortured. — Ed

[233] This conjecture not countenanced by any MSS. that are considered to have much weight. What has led to this conjecture has evidently been a misunderstanding as to the import of the word in this connection. Being a word of general import, it has been viewed as inappropriate here among words of specified meaning: it refers to the temptation or trial to which those who were condemned for their religion were commonly exposed — the offer of life and of favors and recantation: that seems to have been the special temptation here intended. — Ed.

goatskins I do not think that tents made of skins are meant, but the mean and rough clothing of the saints which they put on when wandering in deserts.

Now though they say that Jeremiah was stoned, that Isaiah was sawn asunder, and though sacred history relates that Elijah, Elisha, and other Prophets, wandered on mountains and in caves; yet I doubt not but he here points out those persecutions which Antiochus carried on against God's people, and those which afterwards followed.

Not accepting deliverance, etc. Most fitly does he speak here; for they must have purchased a short lease of life by denying God; but this would have been a price extremely shameful. That they might then live forever in heaven, they rejected a life on earth, which would have cost them, as we have said, so much as the denial of God, and also the repudiation of their own calling. But we hear what Christ says, that if we seek to save our lives in this world, we shall lose them for ever. If, therefore, the real love of a future resurrection dwells in our hearts, it will easily lead us to the contempt of death. And doubtless we ought to live only so as to live to God: as soon as we are not permitted to live to God, we ought willingly and not reluctantly to meet death. Moreover, by this verse the Apostle confirms what he had said, that the saints overcome all sufferings by faith; for except their minds had been sustained by the hope of a blessed resurrection, they must have immediately failed.[234]

We may hence also derive a needful encouragement, by which we may fortify ourselves in adversities. For we ought not to refuse the Lord's favor of being connected with so many holy men, whom we know to have been exercised and tried by many sufferings. Here indeed are recorded, not the sufferings of a few individuals, but the common persecutions of the Church, and those not for one or two years, but such as continued some-

---

[234] The verse concludes with these words "that they might obtain a better resurrection," — better than what? Better than the resurrection referred to at the beginning of the verse, when it is said that "women received their dead raised to life again;" or better than the life promised by persecutors to those doomed to die, in case they renounced their religion. The former is the view taken by Scott and Stuart, and the latter by Doddridge: but as deliverance and no deliverance are facts in contrast, the first is the most obvious meaning.—*Ed.*

times from grandfathers even to their grandchildren. No wonder, then, if it should please God to prove our faith at this day by similar trials; nor ought we to think that we are forsaken by him, who, we know, cared for the holy fathers who suffered the same before us.[235]

38. *Of whom the world was not worthy, etc.* As the holy Prophets wandered as fugitives among wild beasts, they might have seemed unworthy of being sustained on the earth; for how was it that they could find no place among men? But the Apostle inverts this sentiment, and says that the world was not worthy of them; for wherever God's servants come, they bring with them his blessing like the fragrance of a sweet odor. Thus the house of Potiphar was blessed for Joseph's sake, (Genesis xxxix. 5;) and Sodom would have been spared had ten righteous men been found in it. (Genesis xviii. 32.) Though then the world may cast out God's servants as offscourings, it is yet to be regarded as one of its judgments that it cannot bear them; for there is ever accompanying them some blessing from God. Whenever the righteous are taken away from us, let us know that such events are presages of evil to us; for we are unworthy of having them with us, lest they should perish together with us.

At the same time the godly have abundant reasons for consolation, though the world may cast them out as offscourings; for they see that the same thing happened to the prophets, who found more clemency in wild animals than in men. It was with this thought that Hilary comforted himself when he saw the church taken possession of by sanguinary tyrants, who then

---

235 The conclusion of the 37th verse is, "being destitute, afflicted, tormented:" this is said of those who "wandered about in sheep skins and goat skins." They were destitute, they had been oppressed or persecuted and unjustly dealt with. Wrong treatment and oppression or persecution drove them from there homes and destitution followed. This is the way in which things are often stated in Scripture; the effect or the present state first, and then the cause or what led to it. The words are rendered "destitute, afflicted, maltreated," by Macknight, — and "suffering want, afflicted, injuriously treated," by Stuart. The second word often means oppression or persecution. The third word is found only here and chapter xiii. 2 where it is rendered "suffer adversity." It is found in the Sept., in 1 Kings ii. 26, twice and xi. 39. It is used by Aqula in Exodus xxii. 22, and in Job xxxvii. 23. Its meaning properly is, to be ill or wrongfully treated. — *Ed.*

employed the Roman emperor as their executioner; yea, that holy man then called to mind what the Apostle here says of the Prophets; — "Mountains and forests," he said, "and dungeons and prisons, are safer for me than splendid temples; for the Prophets, while abiding or buried in these, still prophesied by the Spirit of God." So also ought we to be animated so as boldly to despise the world; and were it to cast us out, let us know that we go forth from a fatal gulf, and that God thus provides for our safety, so that we may not sink in the same destruction.

39. *And these all, etc.* This is an argument from the less to the greater; for if they on whom the light of grace had not as yet so brightly shone displayed so great a constancy in enduring evils, what ought the full brightness of the Gospel to produce in us? A small spark of light led them to heaven; when the sun of righteousness shines over us, with what pretense can we excuse ourselves if we still cleave to the earth? This is the real meaning of the Apostle.[236]

---

236 This is materially the view taken by Beza, Doddridge, Scott and Stuart. The "promise" is deemed to be especially that of Christ. The ancients heard of him, believed in his coming, but did not witness it. The "some better thing" is considered to be the same with the promise, or to be the Gospel as revealed, or in the words of Stuart, "the actual fulfillment of the promise respecting the Messiah."

Still there is something unsatisfactory in this view as to "the promise," as Stuart seems to intimate. There are two verses, chapter x. 36, and ix. 15, which seem to throw light on this subject: by the first we find that "the promise" is future to us as well as to the ancient saints; and by the second, that "the better thing" is the atoning death of Christ, which was to the ancient saints an unfulfilled event, but to us fulfilled and clearly revealed, and yet its benefits extended to them as well as to us.

The "promise" throughout this Epistle is that of "the eternal inheritance" and "the promises" in verse 13 include this and others, and especially "the better things," that is the Gospel, or fulfillment of what was necessary to attain the inheritance, even the death and resurrection of Christ; or we may say that it is "the better hope," (chapter vii. 19) or the "better covenant, which was established on better promises," (chapter viii. 6.) The verses may be thus rendered —

"And all these, having obtained a good report through faith, have not received the promise: 40. God having foreordained as to

I know that Chrysostom and others have given a different explanation, but the context clearly shows, that what is intended here is the difference in the grace which God bestowed on the faithful under the Law, and that which he bestows on us now. For since a more abundant grace is poured on us, it would be very strange that we should have less faith in us. He then says that those fathers who were endued with so remarkable a faith, had not yet so strong reasons for believing as we have. Immediately after he states the reason, because God intended to unite us all into one body, and that he distributed a small portion of grace to them, that he might defer its full perfection to our time, even to the coming of Christ.

And it is a singular evidence of God's benevolence towards us, that though he has shown himself bountifully to his children from the beginning of the world, he yet has so distributed his grace as to provide for the well-being of the whole body. What

---

us something more excellent, so that they without us might not be perfected;" that is, in body as well as in soul.

The sentiment seems to be this, — "the ancient saints believed God's promise, respecting an eternal inheritance after the resurrection: they died in hope of this, they have not yet obtained it, and for this reason, because God had designed to fulfill to us what he had also promised to them, even the coming of a Redeemer; it is necessary that this more excellent thing than what had in this world been vouchsafed to them, should take place, as on it depended everything connected with the promise of the 'heavenly city:' so that without the more excellent thing fulfilled to us, their perfect state, in body as well as in soul, was not to be attained."

Their souls are perfect, for we as Christians are said to have come "to the spirits of just men made perfect," (chapter xii. 23;) they who die in the Lord are said to "rest from their labors," and are pronounced blessed or happy. (Rev. xiv. 13.) But they are not in possession of the inheritance promised them, neither the ancients nor those who now die in the Lord. The promise as to both will not be fulfilled until the glorious day of the resurrection. Then all the saints, whether before or after the coming of Christ, will at the same time, with pure and immortal bodies, united to pure spirits, be together introduced into their eternal inheritance which he promised to Abraham and his seed, when he said that he would be their God. Christ referred to that declaration as an evidence of the resurrection. (Luke xx. 37.) Then the Patriarchs believed that there would be a resurrection. — *Ed.*

more could any of us desire, than that in all the blessings which God bestowed on Abraham, Moses, David, and all the Patriarchs, on the Prophets and godly kings, he should have a regard for us, so that we might be united together with them in the body of Christ? Let us then know that we are doubly and treble ungrateful to God, if less faith appears in us under the kingdom of Christ than the fathers had under the Law, as proved by so many remarkable examples of patience. By the words, that they received not the promise, is to be understood its ultimate fulfillment, which took place in Christ, on which subject something has been said already.

CHAPTER 12

HEBREWS XII. 1-3

1. Wherefore seeing we also are compassed about with so great a cloud of witnesses, let us lay aside every weight, and the sin which doth so easily beset *us*, and let us run with patience the race that is set before us,
2. Looking unto Jesus the author and finisher of *our* faith; who for the joy that was set before him endured the cross, despising the shame, and is set down at the right hand of the throne of God.
3. For consider him that endured such contradiction of sinners against himself, lest ye be wearied and faint in your minds.

1. *Wherefore, seeing we also, etc.* This conclusion is, as it were, an epilogue to the former chapter, by which he shows the end for which he gave a catalogue of the saints who excelled in faith under the Law, even that every one should be prepared to imitate them; and he calls a large multitude metaphorically a *cloud*, for he sets what is dense in opposition to what is thinly scattered.[237] Had they been a few in number, yet they ought to have roused us by their example; but as they were a vast throng, they ought more powerfully to stimulate us.

He says that we are so surrounded by this dense throng, that wherever we turn our eyes many examples of faith immediately meet us. The word *witnesses* I do not take in a general sense, as though he called them the martyrs of God, and I apply

---

[237] A cloud for a large multitude is a classical metaphor, and not scriptural. A cloud of footmen, and a cloud of birds, are used by Homer; and a cloud of footmen and horsemen, by Livy. — Ed.

it to the case before us, as though he had said that faith is sufficiently proved by their testimony, so that no doubt ought to be entertained; for the virtues of the saints are so many testimonies to confirm us, that we, relying on them as our guides and associates, ought to go onward to God with more alacrity.

Let us lay aside every weight, or *every burden, etc.* As he refers to the likeness of a race, he bids us to be lightly equipped; for nothing more prevents haste than to be encumbered with burdens. Now there are various burdens which delay and impede our spiritual course, such as the love of this present life, the pleasures of the world, the lusts of the flesh, worldly cares, riches also and honors, and other things of this kind. Whosoever, then, would run in the course prescribed by Christ, must first disentangle himself from all these impediments, for we are already of ourselves more tardy than we ought to be, so no other causes of delay should be added.

We are not however bidden to cast away riches or other blessings of this life, except so far as they retard our course for Satan by these as by toils retains and impedes us.

Now, the metaphor of a race is often to be found in Scripture; but here it means not any kind of race, but a running contest, which is wont to call forth the greatest exertions. The import of what is said then is, that we are engaged in a contest, even in a race the most celebrated, that many witnesses stand around us, that the Son of God is the umpire who invites and exhorts us to secure the prize, and that therefore it would be most disgraceful for us to grow weary or inactive in the midst of our course. And at the same time the holy men whom he mentioned, are not only witnesses, but have been associates in the same race, who have beforehand shown the way to us; and yet he preferred calling them witnesses rather than runners, in order to intimate that they are not rivals, seeking to snatch from us the prize, but approves to applaud and hail our victory; and Christ also is not only the umpire, but also extends his hand to us, and supplies us with strength and energy; in short, he prepares and fits us to enter on our course, and by his power leads us on to the end of the race.

And the sin which does so easily beset us, or, *stand around us, etc.* This is the heaviest burden that impedes us. And he says that we are entangled, in order that we may know, that no one is fit to run except he has stripped off all toils and snares. He speaks not of outward, or, as they say, of actual sin, but of the very fountain, even concupiscence or lust, which so possesses every part of us, that we feel that we are on every side held by its snares.[238]

Let us run with patience, etc. By this word *patience*, we are ever reminded of what the Apostle meant to be mainly regarded in faith, even that we are in spirit to seek the kingdom of God, which is invisible to the flesh, and exceeds all that our minds can comprehend; for they who are occupied in meditating on this kingdom can easily disregard all earthly things. He thus could not more effectually withdraw the Jews from their ceremonies, than by calling their attention to the real exercises of faith, by which they might learn that Christ's kingdom is spiritual, and far superior to the elements of the world.

2. *Who for the joy that was set before him*, etc. Though the expression in Latin is somewhat ambiguous, yet according to the words in Greek the Apostle's meaning is quite clear; for he intimates, that though it was free to Christ to exempt himself from all trouble and to lead a happy life, abounding in all good things, he yet underwent a death that was bitter, and in every way ignominious. For the expression, *for joy*, is the same as, instead of joy; and joy includes every kind of enjoyment. And he says, *set before him*, because the power of availing himself of this joy was possessed by Christ, had it so pleased him. At the same time if any one thinks that the preposition ἀντὶ denotes the final cause, I do not much object; then the meaning would be, that Christ refused not the death of the cross, because he saw its blessed issue. I still prefer the former exposition.[239]

But he commends to us the patience of Christ on two accounts, because he endured a most bitter death, and because he despised shame. He then mentions the glorious end of his death, that the faithful might know that all the evils which they may endure will end in their salvation and glory, provided they follow Christ. So also says James, "Ye have heard of the patience of Job, and ye know the end." (James v. 11.) Then the Apostle means that the end of our sufferings will be the same with those of Christ, according to what is said by Paul, "If we suffer with him, we shall also reign together." (Romans viii. 17.)

---

238 See Appendix P2.

239 See Appendix Q2.

3. *For consider him, etc.* He enforces his exhortation by comparing Christ with us; for if the Son of God, whom it behoves all to adore, willingly underwent such severe conflicts, who of us should dare to refuse to submit with him to the same? For this one thought alone ought to be sufficient to conquer all temptations, that is, when we know that we are companions or associates of the Son of God, and that he, who was so far above us, willingly came down to our condition, in order that he might animate us by his own example; yea, it is thus that we gather courage, which would otherwise melt away, and turn as it were into despair.

HEBREWS XII. 4-8

4. Ye have not yet resisted unto blood, striving against sin.
5. And ye have forgotten the exhortation which speaketh unto you as unto children, My son, despise not thou the chastening of the Lord, nor faint when thou art rebuked of him:
6. For whom the Lord loveth he chasteneth, and scourgeth every son whom he receiveth.
7. If ye endure chastening, God dealeth with you as with sons; for what son is he whom the father chasteneth not?
8. But if ye be without chastisement, whereof all are partakers, then are ye bastards, and not sons.

4. *Ye have not yet, resisted unto blood, etc.* He proceeds farther, for he reminds us, that even when the ungodly persecute us for Christ's sake, we are then contending against sin. Into this contest Christ could not enter, for he was pure and free from all sin; in this respect, however, we are unlike him, for sin always dwells in us, and afflictions serve to subdue and put it to flight.

In the first place we know that all the evils which are in the world, and especially death, proceed from sin; but this is not what the Apostle treats of; he only teaches us, that the persecutions which we endure for the Gospel's sake, are on another account useful to us, even because they are remedies to destroy sin; for in this way God keeps us under the yoke of his discipline, lest our flesh should become wanton; he sometimes also thus checks the impetuous, and sometimes punishes our sins, that we may in future be more cautious. Whether then he applies remedies to our sins, or anticipates us before we sin, he thus exercises us in the conflict with sin, referred to by the Apostle. With this honor indeed the Son of God favors us, that he by no means regards what we suffer for his Gospel as a punishment for sin. It behooves us still to acknowledge what we hear from the Apostle in this place, that we so plead and defend the cause of Christ against the ungodly, that at the same time we are carrying on war with sin, our intestine enemy. Thus God's grace towards us is twofold — the remedies he applies to heal our vices, he employs for the purpose of defending his gospel.[240]

But let us bear in mind whom he is here addressing, even those who had joyfully suffered the loss of their goods and had endured many reproaches; and yet he charges them with sloth, because they were fainting half way in the contest, and were not going on strenuously to the end. There is therefore no reason for us to ask a discharge from the Lord, whatever service we may have performed; for Christ will have no discharged soldiers, but those who have conquered death itself.

5. *And ye have forgotten, etc.* I read the words as a question; for he asks, whether they had forgotten, intimating that it was not yet time to forget. But he enters here on the doctrine, that

---

240 "Striving against sin," or contending or fighting against sin, — the sin of apostasy, says Grotius, — the sin of their persecutors, say Macknight and Stuart, sin being considered here as standing for sinners, the abstract for the concrete. The Apostle says, that they had not yet resisted — resisted what? This he seems to explain by saying, "contending against sin." It was then, the assault of sin that they had not yet resisted unto blood; and that sin was evidently apostasy, the sin plausibly presented to them, or ready to encompass and entangle them, mentioned in the first verse.

The phraseology here is similar to what is in the preceding verse; a participle ends the sentence, and that qualifies the foregoing verb — "that ye may not become wearied, being faint in your souls." Faintness or despondency in mind would inevitably be accompanied with weariness. Faith or strength of mind is necessary to prevent fatigue or weariness while engaged in contests and great trials; and as a preventive of despondency, we are directed attentively to consider how our savior bore the extreme trials which he had to endure. — *Ed.*

it is useful and needful for us to be disciplined by the cross; and he refers to the testimony of Solomon, which includes two parts; the first is, that we are not to reject the Lord's correction; and in the second the reason is given, because the Lord loves those whom he chastises.[241] But as Solomon thus begins, my "Son", the Apostle reminds us that we ought to be allured by so sweet and kind a word, as that this exhortation should wholly penetrate into our hearts.[242]

Now Solomon's argument is this: — If the scourges of God testify his love towards us, it is a shame that they should be regarded with dislike or hatred. For they who bear not to be chastised by God for their own salvation, yea, who reject a proof of his paternal kindness, must be extremely ungrateful.

6. *For whom the Lord loveth, etc.* This seems not to be a well-founded reason; for God visits the elect as well as the reprobate indiscriminately, and his scourges manifest his wrath oftener than his love; and so the Scripture speaks, and experience confirms. But yet it is no wonder that when the godly are addressed, the effect of chastisements which they feel, is alone referred to. For however severe and angry a judge God may show himself towards the reprobate, whenever he punishes

---

241 "Correction" is the best word for παιδεία, as it stands for מוסר and not "chastening" or chastisement. "Despise" in Hebrew is to regard a thing as trifling or with contempt, and so in Greek it means to regard a thing as little; the meaning is, not stoical; and then the meaning of the next clause is, be not depending. "Fret not," or "be not faint" or despairing, "when reproved" or "chastised." — *Ed*

242 Beza, Grotius, Macknight and Stuart, agree with Calvin in reading the first words interrogatively — "And have ye forgotten?" etc.

Ribera, the Jesuit, in his comment on this verse said, "The Apostle indirectly (*tacite*) reproves them, because they had no recourse to Scripture in their afflictions; compare Romans xv. 4." Capellus, referring to this passage, observed, "I wish the Jesuits were always to speak in this manner, but Ribera ought to have remembered that Paul was addressing the flock rather than the pastors, and that therefore, the Scriptures ought to be read by laymen."

The clear intimation of the passage no doubt is, that the Hebrews ought to have attended to the truths contained in Scripture. — *Ed*.

them; yet he has no other end in view as to the elect, but to promote their salvation; it is a demonstration of his paternal love. Besides, the reprobate, as they know not that they are governed by God's hand, for the most part think that afflictions come by chance. As when a perverse youth, leaving his father's house, wanders far away and becomes exhausted with hunger, cold, and other evils, he indeed suffers a just punishment for his folly, and learns by his sufferings the benefit of being obedient and submissive to his father, but yet he does not acknowledge this as a paternal chastisement; so is the case with the ungodly, who having in a manner removed themselves from God and his family, do not understand that God's hand reaches to them.

Let us then remember that the taste of God's love towards us cannot be had by us under chastisements, except we be fully persuaded that they are fatherly scourges by which he chastises us for our sins. No such thing can occur to the minds of the reprobate, for they are like fugitives. It may also be added, that judgment must begin at God's house; though, then, he may strike aliens and domestics alike, he yet so puts forth his hand as to the latter as to show that they are the objects of his peculiar care. But the previous one is the true solution, even that every one who knows and is persuaded that he is chastised by God, must immediately be led to this thought, that he is chastised because he is loved by God. For when the faithful see that God interposes in their punishment, they perceive a sure pledge of his love, for unless he loved them he would not be solicitous about their salvation. Hence the Apostle concludes that God is offered as a Father to all who endure correction. For they who kick like restive horses, or obstinately resist, do not belong to this class of men. In a word, then, he teaches us that God's corrections are then only paternal, when we obediently submit to him.[243]

7. *For what son is he,* etc. He reasons from the common practice of men, that it is by no means right or meet that God's children should be exempt from the discipline of the cross; for if no one is to be found among us, at least no prudent man and of a sound judgment, who does not correct his children — for without discipline they cannot be led to a right conduct — how much less will God neglect so necessary a remedy, who is the best and the wisest Father?

---

243 See Appendix R2.

If any one raises an objection, and says that corrections of this kind cease among men as soon as children arrive at manhood: to this I answer, that as long as we live we are with regard to God no more than children, and that this is the reason why the rod should ever be applied to our backs. Hence the Apostle justly infers, that all who seek exemption from the cross do as it were withdraw themselves from the number of his children.

It hence follows that the benefit of adoption is not valued by us as it ought to be, and that the grace of God is wholly rejected when we seek to withdraw ourselves from his scourges; and this is what all they do who bear not their afflictions with patience. But why does he call those who refuse correction *bastards* rather than aliens? Even because he was addressing those who were members of the Church, and were on this account the children of God. He therefore intimates that the profession of Christ would be false and deceitful if they withdrew themselves from the discipline of the Father, and that they would thus become bastards, and be no more children.[244]

HEBREWS XII. 9-11

9. Furthermore we have had fathers of our flesh which corrected *us*, and we gave *them* reverence: shall we not much rather be in subjection unto the Father of spirits, and live?
10. For they verily for a few days chastened *us* after their own pleasure; but he for *our* profit, that *we* might be partakers of his holiness.

---

244 There is in this verse the word "sons," to be understood after "all;" that is, "all the sons are partakers:" so Macknight and Stuart. As "sons" conclude the verse, the word is omitted here. Those who have only the name of Christians are called "bastards," or spurious or illegitimate children, because they are not born of God, being only the children of the flesh. They are not Isaac's but Ishmael, whatever their professions may be, and though baptized and partakers of all the outward privileges of the gospel. — *Ed.*

11. Now no chastening for the present seemeth to be joyous, but grievous: nevertheless afterward it yieldeth the peaceable fruit of righteousness unto them which are exercised thereby.

9. *Furthermore, we have had fathers of our flesh, etc.* This comparison has several parts: the first is, that if we showed so much reverence to the fathers from whom we have descended according to the flesh, as to submit to their discipline, much more honor is due to God who is our spiritual Father; another is, that the discipline which fathers use as to their children is only useful for the present life, but that God looks farther, having in view to prepare us for an eternal life; and the third is, that men chastise their children as it seems good to them, but that God regulates his discipline in the best manner, and with perfect wisdom, so that there is nothing in it but what is duly ordered. He then, in the first place, makes this difference between God and men, that they are the fathers of the flesh, but he of the spirit; and on this difference he enlarges by comparing the flesh with the spirit.

But it may be asked, Is not God the Father also of our flesh? For it is not without reason that Job mentions the creation of men as one of the chief miracles of God: hence on this account also he is justly entitled to the name of Father. Were we to say that he is called the Father of spirits, because he alone creates and regenerates our souls without the aid of man, it might be said again that Paul glories in being the spiritual father of those whom he had begotten in Christ by the Gospel. To these things I reply, that God is the Father of the body as well as of the soul, and, properly speaking, he is indeed the only true Father; and that this name is only as it were by way of concession applied to men, both in regard of the body and of the soul. As, however, in creating souls, he does use the instrumentality of men, and as he renews them in a wonderful manner by the power of the Spirit, he is peculiarly called, by way of eminence, the Father of spirits.[245]

---

245 Here is an instance, among many others, in which men's ingenuity is allowed unnecessarily to involve things in difficulties. The comparison here is founded on two palpable facts: there are fathers of our flesh, i.e., the body, and they have for a short time a duty to perform as such; but God, being the Father of our Spirits, which are to continue forever, deals with us in a way correspond-

When he says, *and we gave them reverence,* he refers to a feeling implanted in us by nature, so that we honor parents even when they treat us harshly. By saying, *in subjection to the Father of spirits,* he intimates that it is but just to concede to God the authority he has over us by the right of a Father. By saying, *and live,* he points out the cause or the end, for the conjunction "and" is to be rendered *that,* — "that we may live." Now we are reminded by this word *live,* that there is nothing more ruinous to us than to refuse to surrender ourselves in obedience to God.

10. *For they verily for a few days, etc.* The second amplification of the subject, as I have said, is that God's chastisements are appointed to subdue and mortify our flesh, so that we may be renewed for a celestial life. It hence appears that the fruit or benefit is to be perpetual; but such a benefit cannot be expected from men, since their discipline refers to civil life, and therefore properly belongs to the present world. It hence follows that these chastisements bring far greater benefit, as the spiritual holiness conferred by God far exceeds the advantages which belong to the body.

Were any one to object and say, that it is the duty of parents to instruct their children in the fear and worship of God, and that therefore their discipline seems not to be confined to so short a time; to this the answer is, that this is indeed true, but the Apostle speaks here of domestic life, as we are wont commonly to speak of civil government; for though it belongs to magistrates to defend religion, yet we say that their office is confined to the limits of this life, for otherwise the civil and earthly government cannot be distinguished from the spiritual kingdom of Christ.

Moreover when God's *chastisements* are said to be profitable to make men *partners of his holiness,* this is not to be so taken as though they made us really holy, but that they are helps to sanctify us, for by them the Lord exercises us in the work of mortifying the flesh.

11. *Now no chastening, etc.* This he adds, lest we should measure God's chastisements by our present feelings; for he shows

---

ing to our destiny. The question of instrumentality has nothing to do with the subject. Nor can anything be fairly drawn from this passage as to the useless question of the non-traduction of souls, as some have thought; and it may be justly be called useless, as it is a question beyond the range of human inquiry. — *Ed.*

that we are like children who dread the rod and shun it as much as they can, for owing to their age they cannot yet judge how useful it may be to them. The object, then, of this admonition is, that chastisements cannot be estimated aright if judged according to what the flesh feels under them, and that therefore we must fix our eyes on the end: we shall thus receive the *peaceable fruit of righteousness*. And by the *fruit of righteousness* he means the fear of the Lord and a godly and holy life, of which the cross is the teacher. He calls it *peaceable,* because in adversities we are alarmed and disquieted, being tempted by impatience, which is always noisy and restless; but being chastened, we acknowledge with a resigned mind how profitable did that become to us which before seemed bitter and grievous.[246]

HEBREWS XII. 12-17

12. Wherefore lift up the hands which hang down, and the feeble knees;
13. And make straight paths for your feet, lest that which is lame be turned out of the way; but let it rather be healed.
14. Follow peace with all *men,* and holiness, without which no man shall see the Lord:
15. Looking diligently lest any man fail of the grace of God; lest any root of bitterness springing up trouble *you,* and thereby many be defiled;
16. Lest there *be* any fornicator, or profane person, as Esau, who for one morsel of meat sold his birthright.
17. For ye know how that afterward, when he would have inherited the blessing, he was rejected: for he found no place of repentance, though he sought it carefully with tears.

12. *Wherefore, lift up, etc.* After having taught us that God regards our salvation when he chastises us, he then exhorts us to exert ourselves vigorously; for nothing will more weaken us and more fully discourage us than through the influence of a false notion to have no taste of God's grace in adversities. There

---

246 See Appendix S2.

is, therefore, nothing more efficacious to raise us up than the intimation that God is present with us, even when he afflicts us, and is solicitous about our welfare. But in these words he not only exhorts us to bear afflictions with courage, but also reminds us that there is no reason for us to be supine and slothful in performing our duties; for we find more than we ought by experience how much the fear of the cross prevents us to serve God as it behooves us. Many would be willing to profess their faith, but as they fear persecution, hands and feet are wanting to that pious feeling of the mind. Many would be ready to contend for God's glory, to defend what is good and just in private and in public, and to do their duties to God and their brethren; but as danger arises from the hatred of the wicked, as they see that troubles, and those many, are prepared for them, they rest idly with their hands as it were folded.

Were then this extreme fear of the cross removed, and were we prepared for endurance, there would be nothing in us not fitted and adapted for the work of doing God's will. This, then, is what the Apostle means here, "You have your hands," he says, "hanging down and your knees feeble, because ye know not what real consolation there is in adversity; hence ye are slow to do your duty: but now as I have shown how useful to you is the discipline of the cross, this doctrine ought to put new vigor in all your members, so that you may be ready and prompt, both with your hands and feet, to follow the call of God." Moreover, he seems to allude to a passage in Isaiah, (Isaiah xxxv. 3;) and there the Prophet commands godly teachers to strengthen trembling knees and weak hands by giving them the hope of favor; but the Apostle bids all the faithful to do this; for since this is the benefit of the consolation which God offers to us, then as it is the office of a teacher to strengthen the whole Church, so every one ought, by applying especially the doctrine to his own case, to strengthen and animate himself.[247]

---

247 The words are neither from the Hebrew nor from the Septuagint, but the order is more according to the former than the latter. The Hebrew is "Brace ye up the relaxed hands, and the tottering knees invigorate;" and the Sept., "Be strong, ye relaxed hands and paralyzed knees." The literal rendering of this passage is, "Therefore the enfeebled (or relaxed) hands and the paralyzed knees restore; i.e., to their former vigor, so that you may contend with your enemies and your trials and run your race." They had

13. *And make straight paths, etc.* He has been hitherto teaching us to lean on God's consolations, so that we may be bold and strenuous in doing what is right, as his help is our only support; he now adds to this another thing, even that we ought to walk prudently and to keep to a straight course; for indiscreet ardor is no less an evil than inactivity and softness. At the same time this straightness of the way which he recommends, is preserved when a man's mind is superior to every fear, and regards only what God approves; for fear is ever very ingenious in finding out byways. As then we seek circuitous courses, when entangled by sinful fear; so on the other hand every one who has prepared himself to endure evils, goes on in a straight way wheresoever the Lord calls him, and turns not either to the right hand or to the left. In short, he prescribes to us this rule for our conduct, — that we are to guide our steps according to God's will, so that neither fear nor the allurements of the world, nor any other things, may draw us away from it.[248]

Hence be adds, *Lest that which is lame be turned out of the way,* or, lest halting should go astray; that is, lest by halting ye should at length depart far from the way. He calls it halting, when men's minds fluctuate, and they devote not themselves sincerely to God. So spoke Elijah to the double-minded who blended their own superstitions with God's worship, "How long halt ye between two opinions?" (1 Kings xviii. 21.) And it is a befitting

---

before acted nobly as it is stated in chapter x. 32-34; he now exhorts them to recover their former vigor and strength. It is rendered by Macknight, "Bring to their right position." The verb ἀνοϱθόω literally means no doubt to make straight again, and is so used in Luke xiii. 13; but it has also the meaning of renewing or restoring to a former state, or of rebuilding. See Acts xv. 16. And in this sense Schleusner takes it in this passage. It is used in the Sept. in the sense of establishing confirming, making firm or strong. See Jeremiah x. 12. Hence Stuart gives this version, —
"Strengthen the weak hands and the feeble knees."
But the idea of repairing, or restoring or reinvigorating, gives the passage the most emphatic meaning. The Apostle in this instance only borrows some of the words from Isaiah, and accommodates them to his own purpose. — *Ed.*

248 Having spoken of strength, he now tells them how to use that strength. Be strong, and take a right course; go along the straight way of duty. See Appendix T2. — *Ed.*

way of speaking, for it is a worse thing to go astray than to halt. Nor they who begin to halt do not immediately turn from the right way, but by degrees depart from it more and more, until having been led into a diverse path so they remain entangled in the midst of Satan's labyrinth. Hence the apostle warns us to strive for the removal of this halting in due time; for if we give way to it, it will at length turn us far away from God.

The words may indeed be rendered, "Lest halting should grow worse," or turn aside; but the meaning would remain the same; for what the Apostle intimates is, that those who keep not a straight course, but gradually though carelessly turn here and there, become eventually wholly alienated from God.[249]

14. *Follow peace, etc.* Men are so born that they all seem to shun peace; for all study their own interest, seek their own ways, and care not to accommodate themselves to the ways of others. Unless then we strenuously labor to follow peace, we shall never retain it; for many things will happen daily affording occasion for discords. This is the reason why the Apostle bids us to *follow* peace, as though he had said, that it ought not only to be cultivated as far as it may be convenient to us, but that we ought to strive with all care to keep it among us. And this cannot be done unless we forget many offenses and exercise mutual forbearance.[250]

---

249 This interpretation is given by Grotius, Macknight and Stuart; but Beza, Doddridge and Scott, take the view given in our version regarding the lame or weak person as intended by τὸ χωλὸν. So is the Vulgate, "that no one halting may go astray, but rather be healed." — *Ed*

250 It has been justly observed that διώκω is to follow or pursue one fleeing away from us. It means not only to seek peace but strive to maintain it. Psalm 34, we have pursuing after seeking, "Seek peace and pursue it," i.e., strive earnestly to secure and retain it. Romans xii. 18, is an explanation.

But this strenuous effort as to peace is to be extended to holiness; not chastity, as Chrysostom and some other fathers have imagined, but holiness in its widest sense, purity of heart and life, universal holiness. The word ἁγιασμὸς is indeed taken in a limited sense, and rendered "sanctification" 1 Thessalonians iv. 3, and it may be so rendered here as it is in those places where it evidently means holiness universally, 1 Corinthians i. 30; 2 Thessalonians ii. 13, 1 Peter i. 2. The article is put before it in order to

As however peace cannot be maintained with the ungodly except on the condition of approving of their vices and wickedness, the Apostle immediately adds, that *holiness* is to be followed together with peace; as though he commended peace to us with this exception, that the friendship of the wicked is not to be allowed to defile or pollute us; for holiness has an especial regard to God. Though then the whole world were roused to a blazing war, yet holiness is not to be forsaken, for it is the bond of our union with God. In short, let us quietly cherish concord with men, but only, according to the proverb, as far as conscience allows.

He declares, that without holiness *no man shall see the Lord;* for with no other eyes shall we see God than those which have been renewed after his image.

15. *Looking diligently,* or, *taking care,* or, *attentively providing, etc.*[251] By these words he intimates that it is easy to fall away from the grace of God; for it is not without reason that attention is required, because as soon as Satan sees us secure or remiss, he instantly circumvents us. We have, in short, need of striving and vigilance, if we would persevere in the grace of God.

Moreover, under the word *grace,* he includes our whole vocation. If any one hence infers that the grace of God is not efficacious, except we of our own selves cooperate with it, the argument is frivolous. We know how great is the slothfulness of our flesh; it therefore wants continual incentives; but when the Lord stimulates us by warning and exhortation, he at the same time moves and stirs up our hearts, that his exhortations may not be in vain, or pass away without effect. Then from precepts and exhortations we are not to infer what man can do of himself, or what is the power of freewill; for doubtless the attention or diligence which the Apostle requires here is the gift of God.

---

show its connection with what follows, "and the (or that) holiness, without which no one shall see the Lord." — *Ed*

251 It means properly overseeing and is rendered "taking the oversight," in 1 Peter v. 2, where alone it occurs elsewhere. The word bishop comes from it. It is rendered, "taking heed," by Erasmus; "Diligently attending," by Grotius; "Taking care," by Beza; "Looking to it," by Doddridge; "carefully observing," by Macknight; and "Seeing to it." By Stuart. Considering what follows, "Taking heed" would be the best version. — *Ed.*

Lest any root, etc. I doubt not but that he refers to a passage written by Moses in Deuteronomy xxix. 18; for after having promulgated the Law, Moses exhorted the people to beware, lest any root germinating should bear gall and wormwood among them. He afterwards explained what he meant, that is, lest any one, felicitating himself in sin, and like the drunken who are wont to excite thirst, stimulating sinful desires, should bring on a contempt of God through the alluring of hope of impunity. The same is what the Apostle speaks of now; for he foretells what will take place, that is, if we suffer such a root to grow, it will corrupt and defile many; he not only bids every one to irradiate such a pest from their hearts, but he also forbids them to allow it to grow among them. It cannot be indeed but that these roots will ever be found in the Church, for hypocrites and the ungodly are always mixed with the good; but when they spring up they ought to be cut down, lest by growing they should choke the good seed.

He mentions *bitterness* for what Moses calls gall and wormwood; but both meant to express a root that is poisonous and deadly. Since then it is so fatal an evil, with more earnest effort it behooves us to check it, lest it should rise and creep farther.[252]

16. *Lest there be any fornicator or profane person, etc.* As he had before exhorted them to holiness, so now, that he might reclaim them from defilements opposed to it, he mentions a particular kind of defilement, and says, "Lest there be any fornicator." But he immediately comes to what is general, and adds, "or a profane person;" for it is the term that is strictly contrary to holiness. The Lord calls us for this end, that he may make us holy unto obedience: this is done when we renounce the world; but any one who so delights in his own filth that he continually rolls in it, profanes himself. We may at the same time regard the profane as meaning generally all those who do not value God's grace so much as to seek it and despise the world. But as men become profane in various ways, the more earnest we ought to strive lest an opening be left for Satan to defile us with his corruptions. And as there is no true religion without holiness, we ought to make progress continually in the fear of God, in the mortifying of the flesh, and in the whole practice of piety; for as we are profane until we separate from the world so if we roll again in its filth we renounce holiness.

---

252 See Appendix U2.

As Esau, etc. This example may be viewed as an exposition of the word *profane;* for when Esau set more value on one meal than on his birthright, he lost his blessing. Profane then are all they in whom the love of the world so reigns and prevails that they forget heaven: as is the case with those who are led away by ambition, or become fond of money or of wealth, or give themselves up to gluttony, or become entangled in any other pleasures; they allow in their thoughts and cares no place, or it may be the last place, to the spiritual kingdom of Christ.

Most appropriate then is this example; for when the Lord designs to set forth the power of that love which he has for his people, he calls all those whom he has called to the hope of eternal life his firstborn. Invaluable indeed is this honor with which he favors us; and all the wealth, all the conveniences, the honors and the pleasures of the world, and everything commonly deemed necessary for happiness, when compared with this honor, are of no more value than a morsel of meat. That we indeed set a high value on things which are nearly worth nothing, arises from this, — that depraved lust dazzles our eyes and thus blinds us. If therefore we would hold a place in God's sanctuary, we must learn to despise morsels of meat of this kind, by which Satan is wont to catch the reprobate.[253]

17. *When he would have inherited the blessing, etc.* He at first regarded as a sport the act by which he had sold his birthright, as though it was a child's play; but at length, when too late, he found what a loss he had incurred, when the blessing transferred by his father to Jacob was refused to him. Thus they who are led away by the allurements of this world alienate themselves

---

253 It is said that "for one morsel of meat," literally, "for one eating," or, "for one meal," as rendered by Doddridge, "he sold his birthright," or according to Macknight, "he gave away his birthrights." In this reference the Apostle gives the substance without regarding expressions, though he adopts those of the Septuagint in two instances, — the verb, which means to give away, used in the sense of selling, — and birthrights, or the rights of primogeniture. The word in Hebrew means primogeniture, used evidently by metonymy for its rights and privileges. Not only a double portion belonged to the first-born, but also the paternal blessing, which included things temporal and spiritual. The notion that the priesthood at that time and from the beginning of the world belonged to the first-born, has nothing to support it. Abel was a priest as well as Cain, and a better priest too. — *Ed.*

from God, and sell their own salvation that they may feed on the morsels of this world, without thinking that they lose anything, nay, they flatter and applaud themselves, as though they were extremely happy. When too late their eyes are opened, so that being warned by the sight of their own wickedness, they become sensible of the loss of which they made no account.

While Esau was hungry, he cared for nothing but how he might have his stomach well filled; when full he laughed at his brother, and judged him a fool for having voluntarily deprived himself of a meal. Nay, such is also the stupidity of the ungodly, as long as they burn with depraved lusts or intemperately plunge themselves into sinful pleasures; after a time they understand how fatal to them are all the things which they so eagerly desired. The word "rejected" means that he was repulsed, or denied his request.

For he found no place of repentance, etc.; that is, he profited nothing, he gained nothing by his late repentance, though he sought with tears the blessing which by his own fault he had lost.[254]

---

254 Though many such as Beza, Doddridge, Stuart etc. regard this "repentance" as that of Isaac, yet the phrase seems to favor the views of Calvin, "he found not the place of repentance," that is the admission of repentance; it was inadmissible, there was no place found for it. The word τόπος has this meaning in chapter viii. 7, "there should be no place (or admission) have been sought for the second." The same sense is given to the word in Ecclesiasticus xxxviii. 12, "give place" (or admission) to the physician — ἰατρῷ δὸς τόπον. We may give this rendering, "for he found not room for repentance;" he seemed to repent of his sin and folly, but his repentance availed nothing, for it could not be admitted; there was in his case no repentance allowed, as the account given in Genesis testifies.

The difficulty about "it" in the following clause is removed, when we consider that here, as in some previous instances, the Apostle arranges his sentences according to the law of parallelism; there are here four clauses; the first and last are connected, and also the middle clauses, —

"For ye know,
That even afterwards wishing to inherit the blessing,
He was rejected,
For he found no room for repentance,

Now as he denounces the same danger on all the despisers of God's grace, it may be asked, whether no hope of pardon remains, when God's grace has been treated with contempt and his kingdom less esteemed than the world? To this I answer, that pardon is not expressly denied to such, but that they are warned to take heed, lest the same thing should happen to them also. And doubtless we may see daily many examples of God's severity, which prove that he takes vengeance on the mockings and scoffs of profane men: for when they promise themselves tomorrow, he often suddenly takes them away by death in a manner new and unexpected; when they deem fabulous what they hear of God's judgment, he so pursues them that they are forced to acknowledge him as their judge; when they have consciences wholly dead, they afterwards feel dreadful agonies as a punishment for their stupidity. But though this happens not to all, yet as there is this danger, the Apostle justly warns all to beware.

Another question also arises, Whether the sinner, endued with repentance, gains nothing by it? For the Apostle seems to imply this when he tells us that Esau's repentance availed him nothing. My reply is, that repentance here is not to be taken for sincere conversion to God; but it was only that terror with which the Lord smites the ungodly, after they have long indulged themselves in their iniquity. Nor is it a wonder that this terror should be said to be useless and unavailing, for they do not in the meantime repent nor hate their own vices, but are only tormented by a sense of their own punishment. The same thing is to be said of *tears;* whenever a sinner sighs on account of his sins, the Lord is ready to pardon him, nor is God's mercy ever sought in vain, for to him who knocks it shall be opened, (Matthew vii. 8;) but as the tears of Esau were those of a man past hope, they were not shed on account of having offended God; so the ungodly, however they may deplore their lot, complain and howl, do not yet knock at God's door for mercy, for

---

Though with tears he sought it, (i.e., the blessing.)"

Though Macknight gave the other explanation of "repentance" yet he considered the blessing as the antecedent to "it" in the last line. Though with the tears of repentance he sought the blessing, yet he was rejected: the door to repentance was as it were closed up, and it could not be opened — Ed.

this cannot be done but by faith. And the more grievously conscience torments them, the more they war against God and rage against him. They might indeed desire that an access should be given them to God; but as they expect nothing but his wrath, they shun his presence. Thus we often see that those who often say, as in a jest, that repentance is sufficiently in time when they are drawing towards their end, do then cry bitterly, amidst dreadful agonies, that the season of obtaining repentance is past; for that they are doomed to destruction because they did not seek God until it was too late. Sometimes, indeed, they break out into such words as these, "Oh! if — oh! if;" but presently despair cuts short their prayers and chokes their voice, so that they proceed no farther.

HEBREWS XII. 18-24

18. For ye are not come unto the mount that might be touched, and that burned with fire, nor unto blackness, and darkness, and tempest,
19. And the sound of a trumpet, and the voice of words; which *voice* they that heard intreated that the word should not be spoken to them any more:
20. (For they could not endure that which was commanded, And if so much as a beast touch the mountain, it shall be stoned, or thrust through with a dart:
21. And so terrible was the sight, *that* Moses said, I exceedingly fear and quake:)
22. But ye are come unto mount Sion, and unto the city of the living God, the heavenly Jerusalem, and to an innumerable company of angels,
23. To the general assembly and church of the firstborn, which are written in heaven, and to God the Judge of all, and to the spirits of just men made perfect,
24. And to Jesus the mediator of the new covenant, and to the blood of sprinkling, that speaketh better things than *that of* Abel.

18. *For ye are not come, etc.* He fights now with a new argument, for he proclaims the greatness of the grace made known by the

Gospel, that we may reverently receive it; and secondly, he commends to us its benign characters that he might allure us to love and desire it. He adds weight to these two things by a comparison between the Law and the Gospel; for the higher the excellency of Christ's kingdom than the dispensation of Moses, and the more glorious our calling than that of the ancient people, the more disgraceful and the less excusable is our ingratitude, unless we embrace in a becoming manner the great favor offered to us, and humbly adore the majesty of Christ which is here made evident; and then, as God does not present himself to us clothed in terrors as he did formerly to the Jews, but lovingly and kindly invites us to himself, so the sin of ingratitude will be thus doubled, except we willingly and in earnest respond to his gracious invitation.[255]

Then let us first remember that the Gospel is here compared with the Law; and secondly, that there are two parts in this comparison, — that God's glory displays itself more illustriously in the Gospel than in the Law, — and that his invitation is now full of love, but that formerly there was nothing but the greatest terrors.

Unto the mount that might be touched, [256] *etc.* This sentence is variously expounded; but it seems to me that an earthly moun-

---

[255] The connection of this part has been viewed by some to be the following: — Having exhorted the Hebrews to peace and holiness, and warned them against apostasy and sinful indulgences, the Apostle now enforces his exhortations and warnings by showing the superiority of the Gospel over the Law. This is the view of Doddridge and Stuart. It appears that Scott connected this part with chapter x. 28-31, and that he considered that the object of the apostle was to bring forward an instance, in addition to former ones, of the superiority of the Gospel, in order to show that the neglect of it would involve a greater guilt than that of the Law. And this appears to have been the view of Calvin, which seems to be favored by the concluding part of the chapter. The word γὰρ may be rendered "moreover." — *Ed*

[256] It has been conjectured that μὴ has been omitted before "touched;" for in that case the passage would more exactly correspond with the account given in Exodus, for the people were expressly forbidden to touch the mountain. An omission of this kind was surely not impossible. The phrase as it is hardly admits of a grammatical construction: it has been found necessary to give the sense of an adjective to the participle. There would not

tain is set in opposition to the spiritual; and the words which follow show the same thing, *that burned with fire, blackness, darkness, tempest,* etc.; for these were signs which God manifested, that he might secure authority and reverence to his Law.[257] When considered in themselves they were magnificent and truly celestial; but when we come to the kingdom of Christ, the things which God exhibits to us are far above all the heavens. It hence follows, that all the dignity of the Law appears now earthly: thus mount Sinai might have been touched by hands; but mount Sion cannot be known but by the spirit. All the things recorded in the nineteenth chapter of Exodus were visible things; but those which we have in the kingdom of Christ are hid from the senses of the flesh.[258]

Should any one object and say, that the meaning of all these things was spiritual, and that there are at this day external exercises of religion by which we are carried up to heaven: to this I answer, that the Apostle speaks comparatively; and no one can doubt but that the Gospel, contrasted with the Law, excels in what is spiritual, but the Law in earthly symbols.

19. *They that heard entreated, etc.* This is the second clause, in which he shows that the Law was very different from the Gospel; for when it was promulgated there was nothing but terrors on every side. For everything we read of in the nineteenth chapter of Exodus was of this kind, and intended to show to the people that God had ascended his tribunal and manifested himself as a strict judge. If by chance an innocent beast approached, he commanded it to be killed: how much heavier

---

be this necessity were the words rendered "To a mount not to be touched and burning with fire, and to," etc. — *Ed*

257 The words used here are not taken literally from the Hebrew nor from the Sept. the four things mentioned in this verse, and the two things mentioned in the following verse, are found in the narrative in Exodus 19 and 20; but not consecutively as here; nor are the same terms used. "Blackness" γνόφῳ, should be "a dark or thick cloud," Exodus xix. 16. "Tempest," θυέλλη, is not mentioned in Exodus or in Deuteronomy; but it includes evidently "the thunders and lightnings" mentioned twice at least in Exodus, though not once in Deuteronomy. — *Ed*

258 "The Hebrews," says Grotius, "came in the body to a material mountain, but we in spirit to that which is spiritual."

punishment awaited sinners who were conscious of their guilt, nay, who knew themselves to be condemned to eternal death by the Law? But the Gospel contains nothing but love, provided it be received by faith. What remains to be said you may read in the third chapter of the Second Epistle to the Corinthians.

But by the words the people *entreated*, etc., is not to be understood that they refused to hear God, but that they prayed not to be constrained to hear God himself speaking; for by the interposition of Moses their dread was somewhat mitigated.[259] Yet interpreters are at a loss to know how it is that the Apostle ascribes these words to Moses, *I exceedingly fear and quake;* for we read nowhere that they were expressed by Moses. But the difficulty may be easily removed, if we consider that Moses spoke thus in the name of the people, whose requests as their delegate he brought to God. It was, then, the common complaint of the whole people; but Moses is included, who was, as it were, the speaker for them all.[260]

22. *Unto mount Sion, etc.* He alludes to those prophecies in which God had formerly promised that his Gospel should thence go forth, as in Isaiah ii. 1-4, and in other places. Then he contrasts mount Sion with mount Sinai; and he further adds, *the heavenly Jerusalem,* and he expressly calls it heavenly, that the Jews might not cleave to that which was earthly, and which had flourished under the Law; for when they sought perversely to continue under the slavish yoke of the Law, mount Sion was turned into mount Sinai as Paul teaches us in the fourth chapter

---

259 The words at the end of verse 20, "or thrust through with a dart," are not deemed genuine, being not found in the best MSS., and none of any authority containing them. — Ed.

260 It is supposed by some that the reference here is to what is found in Exodus xix. 16, 17. It is said in the former verse that all the people in the camp trembled; and it is concluded that Moses was at the time with them, for it is said in the next verse that he brought them forth out of the camp. But the passage that seems most evidently to intimate what is here said in the 19th verse, where we are told, that when the trumpet sounded long, and waxed louder and louder. "Moses spake" and that "God answered him by a voice." Now we are not told what he said, nor what the answer was which God gave. It is however, natural to conclude, that under the circumstances mentioned, Moses expressed his fears, and that God removed them. —Ed.

of the Epistle to the Galatians. Then by the heavenly Jerusalem he understood that which was to be built throughout the whole world, even as the angel, mentioned by Zechariah, extended his line from the east even to the west.

To an innumerable company of angels, etc. He means that we are associated with angels, chosen into the ranks of patriarchs, and placed in heaven among all the spirits of the blessed, when Christ by the Gospel calls us to himself. But it is an incalculable honor, conferred upon us by our heavenly Father, that he should enroll us among angels and the holy fathers. The expression, *myriads of angels,* in taken from the book of Daniel, though I have followed Erasmus, and rendered it *innumerable company of angels.* [261]

23. *The firstborn, etc.* He does not call the children of God indiscriminately the firstborn, for the Scripture calls many his children who are not of this number; but for the sake of honor he adorns with this distinction the patriarchs and other renowned saints of the ancient Church. He adds, which are written in heaven, because God is said to have all the elect enrolled in his book or secret catalogue, as Ezekiel speaks.[262]

---

[261] Calvin follows the Vulg. And connects πανηγύρει with "angels." It means a whole or a general assembly, and occurs in the Sept., and stands for מוֹעֵד often rendered a solemn assembly: it was a solemnity observed by the whole people. Both as to sense construction, it is better to adopt the arrangement of our version. — Ed

[262] To keep this clause distinct from the next but one, "the spirits of just men," etc. has been difficult. The distinction which Calvin seems to make as well as Doddridge, Scott and Stuart, is this, — that those mentioned here, "the first-born," were the most eminent of the ancients; but that "the spirits of just men" include the godly generally. The people of Israel were called "the first born," Exodus iv. 22, because they were God's chosen people. Ephraim is also called, "the first born," Jeremiah xxxi. 9, because of the superiority granted to that tribe; and the Messiah is so called, Psalm lxxxix. 27, on account of his eminence. The first born is one possessed of peculiar privileges. The word here seems to designate the saints, believers, Christians, as they are God's chosen people and highly privileged. We hence see the propriety of "the whole assembly," or the whole number of the faithful, composed of Jews or Gentiles. The Apostle says, "We are part of this whole assembly," and in order to point out his meaning more distinctly

The judge of all, etc. This seems to have been said to inspire fear, as though he had said, that grace is in such a way altered to us, that we ought still to consider that we have to do with a judge, to whom an account must be given if we presumptuously intrude into his sanctuary polluted and profane.

The spirits of just men, etc. He adds this to intimate that we are joined to holy souls, which have put off their bodies, and left behind them all the filth of this world; and hence he says that they are consecrated or "made perfect", for they are no more subject to the infirmities of the flesh, having laid aside the flesh itself. And hence we may with certainty conclude, that pious souls, separated from their bodies, still live with God, for we could not possibly be otherwise joined to them as companions.

24. *And to Jesus the Mediator, etc.* He adds this in the last place, because it is he alone through whom the Father is reconciled to us, and who renders his face serene and lovely to us, so that we may come to him without fear. At the same time he shows how Christ becomes our Mediator, even through his own *blood*, which after the Hebrew mode of speaking he calls the blood of *sprinkling*, which means sprinkled blood; for as it was once for all shed to make an atonement for us, so our souls must be now cleansed by it through faith. At the same time the Apostle alludes to the ancient rite of the Law, which has been before mentioned.

That speaketh better things, etc. There is no reason why *better* may not be rendered adverbially in the following manner, — "Christ's blood cries more efficaciously, and is better heard by God than the blood of Abel." It is, however, preferable to take the words literally: the blood of Christ is said to speak *better things*, because it avails to obtain pardon for our sins. The *blood of Abel* did not properly cry out; for it was his murder that called for vengeance before God. But the blood of Christ cries out, and the atonement made by it is heard daily.[263]

---

he calls it "the Church." The reference here seems to be the saints on earth, and at the end of the verse to departed saints. And they are said to be "made perfect," because freed from guilt, sin, and every pollution, having "washed their robes in the blood of the Lamb." — *Ed.*

263 See Appendix X2.

HEBREWS XII. 25-29

25. See that ye refuse not him that speaketh. For if they escaped not who refused him that spake on earth, much more *shall not* we *escape,* if we turn away from him that *speaketh* from heaven:
26. Whose voice then shook the earth: but now he hath promised, saying, Yet once more I shake not the earth only, but also heaven.
27. And this *word,* Yet once more, signifieth the removing of those things that are shaken, as of things that are made, that those things which cannot be shaken may remain.
28. Wherefore we receiving a kingdom which cannot be moved, let us have grace, whereby we may serve God acceptably with reverence and godly fear:
29. For our God *is* a consuming fire.

25. *See that ye refuse not him that speaketh, etc.* He uses the same verb as before, when he said that the people entreated that God should not speak to them; but he means as I think, another thing, even that we ought not to reject the word destined for us. He further shows what he had in view in the last comparison, even that the severest punishment awaits the despisers of the Gospel, since the ancients under the Law did not despise it with impunity. And he pursues the argument from the less to the greater, when he says, that God or Moses spoke then on earth, but that the same God or Christ speaks now from heaven. At the same time I prefer regarding God in both instances as the speaker. And he is said to have spoken on earth, because he spoke in a lower strain. Let us ever bear in mind that he refers to the external ministration of the Law, which, as compared with the gospel, partook of what was earthly, and did not lead men's minds above the heavens unto perfect wisdom; for though the Law contained in it the same truth, yet as it was only a training school, perfection could not belong to it.[264]

---

264 By "him that speaketh," is by some understood Christ, but more properly God, as his is the leading subject in the foregoing and the following verses. The words which follow are brief; and the first clause is explained more fully in chapter x. 28, and the sec-

26. *Whose voice then shook the earth, etc.* Though God shook the earth when he published his Law, yet he shows that he now speaks more gloriously, for he shakes both earth and heaven. He quotes on the subject the testimony of the Prophet Haggai, though he gives not the words literally; but as the Prophet foretells a future shaking of the earth and the heaven, the Apostle borrows the idea in order to teach us that the voice of the Gospel not only thunders through the earth, but also penetrates above the heavens. But that the Prophet speaks of Christ's kingdom, is beyond any dispute, for it immediately follows in the same passage, "I will shake all nations; and come shall the desire of all nations, and I will fill this house with glory." It is however certain that neither all nations have been gathered into one body, except under the banner of Christ, nor has there been any desire in which we ought to acquiesce but Christ alone, nor was the temple of Solomon exceeded in glory until the magnificence of Christ became known through the whole world. The Prophet then no doubt refers to the time of Christ. But if at the commencement of Christ's kingdom, not only the lower parts of the world were shaken, but his power also reached the heaven, the Apostle justly concludes that the doctrine of the Gospel is

---

ond in chapter i. 2. God spake "on earth" by Moses, but "from heaven" by his son, who came from heaven, ascended into heaven and sent his spirit down from heaven. The comparison here is between speaking on earth and speaking from heaven; but included in this, as previously explained in the Epistle, are the agents employed. God in delivering the Law fixed on a place on earth, and then as it were descended and employed an earthly agent, a mere man as his mediator; but in delivering the gospel, he did not descend from heaven, but employed a heavenly agent, his own son; thus manifested the superiority of the Gospel over the law. And that God is meant throughout this verse is evident from the following verse, "Whose voice," etc. The passage may be thus rendered, —

"See that ye reject not him who speaketh; for if they escaped not who rejected him when speaking on earth, how much more shall not we, if we turn away from him when speaking from heaven?"

We have no single word to express χρηματίζοντα — oraculizing, rendered by Doddridge, "giving forth oracles;" by Macknight, "delivering an oracle;" and by Stuart, "warning." But the best word we can adopt here is "speaking." — *Ed*

sublimer than that of the Law, and ought to be more distinctly heard by all creatures.[265]

27. *And this word, yet once more, etc.* The words of the Prophet are these, "Yet a little while;" and he means that the calamity of the people would not be perpetual, but that the Lord would succor them. But the Apostle lays no stress on this expression; he only infers from the shaking of the heaven and the earth that the state of the world was to be changed at the coming of Christ; for things created are subject to decay, but Christ's kingdom is eternal; then all creatures must needs be brought into a better state.[266]

He makes hence a transition to another exhortation, that we are to lay hold on that kingdom which cannot be shaken; for the Lord shakes us for this end, that he may really and forever establish us in himself. At the same time I prefer a different reading, which is given by the ancient Latin version, "Receiving a kingdom, we have grace," etc. When read affirmatively, the passage runs best, — "We, in embracing the Gospel, have the gift of the Spirit of Christ, that we may reverently and devoutly worship God." If it be read as an exhortation, "Let us have," it is a strained and obscure mode of speaking. The Apostle means in short, as I think, that provided we enter by faith into Christ's kingdom, we shall enjoy constant grace, which will effectually retain us in the service of God; for as the kingdom of Christ is above the world, so is the gift of regeneration.[267]

---

265 The quotation is literally neither from Hebrew nor from the Sept., but is substantially the same. "The earth and the heaven" may be deemed a phrase used to designate the whole state of things, as they include the whole of the visible creation. The whole Jewish polity, civil and religious, is generally supposed to be intended here. But as the shaking of the nations is mentioned in Haggai ii. 6, 7, Macknight thought that by "the earth" is meant heathen idolatry, and by "heaven" the Jewish economy, so called because it was divinely appointed. If this be allowed, then we see a reason for the change which the Apostle has made in the words: the original is both in Hebrew and in the Sept., "I shake (or will shake) the heaven and the earth;" but the Apostle says: "I shake not only the earth, but the heaven also." — *Ed.*

266 See Appendix Y2.

267 See Appendix Z2.

By saying that God is to be served *acceptably*, εὐαρέστως, *with reverence and fear,* he intimates that though he requires us to serve with promptitude and delight, there is yet no service approved by him except it be united with humility and due reverence. Thus he condemns froward confidence of the flesh, as well as the sloth which also proceeds from it.[268]

29. *For our God, etc.* As he had before kindly set before us the grace of God, so he now makes known his severity; and he seems to have borrowed this sentence from the fourth chapter of Deuteronomy. Thus we see that God omits nothing by which he may draw us to himself; he begins indeed with love and kindness, so that we may follow him the more willingly; but when by alluring he effects but little, he terrifies us.

And doubtless it is expedient that the grace of God should never be promised to us without being accompanied with threatening; for we are so extremely prone to indulge ourselves, that without the application of these stimulants the milder doctrine would prove ineffectual. Then the Lord, as he is propitious and merciful to such as fear him unto a thousand generations; so he is a jealous God and a just avenger, when despised, unto the third and the fourth generation.[269]

---

268 The Vulgate is, "with fear and reverence;" Beza's "with modesty and reverence and religious fear;" Schleusner's, "with reverence and devotion." Stuart has adopted our version. See Appendix A3. — *Ed.*

269 The conjunction καὶ at the beginning of this verse is commonly omitted by translators, but Macknight has retained it, "For even our God," etc. The intimation clearly is, that under the Gospel no less than under the Law God is a consuming fire to apostates; and apostasy or idolatry is the sin especially referred to in Deuteronomy iv. 24, from which this passage is taken. — *Ed*

CHAPTER 13

HEBREWS XIII. 1-6

1. Let brotherly love continue.
2. Be not forgetful to entertain strangers: for thereby some have entertained angels unawares.
3. Remember them that are in bonds, as bound with them; *and* them which suffer adversity, as being yourselves also in the body.
4. Marriage *is* honourable in all, and the bed undefiled: but whoremongers and adulterers God will judge.
5. *Let your* conversation *be* without covetousness; *and be* content with such things as ye have: for he hath said, I will never leave thee, nor forsake thee.
6. So that we may boldly say, The Lord *is* my helper, and I will not fear what man shall do unto me.

1. *Let brotherly love, etc.* Probably he gave this command respecting brotherly love, because a secret hatred arising from the haughtiness of the Jews was threatening to rend the Churches. But still this precept is generally very needful, for nothing flows away so easily as love; when everyone thinks of himself more than he ought, he will allow to others less than he ought; and then many offenses happen daily which cause separations.[270]

He calls love *brotherly,* not only to teach us that we ought to be mutually united together by a peculiar and an inward feeling of love, but also that we may remember that we cannot be Christians without being brethren; for he speaks of the love

---

[270] "Continue" or remain, implies that they had manifested this love, chapter vi. 10; as though he had said, "Let the love of the brethren be such as it has been." — *Ed.*

which the household of faith ought to cultivate one towards another inasmuch as the Lord has bound them closer together by the common bond of adoption. It was therefore a good custom in the primitive Church for Christians to call one another brothers; but now the name as well as the thing itself is become almost obsolete, except that the monks have appropriated to themselves the use of it when neglected by others, while at the same time they show by their discords and intestine factions that they are the children of the evil one.

2. *Be not forgetful to entertain strangers, etc.* This office of humanity has also nearly ceased to be properly observed among men; for the ancient hospitality, celebrated in histories, is unknown to us, and Inns now supply the place of accommodations for strangers. But he speaks not so much of the practice of hospitality as observed then by the rich; but he rather commends the miserable and the needy to be entertained, as at that time many were fugitives who left their homes for the name of Christ.

And that he might commend this duty the more, he adds, that angels had sometimes been entertained by those who thought that they received only men. I doubt not but that this is to be understood of Abraham and Lot; for having been in the habit of showing hospitality, they without knowing and thinking of any such thing, entertained angels; thus their houses were in no common way honored. And doubtless God proved that hospitality was especially acceptable to him, when he rendered such a reward to Abraham and to Lot. Were any one to object and say, that this rarely happened; to this the obvious answer is, — That not mere angels are received, but Christ himself, when we receive the poor in his name. In the words in Greek there is a beautiful alliteration which cannot be set forth in Latin.

3. *Remember them that are in bonds,* or, *Be mindful of the bound, etc.* There is nothing that can give us a more genuine feeling of compassion than to put ourselves in the place of those who are in distress; hence he says, that we ought to think of those in bonds as though we were bound with them. What follows the first clause, *As being yourselves also in the body,* is variously explained. Some take a general view thus, "Ye are also exposed to the same evils, according to the common lot of humanity;" but others give a more restricted sense, "As though ye were in their body." Of neither can I approve, for I apply the words to the body of the Church, so that the meaning would be this, "Since ye are members of the same body, it behooves you to feel in common for each other's evils, that there may be nothing disunited among you."[271]

4. *Marriage is honourable in all, etc.* Some think this an exhortation to the married to conduct themselves modestly and in a becoming manner, that the husband should live with his wife temperately and chastely, and not defile the conjugal bed by unbeseeming wantonness. Thus a verb is to be understood in the sense of exhorting, "Let marriage be honorable." And yet the indicative *is* would not be unsuitable; for when we hear that marriage is honorable, it ought to come immediately to our minds that we are to conduct ourselves in it honorably and becomingly. Others take the sentence by way of concession in this way, "Though marriage is honorable, it is yet unlawful to commit fornication"; but this sense, as all must see, is rigid. I am inclined to think that the Apostle sets marriage here in opposition to fornication as a remedy for that evil; and the context plainly shows that this was his meaning; for before he threatens that the Lord would punish fornicators, he first states what is the true way of escape, even if we live honourable in a state of marriage.

Let this then be the main point, that fornication will not be unpunished, for God will take vengeance on it. And doubtless as God has blessed the union of man and wife, instituted by himself, it follows that every other union different from this is by him condemned and accursed. He therefore denounces punishment not only on adulterers, but also on fornicators; for both depart from the holy institution of God; nay, they violate and subvert it by a promiscuous intercourse, since there is but one legitimate union, sanctioned by the authority and approval of God. But as promiscuous and vagrant lusts cannot be restrained without the remedy of marriage, he therefore commends it by calling it "honorable".

What he adds, *and the bed undefiled,* has been stated, as it seems to me, for this end, that the married might know that ev-

---

271 What Beza says of this opinion is, "I by no means reject it, though I regard the other (first mentioned here) as the most obvious." It has been said that whenever Paul mentions the mystical body, it is in connection with Christ, Romans xii. 5, and that "in the body" is to be understood literally, 2 Corinthians v. 6. It is so taken here by Grotius, Doddridge, Scott, and Stuart. — *Ed.*

erything is not lawful for them, but that the use of the legitimate bed should be moderate, lest anything contrary to modesty and chastity be allowed.[272]

By saying *in all men,* I understand him to mean, that there is no order of men prohibited from marriage; for what God has allowed to mankind universally, is becoming in all without exception; I mean all who are fit for marriage and feel the need of it.

It was indeed necessary for this subject to have been distinctly and expressly stated, in order to obviate a superstition, the seeds of which Satan was probably even then secretly sowing, even this, — that marriage is a profane thing, or at least far removed from Christian perfection; for those seducing spirits, forbidding marriage, who had been foretold by Paul, soon appeared. That none then might foolishly imagine that marriage is only permitted to the people in general, but that those who are eminent in the Church ought to abstain from it, the Apostle takes away every exception; and he does not teach us that it is conceded as an indulgence, as Jerome sophistically says, but that it is honourable. It is very strange indeed that those who

---

[272] If the whole verse be rightly considered, the construction of the first part will become evident. Two things are mentioned, "marriage" and "bed" — the conjugal bed. Two characters are afterwards mentioned, "fornicators and adulterers." The first disregard marriage and the second defile the conjugal bed. Then the first clause speaks of marriage as in itself honorable, in opposition to the dishonor put on it by fornicators, who being unmarried, indulge in illicit intercourse with women; and the second speaks of the conjugal bed as being undefiled, when not contaminated with adultery. This being evidently the meaning, the declarative form seems most suitable. Besides, the particle δὲ, "but" in the second part, as Beza observes, required this construction.

But if γὰρ be the reading, as found in some copies, then the perceptive form seems necessary, though even then the sense would be materially the same, — that marriage ought to be deemed honorable in all, that is in all ranks and orders of men, as Grotius observes, and that the conjugal bed ought to be undefiled. —

"Let marriage be deemed honorable among all, and the marriage bed be undefiled; for God will condemn fornicator and adulterer."

Hammond, Macknight, and Stuart adopt the perceptive form; but Beza, Doddridge and Scott, the declarative. — *Ed.*

introduced the prohibition of marriage into the world, were not terrified by this so express a declaration; but it was necessary then to give loose reins to Satan, in order to punish the ingratitude of those who refused to hear God.

5. *Let your conversation be without covetousness, etc.* While he seeks to correct covetousness, he rightly and wisely bids us at the same time to be content with our present things; for it is the true contempt of money, or at least a true greatness of mind in the right and moderate use of it, when we are content with what the Lord has given us, whether it be much or little; for certainly it rarely happens that anything satisfies an avaricious man; but on the contrary they who are not content with a moderate portion, always seek more even when they enjoy the greatest affluence. It was a doctrine which Paul had declared, that he had learned, so as to know how to abound and how to suffer need. Then he who has set limits to his desire so as to acquiesce resignedly in his lot, has expelled from his heart the love of money.[273]

For he has said, etc. Here he quotes two testimonies; the first is taken, as some think, from the first chapter of Joshua, but I am rather of the opinion that it is a sentence drawn from the common doctrine of Scripture, as though he had said, "The Lord everywhere promises that he will never be wanting to us." He infers from this promise what is found in Psalm 118, that we have the power to overcome fear when we feel assured of God's help.[274]

Here indeed he plucks up the evil by the very roots, as it is necessary when we seek to free from it the minds of men. It is certain that the source of covetousness is mistrust; for whosoever has this fixed in his heart, that he will never be forsaken by the Lord, will not be immoderately solicitous about present things, because he will depend on God's providence. When therefore the Apostle is seeking to cure us of the disease of covetousness, he wisely calls our attention to God's promises, in which he testifies that he will ever be present with us. He hence infers afterwards that as long as we have such a helper there is no cause to fear. For in this way it can be that no depraved desires will importune us; for faith alone is that which can quiet the minds of men, whose disquietude without it is too well known.

---

273 See Appendix B3.

274 See Appendix C3.

HEBREWS XIII. 7-9

7. Remember them which have the rule over you, who have spoken unto you the word of God: whose faith follow, considering the end of *their* conversation.
8. Jesus Christ the same yesterday, and to day, and for ever.
9. Be not carried about with divers and strange doctrines. For *it is* a good thing that the heart be established with grace; not with meats, which have not profited them that have been occupied therein.

7. *Remember, etc.* What follows refers not so much to morals as to doctrine. He first sets before the Jews the example of those by whom they had been taught; and he seems especially to speak of those who had sealed the doctrine delivered by them by their own blood; for he points out something memorable when he says, *considering the end of their conversation;* though still there is no reason why we should not understand this generally of those who had persevered in the true faith to the end, and had rendered a faithful testimony to sound doctrine through their whole life as well as in death. But it was a matter of no small importance, that he set before them their teachers for imitation; for they who have begotten us in Christ ought to be to us in the place as it were of fathers. Since then they had seen them continuing firm and unmoved in the midst of much persecutions and of various other conflicts, they ought in all reason to have been deeply moved and affected.[275]

8. *Jesus Christ the same, etc.* The only way by which we can persevere in the right faith is to hold to the foundation, and not in the smallest degree to depart from it; for he who holds not to Christ knows nothing but mere vanity, though he may comprehend heaven and earth; for in Christ are included all the treasures of celestial wisdom. This then is a remarkable passage, from which we learn that there is no other way of being truly wise than by fixing all our thoughts on Christ alone.

Now as he is dealing with the Jews, he teaches them that Christ had ever possessed the same sovereignty which he holds at this day; *The same,* he says, *yesterday, and today, and forever.*

---

275 See Appendix D3.

By which words he intimates that Christ, who was then made known in the world, had reigned from the beginning of the world, and that it is not possible to advance farther when we come to him. *Yesterday* then comprehends the whole time of the Old Testament; and that no one might expect a sudden change after a short time, as the promulgation of the Gospel was then but recent, he declares that Christ had been lately revealed for this very end, that the knowledge of him might continue the same for ever.

It hence appears that the Apostle is not speaking of the eternal existence of Christ, but of that knowledge of him which was possessed by the godly in all ages, and was the perpetual foundation of the Church. It is indeed certain that Christ existed before he manifested his power; but the question is, what is the subject of the Apostle. Then I say he refers to quality, so to speak, and not to essence; for it is not the question, whether he was from eternity with the Father, but what was the knowledge which men had of him. But the manifestation of Christ as to its external form and appearance, was indeed different under the Law from what it is now; yet there is no reason why the Apostle could not say truly and properly that Christ, as regarded by the faithful, is always the same.[276]

9. *Diverse doctrines, etc.* He concludes that we ought not to fluctuate, since the truth of Christ, in which we ought to stand firm, remains fixed and unchangeable. And doubtless, variety of opinions, every kind of superstition, all monstrous errors, in a word, all corruptions in religion, arise from this, that men abide not in Christ alone; for it is not in vain that Paul teaches us, that Christ is given to us by God to be our wisdom.

The import then of this passage is that in order that the truth of God may remain firm in us, we must acquiesce in Christ alone. We hence conclude that all who are ignorant of Christ are exposed to all the delusions of Satan; for apart from him there is no stability of faith, but innumerable tossings here and there. Wonderful then is the acuteness of the Papists, who have contrived quite a contrary remedy for driving away errors, even by extinguishing or burying the knowledge of Christ! But let this

---

276 Stuart takes the same view with Calvin in this point — that the eternal existence of Christ is not what is here taught, but that he as a Mediator is unchangeably the same. See Appendix E3. — *Ed.*

warning of the Holy Spirit be fixed in our hearts, that we shall never be beyond the reach of danger except we cleave to Christ.

Now the doctrines which lead us away from Christ, he says, are *divers* or various, because there is no other simple and unmixed truth but the knowledge of Christ; and he calls them also *strange* or foreign, because whatever is apart from Christ is not regarded by God as his own; and we are hereby also reminded how we are to proceed, if we would make a due proficiency in the Scripture, for he who takes not a straight course to Christ, goes after strange doctrines. The Apostle farther intimates that the Church of God will always have to contend with strange doctrines and that there is no other means of guarding against them but by being fortified with the pure knowledge of Christ.[277]

For it is a good thing, etc. He now comes from a general principle to a particular case. The Jews, for instance, as it is well known, were superstitious as to distinctions in meats; and hence arose many disputes and discords; and this was one of the strange doctrines which proceeded from their ignorance of Christ. Having then previously grounded our faith on Christ, he now says that the observance of meats does not conduce to our salvation and true holiness. As he sets *grace* in opposition to *meats*, I doubt not but that by grace he means the spiritual worship of God and regeneration. In saying *that the heart may be established*, he alludes to the word, *carried about*, as though he had

---

[277] "Doctrines" were said to be "various" because of their number; there were then as now many false doctrines; and "strange" because they were new or foreign to the truth, not consistent with the faith, but derived from abroad as it were, borrowed from traditions, ceremonies, or other foreign sources. Stuart gives another meaning to the first word, that is "different" from Christian doctrine; but it has no such meaning. Still less warranted is Macknight in saying that it means what is "discordant." What is meant by "diverse diseases" and "diverse lusts" is that they were of various kinds, or that they were many. The same author gives an unprecedented meaning to the second word. "foreign," that is, taught by unauthorized teachers! Stuart says, that it means "foreign" to Christian doctrine. The word is indeed used in Acts xvii. 18, and in 1 Peter iv. 12, in the sense of "new," a thing unusual, not heard of before; nor is this meaning unsuitable here. See Ephesians iv. 14, where the same subject is handled. See also Matthew xv. 9. — *Ed.*

said, "It is the spiritual grace of God, and not the observance of meats, that will really establish us.[278]

Which have not profited them that have been occupied therein. It is uncertain to whom he here refers; for the fathers who lived under the Law had no doubt a useful training, and a part of it was the distinction as to meats. It seems then that this is to be understood rather of the superstitious, who, after the Gospel had been revealed, still perversely adhered to the old ceremonies. At the same time were we judiciously to explain the words as applied to the fathers, there would be no inconsistency; it was indeed profitable for them to undergo the yoke laid on them by the Lord, and to continue obediently under the common discipline of the godly and of the whole Church; but the Apostle means that abstinence from meats was in itself of no avail. And no doubt it is to be regarded as nothing, except as an elementary instruction at the time when God's people were like children as to their external discipline. To be *occupied in meats* is to be taken as having a regard to them, so as to make a distinction between clean and unclean. But what he says of meats may be extended to the other rites of the Law.

HEBREWS XIII. 10-15

10. We have an altar, whereof they have no right to eat which serve the tabernacle.
11. For the bodies of those beasts, whose blood is brought into the sanctuary by the high priest for sin, are burned without the camp.
12. Wherefore Jesus also, that he might sanctify the people with his own blood, suffered without the gate.
13. Let us go forth therefore unto him without the camp, bearing his reproach.
14. For here have we no continuing city, but we seek one to come.
15. By him therefore let us offer the sacrifice of praise to God continually, that is, the fruit of *our* lips giving thanks to his name.

---

278 See Appendix F3.

10. *We have an altar, etc.* This is a beautiful adaptation of an old rite under the Law, to the present state of the Church. There was a kind of sacrifice appointed, mentioned in the sixteenth chapter of Leviticus, no part of which returned to the priests and Levites. This, as he now shows by a suitable allusion, was accomplished in Christ; for he was sacrificed on this condition, that they who serve the tabernacle should not feed on him. But by the *ministers of the tabernacle* he means all those who performed the ceremonies. Then that we may partake of Christ, he intimates that we must renounce the tabernacle; for as the word *altar* includes sacrificing and the victim; so *tabernacle*, all the external types connected with it.

Then the meaning is, "No wonder if the rites of the Law have now ceased, for this is what was typified by the sacrifice which the Levites brought without the camp to be there burnt; for as the ministers of the tabernacle did eat nothing of it, so if we serve the tabernacle, that is, retain its ceremonies, we shall not be partakers of that sacrifice which Christ once offered, nor of the expiation which he once made by his own blood; for his own blood he brought into the heavenly sanctuary that he might atone for the sin of the world."[279]

13. *Let us go forth, therefore, etc.* That the preceding allegory or mystical similitude might not be frigid and lifeless, he connects with it an important duty required of all Christians. And this mode of teaching is what Paul also usually adopts, that he might show to the faithful what things God would have them to be engaged in, while he was endeavoring to draw them away from vain ceremonies; as though he had said, "This is what God demands from you, but not that work in which you in vain weary yourselves." So now our Apostle speaks; for while he invites us to leave the tabernacle and to follow Christ, he reminds us that a far different thing is required of us from the work of serving God in the shade under the magnificent splendor of the temple; for we must go after him through exiles, flights, reproaches, and all kinds of afflictions. This warfare, in which we must strive even unto blood, he sets in opposition to those shadowy practices of which alone the teachers of ceremonies boasted.

---

279 The verb ἁγιάζω means here expiation, as in chapter ii. 11, x. 10, and other places in this Epistle; and so it is taken by Calvin and the rendering of Stuart is "that he might make expiation," etc. — Ed

14. *For here we have no continuing city, etc.* He extends still further the going forth which he had mentioned, even that as strangers and wanderers in this world we should consider that we have no fixed residence but in heaven. Whenever, therefore, we are driven from place to place, or whenever any change happens to us, let us think of what the Apostle teaches us here, that we have no certain shade on earth, for heaven is our inheritance; and when more and more tried, let us ever prepare ourselves for our last end; for they who enjoy a very quiet life commonly imagine that they have a rest in this world: it is hence profitable for us, who are prone to this kind of sloth, to be often tossed here and there, that we who are too much inclined to look on things below, may learn to turn our eyes up to heaven.

15. *By him, therefore, let us offer the sacrifice of praise to God, etc.* He returns to that particular doctrine to which he had referred, respecting the abrogation of the ancient ceremonies; and he anticipates an objection that might have been made; for as the sacrifices were attached as appendages to the tabernacle, when this was abolished, it follows that the sacrifices also must have ceased. But the Apostle had taught us that as Christ had suffered without the gate, we are also called thither, and that hence the tabernacle must be forsaken by those who would follow him.

Here a question arises, whether any sacrifices remained for Christians; for this would have been inconsistent, as they had been instituted for the purpose of celebrating God' worship. The Apostle, therefore, in due time meets this objection, and says that another kind of sacrifice remains for us, which no less pleases God, even the offering of the calves of our lips, as the Prophet Hoses says.[280] (Hosea xiv. 2.) Now that the sacrifice of praise is not only equally pleasing to God, but of more account than all those external sacrifices under the Law, appears evi-

---

280 The words in Hosea are not regimen, but in apposition. "So will we render calves, our lips." Such is the meaning given by the Targum, though the Vulg. puts the words in construction, "the calves of our lips." Instead of the calves offered in sacrifices, the promise made was to offer their lips, that is, words which they were required to take, "Take with you words". The Sept., Syr., and Arab. Render the phrase as here given, "the fruit of our lips," only the Apostle leaves out "our". There is the same meaning, though not exactly the same words. — *Ed.*

dent from the fiftieth Psalm; for God there repudiates all these as things of nought, and bids the sacrifice of praise to be offered to him. We hence see that it is the highest worship of God, justly preferred to all other exercises, when we acknowledge God's goodness by thanksgiving; yea, this is the ceremony of sacrificing which God commends to us now. There is yet no doubt but that under this one part is included the whole of prayer; for we cannot give him thanks except when we are heard by him; and no one obtains anything except he who prays. He in a word means that without brute animals we have what is required to be offered to God, and that he is thus rightly and really worshipped by us.

But as it was the Apostle's design to teach us what is the legitimate way of worshipping God under the New Testament, so by the way he reminds us that God cannot be really invoked by us and his name glorified, except through Christ the mediator; for it is he alone who sanctifies our lips, which otherwise are unclean, to sing the praises of God; and it is he who opens a way for our prayers, who in short performs the office of a priest, presenting himself before God in our name.

HEBREWS XIII. 16-19

16. But to do good and to communicate forget not: for with such sacrifices God is well pleased.
17. Obey them that have the rule over you, and submit yourselves: for they watch for your souls, as they that must give account, that they may do it with joy, and not with grief: for that *is* unprofitable for you.
18. Pray for us: for we trust we have a good conscience, in all things willing to live honestly.
19. But I beseech *you* the rather to do this, that I may be restored to you the sooner.

16. *But to do good, etc.* Here he points out even another way of offering a due and regular sacrifice, for all the acts and duties of love are so many sacrifices; and he thereby intimates that they were foolish and absurd in their wishes who thought that something was wanting except they offered beasts to God according to the Law, since God gave them many and abundant opportunities for sacrificing. For though he can derive no benefit from us, yet he regards prayer a sacrifice, and so much as the chief sacrifice, that it alone can supply the place of all the rest; and then, whatever benefits we confer on men he considers as done to himself, and honors them with the name of sacrifices. So it appears that the elements of the Law are now not only superfluous, but do harm, as they draw us away from the right way of sacrificing.

The meaning is, that if we wish to sacrifice to God, we must call on him and acknowledge his goodness by thanksgiving, and further, that we must do good to our brethren; these are the true sacrifices which Christians ought to offer; and as to other sacrifices, there is neither time nor place for them.

For with such sacrifices God is well pleased. There is to be understood here an implied contrast, — that he no longer requires those ancient sacrifices which he had enjoined until the abrogation of the Law.

But with this doctrine is connected an exhortation which ought powerfully to stimulate us to exercise kindness towards our neighbors; for it is not a common honor that God should regard the benefits we confer on men as sacrifices offered to himself, and that he so adorns our works, which are nothing worth, as to pronounce them holy and sacred things, acceptable to him. When, therefore, love does not prevail among us, we not only rob men of their right, but God himself, who has by a solemn sentence dedicated to himself what he has commanded to be done to men.

The word *communicate* has a wider meaning than *to do good*, for it embraces all the duties by which men can mutually assist one another; and it is a true mark or proof of love, when they who are united together by the Spirit of God communicate to one another.[281]

---

281 The words may be thus rendered, "And forget not benevolence (or, literally, well-doing) and liberality." The δὲ here should be rendered "and," for this is enjoined in addition to what is stated in the previous verse. The word εὐποιΐα means kindness, benevolence, beneficence, the doing of good generally; but κοινωνία refers to the distribution of what is needful for the poor. See Romans xv. 26, 2 Corinthians ix. 13. So that Calvin in this instance has reserved their specific meaning. Stuart's version is "Forget not kindness also and liberality;" and he explains the clause thus,

17. *Obey them, etc.* I doubt not but that he speaks of pastors and other rulers of the Church, for there were then no Christian magistrates; and what follows, *for they watch for your souls,* properly belongs to spiritual government. He commands first obedience and then honor to be rendered to them.[282] These two things are necessarily required, so that the people might have confidence in their pastors, and also reverence for them. But it ought at the same time to be noticed that the Apostle speaks only of those who faithfully performed their office; for they who have nothing but the title, nay, who use the title of pastors for the purpose of destroying the Church, deserve but little reverence and still less confidence. And this also is what the Apostle plainly sets forth when he says, that they *watched* for their souls, — a duty which is not performed but by those who are faithful rulers, and are really what they are called.

Doubly foolish, then, are the Papists, who from these words confirm the tyranny of their own idol: "The Spirit bids us obediently to receive the doctrine of godly and faithful bishops, and to obey their wholesome counsels; he bids us also to honor them." But how does this favor mere apes of bishops? And yet not only such are all those who are bishops under the Papacy, but they are cruel murderers of souls and rapacious wolves. But to pass by a description of them, this only will I say at present, that when we are bidden to obey our pastors, we ought carefully and wisely to find out those who are true and faithful rulers; for if we render this honor to all indiscriminately, first, a wrong

---

"Beneficence or kindness toward the suffering and liberality toward the needy." — *Ed*

282 Grotius renders the second verb, ὑπείκετε, "concede" to them, that is, the honor due to their office; Beza, "be compliant," (*obsecundate*;) and the directions of your guides and submit to their admonitions." Doddridge gives the sentiment of Calvin, "Submit yourselves to them with becoming respect."

The words may be rendered, "Obey your rulers and be submissive;" that is cultivate an obedient, compliant and submissive spirit. He speaks first of what they were to do — to render obedience and then of the spirit with which that obedience was to be rendered; it was not merely to be an outward act, but proceeding from a submissive mind. Schleusner's explanation is similar, "Obey your rulers and promptly (or willingly) obey them." — *Ed.*

will be done to the good; and secondly, the reason here added, to honor them because they watch for souls, will be rendered nugatory. In order, therefore, that the Pope and those who belong to him may derive support from this passage, they must all of necessity first prove that they are of the number of those who watch for our salvation. If this be made evident, there will then be no question but that they ought to be reverently treated by all the godly.[283]

For they watch, etc. His meaning is, that the heavier the burden they bear, the more honor they deserve; for the more labor anyone undertakes for our sake, and the more difficulty and danger he incurs for us, the greater are our obligations to him. And such is the office of bishops, that it involves the greatest labor and the greatest danger; if, then, we wish to be grateful, we can hardly render to them that which is due; and especially, as they are to give an account of us to God, it would be disgraceful for us to make no account of them.[284]

He further reminds us in what great a concern their labor may avail us, for, if the salvation of our souls be precious to us, they ought by no means to be deemed of no account who watch for it. He also bids us to be teachable and ready to obey, that what pastors do in consequence of what their office demands, they may also willingly and *joyfully* do; for, if they have their minds restrained by grief or weariness, though they may be sincere and faithful, they will yet become disheartened and careless, for vigor in acting will fail at the same time with their cheerfulness. Hence the Apostle declares, that it would be *unprofitable* to the people to cause sorrow and mourning to their pastors by their ingratitude; and he did this, that he might intimate to us that we cannot be troublesome or disobedient to our pastors without hazarding our own salvation.

---

283 "The Greek interpreters," says Estius, "teach that obedience is due to a bishop, though he be immoral in his conduct; but not if he perverts the doctrine of faith in his public preaching, for in that case he deprives himself of power, as he declares himself to be an enemy to the church." Poole, who quotes this passage, adds, "Let the Papisticals note this, who vociferously claim blind obedience in behalf of their pastors." — *Ed.*

284 See Appendix G3.

As hardly one in ten considers this, it is hence evident how great generally is the neglect of salvation; nor is it a wonder how few at this day are found who strenuously watch over the Church of God. For besides, there are very few who are like Paul, who have their mouth open when the people's ears are closed, and who enlarge their own heart when the heart of the people is straitened. The Lord also punishes the ingratitude which everywhere prevails. Let us then remember that we are suffering the punishment of our own perverseness, whenever the pastors grow cold in their duty, or are less diligent than they ought to be.

18. *For we trust, etc.* After having commended himself to their prayers, in order to excite them to pray, he declares that he had a *good conscience.* Though indeed our prayers ought to embrace the whole world, as love does, from which they flow; it is yet right and meet that we should be peculiarly solicitous for godly and holy men, whose probity and other marks of excellency have become known to us. For this end, then, he mentions the integrity of his own conscience, that is, that he might move them more effectually to feel an interest for himself. By saying, I am persuaded, or I *trust,* he thus partly shows his modesty and partly his confidence. *In all,* may be applied to things as well as to men; and so I leave it undecided.[285]

19. *But I beseech you, etc.* He now adds another argument, — that the prayers they would make for him, would be profitable to them all as well as to himself individually, as though he had

---

[285] The Greek fathers connect it with the preceding clause, "For we trust we have a good conscience towards all," that is towards Jews and Gentiles; but the Vulg. connects it with the following, "willing in all things to live well;" that is honorably. "Willing in all things to behave well" Macknight; "determined in all things to behave honorable" Doddridge; "being desirous in all things to conduct ourselves uprightly," Stuart. To keep the alliteration in the text, the words may be rendered thus — "We trust that we have a good conscience, being desirous to maintain a good conduct." A good conscience is a pure conscience, free from guilt and sinister motives: and to behave or live goodly, as the words are literally, is not to behave honorably or honestly, but to behave or live uprightly according to the rule of God's word; so that the best version is, "Willing in all things to live uprightly." "We trust," is rendered by Doddridge and Macknight, "we are confident;" but our version is preferable. — *Ed.*

said, "I do not so much consult my own benefit as the benefit of you all; for to be restored to you would be the common good of all."

A probable conjecture may hence perhaps be gathered, that the author of this Epistle was either beset with troubles or detained by the fear of persecution, so as not to be able to appear among those to whom he was writing. It might however be, that he thus spoke, though he was free and at liberty, for he regarded man's steps as being in God's hand; and this appears probable from the end of the Epistle.

HEBREWS XIII. 20-25

20. Now the God of peace, that brought again from the dead our Lord Jesus, that great shepherd of the sheep, through the blood of the everlasting covenant,
21. Make you perfect in every good work to do his will, working in you that which is well pleasing in his sight, through Jesus Christ; to whom *be* glory for ever and ever. Amen.
22. And I beseech you, brethren, suffer the word of exhortation: for I have written a letter unto you in few words.
23. Know ye that *our* brother Timothy is set at liberty; with whom, if he come shortly, I will see you.
24. Salute all them that have the rule over you, and all the saints. They of Italy salute you.
25. Grace *be* with you all. Amen.

Written to the Hebrews from Italy, by Timothy.[286]

20. *Now the God of peace, etc.* To render mutual what he desired them to do, he ends his Epistle with prayer; and he asks of God to *confirm*, or to fit, or to perfect them in *every good work;* for such is the meaning of καταρτίσαι. We hence conclude, that we are by no means fit to do good until we are made or formed for the purpose by God, and that we shall not continue long in doing

---

[286] This forms no part of the Epistle; and the subscriptions to the other Epistles must be viewed the same. Some of them are indeed manifestly erroneous, as the case with this. See verse 23. — Ed.

good unless he strengthens us; for perseverance is his peculiar gift. Nor is there a doubt but that as no common gifts of the Spirit had already, as it seems, appeared in them, the first impression with which they began, is not what is prayed for, but the polishing, which they were to be made perfect.

That brought again from the dead, etc. This clause was added for the sake of confirmation; for he intimates that God is then only prayed to aright by us, to lead us on to perfection, when we acknowledge his power in the resurrection of Christ, and acknowledge Christ himself as our pastor. He, in short, would have us to look to Christ, in order that we may rightly trust in God for help; for Christ was raised from death for this end, that we might be renewed unto eternal life, by the same power of God; and he is the great pastor of all, in order that we may protect the sheep committed to him by the Father.

Through the blood, etc. I have rendered it, "In the blood;" for as ב "in," is often taken in the sense of *with*, so I prefer to regard it here. For it seems to me, that the Apostle means, that Christ so arose from the dead, that his death was not yet abolished, but that it retains its efficacy forever, as though he had said, "God raised up his own son, but in such a way that the blood he shed once for all in his death is efficacious after his resurrection for the ratification of the everlasting covenant, and brings forth fruit the same as though it were flowing always."[287]

21. *To do his will, etc.* He now gives a definition of good works by laying down God's *will* as the rule; for he thus intimates, that no works are to be deemed good, but such as are agreeable to the will of God, as Paul also teaches us in Romans xii. 2, and in many other places. Let us then remember, that it is the perfection of a good and holy life, when we live in obedience to his will. The clause which next follows is explanatory, *working* (or doing) *in you what is well pleasing in his sight.* He had spoken of that will which is made known in the Law; he now shows, that in vain is obtruded on God what he has not commanded; for he values the decrees of his own will far more than all the inventions of the world.

Through Jesus Christ, etc. This may be explained in two ways, — "Working through Jesus Christ", or, "Well-pleasing through Jesus Christ." Both senses are suitable. For we know that the spirit of regeneration and also all graces are bestowed on us

---

287 See Appendix H3.

through Christ; and then it is certain, that as nothing can proceed from us absolutely perfect, nothing can be acceptable to God without that pardon which we obtain through Christ. Thus it comes, that our works, performed by the odor of Christ's grace, emit a sweet fragrance in God's presence, while otherwise they would have a fetid smell. I am disposed to include both meanings.

To whom be glory, etc. This I refer to Christ. And as he here ascribes to Christ what peculiarly belongs to God alone, he thus bears a clear testimony to his divinity; but still if anyone prefers to explain this of the Father, I do not object; though I embrace the other sense, as being the most obvious.

22. *And I beseech you, etc.* Some understand this as though he was soliciting them to hear him; but I take another view; for he mentions, as I think, that he had written in a *few words*, or briefly, in order that he might not appear as though he wished to lessen in any degree the ordinary practice of teaching. Let us hence learn that the Scripture has not been committed to us in order to silence the voice of pastors, and that we are not to be fastidious when the same exhortations often sound in our ears; for the holy Spirit has so regulated the writings which he has dictated to the Prophets and the Apostles, that he detracts nothing from the order instituted by himself; and the order is, that constant exhortations should be heard in the Church from the mouth of pastors. And probably he recommends the *word of exhortation* for this reason, that though men are by nature anxious to learn, they yet prefer to hear something new rather than to be reminded of things known and often heard before. Besides, as they indulge themselves in sloth, they can ill bear to be stimulated and reproved.

23. *Know ye that our brother, etc.* Since the termination of the Greek verb γινώσκετε, will admit of either renderings, we may read, "Ye know," or, "Know ye;" but I prefer the latter reading, though I do not reject the other.[288] The probability is, that he was informing the Jews on the other side of the sea of what they did not know. Now, if this *Timothy* was the renowned companion of Paul, which I am inclined to think, it is very probable that either Luke or Clement was the author of this Epistle. Paul, indeed, more usually calls him his son; and then what immediately fol-

---

288 The Vulgate Beza and almost all expounders, render it as an imperative, "Know ye." — *Ed.*

lows does not apply to Paul; for it appears that the writer was at liberty and at his own disposal; and besides, that he was then anywhere rather than at Rome; nay, it is very probable, that he was going round through various cities, and was then preparing to pass over the sea. Now all these particulars might have been suitable to the circumstances either of Luke or of Clement after the death of Paul.[289]

24. *Salute, etc.* As he writes his Epistle generally to the Hebrews, it is strange that he bids some, separate from the rest, to be saluted; but he sends this salutation, as I think, more particularly to the rulers, as a mark of honor, that he might conciliate them, and gently lead them to assent to his doctrine. And he adds, —

And all the saints. He either means the faithful from among the Gentiles, and refers to them that both Jews and Gentiles might learn to cultivate unity among themselves; or his object was to intimate, that they who first received the Epistle, were to communicate it to others.

---

[289] The words ἀπολελυμένον in this verse, has been rendered by Macknight and some others, "sent away." It is no doubt used in the sense of dismissing, dissolving, or sending away an assembly or a multitude, but not of sending away a person on a message. The two things are wholly distinct. The verb means to set loose, to loosen to release and hence to dismiss, to set at liberty, to make free, and never in the sense of sending a person to a place on business, or with an errand or message. The objection that we do not read elsewhere of Timothy's imprisonment is of no weight for the history we have of those times is very brief; and if we judge from the state of things at that period, there is nothing more probable than that Timothy shared the lot of Paul and of others. It is also probable that he was not imprisoned at Rome, where Paul was, but at some other place, for Paul says he expected him soon; and he does not say "If he returns quickly," but "if he come quickly." —*Ed.*

APPENDIX OF ADDITIONAL ANNOTATIONS

APPENDIX A

Chapter i. 3 *Who being the brightness, etc.* The words are rendered by *Beza,* "the effulgence of his glory, and the impress of his person;" by *Doddridge,* "the effulgent ray of his glory, and the express delineation of his person;" by *Macknight,* "an effulgence of his glory, and an exact image of his substance;" and by *Stuart,* "the radiance of his glory, and the exact image of his substance." The word "brightness," does not adequately express the meaning of the first word, ἀπαύγασμα, which signifies an emitted light, a splendor proceeding from an object. The most suitable word would be, outshining, or irradiation, "the outshining of his glory." The "express image" of our version is the impress, the engraven or impressed form, derived from the archetype. And "impress," as given by *Beza,* fully expresses it.

The words are doubtless metaphorical, but the idea is this — that Christ, as a Mediator, as the Son of God in human nature, exactly represents what God is, being the very image of him who is invisible. "Substance," or essence, is the divine nature in all its glorious and incomprehensible attributes of power, wisdom, holiness, justice, and goodness. These and other perfections are exhibited in Christ perfectly, and in such a way that we can look on them, and in a measure understand them. Hence he said, "He that hath seen me, hath seen the Father," John xiv. 9.

The word ὑπόστασις, does not mean a "person," either in Scripture or in classic writers. It is a meaning invented by the fathers during the Arian controversy. As used in the *Sept.* and in the New Testament, it means foundation or basis, Ezekiel xliii. 11, — substance, Psalm cxxxix. 15, — expectation, Psalm xxx-

viii. 11, — and confidence, 2 Corinthians ix. 4. Its classic meaning, according to *Stuart*, is foundation, steadfastness, courage, purpose, resolution, determination, substance, essence, being. There is in Colossians i. 15, a phrase of a similar import, with "the impress of his substance," where Christ is said to be "the image (εἴχων — the likeness) of the invisible God." The substance or essence is "the invisible God," and "the impress" is "the image."

"In the opinion," says *Stuart*, "that the verse now under consideration relates to the incarnate Messiah, and not to the Logos in his divine nature simply considered, I find that Scott and Beza concur, not to mention others of the most respectable commentators."

It was the mistaken view which the fathers took of the passage that led them to invent a new meaning to the word ὑπόστασις; and many have followed them.

APPENDIX B

Chapter i. 5. *Thou art my Son, etc.* It is to be observed that Christ *is* called a Son when his prophetic office is referred to, ver. 2, when spoken of as a king, ver. 8, when his priesthood is mentioned, chapter v. 5, and when a comparison is made between him and Moses, chapter iii. 6. But as a king over his people is he represented here as superior to angels; and David as his type was also called a son because he was a king. Christ is said here to have derived his name by "inheritance" — from whom? The Apostle refers throughout to the Old Testament; and what does Peter say That David, being a Prophet, knew that God "would raise up Christ to sit *on his* throne," Acts ii. 30. Then the inheritance in this instance was from David. Christ is God's *only-begotten* Son as to his divine nature; but he is also a Son in a peculiar manner, superior to all others, that is, as a Prophet, Priest, and King. There were types of him in these offices; but they were only types, and therefore far inferior to him even as to these offices. And angels never sustained such offices.

APPENDIX C

Chapter i. 6 *And again when he bringeth, etc* Critics have found some difficulty in the order in which the particles are arranged here, and have proposed a transposition, which is not at all necessary. The word "first-begotten," or first-born, seems to have been used on account of what the previous verse contains. The words, "Today have I begotten thee," refer clearly to the resurrection; and Christ is said to have been "the first-born from the dead," Colossians i. 18. Having then referred to Christ's resurrection, he now as it were goes back to his birth, or to the announcement made in prophecy of his coming into the world, and seems to say, that not only when he became the first-born from the dead he attained a manifested superiority over angels, but even at his first introduction into the world, for they were commanded even to worship him. "And when again," or also, or moreover, "he introduces," etc.; as though he had said, "God owned him as his Son by raising him from the dead; and again, or in addition to this, when he introduced him into the world, he commanded the angels to worship him." So that the subordination of angels was evident before his resurrection, even at his very introduction into the world.

Stuart considers his introduction to be his birth, and regards the words, "and let all the angels of God worship him," as borrowed, though not literally, from Psalm xcvii. 7, to express what is intimated in the account of his birth, Luke ii. 10-14. The Hebrews, written to, were, he supposes, acquainted with that event.

This is the view taken by some of the fathers, *Chrysostom* and others. But some, as *Mede,* thinking the quotation a prophecy, consider that his second coming is intended, as the contents of the Psalm were deemed to be descriptive of the day of judgment. A third party, as Dr. *Owen,* view the introduction to be Christ's birth, and consider the Psalm as giving an allegorical description of the progress of the Gospel in the world; and this seems to be the view taken by *Calvin,* and is apparently the most consistent.

The difference in the quotation is quite immaterial. The words in the Psalm are, "Worship him all gods," or rather angels; for so is the word sometimes rendered. The version of the *Sept.* is, "Worship him all ye his angels;" and here "God "is put instead of "his."

APPENDIX D

Chapter i. 10. *Thou, Lord, etc.* The quotation is literally from the *Sept.*, only the order of the words in the first sentence is changed; and it is literally the Hebrew, except that σὺ χύζιε are added. The Hebrew is, "Of old the earth hast thou founded, and the work of thy hands are the heavens."

Nothing can more clearly prove the *divine* nature of Christ than this quotation; and it settles at once the meaning of αἰωϙνας; in the 2nd verse, as it confirms the truth that Christ, the Messiah, being not only the Son but also the only-begotten of God, is the Creator of the world, even the earth and the heavens, as here stated. Nor can the word have any other meaning in chapter ix. 26, and xi. 3

It is generally admitted that this Psalm refers to Christ; and Dr. *Owen* mentions three particulars in proof of this, — the redemption of the Church, verses 13 and 16, — the call of the Gentiles, verses 15, 21, and 22, — and the creation of a new people, verse 18; and he adds, that the Jews themselves refer the last thing to the time of the Messiah.

Referring to the words, "as a vesture," the same author beautifully observes, that the whole creation is like God's vesture, by which he shews himself to men in his power and wisdom, and that hence it is said, that he "clothes himself with light as with a garment," Psalm civ. 2.

APPENDIX E

Chapter i. 14 *Are they not all ministering spirits, etc* It is said of Christ also, that he was a minister or a servant; but while he was a servant, he was at the same time the Lord of all, which cannot be said of angels. Yet as a servant he was superior to them; for he became so in a work which they were not capable of doing. So that as a servant a superiority belongs to him. But his office as a servant is not contemplated here. Indeed all the names given to him, in common either with men on earth or with angels in heaven, mean very different things when applied to him; such as son, servant, priest, king, Savior, etc.

It ought to be born in mind that throughout this chapter Christ is spoken of in his character of a Mediator, and not as to his divine nature simply considered, and that the reference is made, as to his superiority over angels, to the testimonies in the Old Testament. He is in this chapter represented as superior to angels, —

1. Because he is called in a peculiar respect a Son.
2. Because angels were commanded to worship him.
3. Because he is addressed as having an eternal throne, and being honored more than all his associates as a king.
4. Because he is the Creator of the world.
5. And lastly, because there is a promise made to him that all his enemies shall be finally subdued, while angels are only employed in ministering to his people.

Who, after duly considering all these things, can possibly come to any other conclusion than that the Messiah is a divine person as well as human? Angels are commanded to worship him, his throne is eternal, he created this world, and all his enemies shall finally be made his footstool. That he is sometimes spoken of as having a delegated power, as in verse 2, "by whom he (God) made the world," and sometimes as acting independently, as in verse 10, "Thou, Lord, hast founded the earth;" all this only proves, that as he is inferior to the Father in his mediatorial office, so he is one with the Father as his only-begotten Son. Creation is what God claims as peculiarly his own work; and were not the Son one in essence with the Father, creation could not have been ascribed to him.

APPENDIX F

Chapter ii. 1. *Lest at any time we should let them slip.* Much has been written as to the meaning of the verb here used. It is said by *Schleusner* that it signifies two things, "to flow through," as waters through a sieve or a leaky vessel, and "to flow by," as a river. It is used mostly in the latter sense. *Chrysostom* and others, both ancient and modern, give it the sense of falling away or perishing; but, according to *Stuart,* there is no instance either in Scripture or the classics which countenances such a meaning. As it was often the case, so here, the fathers gave what they conceived to be the general sense, without attending to the precise meaning of the word used; and thus their propositions are often very loose. Besides, most of them were wholly ignorant of the language of the Old Testament.

To flow by, in the sense of escaping, is its meaning in classical authors; and *Stuart* says that all the examples commonly referred to apply only to *things*, and not to *persons*. The word only occurs here in the New Testament, and once in the *Sept.*; and there also it refers to a person, and is clearly used *transitively*. The passage is Proverbs iii. 21, "O son, pass not by (or disregard not, μὴ παραῤῥυῶς, flow not by,) but keep (or retain, τήρησον) my counsel and thought." The form of the sentence is different in Hebrew, but the idea is here preserved, "My son, let them not depart from thine eyes; keep (retain) sound wisdom and discretion." Not to suffer them to depart from the eyes, is the same as not to pass them by or disregard them. There is no other idea compatible with the context; and it is what exactly suits this passage. Then the sentence would be, "Lest we should at any time disregard (or neglect) them."

It is justly observed by *Stuart*, that everything in the whole passage is in favor of this meaning: it is the opposite of "taking heed;" and it is often the case in Scripture that the negative idea is stated as well as the positive, and *vice versa*. Besides, in verse 3 the same idea is presented to us on the same subject, "If we *neglect*," etc. Indeed, to disregard or neglect may be deemed as the *consequence* of not taking heed or attending to a thing. Inattention to truth is followed by the neglect of what it teaches and inculcates. Unless we earnestly attend to what we hear, we shall inevitably neglect what is required. There may be some attention without performance; but there can be no performance without attention.

APPENDIX G

Chapter ii. 7 *Thou madest him, etc* The reference is to Psalm 8, and has been variously explained. There are especially three opinions on the subject. Some, like *Calvin* and *Doddridge*, consider that the case of "man," as described in the Psalm, is *alluded* to, or accommodated to Christ. Others, like *Grotius*, hold that "man," in the Psalm, is to be understood historically and mystically. The third party, as most of the Fathers, as well as some later divines, such as *Beza*, *Dr. Owen.*, and *Stuart*, maintain that the Psalm is strictly prophetic. What makes it difficult to regard it in this light is the exclamation, "What is man?" and also the dominion over the brute creation, which is the only thing mentioned in the Psalm as constituting the glory and honor of man.

All critics refer on this subject to the grant given to Adam in Genesis i. 28. But this grant, forfeited no doubt by Adam's sin and fall, was afterwards renewed to Noah and his sons, when they came out of the ark, and was even enlarged, as the permission to eat animal food was given them. Genesis ix. 1-3. It was this grant no doubt the Psalmist had in view. Noah and his sons were men of faith; Noah is distinctly said to have been a righteous man. It was to them as bearing this character that the grant was made. What Adam forfeited was restored to those restored to God's favor, that is, the dominion over the brute creation and the inheritance of this lower world. But as Canaan was afterwards to the Israelites a type of heaven, and also a pledge to those who were Israelites indeed, so might be regarded the possession of the earth granted to Noah and his sons, though dominion in which "glory and honor" consisted, is what is expressly mentioned in the Psalm; and dominion is the special subject handled by the Apostle, verse 5.

Though man, as to his nature, is inferior to the angels, yet in that nature God has granted him a dominion never granted to angels. The power over every living thing in the world was bestowed, not on angels, but on man, according to the testimony of the Old Testament; so that the power ascribed by the Jews to angels was not warranted by their own Scriptures. This fact seems to have been referred to as an introduction to what the Apostle was proceeding to say respecting Christ, and as an evidence that his human nature, though in itself inferior to that of angels, did not detract from his superiority; as though he had said, "It is no objection that he became man, for even to man, not to angels, has been granted the dominion of the world."

Then the Apostle extends the idea, and refers to Christ as one who was to make good the grant made. The dominion promised to man, especially what that dominion was a pledge of, was not attained by man; but Christ, who has assumed his nature, and in this respect became lower than the angels, will yet attain it for him. It is through Christ indeed that we obtain a right to the things of this world as well as to the things of the next world. God promises both to his people; but in Christ only are his promises, yea and amen. The promise made to man as a believer, both as to this world and the next, is as it were made good only through Christ, who assumed his nature for this very purpose.

By taking this view we avoid the necessity of making that prophetic which has no appearance of being so, or of supposing that the Psalm is referred to by way of accommodation. The fact respecting man restored to God's favor is stated, and the Apostle teaches us that the dominion granted to him can only be realized through Christ, who has already attained that dominion in his own person, and will eventually confer it on all his people.

APPENDIX H

Chapter ii. 9. *That he by the grace of God, etc* How to connect the different parts of this verse has been a difficulty which critics have in various ways attempted to remove. There is hardly a sense in our version. We must either regard a transposition in the words, or, like *Stuart*, give the meaning of *when* to ὅπως, "when by the grace of God he had tasted death for all." But this is an unnatural meaning, and therefore not satisfactory. *Doddridge* supposes a transposition, and gives this version, —

"But we see Jesus, who was made a little lower than the angels for the suffering of death, that by the grace of God he might taste death for every man, crowned with glory and honor."

Macknight more properly connects "the suffering of death" with "crowned with glory and honor," while he makes a similar transposition. *Bloomfield* considers that there is an ellipsis in the last clause, and gives this rendering, —

"But him, who was made a little lower than the angels, even Jesus, we behold, on account of having suffered death, crowned with glory and honor, which suffering he bore, in order that by the grace of God he might taste of death for every man."

This borders on tautology, and cannot be admitted. That the transposition made by *Doddridge* and *Macknight* gives the real meaning, admits hardly of a doubt; and such a version would be the most suitable in our language. But how to account for the arrangement in the Apostle's words seems to be this, it is a construction according to the system of Hebrew parallelism; the first and the last clause are connected, and the second and the third. Let the verse be arranged in lines, and this will become quite evident, —

"But him, who was made a little lower than angels, — We behold, *even* Jesus, for the suffering of death, Crowned with glory and honor, — That by God's grace he might for all taste death."

The meaning is clearly this, — that he was made lower than angels in order to die for all, and that on account of his atoning death he was crowned with glory and honor; which perfectly accords with what the Apostle teaches us in Philippians ii. 8-10. See a similar arrangement in Matthew vii. 6, and 1 Corinthians vi. 11.

APPENDIX I

Chapter ii. 14 *The power of death, etc* This is rendered by *Stuart* "deadly power." The genitive after χράτος; is no doubt in several instances rendered adjectively, as "the power of his glory," in Colossians i. 11, "his glorious power;" and "the power of his might," in Ephesians vi. 10, may be rendered "His mighty power." But there is here an antithesis which ought to be preserved, — the death of Christ and the death over which Satan is said to have power. Christ by his death deprived Satan of his power to cause death.

To "destroy" does not suitably express what is meant by the verb here used. It means to render void, useless, inefficacious, and hence to overcome, to subdue. When applied to the Law, it means to render void or to abolish: but when it refers to a person, as here, or to a hostile power, as in 1 Corinthians xv. 24, it means to subjugate, to put down, or to overcome. So here, the rendering most suitable would be, "that by death he might overcome (or subdue) him who had the power of death," that is, the power of causing eternal ruin; for death here must mean the second death. And hence the Rabbinical notion about the angel of death, that is, of temporal death, has no connection with this passage.

There is here evidently an allusion to Genesis iii. 13. The originator of death is Satan, both as to the soul and the body; and hence our Savior calls him a murderer. To subdue this murderer was to remove the sin which he introduced, by means of which he brought in death; and this removal of sin was effected by death, so that the remedy for sin was the same with the effect which sin produced.

APPENDIX K

Chapter ii. 16 *For verily he took not, etc* The words may be rendered, "For verily he lays not hold on angels, but on the seed of Abraham does he lay hold." Both early and later divines have supposed "nature" to be understood; but some moderns, following *Cameron* of an earlier age, regard the verb in the sense of bringing aid or help. So *Stuart* and *Bloomfield*. The first renders the verse thus, —

"Besides, he doth not at all help the angels, but he helpeth the seed of Abraham."

The present, the historical present, is used for the past; or if we render οὐ γὰρ δήπου "for nowhere," the reference is to Scripture; nowhere in Scripture is such a thing recorded.

But to "take hold on" is sufficiently plain and very expressive. Christ took hold on Peter when he was sinking, (Matthew xiv. 31:) it is the same verb. Our Savior took not hold on the angels when sinking into ruin, but he did take hold on the seed of Abraham to save them from perdition. The connection seems to be with the preceding verses; therefore γὰρ ought to be rendered "for" and not "besides," as by *Stuart,* nor "moreover," as by *Macknight.* A reason is given why Christ became partaker of flesh and blood; and the reason was, because he did not come to deliver angels but the seed of Abraham; that is, his spiritual, not his natural seed, for he speaks throughout of God's sons and God's children. See John i. 12, 13, where the born of God are represented to be those to whom Christ grants the privilege of children.

APPENDIX L

Chapter iii. 4 *He that built, etc.* This verse has been considered as difficult with respect to the connection it has with the argument of the Apostle. *Stuart* states thus the difficulty, — "Moses as the *delegate* of God was the founder of the Jewish institution, and Christ is merely declared to be only a *delegated founder,* then in what way does the writer make out the superiority of Christ to Moses. Both were delegates of the same God, and both the founders of a new and divine dispensation. If Christ, then, is not here asserted to be founder in some other character than that of a *delegate,* I am unable to perceive any force in the writer's argument." Hence the Professor comes to the conclusion, that Christ is meant by the Apostle when he says, "He who built (or formed) all things is God," conceiving that the argument is otherwise inconclusive.

Now, the mistake of the Professor is this, that he makes delegation to be the comparison and not the *character* of the delegation. That Christ's power was delegated is quite evident from this passage: Christ is said to have been "appointed" in verse 2, and is said to be "faithful," which implies that he had an office delegated to him. Then the delegation is undeniable; and what the Apostle evidently dwells upon is the superiority of the delegated power: Moses was faithful as a servant in God's house; the people of Israel were previously Gods adopted people; but Christ has power, a delegated power, to make as it were a new people; he builds his own house. Moses was a part of the house in which he served; but as Christ builds his own house, he is worthy of more glory than Moses. These are the comparisons made by the Apostle.

Then this verse is introduced, and that for two reasons, — first, to shew that God built the house in which Moses served; and secondly, to intimate the divine power of Christ, as none but God builds all things. Moses' house is called God's house in verse 2; and Christ's house is called his own in verse 5. Hence the obvious inference is, that he is one with God, as God only builds all things, though in his Mediatorial character he acts as God's Apostle and high priest. The same kind of representation we find in the first chapter: it is said that by him God made the world; and afterwards that the Son is the Creator, who had founded the earth, and whose work are the heavens. Creative power, though exercised by Christ as a Mediator, must yet be a divine power.

APPENDIX M

Chapter iii. 9. *Tempted, etc.* To understand this passage we must bear in mind the event referred to. The same year in which the people of Israel came forth from Egypt, they were distressed for water at Rephidim, (Exodus xvii. 1;) and the place had two names given to it, Massah and Meribah, because the people tempted God and chided with Moses. The Lord did not swear *then* that they should not enter into the land of Canaan; but this was on the following year, after the return of the spies. (Numbers xiv. 20-38.) And God said then that they had tempted him "ten times;" that is, during the short time since their deliverance from Egypt. It was after *ten* temptations that God deprived them of the promised land.

Bearing in mind these facts, we shall be able to see the full force of the passage. The "provocation" or contention, and "temptation" refer clearly to the latter instance, as recorded in Numbers 14, because it was then that God swear that the people should not enter into his rest. The people's conduct was alike in both instances.

To connect "forty years" with "grieved" was the work of the Punctuists, and this mistake the Apostle corrected; and it is to be observed that he did not follow in this instance the *Septuagint*, in which the words are arranged as divided by the Masorites. Such a rendering as would correspond with the Hebrew is as follows, — "Today when ye hear his voice,

8. Harden not your hearts as in the provocation, In the day of temptation in the wilderness.

9. When your fathers tempted me, they proved me And saw my works forty years:

10 I was therefore offended with that generation and said, Always do they go astray in heart, And they have not known my ways;

11. So that I swear in my wrath, They shall by no means enter into my rest.'"

The meaning of the ninth verse is, that when the children of Israel tempted God, they proved him, *i.e.*, found out by bitter experience how great his displeasure was, and saw his works or his dealings with them for forty years. He retained them in the wilderness during that period until the death of all who disbelieved his word at the return of the spies; he gave them this proof of his displeasure. "Therefore" in verse 11 is connected with "tempted;" it was because they tempted him that he was offended with them so as to swear that they should not enter into his rest. There is evidently a ו left out in Hebrew, found only in one MS.; but it is required by the future form of the verb. To "go astray in heart" was to disbelieve God's word, (see verse 12, and Numbers xiv. 11;) and not to have known Gods ways, was not to recognize his power, and goodness, and faithfulness in their deliverance from Egypt. See Numbers xiv. 22. Not to know here does not mean what *Stuart* says, not to approve, but not to comprehend or understand God's ways, or not to recognize them as his ways or doings.

The last line is in the form of an oath, "If they shall enter," etc.; but when in this defective form, the "if" may be rendered as a strong negative, "by no means." *Doddridge* has "never," and *Macknight* "not," in which he has been followed by *Stuart*.

APPENDIX N

Chapter iii. 15 *While it is said, etc.* No doubt the connection first referred to in the note is the most suitable. This verse is as it were the heading of what follows; but to put the sixteenth verse in an interrogatory form, as is done by *Stuart*, seems not suitable to the passage. I would render the words thus, —

15. With regard to what is said, "Today, when ye hear his

16. voice, harden not your hearts as in the provocation," some indeed when they heard did provoke, but not all who came

17. out of Egypt under Moses: but with whom was he offended for forty years? was it not with those who sinned, whose

18. carcasses fell in the wilderness? And to whom did he swear that they should not enter into his rest, but to those who did not believe?

The "provocation" is the subject; who offered it are then mentioned; and afterwards the cause of it, the want of faith.

APPENDIX O

Chapter iv. 2 *For unto us was the Gospel preached, etc.* Literally it is, "For we have been evangelized." *Doddridge* has, "For we are made partakers of the good tidings;" *Macknight*, "For we also have received the good tidings;" and *Stuart*, "For to us also blessings are proclaimed." Perhaps the most literal version would be, "For we also have had good tidings." The same form of words occurs again in verse 6, "And they to whom it was first preached," etc.; rather, "And they who had first good tidings," etc. The good tidings were evidently the promise of rest.

"The word preached" is literally "the word of hearing;" that is, the word heard, a noun being put for a participle, a common thing in Hebrew.

Though there are several MSS. and the Greek fathers in favor of "mixed" being in the accusative case, agreeing with "them," "who united not by faith with those who heard," *i.e.*, obeyed; yet the *Vulgate* and the *Syriac* countenance our present reading, which has been adopted by *Erasmus, Beza,* Dr. *Owen,* and most modern divines, as being most suitable to the passage.

Our version is followed by *Doddridge* and *Macknight*. The version of *Stuart* is the same with that of *Calvin*, "being not connected with faith in those who heard it." The *Syriac* seems the most literal, "being not mingled with faith by them who heard it." They had not the ingredient of faith to mix up as it were with it. Instead of receiving the promise, they refused and rejected it, as though it were an unwholesome and disagreeable draught. The word is used in 2 Macc. xv. 39, of wine *mingled* with water.

APPENDIX P

Chapter iv. 12. *For the word of God, etc.* Some, as *Stuart* and *Bloomfield*, view "the word" here as minatory, being a threatening to the unbelievers before mentioned. Though it may be so viewed, yet it seems not to be right to translate λόγος; "threatening," as done by *Stuart*.

APPENDIX Q

"Quick" or living, and "powerful" or efficacious, are regarded by many as meaning nearly the same thing; but "living" designates what is valid, what continues in force, as opposed to what is dead and no longer existing; and "efficacious" refers to the effect, capable of producing the effect designed. Exclusion from rest as to unbelievers was still living, still in force, abiding the same without any change. See 1 Peter i. 23, 25. It was also in full power so as effectually to exclude from rest all who did not believe. And then to prevent every evasion, so that no one might think a mere profession sufficient, or rather to guard against the incipient seduction of sin, he compares this "word" to a sword which can dissect the whole well-compacted frame of man, so that even the very marrow may be discovered; and then passing from this simile, he says that this "word" is capable of judging the thoughts and purposes of the heart. And in order to identify as it were this "word" with God himself; he immediately refers to God's omniscience. The design of the Apostle seems to have been to guard the Hebrews against the deceitfulness of sin; so that they might not give heed to any of its hidden suggestions.

Stuart makes the transition from the "word" to God at the end of the twelfth verse, and renders the clause thus, "He also judgeth the thoughts and purposes of the heart." But this clause may more properly be viewed as explanatory of what is said of the two-edged sword.

APPENDIX R

Chapter iv. 12. *Two-edged sword, etc* Whether the penetrating, or convincing, or killing power of the "word" is set forth by the metaphor of the "sword," has been controverted. *Beza* and *Scott*, as well as *Calvin*, regard its convincing *and* killing power as intended. "It enters," says *Beta*, "into the inmost recesses of the soul, so that it indicts on the perverse a deadly wound, and by killing the old man quickens into life the elect." *Stuart* views its killing power as alone intended: "The sense is," he observes, "that the divine commination is of *most deadly* punitive efficacy."

Now, if the whole passage be duly considered in connection with what is gone before, there will appear a sufficient reason to conclude, that the metaphor of "the sword "is only intended to shew that the "word" reaches to all the inward workings of the soul, that it extends to the motives and the most hidden thoughts and purposes of the heart. The last clause in the 12th verse clearly explains what is meant by the "sword;" and this is further confirmed by the following verse, where it is said that all things are naked and open to God, of whose word he speaks, and with whom we have to do. All this seems to concur with the purpose for which the words were introduced, that is, to warn the Hebrews of the danger of listening to the seductive and deceiving power of sin.

As to the 13th verse, *Bloomfield* suggests a transposition which would render the transition from God's word to God himself much more easy, "Moreover there exists no creature that is not manifest in the sight of him with whom we have to do; but all things are naked and exposed to his eyes." But the construction here is similar to what we have noticed in two previous instances, chapter ii. 9, and 17, 18; the first and the last clause are connected, and the two middle clauses.

The last sentence is rendered by *Grotius*, "of whom is our word, *i.e.*, of whom we speak; by *Beza*, "with whom we have to do; by *Doddridge, Macknight*, and *Stuart*, "to whom we must give an account." Wherever λόγος signifies "account," the verb "to render," or a similar verb is connected with it. There are two instances in the *Sept.* where it stands alone with a pronoun in the dative case as here, and it means *business, affair,* or *concern:* see Judges xviii. 28, and 2 Kings ix. 5. In the last passage it is connected also, as here, with the preposition πρὸς. There can therefore be no doubt but that our version is the right one, "with whom we have to do," or literally, "with whom *there is* to us a concern." There is no *usus loquendi*, as pleaded by some, in favor of the other meaning.

APPENDIX S

Chapter vi. 1 *Therefore leaving, etc* Authors differ as to the character of this passage, whether it be hortatory or didactic, that is, whether the Apostle, putting himself as it were with them, exhorts them to advance in knowledge, or, discharging the office of a teacher, he intimates the course which he means to pursue. *Stuart* and some others, as well as *Calvin,* take the first view, as though the Apostle had said, "As the perfect or grown up are alone capable of receiving strong food, it behooves us to quit the state of childhood and to advance into the state of manhood, so as to attain perfect knowledge." It is said that this view comports better with what follows, "for it is impossible," etc.

But there are especially two things in the passage which militate against this view, first, "not laying the foundation," etc. which refers evidently to teaching; and secondly, the third verse, which also refers to teaching.

It is usual with the Apostle to speak of himself in the plural number: see, for instance, the 9th verse. "Therefore" is a general inference from what he had been saying, and not from a particular clause, as though he had said, "Such being the case with you, let me now therefore, in order to draw you onward, leave the first principles, and proceed to state things which are suitable to advanced Christians: it is not my purpose now to preach repentance and faith in which you have been already taught, and to do this is unavailing as to those who have fallen away; 'for it is impossible,'" etc. His object was not to convert them to the faith, but to confirm and advance them in it.

Or the whole argument may be more fully stated thus, — "What I design now to do is not to call you to repentance and faith, to require you to be baptized that you might receive the miraculous gift of the Holy Ghost, and to teach you the doctrine of the resurrection as confirmed by our Savior's resurrection, and of the day of judgment, when a sentence shall be pronounced on the just and unjust which shall never be reversed; for all these things have been long known to you, and you have made a long profession of them: there is therefore no need of taking such a course, nor is it of any benefit, for if you fall away, it is impossible to restore you again to repentance." But instead of making the case personal to them, he states it generally. He thus most powerfully stimulated them to make advances in the knowledge of divine truths; for not to advance is to retrograde, and to retrograde is the direct way to apostasy.

APPENDIX T

Chapter vi. 5. *And the powers of the world to come.* The *five* things mentioned here have been variously explained.

1 *Enlightened*, — baptized, say most of the fathers, and some moderns too, but without any countenance from the use of the word in Scripture, either in the New Testament or in the *Sept.* It means to emit light, to bring to light, to enlighten, and hence to instruct, to teach. It is often used in the *Sept.* for a word that means to teach in Hebrew. The taught, the instructed in the duty and necessity of repentance and in Christian truth generally, were no doubt "the enlightened." This is the meaning given to it by *Crotius, Beza, Dr Owen, Doddridge, Scott, Stuart, etc.*

2 *The heavenly* gift, — faith — Christ — the Holy Spirit — pardon of sins — peace of conscience — eternal life: all these have been stated, but the first, "faith towards God," mentioned in the first verse, is no doubt what is meant.

3. *Partakers of the Holy Ghost;* that is, in his miraculous powers, as understood by most; it is what is evidently intimated by "baptisms and laying on of hands" in the second verse.

4 *The good word of God,* — the Gospel — the Gospel covenant — the promises of the Gospel — the heavenly inheritance: such have been the explanations given. There are but two places where the phrase "the good word" occurs, and that is in Jeremiah xxix. 10, and in xxxiii. 14; and there it means the promise of restoration given to the Jews, and here it clearly means the promise of the resurrection mentioned in the second verse.

5. *The powers of the world to come;* that is, miraculous powers, say most; but αἰὼν ὁ μέλλων, "the world to come," says *Schleusner* never means in the New Testament the time of the Gospel, but the future world. See Matthew xii. 32; Luke xviii. 30; Ephesians i. 21. He therefore explains the clause thus, "The power and efficacy of the doctrine respecting the future felicity of Christians in heaven." It would have comported more with the "eternal judgment" in these converse, had he said, "respecting the future state both of the saved and of the lost in the next world;" for eternal judgment refers to both.

To "taste," according to the usage of Scripture, is to know, to partake of, to experience, to possess, to enjoy. It does not mean here, as some have thought, slightly to touch a thing, or to sip it, but to know, to know experimentally, to feel, or to enjoy.

Thus we see that there is a complete correspondence between the particulars mentioned here and the things stated in verses 1 and 2.

APPENDIX U

Chapter vi. 4-9. On the subject handled in these verses, *Stuart* asks and answers a question thus, "Does the whole paragraph pertain to real Christians, or to those who are such only by profession? To the former beyond all reasonable doubt." The question is not suitable, for the Apostle only speaks of those who had enjoyed certain privileges, and as to whether they were real or merely professing Christians, he does not treat of. Paul addressed the Corinthians as "the Church of God;" and it might in the same way be asked, "Did he address them as real Christians, or as those who were only such by profession t" and it might be answered, "Doubtless as real Christians." And yet we find that he says, "Examine yourselves, whether ye be in the faith." What is spoken of here is the *enjoyment* of certain privileges and the danger of not making a right use of them, and even the awful doom of those who disregarded them and turned away from the truth.

Our author indeed fully admits the doctrine of the perseverance of the saints; but a question of this kind, not relevant to the subject, tends only to create embarrassment. He indeed afterwards somewhat modifies it by saying, that "God treats Christians as free agents and rational beings, and guards them against defection, not by mere *physical* force, but by *moral* means adapted to their nature as free and rational agents." No doubt God thus acts according to the whole current of Scripture; but this in no way contravenes the truth, clearly taught in many passages, that his elect people, real Christians, shall never perish.

APPENDIX X

Chapter vi. 10. *And labor of love, etc* Though *Griesbach* and others have excluded τοῦ χόπου, "labor," from the text, yet *Bloomfield* thinks that there are sufficient reasons for retaining the words. The greatest number of MSS. contain them, and they seem necessary to render the passage complete, though the meaning without them would be the same. There is here an instance of an arrangement similar to what is found often in the Prophets, as will be seen by putting the verse in lines, —

"For not unrighteous is God, To forget your work, And the labor of that love Which ye have shewed to his name, Having ministered and ministering to the saints."

Excluding the first line, we see that the first and last are connected, and the two middle lines. Their "work" was to minister to the saints; and in addition to this there was "the labor of that love" which they manifested towards God. He would not forget their work in aiding the saints, nor the love which they had shewn towards his name by an open profession of it, and activity and zeal in God's service. *Grotius* says that "the labor of love" was in behalf of the Christian faith.

Stuart says that "work" was the outward act, and that "love" was the principle from which it emanated. Examples of this kind no doubt occur often in Scripture, the not being first stated, and then the inward principle or motive; but if "labor" be retained, this view cannot be maintained.

APPENDIX Y

Chapter vi. 11. *To the full assurance, etc.* The preposition πρὸς, "to," may be rendered "with regard to, in respect of." If this meaning be given to it, then the diligence required was with reference to the full assurance of hope: they were to exercise diligence in order that they might enjoy the assurance of hope to the end. But if the preposition be rendered "for the sake of," as by *Stuart*, then the meaning is, that they were to exercise the same diligence as they had already exhibited in the work and labor of love, for the purpose of attaining the full assurance of hope.

Now *Calvin* takes the first meaning; he considers that the Apostle now refers to the full assurance of hope or of faith as he regards it, as he had before spoken of the works of benevolence. What follows seems to favor this view, for the Apostle proceeds to speak of faith and patience as exemplified by the fathers, especially by Abraham.

Some, as *Beza*, connect "to the end" with "shewing the same diligence," but it is more suitable to connect them with "the assurance of hope," as it is done by most.

The remarks of *Scott* on the difference of "the assurance of hope," of "the understanding," and of "faith," are so clear and discriminating that they shall be added, —

"He who so understands the Gospel as to perceive the relation of each part to all the rest, and its use as a part of some great design, in something of the same manner that a skillful anatomist understands the use and office of every part of the human body, in relation to the whole, has *the full assurance of understanding;* and those things willful appear inconsistent, useless, or superfluous to others, he perceives essentially necessary to the system or the great design. The man who is fully convinced that this consistent and harmonious though complicated design is the work and revelation of God, and has no doubt the things testified are true, that the promises and threatenings will be fulfilled, and that Christ will certainly save all true believers, has *the full assurance of faith,* though he may through misapprehension, or temptation, or other causes, doubt of his own personal interest in this salvation. But he, who beyond doubt or hesitation is assured that he himself is a true believer, interested in all the precious promises, sealed by the sanctifying Spirit, and 'a partaker of the glory that shall be revealed,' has *the full assurance of hope."*

APPENDIX Z

Chapter vii. 14. *For under it the people received the Law, etc* These words are variously explained. The preposition ἐπὶ often means "for," or "on the account of," as ἐπ᾽ ἐλπίδι, "for the hope," (Acts xxvi. 6;) and so *Macknight* renders it here "on account of it the people received the Law." It is not true that the people were under the priesthood when they were subjected to the Law; for the Law was given before the Levitical priesthood was established: it was after the tabernacle was made and set up that Aaron and his sons were consecrated priests. See Exodus xl. 12-15

Stuart gives another rendering, "For the Law was given to the people in connection with this," or "on this condition," as he explains himself in a note. And he observes, "The meaning is, that the Levitical priesthood and the Mosaic Law are closely and inseparably linked together."

As the Apostle speaks afterwards of the change of the Law, that is, respecting the priesthood, it is more consistent to regard the same law as intended here, "though the people had received a law respecting it," that is, the priesthood. This is parenthetically put in for two reasons, — to anticipate an objection on the ground of a divine appointment, and to introduce the subject for the purpose of shewing that it was an appointment intended to be changed.

APPENDIX A2

Chapter vii. 11-17. This passage may be thus rendered, —

11. "Now if indeed perfection were by the Levitical priesthood, (though the people had received a law respecting it,) what need was there still that another priest should rise after the order of Melchisedec, and not to be named after the order

12. of Aaron? The priesthood then being changed, there is of

13. necessity a change also of the law; for he of whom these things are said belongs to another tribe, from whom no one
14. attended at the altar. It is indeed evident that our Lord sprang from Judah, of which tribe Moses said nothing
15. respecting the priesthood. And this is still more manifest, since according to the likeness of Melchisedec rises another
16. priest; who is made, not according to the law of carnal
17. precept, but according to the power of perpetual life; for he testifies, 'Thou art a priest for ever, according to the order of Melchisedec.'"

"The law of carnal precept" is the rule that refers to the present life, life in the flesh, which is frail and uncertain; and contrasted with it is "perpetual life, which belongs to Christ as a priest, according to the quotation which follows. The meaning is, that Christ was not made a priest according to that law which regulates things belonging to dying men, (see verse 23,) but in accordance with what was suitable to one endued with permanent life or existence.

The argument of the whole passage seems to be as follows, — There is no perfection in the Levitical priesthood, for another priest has been appointed. This being the case, the law respecting the priesthood must necessarily be changed; and that it is changed is proved by two things, — by the fact that Christ did not spring from the tribe of Levi, and by the prophetic announcement that he was to be a priest according to the order of Melchisedec, and consequently a perpetual priest, and not like the sons of Aaron, who were priests in succession, being all subject to death.

APPENDIX B2

Chapter vii. 19. *But the bringing in, etc.* Theophylact, Luther, Capellus, and others have rendered this noun as in the same predicament with "disannulling" or abrogation in the former verse, —

18. "There is therefore an abrogation of the preceding commandment, on account of its weakness and uselessness, (for
19. the law perfected nothing,) and an introduction of a better hope, through which we draw nigh to God."

This passage forms an inference or a conclusion from what has been said. The "commandment" abrogated was respecting the Levitical priesthood. Its "weakness" was, that it could not really atone for sin; and its uselessness, that it could not make men holy or confer life. The same thing is expressed in the words included in the parenthesis. But what has been said does not only prove that the Levitical priesthood is abolished, but also that there is brought in or introduced a better hope; which means that a better thing than the Levitical priesthood, which was an object of hope to the ancient saints, is introduced after that priesthood, and was expressly mentioned by David in the Psalms many years after the Levitical priesthood was established. This appears to be the genuine meaning of the passage.

Then the following verses come in very suitably, as the "introduction" is mentioned here, —

20. "And inasmuch as *it was* not without an oath, (for they
21. indeed were made priests without an oath, but he with an oath, *made by* him who said to him, 'The Lord hath sworn and will not repent, Thou art a priest for ever, according
22. to the order of Melchisedec,') of a covenant so much the
23. better is Jesus the surety. They are also many who are made priests, because they are not suffered by death to continue; but he, because he abideth for ever, hath a priesthood that passeth not to another, (or more literally, hath an intransmissible priesthood.)"

What was not "without an oath" was "the introduction," etc. There are here two additional things stated as proving the superiority of Christ's priesthood: the oath proved that he was the surety of a better covenant; and his priesthood, unlike that of Aaron, which passed from one to another, was intransmissible or unsuccessive, as the word means, and not "unchangeable," as in our version.

APPENDIX C2

Chapter vii. 27. *Who needeth not daily, etc* A difficulty has been raised as to this verse. It is said that Christ did not, like the priests, offer up a daily sacrifice, first for his own sins and then for the sins of the people, "for this he did once when he offered up himself." It seems hence, it is said, that he offered a sacrifice for himself as well as for the people. In order to explain this, it has been proposed to take in the following verse; and it has been said that there is here an arrangement similar to what often occurs in the Prophets; that is, when two things are stated, the last is first referred to, and then the first. The two things here are the priest's own sins and those of the people. The Apostle is supposed to speak first of what Christ did as to the sins of the people, and then that in the following verse he shews that Christ had no sins of his own, for he became or was made "a perfect priest," and that "for ever," being sinless not only when he actually offered the great sacrifice, but also sinless as our intercessor in heaven.

This is the explanation of Bishop *Jebb*, and is adopted by *Bloomfield*. That arrangements of this kind are found in the New Testament, and even in this Epistle is what cannot be doubted. But the last word, "perfected," will not admit of the meaning given to it, "he *is* and *was*, and *shall be* everlastingly perfect and free from sin." Were this its meaning, there would be a complete correspondence with the former part. Perfection is twice before applied to Christ in this Epistle, (chapter ii. 10; v. 9,) but not in the sense above stated. When Christ is said to be perfected or made perfect, the meaning is that he is completely fitted and qualified for his undertaking, or that he has fully completed his work of expiation. Here the meaning seems to be that he is for ever made perfect as a priest, having not only once for all made an adequate atonement for the sins of his people, but also continues a priest for ever.

As to the 27th verse, it may be thus rendered, —

27. "Who has no need daily to offer sacrifices, as the high priests, (first for their own sins, and then for those of the people:) for this he did once for all, when he offered up himself"

"This he did" refers only to the offering of a sacrifice, and "for their own sins," etc., apply only to the high priests. Thus we avoid the difficulty alluded to.

From an idea that the high priest offered sacrifices only once a year, *i.e., on* the day of expiation, *Macknight* renders καθ ἡμέραν "from time to time," etc. He considers it as equivalent to κατ ἐναυτὸν "from year to year," in chapter x. 1, and refers to Exodus xiii. 10, where "from year to year" is in Hebrew from "days to days," and the same in the *Sept.*, ἀφ᾽ ἡμερῶν εἰς ἡμέρας. Whether the high priest offered sacrifices daily, is what cannot be ascertained from Scripture, though *Stuart* refers to Leviticus vi. 19-22, and Numbers xxviii. 3, 4, where nothing satisfactory is found. He quotes indeed some words from *Philo*, who says that this was the case. *Scott* considered that what was done daily by the priests is here attributed to the high priest, they being his coadjutors. But *Macknight's* explanation *is* the most satisfactory, especially as the comparison throughout is between Christ and the high priest.

The 28th verse may be thus rendered,—

"For the law made men high priests, who have infirmity; but the word of the oath, the Son, perfected for ever."

"Perfected," or completely qualified, that is, as a priest. The word, perfected, depends as to its specific meaning on the context. The subject here is the perpetuity of the priest. The high priests under the Law did not continue because of death, (verse 23,) and this is the "infirmity" mentioned here, though in another place, (chapter v. 2,) it means sinfulness. Then the perfection of the Son is the perpetuity of his life, referred to in verses 16 and 24. The high priests died, and hence were not fitted for their work; but Christ lives, and therefore continues for ever fully qualified for his office. See verse 26.

APPENDIX D2

Chapter viii. 1. *This is the sum, etc* Many think that the word κεφάλαιον does not mean here a sum in the sense of a summary, but a principal thing. So *Chrysostom* understood it. *Macknight's* version is, "Now of the things spoken the chief is;" *Stuart's* is substantially the same. But the idea seems to be somewhat different: the literal rendering is, "Now the head as to the things said is," etc.; that is, the sum total, the whole amount.

Parkhurst quotes a passage from *Menander* which is very similar to the first part of this verse, Τὸ δὲ κεφάλιον τῶν λόγων Ἄνθρωπος εἶ— "But the sum of my discourse is, Thou art a man," etc. The word means here the substance or the sum total. The word ראש, read, in Hebrew, has a like meaning, the total number of the people, Exodus xxx. 12; Numbers iv. 2

APPENDIX E2

Chapter viii. 9. *And I regarded them not, etc* The Apostle here follows the *Sept.*, though in some other parts of this quotation he follows more closely the Hebrew. Our version in Jeremiah xxxi. 32, is, "although I was a husband to them," which is not countenanced by any of the earlier versions. The phrase is peculiar, not found anywhere else except in Jeremiah iv. 17; which is rendered by *Kimchi*, "I have abhorred them."

The verb means to have, to possess, to rule, to exercise dominion, to marry; and *Pocock* and some others think, that it means to loathe, to disdain, to abhor, when followed as here by the preposition ב and it is said that its cognate in Arabic has this meaning. The *Vulg.* here is, "and I have ruled over them;" and the *Syr.*, "and I have despised them." The expression is softened by the *Sept.*, "and I have disregarded (or cared not) for them." The same is done as to the preceding clause, "because they continued not in my covenant," which is in Hebrew, though not as rendered in our version, "because they broke my covenant." So אשר rendered by the *Syr.* and the *Targ.* "Which my covenant" has been derived from the *Vulg.*, and is a construction which the original will not bear.

Still the most probable and the easiest solution is, to suppose a typographical mistake in Jeremiah xxxi. 32, the word בעלתי: being used instead of בחלתי: there being only one letter different. The reasons for this supposition are these: — All the versions are different here from what they are in Jeremiah iv. 17, where the same phrase is supposed to occur, — and this latter verb is found in Zechariah xi. 8, followed by: as here, and means to "abhor," or according to some, to "reject."

There is also another word, נעלתי which has been mentioned, and has but one letter different; and as it is used by Jeremiah himself in chapter xiv. 19, and with ב, in the sense of abhorring or loathing, it may justly be deemed as the most probable word.

But *Newcome* suggests another thing, a typographical mistake in the Greek. There is another reading in some copies of the *Sept.*, and that is, εμελησα, "I have cared for them;" and this would in substance agree with "I was a husband to them." This conjecture is less probable; for it involves a mistake both in the *Sept.* and in this Epistle. But either of these suppositions would reconcile the passages; and it is singular that in both cases the change required is only in *one* letter!

APPENDIX F2

Chapter ix. 2 *The first, etc. Doddridge, Macknight,* and *Stuart,* connect "the first" with "tabernacle," but improperly. The rendering ought to be no doubt as in our version, or as follows, "For a tabernacle was made; the first, in which were the candlestick, and the table, and the shew-bread, which is called holy." We find in verse 3, that "the Holy of holies" is also called a tabernacle, which was as it were the second tabernacle, or the second part of it, see verse 7. The word "holy," followed by "of holies," is an adjective agreeing in gender with tabernacle; and "of holies" seem to mean holy things; so that it might be rendered, "The holy tabernacle of holy things." The accents are of no authority. The word "holy" in the plural with an article, as in verse 8 and 12, designates the Holy of holies; or it may refer to both places, the sanctuary and the Holy of holies, for the people were excluded from both; and no access, strictly speaking, applied to them only.

APPENDIX G2

Chapter ix. 9, 10. These two verses have greatly tried the ingenuity of critics, not as to the general meaning, but as to the construction. All agree as to the general import of the passage, and yet they find a difficulty in the syntax. This has arisen from not apprehending the style of the Apostle; he often arranges his sentences according to the practice of the ancient prophets. So he does here. In verse ninth he mentions two things, "gifts" or oblations and "sacrifices;" then he refers first to "sacrifices," and afterwards to the "gifts." Of the "sacrifices," he says, that they could not perfect or justify "the worshipper," for so λατρευόντα ought to be rendered here; but of "the gifts," together with meats, etc., he says, that they were only imposed until the time of reformation. Here syntax is satisfied. The two verses may be thus rendered, —

9. "Which is a type for the present time, while gifts and sacrifices are offered, which (sacrifices) cannot perfect the

10. worshipper as to his conscience, being imposed (gifts) only, together with meats, and drinks, and divers washings, even ordinances of the flesh, until the time of reformation."

Now, there is here a consistency in every part; δυνάμεναι is in the same gender with θυσίαι, and what is said is suitable to sacrifices, they being not able to atone for sin; and then ἐπικείμενα *is* of the same gender with δῶρά, and what is said of them is also suitable, that they were imposed or required only, together with meats, etc., which were rituals referring to the flesh or body, and not to the conscience or the soul, until the time of reforming or rectifying all things came.

Doddridge rightly states the efficacy of the Jewish sacrifices when he says, that they averted "temporal evils," but did expiate offenses in the court above; they removed offenses against the government under which the Jews lived, and restored them to the privileges of eternal communion with the Church; and thus they were types and symbols of the efficacy of the true sacrifices by which we are restored to the favor of God, and to a spiritual communion with him.

APPENDIX H2

Chapter ix. 16, 17. Much has been written on the meaning of the word διαθήκη in this passage. It is rendered "covenant" throughout by *Doddridge, Macknight, Scholefield, etc.;* and *Scott* is disposed to take the same view. *Macknight's* version is this, —

16. "For where a covenant is, there is a necessity that the

17. death of the appointed sacrifice be brought in; for a covenant is firm over dead sacrifices, since it never hath force whilst the appointed sacrifice liveth."

The difficulty here is as to the word διαθέμενος, rendered above, "the appointed sacrifice," — by *Doddridge,* "he by whom the covenant is confirmed," — and by *Scholefield,* "the mediating sacrifice." But the word is never found to have such meanings in the New Testament, in the *Sept.,* or in the classics. It is therefore impossible to accede to such a view of the passage.

It is then said, on the other hand, that διαθήκη does not mean a testament or a will in the New Testament nor in the *Sept.* This is not true; for it clearly means a testament or a will in Galatians iii. 15, and in connection, too, with its common meaning, a covenant, see verse 17. Besides it has commonly, if not always, this meaning in the classics.

These two verses are to be viewed as an illustration, and may be regarded as parenthetic; and were γὰρ rendered "in fact," or indeed, this would appear more evident, "Where indeed a testament is," etc. As an illustration, a reference to a testament is exceedingly suitable; for with regard to Christ, his death was really the ratification of the covenant; as by death a Will attains its validity, so by Christ's death the covenant of which he is the Mediator. Death in both instances has a similar effect. And this, and no more than this, seems to have been the intention of the Apostle. The different meaning of the same word in the same passage is to be found out by words connected with it; in the present instance διαθέμενος is sufficient, independently of the 17th verse, which can be rightly applied to nothing but to a will or a testament.

Many agree with *Calvin* on these verses, such as *Erasmus, Beza, Schleusner, Stuart, Bloomfield,* etc.

APPENDIX I2

Chapter x. 5 *But a body hast thou prepared me* The words in the Psalm are, "Mine ears hast thou opened," xl. 6; or more literally, "Ears hast thou opened for me." *Calvin* seems to have discarded the idea of an allusion to the boring of the ear in sign of servitude. The two verbs are certainly different. He evidently refers to Isaiah l. 5, "The Lord hath opened mine ear, and I was not rebellious;" which clearly applies to Christ. He therefore makes the meaning of the phrase to be, "Thou hast made me teachable and obedient." This view has been adopted by *Merrick, Bishop Horne,* and *Stuart.* But how to make the words, "a body hast thou prepared for me," to bear an analogous meaning, does not very clearly appear. *Bishop Horne* gives this version, "Thou hast prepared" or fitted "my body," that is, to be obedient and to do thy will.

Mede conceived that the allusion is to the practice of boring the ear in token of servitude, mentioned in Exodus xxi. 6; and that as that practice was unknown to the Greeks, the *Seventy* rendered the words in conformity with what they did as to their slaves; which was, to set a mark on the body; "Thou hast fitted (or adapted) a body for me;" that is, that I might be thy servant. That Christ assumed "the form of a servant," is expressly declared in Philippians ii. 7. There is in this case an agreement as to meaning; but the difficulty is: as to the verb כרה which does not mean to bore or to perforate, but to dig, to hollow out, and in a secondary sense, to form or to make a thing, such as a well, a pit, a grave, or a cave. As to "ears" instead of an "ear," as in Exodus xxi. 6, that might be accounted for by saying, that the object was to shew the *entire* willingness of Christ to become a servant.

These have been the two ways proposed to reconcile the passages as they now stand. There are no different readings in Hebrew, nor in the *Sept.*, nor in this Epistle. Proposals have therefore been made as to a change in the texts on the supposition of typographical mistakes.

Some, as *Grotius, Hammond,* and *Dr. Owen,* have proposed ὠτία, ears, instead of σῶμα, body, in the *Sept.* When did this change take place? Before or after the Apostle's time? If before, then the Apostle adopted a false reading; if after, then the same mistake must have been made in the *Sept.* and in this Epistle; which is not credible.

Others have supposed a mistake in the Hebrew text; and this conjecture has been approved by *Kennicott, Doddridge,* Bishop *lowth,* Adam *Clarke,* and Pye *Smith.* It is no objection to say that the *Syr., Vulg.,* and the *Targ.,* confirm the present reading; for the mistake might have been made long before any of these were in existence. Such a change might indeed have been made in the first ages of Christianity, and might have been made intentionally, through a wish to obscure the testimony of Scripture respecting Christ.

The words are supposed to have been אז גוה instead of אז ניים, as the text now is. There would in this case be a literal agreement; the passage in the Psalm might then be thus rendered, —

6. "Sacrifice and offering thou hast not delighted in, Then a body hast thou formed for me; Burnt-offering and sin-offering thou hast not required,

7. Then I said, Behold, I am coming." —

There is here a consistency throughout. "Behold, I am coming," that is, in the body designed for him. And then the Apostle says, "When coming into the world, he saith," etc., clearly referring to our Saviors incarnation. And this "body" is afterwards expressly mentioned in verse 10, in opposition to sacrifices. It is true that in his argument in verse 9, he dwells on the words, "I come;" but then his coming was in the body prepared for him.

APPENDIX K2

Chapter x. 14 *He hath perfected, etc* The word simply means to complete, to finish, to perfect; and it depends on the context what that completion or perfection means. To perfect the sanctified or the expiated, or those atoned for, was completely to free them from the imputation of sin, to make them fully clear from guilt, or in other words, fully to take away their sins, which was never done by the sacrifices of the law, verse 11. This is the point here handled. Stuart gives the real meaning by the following free translation, — "By one offering, then, he hath fully accomplished for ever what was needed by those for whom expiation is (was) made."

The perfecting "for ever" by one offering in this verse, proves that "for ever," εἰς τὸ διηνεκὲς, in verse 12, is to be connected with the offering of one sacrifice, and not with the sitting on God's right hand; the verse may be thus rendered, —

12. "But he, having offered one sacrifice for sins for perpetuity, (or, according to Beza and Stuart, 'one perpetual sacrifice for sins,') sat down on the right hand of God, henceforth waiting until his enemies be made his footstool."

Some copies have αὐτὸς; — "he;" and some, οὗτος; — "this." If the latter be adopted, it ought not to be rendered "this man," but "this priest," such being the word used before. As *one* sacrifice is opposed to *many* sacrifices, so a *perpetual* sacrifice, that is, a sacrifice perpetually efficacious, is opposed to those sacrifices which were *often* made.

APPENDIX L2

Chapter x. 19 21. Of these verses the following rendering is offered, —

19. "Having then, brethren, liberty as to an entrance into the

20. holiest through the blood of Jesus, which he has consecrated for us, a way new and leading to life, through the

21. veil, that is, his flesh, — and having a great priest over the house of God, let us approach," etc.

It is rather "liberty" or freedom than "boldness," and so it is rendered by Beza, Doddridge, and Stuart. The *Vulgate* has "confidence." The word for "consecrated" is literally "initiated:" Christ first opened the way, and opened it for his people. The "way" is in apposition with "entrance." It was "new," in contrast with the old under the Law, and living or "leading to life:" so ζῶσαν evidently means here. It has often a causative sense. The "living bread" in John vi. 51, is said in verse 33 to be the bread that "giveth life." So here the living way may be said to be that which leads to life.

There is a division of opinion as to the "veil." *Calvin, Doddridge, Stuart,* and others, take the veil as a figurative expression for the human nature of Christ; and they ground their opinion on the following texts, John i. 14; 1 Timothy iii. 16; Philippians ii. 6. Others give this explanation, "As the veil was removed for the entrance of the high priest, so Christ s body was removed by death, in order to open an entrance into heaven." But the easiest and the most natural way is to consider it an allusion to what took place at our Saviors death, the rending asunder of the veil of the temple, (Matthew xxvii. 51,) which was a significant intimation and a striking symbol of what was done by Christ when he died on the cross. It was by his flesh or body being torn and rent, when suffering for us, that a way to the holiest was opened to us, and the same is ascribed to his blood in the former verse, so that one part corresponds with the other. The way was opened through the veil being rent, which symbolized his rent or torn flesh.

APPENDIX M2

Chapter x. 22. *With pure water* It is evident that baptism is not here referred to, because the Apostle is instructing the Hebrews, who had been baptized, how they were daily to draw nigh to God.

The words "pure water" are not found elsewhere in the New Testament, nor in the *Sept.* but once, Ezekiel. xxxvi. 25, where our version is "purifying water," and no doubt correctly, though the early versions have "pure water." It was a command as to Aaron, "He shall wash (λούσεται) with water his whole body (πᾶν τὸ σῶμα;)" So the *Sept.,* but the Hebrew is "his flesh," (בשרו,) though the Samaritan text has "all," (כל) before it, Leviticus xvi. 4. See also Leviticus xvi. 24. The terms here used are sacerdotal or Levitical. The "sprinkled" with blood were the priests at their consecration, and not those who brought their offerings. See Leviticus viii. 30. In no other case were any sprinkled with blood except the lepers, and the people when the covenant was made. Washing with water was also done by the priests at their consecration, (see Leviticus viii. 6,) and whenever they ministered. (Exodus xxx. 20, 21.)

The reason of this allusion especially to what was done as to the priests, seems to have been this, to shew that all who now draw nigh to God through Christ are priests, for they all serve God as it were in the sanctuary, and like the high priest, enter as it were into the holiest, not once a year, but daily and constantly, whenever they hold communion with God.

As sprinkling in the case of Christians is continually needed, so is washing, as the daily washing of the priests before they engaged in their duties. (Exodus xl. 32.) The sprinkling betokens forgiveness, and washing, sanctification or cleansing. See 1 Peter i. 2; and 2 Corinthians vii. 1; 1 Thessalonians v. 23.

It may be added that as (ζῶσαν, living, seems to have been used in verse 20 in a causative sense, so καθαρὸν in this passage; and it may be rendered, as in Ezekiel xxxvi. 25, "purifying." The priests after washing were said to be clean, and were deemed to have been thereby purified, which proves that washing was nothing more than a symbol. Pure or purifying water signifies the sanctifying effect of divine grace.

APPENDIX N2

Chapter x. 26. *Willfully, etc.* It is rendered by the *Vulg.*, "*voluntarie* — voluntarily;" by *Beza*, "*ultro* — of one's own accord;" by *Doddridge* and *Macknight*, as in our version, and by *Stuart*, "voluntarily."

It occurs in one other place, (1 Peter v. 2,) and is rendered "willingly;" it is found as an adjective in Philemon 14, and is rendered willingly; and in both instances in opposition to "constraint." So that *Schleusner's* explanation seems right, "with no compelling force — *nulla vi cogente*." It is used in the *Sept.* for a Hebrew word which means freely, with free will, spontaneously. We may therefore thus render the words, "For if we sin of our own free will, (that is, renounce the faith, which is clearly the sin intended,) after having received the knowledge of the truth, there remains no more a sacrifice for sins."

According to this verse the case of the persecuted is not here contemplated, for they are under constraint; but such are spoken of here as renounced the faith willingly, freely, by their own free choice; so that "willfully" is not what is meant, but spontaneously, without any outward constraining force or influence.

The fathers, such as *Chrysostom, Theophylact,* and *Augustine,* sadly blundered on this passage, because they did not understand the sin that is here intended, though it be evidently that of apostasy according to the drift of the whole context; and hence they said some strange things about sin after baptism, though baptism is neither mentioned nor alluded to in the whole passage. How many errors and absurdities have been introduced by the fathers into the world!

APPENDIX O2

Chapter x. 30 *The Lord shall judge* The same meaning is given to "judge" here by *Beza* as by *Calvin;* but *Doddridge, Grotius,* and *Macknight* think it means to avenge, to vindicate, or defend. The argument is considered to be this, — "If God would avenge the injury done to his people, much more the injury or reproach done to his Son and the Holy Spirit." *Stuart* and *Bloomfield* give the verb the sense of condemning or punishing; that is, his apostatizing people, — "The Lord will condemn (or punish) his people."

The two quotations are connected in Deuteronomy xxxii. 35, 36. "Vengeance" refers to idolaters; and lest an advantage should have been taken of this, he added, as it seems, these words, "The Lord will judge his people;" that is, he will call his people to an account, so as to reward some, and to punish others. The apostates might have said, "Though we leave the Christian, and turn to the Jewish religion, we shall not be idolaters; therefore the vengeance you threaten will not belong to us. To prevent this kind of evasion, the Apostle adds, "The Lord will summon to judgment his own people, and give to each according to their works. The fact, that God is a judge, who will reward some and punish others, is what is meant; and this view accords with the passage in Deuteronomy, and also with the design of the Apostle here.

The two verbs also, the Hebrew ידין, and the Greek κρινεῖ, will admit of this meaning. The first, indeed, though not the second, often means to vindicate, to defend; but the context in Deuteronomy xxxii. 36, requires its sense to be that of executing what is right and just to all. See Genesis xxx. 6

APPENDIX P2

Chapter xii. 1. *Which doth so easily beset us, etc.* Calvin follows the *Vulg.*, "which surrounds us, or stands around us. It is rendered by *Chrysostom*, "which easily surrounds us; by *Beza*, "which is ready to encompass us;" by *Doddridge*, "which in present circumstances hath the greatest advantage against us;" by *Macknight*, "easily committed."

The word εὐπερίστατον means literally, "well-standing-around." But εὐ in composition often means readily, easily, aptly. Then we may render it, "the readily surrounding sin," that *is*, the sin which readily surrounds us, and thereby entangle us, so as to prevent as, like long garments, to run our course. The runners threw aside every weight or burden, and also their long garments. These two things seem to have been alluded to. Therefore the second clause is not explanatory of the preceding, as some consider it, but is wholly a distinct thing; there was the burden and the readily entangling sin. The burden was probably worldly cares, or as *Theophylact says*, "the baggage of earthly concerns;" and the easily encircling sin seems to have been the fear of persecution as *Doddridge* suggests; which, if allowed to prevail, would lead them to apostasy.

If the word be taken in an active sense, then what is meant is the deceptive power of sin, it being that which readily surrounds and allures us; but if it be taken passively, then what *is* specifically meant *is*, that the sin referred to is that which stands fairly and plausibly around us; for "well-standing-around" is what presents on every side a fair and plausible appearance. And apostasy might have been so represented; for the Jews could produce many plausible arguments. *Scapula* says that ἀπερίστατος is applied by the Greek rhetoricians to a question barely or briefly stated, unaccompanied with any circumstances; then, if instead of the negative, ευ, well, be prefixed to it, the meaning would be that it is something well stated and plausibly represented. The version in this case would be, "the sin that plausibly presents itself." If this meaning be received, then there seems to be a striking contrast in the passage; we are surrounded by a throng of witnesses, and also by sin with its plausible pretenses. It *is* usual with Paul to personify sin.

APPENDIX Q2

Chapter xii. 2. *Who for the joy, etc.* Hardly any agree with *Calvin* in the view he takes of this clause. The preposition is, indeed, used in both senses; but the words, "set before him," and the argument, evidently favor the other view. The subject handled is, that the prospect of future glory ought to sustain us under the evils of the present life; and Christ is referred to as an example; and the Apostle says, that he for the sake of the joy set before him endured the cross. The same word is here used and rendered, "set before him," as in chapter vi. 18

The first clause of the verse is rendered by *Calvin,* "the prince and perfecter of the faith;" by *Beza,* "the leader and consummator of the faith;" by *Doddridge,* "the leader and finisher of *our* faith;" by *Macknight,* "the captain and perfecter of the faith," and by *Stuart,* "the author and perfecter of *our* faith." The first word is rendered "author" by the *Vulg.,* and "the beginner" by *Erazmus.* Following this meaning we may render thus, "the beginner and perfecter of the faith," that is, of the Gospel, or of the religion we profess. Christ being the author or originator, and also the complete revealer of the faith, of what we profess to believe, may fitly be set forth as our example. This is the view of *Stuart.*

Doddridge takes faith as a principle, that is, subjective faith, faith in us; so *Theophylact* did, "He at first gives us faith, and afterwards brings it to perfection." *Scott* mentions this view, and then adds, "From him as the great Prophet, the *doctrine* of faith had been delivered from the beginning, and perfected in the revelation made in the Gospel; and this none would ever be authorized to change, add to, or deduct from."

But the reference here seems to be to what Christ did in his own person, as it appears from what follows; he endured the cross, which seems to refer to the first word, "leader;" and his sitting down at God's right hand appears to be explanatory of his being the consummator of the faith. The Apostle's subject is the race, that is, the race of faith, or in behalf of the faith we profess. Christ is the captain or leader in this race of faith; and though he had the cross to endure, he yet completed it, and is now at God's right hand. This is the example that is presented to us. *Schleusner* explains τελειωτὴν as one who brings anything to an end, a finisher, a completer. Christ is the captain or leader in the contest of faith, and the completer of it, having brought it to a triumphant issue.

APPENDIX R2

Chapter xii. 6 *For whom the Lord loveth, etc* The quotation is from Proverbs iii. 11, 12, made from the *Sept.*, consistently with the Hebrew, except in the last clause; which in Hebrew is, "As a father, the Son in whom he delights." Some have unwisely attempted to amend one of the words in Hebrew, while there are *three* words which must be altered if we attach importance to verbal identity; and even the amended word can hardly answer the purpose, a sense being given to it, which it has nowhere else.

If we make כאב: a verb, it will not be suitable, for its meaning is to be sore, to be sad, to be sorrowful, and is ever used intransitively; and if like *Schleusner*, we make it a יכאיב, it will hardly bear the meaning here required; it is used in the sense of making sore, sad, or sorrowful. This, indeed, approaches to a verbal identity; but then there is "every" to be put in, and "delights in" is to be changed into "receiveth." To be over-scrupulous about words, when the general meaning is the same, is neither wise nor reasonable, but wholly puerile; it is a disposition clearly discountenanced by the usage of Scripture, there being many passages in which the meaning *is* given but not the words. Even in this Epistle the same passage *is* quoted twice, but in different words. See chapter viii. 12; x. 17

The *Vulg.*, the *Syr.*, and the *Targ.*, materially agree with the Hebrew text as it *is*. The *Arab.* alone favors the *Sept. Macknight* quotes *Hallet* as saying, that the *Syr.* and the *Targ.*, as well as the *Arab.*, coincide with the *Sept.*; which is quite a mistake. The *Syr.* is, "For whom the Lord loveth he correcteth, like a father who correcteth his own son;" and the *Targ.* is nearly the same, the word "father" being retained. And then what this author says as to the meaning of the verb כאב: is not true; there is no instance in which it is used in the sense of scourging. We must not pervert the meaning of words, or invent a new meaning, to gratify a fond desire for verbal agreement.

But there is in this quotation what deserves special notice. "Correction" was by the rod; so we find the rod and correction joined together in Proverbs xxii. 15. In Hebrew it is "the rod of correction (מוסר)," and in the *Sept.*, "rod and correction (παιδεία.)" In Proverbs xxiii. 13, correction and beating with the rod are represented as the same thing. Bearing this in mind, we shall understand the connection and meaning of this passage,

—

11. The correction of the Lord, my Son, despise not, — And fret not at his chastisement;

12. For whom the Lord loveth he chastiseth, And *corrects* as a father the Son he graciously accepts.

The middle lines are *evidently* connected; chastisement is the subject of both, the noun and the verb are from the same root. Then the first and the fourth are also connected; the "Son" is mentioned in both; and the verb in the last line must be borrowed from the subject of the first line, and that is correction. We hence see the reason why μαστιγοῖ is introduced, it being nothing more than to supply what is left to be understood in Hebrew.

APPENDIX S2

Chapter xii. 11. *Peaceable fruit of righteousness, etc* This is a phrase which is commonly understood as to its general import, and yet it is difficult to explain it satisfactorily. Some take "of righteousness" as the exegetic genitive case, "the peaceable fruit," that is, as *Macknight* explains it, "which is righteousness;" and he adds, "Righteousness is denominated *peaceful*, because it is productive of inward peace to the afflicted person himself, and of outward peace to them with whom he lives; also it is called the fruit of God's chastisements, because afflictions have a natural tendency to produce virtues in the chastised, which are the occasion of joy far greater than the pain arising from the chastisement." Psalm cxix. 67, 71, 75

Doddridge also seems to have understood the phrase in the same sense, for he says, that chastisement "produces and improves those virtues which afford joy and peace to the mind." To the same effect are the remarks of *Scott*, and *Calvin's* view seems to be similar.

The phrase admits of another meaning: "The fruit of righteousness," according to the more frequent usage of Scripture, means the fruit which belongs to righteousness, or in the words of *Stuart*, "such as righteousness produces," or in the words of an author quoted by *Poole*, "which proceeds from righteousness." Righteousness seems to mean here what is just and right, or what ought to be done according to the will of God, as when our Savior says, "For thus it becometh us to fulfill all righteousness," Matthew iii. 15. What may be deemed as especially referred to here, is submission or subjection to the divine will mentioned in verse 9. This subjection was righteousness; it was right according to the statement in verse 7. It was said before that the object of correction is to make us partakers of God's holiness; now he mentions righteousness; they are connected. We must be made holy, we must be cleansed from pride, worldliness, and self-will, in order that we may do what is right and just, that is, submit to God's will when he chastises us; and when this submission or righteousness takes place, then correction produces a peaceable or a blessed fruit, that is, such an effect, or such a blessing, as peace or happiness. Peace and happiness are both signified by the word; but "blessed" or happy is more suitably applied to "fruit" than "peaceable" or peaceful.

Then the meaning may be thus conveyed, "but it afterwards yields to those who are exercised (or trained, that is, unto holiness) by it, a blessed fruit, such as righteousness (that is, subjection to our Father's will) brings forth."

APPENDIX T2

Chapter xii. 13. *And make straight paths, etc.* If this be a quotation, and not an appropriation of certain words, it is taken from Proverbs iv. 26, where the Hebrew *is*, "Make direct the path of thy feet;" and the *Sept.*, "Make straight the paths for thy feet," the very words of this passage. That the verb in Hebrew means to "make direct," and not to "ponder," as in our version, is evident from a similar phrase in Psalm lxxviii. 50, "He made (or made direct) a way to his anger." The verb is the same as in Proverbs. The noun means a balance, or rather the beam of a balance, (see Proverbs xvi. 11,) which is straight, and is used to equalize what is weighed. The verb may therefore include the idea of making straight or of making even. The verse that follows in Proverbs iv. 26, favors this idea of a straight path, "Turn not to the right hand nor to the left," which implies that it is a straight course that is to be taken. See verse 25

"Make direct the path of thy feet," or "Make straight the paths for thy feet," evidently means, "Let the path or paths along which you go, be direct or straight." The ways of error and sin are called crooked paths: see Proverbs ii. 15; Isaiah lix. 8. So the way of truth and holiness is compared to a straight line, from which we are not to deviate either to the right hand or to the left.

It is remarkable what the Apostle says in Galatians ii. 14, of Peter and those who dissembled with him, that they "did not walk uprightly (or literally, did not foot straightly, οὐκ ὀρθοποδοῦσι) according to the truth of the Gospel;" they deviated from the straight line prescribed by the Gospel. The idea, therefore, of removing impediments, of making their paths plain or smooth, as *Macknight* and others render it, seems not to be here intended; nor does it comport with what follows, "that the lame," or the feeble, "may not turn aside, but rather be healed," that is, of his lameness, or his weakness. For were those reputed strong in the faith not to walk straightly, but to turn into the crooked ways of dissimulation, like Peter and others at Antioch, the lame, the weak in faith, would be tempted to do the same, instead of having their lameness healed, or their weakness strengthened by the example of others walking in a straight course.

The idea of dislocation given to ἐκτραπῶ by *Schleusner, Macknight,* and others, is one invented for the purpose of suiting what they conceived to be the meaning of this passage, which is by no means necessary, and is indeed inappropriate to the context when rightly understood. "That which is lame," τὸ χωλὸν, is a neuter instead of a masculine, an idiom we often meet with in the New Testament.

APPENDIX U2

Chapter xii. 15 *Lest any root, etc* This quotation, made from Deuteronomy xxix. 18, seems to be an adoption of some words, and nothing more; for it is neither literally the Hebrew nor the *Sept.* "Root" refers not to a principle in Deuteronomy, but to an individual, to a person given to idolatry. A person also seems to be intended here. The clause in Hebrew is, "Lest there be among you a fruit-bearing root, hemlock or wormwood;" and in the *Sept.,* "Lest there be among you a root springing up in gall and bitterness." As the idea only of a growing bitter or poisonous root is borrowed, it is not necessary to suppose that the application here is the same as in Deuteronomy. What is there applied to an idolater, is here applied to a person disturbing the peace of the Church.

Some understand this passage as referring to defection or apostasy; and therefore render the first clause, "Lest any one recede (or depart) from the grace of God," that is, the Gospel, or Christian faith. But the words can hardly admit of this meaning. Hence most give this version, "Lest any one fall short of the grace of God." But what is this "grace of God?" Various answers have been given, — God's favor to those who cultivate holiness; God's mercy offered in the Gospel; the promised rest; eternal life. But taking this verse, as we certainly ought, in connection with the preceding, we may justly say, that it is God's sanctifying grace, or "the holiness "mentioned before; and then, according to the inverted order which we often find in Scripture, the next clause refers to "peace," "lest any root of bitterness, growing up, should disturb you, and many by it (or by this) be polluted (or infected.)"

Then follow examples of these two evils in the same order: the first, "the fornicator," is the violator of "holiness," or is deficient as to this grace of God; and the second, "the profane," is a disturber of the peace of the Church, as Esau was, of the peace of his own family, being "a root of bitterness."

But observe, "peace" was to be with "*all* men;" yet the example as to the disturber of it refers to the peace of the Church; so with respect to "holiness," what is universal is inculcated; but the example as to the violator of it is particular. For want of seeing this, no doubt some of the fathers regarded "holiness" in the former verse us meaning chastity.

Esau became "a root of bitterness" by being profane; and to be profane in this instance was to despise holy things, to regard them of no value, so as to prefer to them the gratification of the flesh. This was Esau's profaneness, which led eventually to a dreadful discord in his family; and to shew the evil which follows such profaneness, the Apostle points out the loss he sustained as a warning to others.

APPENDIX X2

Chapter xii. 18-24. In this comparison between the Law and the Gospel, it would no doubt be more consonant to what is said in

Exodus and also to the comparison here made, to regard μὴ as a part of the text, though omitted in all the copies already examined. Very seldom indeed is there any sufficient ground for a conjecture of this kind; nor can it be said that there is here an indispensable necessity for it, only that the comparison would be more complete, — "Ye are not come to a mount not to be touched under the peril of destruction; but to a mount to which you have a free access." So terrible was the delivery of the Law, that to touch the mountain was instant death; to approach Sion is what we are graciously invited to do, it being the city of God, who giveth life." The participle ζῶν seems to have this meaning here, as there appears no other reason why the word is here applied to God.

In describing the superiority of the Gospel to the Law, the Apostle borrows expressions from the former dispensation; and though Mount Sion and Jerusalem seemed to belong to the Law, yet they are taken here in contrast with Sinai, where the Law was proclaimed. Sion is, indeed, an evangelical term, and the whole ceremonial Law, though added to the Law proclaimed on Mount Sinai, was yet the Gospel typically, and existed in part before the Law was given.

The contrast here is very striking: terror and death were to the Israelites at Sinai; but a free approach and life are to those who come to Sion: there were on Sinai angels, surrounded with fire, darkness, and tempest; but myriads of them, an innumerable host, are now ministering spirits to the inhabitants of Sion: the whole assembly at the foot of Sinai were only the children of Israel; but the assembly in Sion is the general assembly and Church of the firstborn, the saints of God gathered from all nations: God appeared on Sinai as the judge, ruler, and governor of one people; but the God of Sion is the judge and governor of all who come there from all the various nations of the earth: to those at Sinai the state of departed saints was imperfectly known; but to those who are come to Sion their condition is well known, they being a part of that body — the Church — of which Christ is the head: the mediator at Sinai was Moses, a faithful servant, and no more; but the Mediator of the New Covenant, which belongs to Sion, *is* Jesus, by virtue of whose blood all sins are forgiven, and all pollutions removed — a blood which pleads for mercy and not for vengeance as the blood of Abel. All the parts of the first contrast are not mentioned, but they may easily be gathered from the second.

That the Church on earth is here meant by Sion, seems very clear. The Church is often called the kingdom of heaven, and its subjects are called the citizens of heaven. That angels and saints departed are mentioned as those to whom we are come, is no objection, because everything that belongs to Sion is seen only by faith. Our connection with distant believers, living on the earth, is maintained only by faith, exactly in the same manner as our connection with angels or departed spirits. Whether the angels mentioned here are ministering spirits, or the hosts above who serve God in heaven, it makes no difference, as they are fellow-servants and fellow-citizens as it were with all the family on earth. See Colossians i. 16, 17. It is the same company, though one is now on earth and the other in heaven; they will finally be more closely united.

To the notion that some, as *Macknight* and others, have entertained, that Sion here means the Church in its glorified state after the resurrection, there are insuperable objections: the contrast in that case would not be suitable; for the object of the Apostle is evidently to set forth the excellency of the Gospel dispensation in comparison with that of the Law; no satisfactory difference on such a supposition could be made between the Church of the firstborn and the spirits of just men made perfect; the expression, "the enrolled in heaven," is more suitably applied to those on earth than to those in glory; and there would be no propriety in that case in mentioning Christ as the Mediator, or that his blood speaks a language different from that of Abel.

APPENDIX Y2

Chapter xii. 27 *As of things that are made, etc* The meaning of ὡς πεποιημένων, as given by *Doddridge, Scott,* and *Stuart, is,* that they were things created, and therefore perishable, appointed only for a time. *Macknight* considered the expression elliptical for things "made with hands;" which denotes what is of an imperfect nature. But the explanation of *Schleusner* is the most natural and most suitable to the passage. He says that ποιέω means sometimes to accomplish, to finish, to bring to an end. (Romans iv. 21; ix. 28; Ephesians iii. 11; 1 Thessalonians v. 24.)

Then the rendering would be, "as of things to be completed," or brought to an end. They were things to be shaken or changed, as things to be finished or terminated. The corresponding verb in Hebrew, עשה, has evidently this meaning, "all his works which he had made," (עשה,) or completed, or finished. (Genesis ii. 2; see Isaiah xli. 4.)

APPENDIX Z2

Chapter xii. 28. *let us have grace, etc* So *Beza, Grotius, Doddridge,* and *Scott.* The *Vulg.* and *Calvin* are no doubt wrong. The authority as to MSS. is altogether in favor of the verb being in the imperative mood. *Macknight* gives this singular rendering, "Let us hold fast a gift whereby we can worship God," etc. He explains the "gift" as denoting the dispensation of religion. No less unsuitable is the version of *Stuart,* though countenanced by some of the fathers, "Let us manifest gratitude (by which we may serve God acceptably) with reverence and godly fear." When "χάρις" means gratitude, it is ever followed by a dative case, which is not the case here. To have faith, ἔχειν πίστιν is to possess it, (Matthew xvii. 20;) to have eternal life is to possess it, (Matthew xix. 16;) to have hope is to enjoy or possess it, (Romans xv. 4;) and so to have grace is to possess it. And this alone comports with what follows; it is the possession of that by which we may "serve God acceptably." By "grace" we are to understand the gracious help and assistance which God promises to all who seek it.

To receive a kingdom is to obtain a right or a title to it; and having the promise of this kingdom we ought to seek, attain, and possess that grace, that divine help, by which we may in the meantime serve God acceptably. This is the obvious meaning of the passage.

APPENDIX A3

Chapter xii. 28. *With reverence and godly fear* The first word, αἰδώς, means "modesty," as rendered in 1 Timothy ii. 9, and it is not found elsewhere in the New Testament. It has in the classics the meaning of respect and reverence. The second word, εὐλαθεία, properly means caution, circumspection, awfulness, and hence dread and fear. It is found only here, and chapter v. 7. It occurs as a passive participle twice, in Acts xxiii. 10, and in chapter xi. 7, and means to be influenced or moved with fear. Neither "godly" nor "religious" ought to be added to it.

It may seem difficult to reconcile this "fear" or dread with that love, and confidence, and delight with which God is to be served according to the evident testimony of Scripture, especially of the New Testament. But were we to take the first word as meaning "modesty," (or humility,) as rendered by *Beza*, we might regard the words as describing what we ought to feel in considering what we are in ourselves, and what the danger is to which we are exposed. The meaning then would be, that we are to serve God under a deep consciousness of our own weakness, and under a fear or dread of the danger of apostasy, though that dread may arise in part from an apprehension of what God will be to apostates, according to what is said in the following verse. Without these two feelings it is indeed impossible for us in our present state to serve God acceptably; for without humility arising from a sense of unworthiness and weakness, we shall not be capable of appreciating his mercy; and without the dread of sin, and especially of apostasy, we shall never depend as we ought on God's power to preserve us.

These feelings do not in the least degree interfere with the exercise of love, gratitude, or confidence, but on the contrary strengthen them. The weak shall be supported, but he must feel his weakness; and those who dread sin (not God) shall be kept and preserved; but they must feel this dread. And the more our weakness is felt, the stronger we shall be, as Paul says, "When I am weak, then am I strong;" and the more we fear and dread sin, the safer we shall be. But, like Peter, we shall stumble and fall if we become self-confident and exempt from the dread of sin.

No other meaning but that of fear or dread belongs to εὐλαθεία, wherever found, either as a noun or a participle. It is the fear of evil and not the fear of God. See the *Sept.*, in Joshua xxii. 24; and 1 Macc. iii. 30; xii. 42. There is no place found where it denotes the fear of God.

APPENDIX B3

Chapter 13:5 *let your conversation, etc.* It is rendered by *Macknight* "behavior;" and by *Stuart* "conduct." But τρόπος; means not only way, manner, conduct, but also a turn as it were of the mind, disposition, *ingenium*, as given by *Schleusner*. *Parkhurst* quotes a passage from *Demosthenes*, in which it evidently bears this sense. This version may then be given, "Let there be no moneyloving disposition;" or, "Let your disposition be free from the love of money." The *Syr.* is, "Let not your heart love money." The *Vulg.* gives a loose version, "Let the conduct be without avarice." *Beza's* is nearly the same. "Be content," or "be satisfied, with what you have;" that is, deem what you have sufficient or enough.

APPENDIX C3

Chapter xiii. 5 *I will never leave thee, etc* There are three places where these words with some variety are found, Deuteronomy xxxi. 6; Joshua i. 5; 1 Chronicles xxviii. 20. In the first, they are the words of Moses to the people of Israel; in the second, the words of God to Joshua; and in the third the words of David to Solomon. The Hebrew in the three places is exactly the same, excepting the change of person; but in none is the version of the *Sept.* the same. The words, as here given, is literally the Hebrew in Joshua i. 5, where the Greek version is wholly different; only the Apostle introduces the treble negatives as found in that version in Deuteronomy xxxi. 6, but not given in that version in either of the two other instances. Then the quotation is from Joshua i. 5, except that the Apostle follows the *Sept.* in Deuteronomy xxxi. 6, as to the three negatives.

The Hebrew could not be rendered as to the verbs more correctly than what is done by the Apostle, which are the same in the *Sept.*, except in Joshua i. 5. The first verb means to relax, and in a transitive sense, to let go, to dismiss, to give up, to surrender; and the second verb means to leave, to forsake, to desert. The verbs in Greek bear a similar meaning. To give a distinct sense to each, we may render the clause thus, —

"I will not dismiss thee,
  Nor will I by any means desert thee."

That is, I will not give thee up so as to separate myself from thee; nor will desert thee, no, by no means, when thou art in difficulties and trials.

The three negatives with the last verb are remarkable. There is in Hebrew what somewhat corresponds with them. The ו when preceded by a negative may often be rendered *and not, nor, neither*. Then the version would be this, "I will not dismiss thee, nor will I, no, forsake thee." It is indeed a promise, that God will continue to be our God, so as not to give us up, and that he will by no means forsake us in time of need.

The quotation in the next verse is from Psalm cxviii. 6, and is literally the *Sept*. The Hebrew is somewhat different, "The Lord is mine, and I will not fear; what can man do to me?" Then the next verse shews that the Lord who was his was also a help to him, "The Lord, mine, is my help, (literally, for my help;) and I shall look on my haters;" a phrase which signifies that he should gain the victory over them. The word "help" is borrowed by the *Sept*. from the seventh verse; and as it was evidently the Apostle's design to confirm the last clause of the previous citation, "I will not forsake thee," he deemed it sufficient to quote the words of the *Sept*.

APPENDIX D3

Chapter xiii. 7 *Rule over you, etc.* The word ἡγούμενοι means properly leaders, conductors, guides, such as lead the way, and according to its secondary meaning, presidents, chiefs, governors, rulers. It is rendered "prefects — *praefectorum*," by the *Vulg.*; "leaders — *ductorum*," by *Beza* and *Stuart*; and "rulers" by *Macknight*; *Doddridge* paraphrases it, "Who have presided over you." The version most suitable to the context is "your leaders;" for they are spoken of as persons to be followed; they were such as took the lead in religion and were examples to others. But in verse 17 the idea of a ruler is most suitable, for they were to be obeyed. The specific meaning of a word which has various senses is ever to be ascertained from the context. The leaders here referred to were those who had finished their course; for they were *to remember* them, and not to observe their conduct then as though they were living; and contemplating the end or conclusion of their life, they were to follow their faith.

The word ἔχθασις; means an outlet, a way of escape, also the end, conclusion, or termination of a thing, or the issue; and ἀναστροφή signifies manner of life, intercourse, behavior, conduct, the way in which one lives. There is no English word that can suitably express it. It may be rendered here "life," — "and contemplating the end of their life, follow their faith;" that *is*, what they believed. They ended their life in peace, and were enabled to triumph over all evils by means of the faith which they professed and possessed.

APPENDIX E3

Chapter xiii. 8 *Jesus Christ the same, etc* The connection of this verse is differently viewed, and also its meaning. Some connect it with the preceding verse thus, — "Jesus Christ is even the same in power, grace, and faithfulness; he supported your leaders and guides, who have completed their trials victoriously; he being still the same will support you." Such is the view taken by *Grotius, Doddridge, Macknight, Scott,* and *Stuart.* Others, as *Scholefield, Bloomfield,* and some German divines, connect the verse with what follows in this sense, — "Jesus Christ is the same, therefore be ye the same, and be not carried about by divers and strange doctrines."

But there is no need of this exclusive connection, as the verse appears connected with the preceding and the following verse. Those who adopt the first view seem to be wrong as to the main subject of the passage. What the Apostle exhorted the Hebrews to do was to follow the *faith* of their leaders who were gone to rest, and the contemplation of their happy and victorious end was introduced for the purpose of encouragement in following their faith. And that this is the particular and the chief point handled here is evident from the ninth verse, where this doctrine is as it were applied, "Be ye not carried about," etc. Then the meaning of the whole passage may be given thus, — "Follow the faith of your departed guides; there is no change in it, Christ is ever the same in his mind, will, and purpose as to the faith: suffer not, therefore, yourselves to be led astray by various and strange doctrines, different from the faith of those who taught you and have attained a happy end." Thus the passage appears consistent throughout and suitably connected, —

7. Remember your leaders, who have spoken to you the word of God, and contemplating the end of their life, follow their

8. faith: Jesus Christ, yesterday and today, *is* the same, and

9. *will be* for ever: Be not carried about by various and strange (new) doctrines; for it is good that the heart should be made firm by grace, not by meats, by which they have not profited who have been so occupied.

If the auxiliary verb be put in at all in the eighth verse, it ought to be put in twice. But the words may be rendered as a nominative case absolute, "Jesus Christ *being* the same yesterday, and today, and for ever;" as though he had said, "I exhort you to follow their faith, inasmuch as Jesus Christ, our teacher, mediator, and Savior never changes, but is ever the same."

The MSS. are more in favor μὴ παραφέρεσθε, "Be ye not carried away," than of μὴ περιφέρεσθε, "Be ye not carried about;" but as the latter verb is used on the same subject in Ephesians iv. 14, it is better to adopt it here: the difference indeed is very trifling.

The passage, as thus explained, bears strongly against every innovation in the faith, in the doctrine of the Gospel, Christ its teacher being ever the same. There are to be no strange or new doctrines; for such is the meaning of strange here, that is, what is alien to the Gospel, and therefore new. And what are all the additions which have been made by the fathers, and especially by the Church of Rome, but various doctrines, foreign to the Gospel, which ever continues the same? Their variety is as great as their novelty. Christ was, is, and will ever be the same as teacher, mediator, and Savior; hence the faith, once delivered to the saints, must continue unchangeably the same.

APPENDIX F3

Chapter xiii. 9. *For it is a good thing, etc* There seems to be some obscurity in the latter part of this verse, and in the following verses. There appears, however, to be an intimation of what the Apostle means in the term "strange" or new, as applied to the doctrines here referred to. There was probably an attempt made to unite some parts of the ceremonial law, especially the feasts, with the Gospel. The distinction of meats was not new, but this kind of mixture might have been so termed, that is, a participation in those sacrifices, part of which was allowed to be eaten by those who presented them, Leviticus vii. 11-21. This was probably one of the strange or new doctrines. Such a compliance must have been made for the sake of avoiding reproach and persecution.

The Apostle says in verse 10, that those who did eat of the sacrifices could not be partakers of what Christians feed on. Then in verse 11, he mentions the sacrifice made annually by the high priest, no part of which was eaten, but the whole was burnt without the camp, (referring to the state of things when the tabernacle was erected in the wilderness,) intimating that the *chief* sacrifice was not partaken of either by the priests or by the people. Taking this fact as an intimation, and a symbol of what was to be, he says that Christ had offered the great and the real sacrifice without the gate, (alluding now to the temple at Jerusalem,) where we are to follow him, bearing the reproach to which he was subjected; and we are not to return as it were to the tabernacle, and to partake of such sacrifices as were there eaten.

As an inducement to bear reproach, he reminds them that life is but short, and that Christians expect their home in another country; and at last he states what sacrifices they were still to offer to God, not the sacrifices of peace-offerings, but those of praise and thanksgiving, and also of good works.

The "meats" according to this view, mentioned in verse 9, must have been the meats eaten when free-will-offerings were presented. Admitting that the great sacrifice for sin had been offered by Christ, some might have still supposed and taught that such offerings as these were still allowed; and to eat of such offerings might have been thought a very profitable thing, calculated to produce a great benefit. In opposition to such a sentiment, the Apostle may be supposed to have said, that it was good that the heart should be strengthened by grace, not by meats, which did not prove profitable to those who usually partook of them.

The "altar" is to be taken for the sacrifices offered on it. He declares that it was not possible to partake of the Christian's food, and of the offerings made on the altar. The literal rendering of the 11th and 12th verses is as follows, —

11. "Moreover, of the animals whose blood for sin is brought into the holiest by the high priest, the bodies of these are

12. burnt without the camp. Therefore Jesus also, that he might make expiation for the people by his own blood, suffered without the gate."

The purpose for which these words seem to have been added, was to shew that no eating, no meats, were connected with the sacrifice for sin; and by saying in the following verse that we are to follow Christ without the camp, bearing his reproach, the Apostle intimates that this reproach ought not to be avoided by joining those in the tabernacle, engaged in offering peace-offerings on which they feasted.

The import of the whole passage, 9-16, may be thus stated: — "Be not led away by various kinds of doctrines, and such as are new; grace, and not eating of offerings, strengthens the heart to enable it to maintain the faith and to endure trials; and this grace, the meat that belongs to our altar, cannot be partaken of by those who are still wedded to the altar of the earthly tabernacle. And as to the annual sacrifice for sin, it is not eaten, but all burnt, not in the tabernacle, but without the camp, — an intimation of what Christ did when he suffered without the gate. Thither we must follow him, and not return again to the tabernacle in order to avoid reproach; and this reproach will not be long, for we are hastening to another world; and instead of presenting free-will offerings and eating of them, what we are to offer now are the sacrifices of praise, of thanksgiving, and of good works."

APPENDIX G3

Chapter xiii. 17 *That they may do it with joy, etc.* There is a difference of opinion as to this sentence. Some, as *Theophylact, Grotius,* and *Doddridge* refer "it," or "this," to watching; others, as *Macknight, Scott,* and *Stuart,* apply "it" to the account that is to be given by ministers. The first view, which *Calvin* evidently takes, is alone consistent with the rest of the passage. The concluding words of the verse are wholly inappropriate, if the account at the day of judgment be considered as intended, but in every way suitable when we regard watching as referred to. To say that an unfavorable account at the last day would be "unprofitable" to the people, would be to use an expression in no way congruous; but to represent the watching of ministers, when rendered "grievous" by the perverseness and refractory conduct of the people, as unprofitable to the people themselves, is altogether appropriate; and it is a very important consideration, and affords a strong argument in favor of obedience. The people by insubordination, not only grieve those who watch over them, but also injure themselves, prevent their own improvement, and render the watching care of their ministers useless. Reference is made by *Macknight* to 1 Thessalonians ii. 19; but "joy" only is mentioned there; and *Doddridge* justly observes, "It is not possible for any perverseness of the people to prevent a faithful minister from giving up his account with joy; nor can any *groans* be mingled with the triumphant songs which God will put into the mouths of all his people." No doubt the "grief" here mentioned shews clearly the meaning of the passage.

APPENDIX H3

Chapter xiii. 20 *Through the blood of the covenant, etc* The *Vulg.*, our version, *Calvin*, and *Scott*, connect the words with "bringing again from the dead;" only the *Vulg.* and *Calvin* render the preposition *in*, and our version and *Scott, through*. The idea conveyed by *in* is explained by *Calvin*, and the same is given by *Theodoret*, and what is meant by *through* is thus explained by *Scott*, — "In order to shew that his ransom was accepted, and that he might perform his gracious work as the great Shepherd of the sheep, God the Father had raised him from the dead 'through the blood of the everlasting covenant.'"

Others, as *Beza, Doddridge* and *Stuart*, connect the words with "the great Shepherd," that is, that Christ became the great Shepherd of the sheep through the blood of an everlasting covenant; and Acts xx. 28, and John x. 11-19, have been referred to as favorable to this view. *Stuart's* version is the following, —

20. "Now may the God of peace, that raised from the dead our Lord Jesus, (who by the blood of an everlasting covenant

21. has become the great Shepherd of the sheep,) prepare you for every good work, that ye may do his will; working in you that which is well-pleasing in his sight, through Jesus Christ, to whom be glory for ever and ever."

But a more literal rendering may be given thus, —

20. "Now the God of peace, who has restored from the dead the Shepherd of the sheep (the chief through the blood of

21. the everlasting covenant) our Lord Jesus, — may he fit you for every good work to do his will, forming in you what is well-pleasing in his sight through Jesus Christ, to whom be glory for ever and ever."

The word μέγας great, means sometimes "chief," *summus*, as given by *Schleusner;* and it has this meaning in chapter iv. 14. In John x. 11, etc., our Savior refers to his death, the shedding of his blood, as an evidence that he was *the* good Shepherd. It may then be rightly said, that he became the chief by or through the blood of the everlasting covenant, that is, through the blood that sealed and rendered effectual a covenant that is permanent, and not temporary like that of Moses.

His prayer was that God would fit, adapt, or prepare them for every good work; and this he afterwards explains, "forming," producing, or creating "in you," etc.; for the verb, ποιέω, to make, is often used in this sense. He means an internal influence or operation, as expressed more fully in Philippians ii. 13, "For it is God who worketh in you both to will and to do (literally, to work) of his good pleasure." And this forming or creating in them what was pleasing in his sight was to be done through Jesus Christ, through him as a Mediator, he having become the chief Shepherd of the sheep by shedding his blood for them.

A TRANSLATION OF CALVIN'S VERSION OF THE EPISTLE TO THE HEBREWS

Chapter 1

1 God having formerly spoken many times and in many ways to the fathers by the prophets,

2 Has in these last days spoken to us by the Son, whom he has constituted the heir of all things, by whom also he made the worlds;

3 Who being the effulgence of his glory, and the impress of his person, and sustaining all things by his powerful word, having by himself effected the purgation of our sins, sat down on the right hand of Majesty on high;

4 Being so much superior to the angels, as he has inherited a name more excellent than they.

5 For to whom of the angels has he ever said, "My Son art thou, I have this day begotten thee?"

6 And again, "I will be to him a Father, and he shall be to me a Son?" and again, when he introduces the first-begotten into the world, he says, "And adore him let all the angels of God.

7 And of the angels he saith, "Who makes his angels spirits, and his ministers a flame of fire:"

8 But of the Son, "Thy throne, O God, is for ever and ever; a scepter of righteousness is the scepter of thy kingdom:

9 Thou hast loved righteousness and hated iniquity; therefore God hath anointed thee, *even* thy God, with the oil of joy above thy companions:"

10 And, "Thou art from the beginning, O Lord, thou hast founded the earth, and the works of thine hands are the heavens;

11 They shall perish, but thou continuest; and all as a garment shall become old,

12 And as a vesture shalt thou roll them up, and they shall be changed: but thou art the same, and thy years shall not fail."

13 But to whom of the angels has he ever said, "Sit at my right hand, until I make thine enemies thy footstool?"

14 Are they not all administrative spirits, who are sent forth to minister for those who are to inherit salvation?

CHAPTER 2

1 Wherefore we ought to attend more to those things which we hear, lest at any time we let *them flow* away.

2 For if the word which had been declared by angels, was sure, and every transgression and disobedience received a just recompense of reward;

3 How shall we escape, if we neglect so great a salvation? which, having first been begun to be declared by the Lord, has been confirmed to as by those who had heard him;

4 While God was at the same time bearing a testimony by signs and wonders and various miracles, and gift distributed by the Holy Spirit, according to his will.

5 For to the angels has he not subjected the future world of which we speak:

6 But one has in a certain place testified, saying, "What is man, that thou art mindful of him" or the son of man, that thou visitest him?

7 Thou hast made him a little inferior to the angels; with glory and honor hast thou crowned him, and hast set him over the works of thine hands:

8 All things hast thou made subject under his feet." Doubtless in making subject all things to him, he left nothing that is not made subject: notwithstanding we do not as yet see all things made subject to him;

9 But we behold Jesus, who was made a little inferior to the angels, (crowned with glory and honor for having suffered death,) that he might by the grace of God taste death for all.

10 For it became him, for whom *are* all things, and through whom *are* all things, in leading many sons to glory, to consecrate the leader of their salvation by sufferings:

11 For he who sanctifies and they who are sanctified are all of one; for which cause he is not ashamed to call them brethren;

12 Saying, "I will declare thy name to my brethren; in the midst of the Church will I sing to thee:" and again, "I will trust in him;"

13 And again, "Behold I and the children whom God has given me."

14 Since then the children partake of flesh and blood, he also in like manner was partaker of the same, that by death he might destroy him who had the power of death, that is, the devil;

15 And might deliver them who through fear of death were all their life subject to bondage.

16 For he nowhere takes hold on angels; but on the seed of Abraham does he take hold.

17 It hence behooved him to become in all things like his brethren, that he might be a merciful and faithful high priest in things respecting God, in order to atone for the sins of the people:

18 For as it happened to him to be tried, he is able to succor them who are tried.

Chapter 3

1 Therefore, holy brethren, partakers of the heavenly calling, consider the Apostle and the High Priest of our profession, Christ Jesus:

2 Who was faithful to him who had appointed him, as Moses also was in his whole house.

3 For of greater glory was he counted worthy than Moses, as the builder has greater honor than the house itself

4 Every house is indeed built by some one; but he who has built all things is God.

5 And Moses was indeed faithful in his whole house as a minister, for a testimony to those things which were afterwards to be declared;
6 But Christ as a Son over his own house; whose house we are, if we hold firm the confidence and the glorying of our hope to the end.
7 Therefore (as the Holy Spirit saith, "Today, if ye will hear his voice,
8 Harden not your hearts, as in the provocation, in the day of temptation in the wilderness,
9 When your fathers tempted me, proved me, and saw my works forty years:
10 I was therefore offended with that generation, and said, They always err in heart, and they have not known my ways;
11 So I swore in my wrath, They shall not enter into my rest")
12 See, brethren, that there be not at any time in any of you the wicked heart of unbelief, by departing from the living God:
13 But exhort one another daily, while it is called today, lest any of you be hardened through the deception of sin.
14 For we are become partakers of Christ, if indeed we hold firm the beginning of our confidence to the end,
15 since it is said, "Today, if ye will hear his voice, harden not your hearts, as in the provocation:"
16 For some, when they had heard, did provoke; but not all who had come out of Egypt by Moses.
17 With whom then was he offended for forty years? was it not with them who had sinned, whose carcasses fell in the wilderness
18 And to whom did he swear that they should not enter into his rest, except to the unbelieving?
19 We then see that they could not enter in on account of unbelief.

Chapter 4

1 Let us then fear, lest, when a promise of entering into his rest remains, any of us should seem to be disappointed of it;

2 For to us has the promise been announced as well as to them; but the word heard did not profit them, for it was not connected with faith in those who heard *it*.

3 For we enter into his rest when we believe; as he has said, "As I have sworn in my wrath, if they shall enter into my rest;" though the works were done at the creation of the world;

4 For he has said thus in a certain place of the seventh day, "And God rested on the seventh day from all his works:"

5 And here again, "If they shall enter into my rest."

6 Seeing then it remains that some do enter into it, but they to whom it was first preached did not enter in on account of unbelief.

7 Again he defines a certain day, saying by David, "Today," after so long a time, (as it is said,) "Today, if ye will hear his voice, harden not your hearts."

8 For if Joshua had given them rest, he would not have spoken of another after those days.

9 Then there remains a Sabbath-rest for the people of God;

10 For he who is entered into his rest, has also himself rested from his own works, as God from his.

11 Let us then strive to enter into that rest, lest no one fail according to the same example of unbelief.

12 For living is the word of God and efficacious, and more penetrating than any two-edged sword, reaching even to the dividing of soul and spirit, and of the joints and marrow, and *is* a discerner of the thoughts and intentions of the heart:

13 For there is no creature which does not appear before him; nay, all things are naked and open to the eyes of him with whom we have to do.

14 Having then a great high priest, who has entered into the heavens, Jesus the Son of God, let us hold fast our profession:

15 For we have not a high priest who cannot sympathize with our infirmities; but *was in* all things tempted like as we are, yet without sin.

16 Let us then come with confidence to the throne of grace, that we may obtain mercy, and find grace for a seasonable help.

Chapter 5

1 For every high priest, taken from men, is appointed for men as to things pertaining to God, that he may offer gifts and sacrifices for sins;

2 Who can render himself gentle to the ignorant and the erring, since he himself is also surrounded with infirmity:

3 And on this account he ought, as for the people, so also for himself, to offer for sins.

4 And no one takes to himself this honor, but he, who is called by God, as Aaron also *was*.

5 *So* also Christ glorified not himself that he became a high priest, but he who said to him, "My Son art thou, I have this day begotten thee;"

6 As also he says in another place, "Thou art a priest for ever according to the order of Melchisedec:"

7 Who in the days of his flesh, when he offered up prayers and supplications, with strong crying and tears, to him who was able to save him from death, and was heard in what he feared;

8 Though he was a Son, yet learned obedience from those things which he suffered;

9 And being sanctified, he became to all who obey him the author of eternal salvation;

10 Having been called by God a priest according to the order of Melchisedec:

11 If whom we have much to say to you, and difficult to be explained, since ye are dull of hearing.

12 For when ye ought for the time to be teachers, ye have again need that one should teach you the elements of the beginning of God's words, and are become such as have need of milk, And not of strong meat:

13 For every one who partakes of milk is inexperienced in the word of righteousness, for he is an infant;

14 But strong meat is for the perfect, who through practice have their senses exercised so as to distinguish between good and evil.

Chapter 6

1 Therefore, passing by the first doctrine of Christ, let us be born onward to perfection, not laying again the foundation of repentance from dead works and of faith in God,

2 (of the doctrine of baptisms and of the imposition of hands,) and of resurrection of the dead, and of eternal judgment;

3 And this we shall do, if God will permit.

4 For it is impossible that those who have been once enlightened, and have tasted the heavenly gift, and have been made partakers of the Holy Spirit,

5 And have tasted the good word of God, and the powers of the world to come,

6 And have fallen away, should be renewed again into repentance, they having again crucified to themselves the Son of God, and exposed him to open shame.

7 For the earth, which drinketh the rain which often cometh upon it, and bringeth forth a blade meet for them by whom it is cultivated, receiveth a blessing from God:

8 But that which beareth thorns and briers is worthless and nigh a curse, the end of which is to be burned.

9 But we are persuaded, beloved, of better things respecting you, and those connected with salvation, though we thus speak:

10 For God is not unjust, that he should forget your work, and the labor of that love which yon have shewed towards his name, since ye have ministered to the saints, and do minister.

11 But we desire that every one of you should shew the same diligence to the full assurance of hope unto the end;

12 So that ye may not become slothful, but be followers of those who by faith and patience have inherited the promises.
13 For when God made a promise to Abraham, since he bad none greater by whom he could swear, he swore by himself,
14 Saying, "Blessing I will bless thee, and multiplying I will multiply thee:"
15 And so after having patiently waited, he obtained the promise.
16 For men indeed swear by one who is greater, and an oath for confirmation is to them an end of all dispute:
17 Therefore God, willing more abundantly to shew to the heirs of salvation the immutability of his counsel, interposed an oath;
18 That by two immutable things, in which it was impossible that God should lie, we might have a strong consolation, who have fled to lay hold on the hope set before us:
19 Which we have as an anchor of the soul, safe and firm, and entering into what is within the veil;
20 Where our forerunner, Jesus, has entered, having been made a high priest for ever, according to the order of Melchisedec.

CHAPTER 7

1 For this Melchisedec, the king of Salem, *was a* priest of the most high God, who met Abraham returning from the slaughter of the kings, and blessed him,
2 To whom also Abraham divided the tenth of all; who is first indeed, by interpretation, called the King of righteousness, and then also the King of Salem, that is, the King of peace;
3 Without father, without mother, without kindred, having neither beginning of days nor end of life, but being made like to the Son of God, he remains a priest perpetually.
4 Now consider how great is he, to whom the patriarch Abraham gave even the tenth of the spoils.

5 And they indeed who receive the priesthood, even those who are of the sons of Levi, have a command to take the tenth, according to the law from the people, that is, from their brethren, though they have come forth from the loins of Abraham:

6 But he whose kindred is not counted from them, took the tenth from Abraham, and blessed him who had the promises:

7 And without all controversy, the less is blessed by the greater.

8 And here indeed men who die receive the tenth; but there he, of whom it is testified that he liveth;

9 And as I may so say, Levi who is wont to receive the tenth, paid the tenth in Abraham;

10 For he was as yet in the loins of his father when Melchisedec met him.

11 If then there was perfection by the Levitical priesthood, (for under it the people received the law,) what need there was still, that another priest should rise after the order of Melchisedec, and should not be called after the order of Aaron?

12 For when the priesthood is changed, there is also necessarily *a* change of the law.

13 Doubtless he of whom these things are said, was from another tribe, from which no one attended at the altar:

14 For it is clear that our Lord descended from the tribe of Judah, of which tribe Moses has said nothing as to the priesthood;

15 And it is still more clear, since another priest was to rise according to the order of Melchisedec;

16 Who was not made according to the law of a carnal command, but according to the power of a permanent life;

17 For he thus testifies, "Thou art a priest for ever, after the order of Melchisedec."

18 For there is an abrogation of the former command, on account of its weakness and uselessness;

19 For the law perfected nothing, but *was* an introduction to a better hope, by which we draw nigh to God;

20 And this *is* better, because it was not done without an oath:

21 For they indeed are made priests without an oath; but he with an oath by him who said to him, "Thou art a priest for ever, according to the order of Melchisedec."
22 Of so much a better covenant is Jesus made the surety.
23 And they indeed being many were made priests, for they were not suffered by death to continue:
24 But he, as he remains perpetually, has an unchangeable priesthood.
25 Hence he is able also to save for ever those who through him come to God, always living, that he may intercede for them.
26 For such a high priest became us, being holy, innocent, undefiled, separated from sinners, and higher than the heavens;
27 Who has no need, as the priests, daily to offer sacrifices, first for their own sins, and then for *the sins* of the people; for this he did once when he offered up himself.
28 The law indeed makes men priests who have infirmity; but the word of the oath, which was after the Law, the Son, made perfect for ever.

Chapter 8

1 Now of the things which have been said the sum is, — Such an high priest have we, that hath sat down on the right hand of the throne of majesty in the heavens,
2 A minister of the sanctuary, even of the true tabernacle, which the Lord has pitched and not man.
3 For every high priest is appointed to offer gifts and sacrifices: it is hence necessary that he also should have that which he might offer.
4 If indeed he were on earth, he could not be a priest, since there are priests who offer gifts according to the law;
5 Who minister in [that which *is*] the exemplar and shadow of heavenly things, as Moses was warned by the oracle, when he was about to make the tabernacle, "See," he says, "that thou make all things according to the pattern which was shewn to thee in the mount."

6 But now he has obtained a more excellent ministry, inasmuch as he is the Mediator of a better covenant, which has been established on better promises.

7 For if the first had been faultless, there would have been no place sought for the second.

8 For finding fault with them, he says, "Behold, the days are coming, saith the Lord, when I shall make with the house of Israel and with the house of Judah a new covenant;

9 Not according to the covenant I made with their fathers in the day when I laid hold on their hand to lead them up from the land of Egypt; because they have not continued in my covenant and I disregarded them, saith the Lord:

10 For this is the covenant which I will make with the house of Israel after those days, saith the Lord, I will put my laws in their mind, and in their hearts will I write them; and I will be to them a God, and they shall be to me a people;

11 And they shall not teach every one his neighbor, and every one his brother, saying, Know thou the Lord; for all shall know me, from the least among them to the greatest;

12 For I will be merciful to their unrighteousness, and their sins and iniquities will I no more remember." By calling it new, he hath made old the first; and that which is old and aged is on the eve of vanishing.

CHAPTER 9

1 The first then had indeed ordinances of worship and a worldly sanctuary:

2 For there was made the first tabernacle in which *were* the candlestick, and the table, and the shew-bread, which is called the sanctuary;

3 And after the second vail, the tabernacle which is called the Holy of holies, which has the golden censer, and the ark

4 Of the covenant covered around with gold, in which is the golden pot which has manna, and Aaron's rod which had budded, and the tables of the covenant;

5 And over it the cherubim of glory overshadowing the mercy-seat: of which it is not for us now to speak particularly.

6 Now these things being thus set in order, into the first tabernacle the priests always enter who perform the service;

7 But into the second, the high priest alone once a year, not without blood, which he offers for the ignorances of himself and of the people;

8 The Holy Spirit intimating this, — That the way to the holiest was not yet made manifest while the first tabernacle was yet standing;

9 Which was a likeness for the time present, in which gifts and sacrifices are offered, which cannot as to conscience sanctify the worshipper,

10 Being imposed only with meats and drinks, and divers washings and sanctifications of the flesh, until the time of emendation.

11 But Christ, having afterwards come a high priest of good things to come, by a greater and more perfect tabernacle, not made with hands, that is, not of this creation,

12 Nor by the blood of goats and calves, but by his own blood, entered once into the holy place, having obtained eternal redemption.

13 For if the blood of bulls and of goats, and the ashes of an heifer sprinkled on the unclean, sanctifies to the purifying of the flesh;

14 How much more shall the blood of Christ, who by the eternal Spirit offered himself, *being* faultless, to God, cleanse your conscience from dead works to serve the living God?

15 And for this reason he is the Mediator of a new testament, that by means of death for the redemption of transgressions under the first testament, they who were called might receive the promise of the eternal inheritance

16 For where a testament is, there must necessarily be the death of the testator:

17 For a testament is of force as to the dead, for it is never valid as long as the testator is living.

18 Hence the first was not dedicated without blood:
19 For when every command according to the law had been spoken by Moses to the whole people, taking the blood of calves and of goats, with water, and scarlet wool, and hyssop, he sprinkled the book and all the people,
20 Saying, "This is the blood of the testament which God hath commanded you."
21 And he sprinkled also in a like manner with blood the tabernacle and all the vessels of the ministry;
22 And nearly all things are cleansed by blood according to the law: and without shedding of blood there is no remission.
23 It is then necessary that the exemplars of those things which are in heaven should be cleansed with these, but the heavenly things themselves with better sacrifices than these.
24 For Christ has not entered into holy places made with hands, the exemplars of the true, but into heaven itself, that he may now appear before God for us;
25 Not indeed that he may often offer himself, as the high priest *who* enters into the holiest every year with another's blood,
26 (for then he must have often suffered since the creation of the world;) but now at the end of the ages hath he once appeared for the destruction of sin by the sacrifice of himself.
27 And as it is appointed to men once to die, and after this the judgment;
28 So Christ, having been once offered, that he might take away the sins of many, will appear the second time without sin unto salvation, to those who wait for him.

Chapter 10

1 For the law, having the shadow of good things to come, not the very living image of things, can never by the sacrifices which are offered continually every year, sanctify those who come;

2 Would they not have otherwise ceased to be offered? because the worshippers, once cleansed, would have no more conscience of sins

3 But in these there is a remembrance of sins every year;

4 For it is impossible that the blood of bulls and goats should take away sins.

5 Therefore when coming into the world, he saith, "Sacrifice and offering thou wouldest not, but a body hast thou prepared for me;

6 Burnt-offerings and *sacrifices* for sin thou hast not approved;

7 Then said I, Lo, I am coming (in the volume of the book it is written of me) that I may do, O God, thy will."

8 After having said above, "Sacrifice and offering, burnt-offering and *sacrifices* for sin thou wouldest not, nor hast thou approved," which are offered according to the law;

9 Then he said, "Lo, I am coming that I may do, O God, thy will," —he takes away the first, that he may establish the second;

10 By which will we are sanctified through the offering of the body of Jesus Christ once *made*.

11 And every priest stands, indeed, daily to minister and to offer often the same sacrifices which can never take away sins;

12 But he, having offered one sacrifice for sins, sits down perpetually at the right hand of God,

13 Henceforth waiting until his enemies be made his footstool:

14 For by one offering he hath consecrated for ever those who are sanctified.

15. Now the Holy Spirit also bears witness to us; for after having previously said,

16 "This is the covenant which I will make with them after those days, saith the Lord; I will put my laws in their hearts, and in their minds will I write them," [he adds,]

17 "And their sins and their iniquities will I remember no more."

18 Now, where there is remission of these, there is no more offering for sin.

19 Having then, brethren, confidence to enter into the holiest by the blood of Jesus,
20 By a new and living way which he hath consecrated for us through the veil, that is, his flesh,
21 And having a great priest over the house of God,
22 Let us draw near with a sincere heart, in a full assurance of faith, sprinkled in our hearts from an evil conscience, and washed in our body with pure water;
23 Let us hold the confession of our hope with out wavering, for faithful is he who has promised;
24 And let us consider one another for the purpose of emulation in love and in good works;
25 Nor let us neglect the assembling of ourselves together, as the custom with some is; but let us exhort *one* another, and so much the more as ye see the day approaching.
26 For to those who willingly sin, after having received the knowledge of the truth, there is no more left a sacrifice for sins,
27 But a dreadful expectation of judgment, and a fiery indignation which shall devour the adversaries.
28 He who cast aside the law of Moses died without mercy under two or three witnesses: of how much heavier punishment,
29 Think ye, shall he be deemed worthy, who has trodden under foot the Son of God, and counted unholy the blood of the testament by which he has been sanctified, and has treated scornfully the Spirit of grace?
30 For we know who says, "Mine is vengeance, I will repay," saith the Lord; and again, "The Lord will judge his people."
31 It is a dreadful thing to fall into the hands of the living God.
32 But remember the former days, in which, after being illuminated, ye endured a great conflict of sufferings; partly when ye were exposed to public shame by reproaches and distresses,
33 And partly when ye became the companions of those who were thus treated:

34 For ye sympathized with me in my bonds, and took the plunder of your goods with joy, knowing that ye have a better and an enduring substance in heaven.
35 Cast not then away your confidence which has a great recompense of reward.
36 Ye have truly need of patience, so that having done the will of God, ye may obtain the promise:
37 For it will yet be a little while, when he who is coming will come, and will not delay.
38 But the just, by faith shall he live; and if he draws back, my soul shall have no delight in him.
39 But we are not of those who draw back to perdition, but of those who believe to the salvation of the soul.

CHAPTER 11

1 Now faith is the substance of things hoped for, the demonstration of things not seen:
2 For by it the elders obtained a testimony.
3 By faith we understand that the worlds were set in order by the Word of God, so that of things not visible they became visible.
4 By faith Abel offered to God a more excellent sacrifice than Cain, by which he obtained a testimony that he was righteous, God bearing a testimony to his gifts; and by it, he being dead, yet speaketh.
5 By faith Enoch was translated, so as not to see death; nor was he found, because God had translated him; for before his translation he had received a testimony that he pleased God.
6 But without faith it is impossible to please him; for he who comes to God must believe that he is, and that he is the rewarder of those who seek him.
7 By faith Noah, having been warned by God of things which did not as yet appear, being moved with fear, prepared an ark for the preservation of his house; by which he condemned the world, and became heir of the righteousness which is by faith.

8 By faith Abraham, when he was called, obeyed, so that he went out into the place which he was to receive for an inheritance; and he went out, not knowing where he was going.

9 By faith he sojourned in the promised land, as though it was a foreign country, dwelling in tents together with Isaac and Jacob, co-heirs to the same promise;

10 For he expected a city having foundations, whose master-builder and maker is God.

11 By faith also Sarah herself received power to conceive seed; and beyond the time of age she brought forth, because she counted him faithful who had promised.

12 Therefore there have been begotten even of one, and him indeed dead, *those* in multitude as the stars of heaven, and as the numberless sand which is on the sea-shore.

13 All these died in faith, not having received the promises, but having afar off seen, and believed, and embraced them, and confessed that they were strangers and pilgrims on the earth:

14 Verily they who say such things shew that they seek a country.

15 And if indeed they had remembered that from which they had come out, they had time to return:

16 But they now desire a better, even that which is heavenly: hence God is not ashamed to be called their God, for he has prepared for them a city.

17 By faith Abraham offered up Isaac, when he was tried; and he offered up the only-begotten after having received the promises,

18 Respecting whom it had been said, "In Isaac shall thy seed be called;"

19 Accounting that God was able to raise him even from the dead; whence also he received him in a type.

20 By faith Isaac blessed Jacob and Esau concerning things to come. By faith Jacob, when dying,

21 Blessed both the sons of Joseph, and worshipped on the head of his couch.

22 By faith Joseph, when dying, made mention of the departure of the children of Israel, and gave an order respecting his bones.

23 By faith Moses, when born, was hid three months by his parents, because they saw that he was a beautiful child, and feared not the decree of the king.
24 By faith Moses, when grown up, refused to be called the son of Pharaoh's daughter,
25 Choosing rather to suffer evils with the people of God than to have the temporary pleasures of sin;
26 Esteeming the reproach of Christ greater riches than the treasures of Egypt; for he looked on the recompense of reward.
27 By faith he left Egypt, having not feared the wrath of the king: for he endured, as seeing him who is invisible.
28 By faith he appointed the passover, and the sprinkling of blood, that he who destroyed the first-born should not touch them.
29 By faith they passed through the Red Sea as through a dry land; which when the Egyptians attempted, they were drowned.
30 By faith the walls of Jericho fell, having been surrounded seven days.
31 By faith Rahab the harlot perished not with the unbelieving, after having received the explorers in peace.
32 And what more shall I say? for the time would fail me to tell of Gideon and Barak, of Samson and Jephthae; of David, and of Samuel, and the Prophets;
33 Who by faith subdued kingdoms, wrought righteousness, obtained promises, closed the mouths of lions,
34 Quenched the violence of fire, escaped the edge of the sword, became strong in weakness, were made valiant in battle, put to flight the armies of aliens:
35 Women, by a resurrection, received their dead; and some were tortured, not having received deliverance, that they might obtain a better resurrection;
36 And others experienced mockings and scourgings, and further, bonds and imprisonment:
37 They were stoned, sawn asunder, tempted, slain with the sword: they wandered in sheep-skins and goat-skins, being destitute, oppressed, ill-treated,

38 (of whom the world was not worthy;) wandering in deserts, and on mountains, and in dens and caves of the earth.

39 And all these, having received a testimony by faith, did not obtain the promise:

40 God having provided some better thing for us, that they might not without us be made perfect.

Chapter 12

1 Therefore, as we are surrounded by such a cloud of witnesses, laying aside every weight, and the sin which besets us, let us also run with patience in the race set before us,

2 Looking to Jesus, the author and finisher of our faith; who, for the joy set before him, endured the cross, having despised shame, and sat down on the right hand of the throne of God:

3 For consider who he was who endured from sinners such contradiction against himself,

4 That ye may not be wearied, being faint in your souls; ye have not as yet resisted unto blood, while striving against sin.

5 And ye have forgotten the exhortation which speaks to you as to children, "My son, despise not the chastening of the Lord, nor be faint when thou art reproved by him:

6 For whom the Lord loveth he chasteneth; and he scourgeth every son whom he receiveth."

7 If ye endure chastening, God dealeth with you as with sons: for what son is he whom the father chasteneth not?

8 But if ye be without chastisement, of which all [sons] are partakers, then ye are bastards, and not sons.

9 Since we had the fathers of our flesh as our chastisers, and we reverenced them, shall we not much more be subject to the Father of spirits, and live?

10 For they indeed for a few days chastised us according to their own will: but he for our benefit, that he may impart to us his holiness.

11 But no chastening seems indeed for the present to be joyful, but grievous; yet afterwards it renders the peaceful fruit of righteousness to those who are by it exercised.

12 Raise ye up, therefore, the remiss hands, and the relaxed knees,

13 And make straight paths for your feet, that halting may not lead you astray, but rather that it may be healed.

14 Follow peace with all, and holiness, without which no one shall see the Lord;

15 Taking heed, lest any one should come short of the grace of God; lest any root of bitterness, growing up, should disturb you, and many be through it defiled;

16 Lest there should be any fornicator or a profane person, like Esau, who for one meal sold his birthright:

17 For ye know that when afterwards he wished to inherit the blessing, he was rejected; for he found no place for repentance, though he sought it with tears.

18 For we have not come to the mount that might be touched, and to the burning fire, and to blackness, and darkness, and tempest,

19 And to the sound of a trumpet, and the voice of words, which they having heard entreated that the word should not be proclaimed to them;

20 For they could not bear what was enjoined, "If a beast touch the mountain, it shall be stoned or pierced through with a dart;"

21 And so terrible was the sight, *that* Moses said, "I fear and tremble."

22 But ye have come to Mount Sion, the city of the living God, the heavenly Jerusalem, and to the company of innumerable angels,

23 And to the Church of the first-born, who are written in heaven, and to God the judge of all, and to the spirits of just men made perfect,

24 And to Jesus the Mediator of the New Testament, and the blood of sprinkling, which speaks better things than that of Abel.

25 See that ye despise not him that speaketh; for if they escaped not who despised him who spoke on earth, how much less we, if we turn away from him *who speaks* from heaven?
26 Whose voice then shook the earth; but now he has promised, saying, "Yet once I shake, not only the earth, but also heaven:"
27 And this, "Set once," signifies the removal of the things shaken, that the things unshaken might remain.
28 Hence we, who receive a kingdom which is not shaken, have grace, by which we serve God acceptably with reverence and fear:
29 "For our God is a consuming fire."

Chapter 13

1 Let brotherly love continue.
2 Be not unmindful of hospitality; for by this some have unawares received angels.
3 Remember those in bonds, as bound with them, *and* the afflicted, as ye yourselves are in the body.
4 Honorable is marriage in all, and the unpolluted bed; but fornicators and adulterers God will condemn.
5 *Let your* conduct *be* without avarice; be content with what ye have; for he has said, "I will not leave thee, nor forsake thee;"
6 So that we may confidently say, "The Lord is to me a helper, nor will I fear what man may do to me."
7 Remember those who are set over you, who have spoken to you the Word of God; whose faith follow, considering the end of their conduct.
8 Jesus Christ, yesterday and today, is even the same for ever;
9 Be not carried about by various and foreign doctrines; for it is good that the heart should be strengthened by grace, not by meats, which have not profited those who have been conversant in them.
10 We have an altar, from which they have no right to eat who serve the tabernacle.

11 For the beasts, whose blood for sin is brought by the high priest into the holiest, their bodies are burnt without the camp.
12 Hence Jesus also, that he might sanctify the people by his own blood, suffered without the camp.
13 Let us then go forth to him without the gate, bearing his reproach.
14 For we have not here an abiding city, but we seek one to come.
15 By him, then, let us continually offer the sacrifice of praise to God, that is, the fruit of our lips, giving thanks to his name:
16 But to do good, and to communicate, forget not; for with such sacrifices God is well pleased.
17 Obey those who are set over you, and be submissive; for they watch for your souls, as those who are to render an account; so that they may do this with joy, and not with grief, for that would be unprofitable to you.
18 Pray for us; for we trust that we have a good conscience, desiring in all things to live honestly:
19 But I beseech you the more to do this, that I may the sooner be restored to you.
20 Now may the God of peace, who brought up from the dead the great pastor of the sheep in the blood of the eternal covenant,
21 Even our Lord Jesus, confirm you in every good work, that ye may do his will, doing in you what is acceptable before him through Jesus Christ, to whom be glory for ever and ever. Amen.
22 But I beseech you, brethren, bear the word of exhortation; for a few words have I written to you.
23 Know ye that brother Timothy is set at liberty; with whom, if he comes shortly, I shall see you.
24 Salute all those who are set over you, and all the saints; they from Italy salute you.
25 Grace be with you all. Amen.

Written to the Hebrews from Italy by Timothy

www.ingramcontent.com/pod-product-compliance
Lightning Source LLC
Chambersburg PA
CBHW011315080526
44587CB00024B/3997